T0247775

Black Conservatives
in the United States

Godfrey Mwakikagile

1

Black Conservatives in the United States
Godfrey Mwakikagile

Second Edition

ISBN 10: 0-9802587-0-7
ISBN 13: 978-0-9802587-0-7

New Africa Press
Dar es Salaam, Tanzania
Pretoria, South Africa

First published in the United States of America. American spelling used in the first edition has not been changed in order to maintain the integrity of the original text.

Contents

Acknowledgements

SPACE does not allow me to name all the individuals and institutions to whom I am deeply indebted for helping me make this work possible. But I must express my profound gratitude to all the sources I have cited to document this study. They are given full attribution in the chapter notes.

The brevity of this acknowledgment should not in any way be misconstrued as a deliberate attempt to ignore or minimize the contribution made by those I have not named here. It is, rather, a genuine effort to convey the depth of my indebtedness to each and everyone of them, including some of whom I may have inadvertently omitted from the main text, however indirect their contribution may be. They have all equally, each in his or her own way, contributed to the success of this effort.

Foremost among them are ideologues on the Right themselves, although they played only a peripheral role in sparking and fueling my interest in the black conservative phenomenon which constitutes the core of this study.

As a black myself, I have always been interested in the subject of black conservatives and their ideological cohorts in the mainstream because of their agenda for black America that is considered by many blacks to be hostile to their well-being. The works of some of them have been an invaluable source of material in the documentation of my study. And for that, I am deeply grateful to them all.

They include Dinesh D'Souza - a "mainstream" conservative who is an immigrant from India - whose book, *The End of*

Racism, helped to refute his own thesis. There is no end to racism, contrary to what he says. It is very much alive. His work inadvertently exposed the empty ideological rhetoric of black conservatives, his ideological compatriots, whose solutions to the problems of black America do not correspond to reality in a color-conscious society.

I must also express my profound gratitude to black conservatives themselves, such as Robert L. Woodson Sr.; Fay M. Anderson (she later left the Republican party in disgust because it continued to ignore blacks, as she stated in *The Washington Post*); Vincent Watkins, Jerry T. Burley, Willie A. Richardson, publisher of *Headway*, a black conservative journal, now defunct; and others like them, who have had the courage to admit that theirs is a lone voice in the wilderness, ignored by the vast majority of African-Americans who see black conservatives as insensitive and irrelevant to their needs and well-being: no more than puppets manipulated at will by mainstream - euphemism for white - conservatives who couldn't care less about the plight and well-being of black America.

I appreciate their candor. They couldn't have done a better job of condemning themselves to irrelevancy in the black American context.

Special thanks must also go to *Headway,* formerly *National Minority Politics*, for being an invaluable source of material on black conservatives I have used in this book; the *National Review*, the flagship of the mainstream conservative movement that also has been a great source of information I have used liberally - not necessarily in the ideological sense - in my work; *The Washington Post*, *The New York Times*, *The Wall Street Journal*, *The Boston Globe*, *The Nation*, and *The Economist* among others, whose coverage of racism helped fortify my thesis.

Other individuals also deserve special mention: Cornel West for his commentary on black conservatives; Ishmael Reed for his analysis of racism in the media conservatives claim is liberal and biased against them and favors blacks; Bruce Shapiro, for his blunt appraisal of police brutality against blacks, in *The Nation* and other forums; and Todd Gitlin, for his incisive analysis of America's racial predicament in his book, *The Twilight of Common Dreams: Why America Is Wracked by Culture Wars.*

I also wish to express my deep gratitude to those who have made a unique contribution to this effort. They include my publisher for bringing this work to fruition; and black America for her indispensable role in the conception and execution of this project as a source of spiritual sustenance. She inspired this study, and she deserves credit more than anybody else. This book could not have been written without her.

And while all credit is due to others for the successful completion of my work, I must take full responsibility for any mistakes which may be found in this book; while always bearing in mind that even the best works we produce have been preceded by others and benefited from the knowledge and experience of our forebears.

Preface

MANY avenues of opportunity have remained narrow and constricted, available only to the relatively few. Today, the hopes and dreams of millions of Americans are stifled, not because of their individual failings, but solely because of their skin color. That is why I, along with other ACLU leaders, believe that the most pervasive, overarching civil-liberties problem in this country is race discrimination.

According to the National Opinion Research Center, a majority of white Americans still believe that blacks and Hispanics are less intelligent, less hardworking, and less patriotic than whites. It would be naive to think these negative streotypes do not influence the decisions made by employers and school administrators (the vast majority of whom are white), translating into milions of lost opportunities. We are still generations away from the color-blind merit system that critics of affirmative action like to think we already have.

Few would disagree with the maxim that a good education is the best path to a better, more economically secure life. But in this country, government spending on public education is clearly linked to race. Schools serving mostly minority, inner-city children receive half as much money per student as schools in the surrounding white suburbs. This unequal distribution of public resources based on skin color denies both the equality of opportunity and equality of results. -- Nadine Strossen, president, American Civil Liberties Union (ACLU), in the conservative journal *Policy Review*, Washington, D.C., September-October 1997, p. 3.

BLACK CONSERVATIVES are some of the most controversial figures in the United States today. But they have yet to win acceptance they so desperately seek from their own people, fellow blacks, to legitimize their views they claim articulate the needs

8

and aspirations of Black America.

They may be genuine in their intentions, but most of the views they express across the spectrum - on political, economic, and social issues - are fundamentally at odds with what the majority of blacks believe to be the reality in their lives in a society where racism remains a major problem; although not as bad as it was before. In fact many blacks, especially those in the middle class, have made significant progress since the sixties.

Blacks don't constitute a monolithic whole; they don't think alike, and they don't act alike, just like other people don't. But the majority of them seem to agree on one thing: America has yet to be what it has always professed to be. Black conservatives disagree. They say America has already achieved that goal.

This work looks at the role black conservatives play in American politics and in the lives of black Americans, also known as African-Americans although black conservatives especially - as well as a significant number of other blacks - don't want to be identified as such; they just want to be called black Americans even if some of them are not ashamed of their African heritage.

The book discusses such topics as the relationship between blacks and the Republican party, and the perspectives black conservatives share on poverty, racism, welfare, self-reliance, affirmative action, and the criminal justice system as it relates to blacks. It is also a critique of *The Bell Curve*, a book which has inflamed passions especially among blacks, and of the views some black conservatives have expressed on racial IQ differences which have fueled debate on this highly explosive subject.

Although racism still is a serious problem in the United States today, it is not an insurmountable obstacle in all cases. Some of the most downtrodden members of society succeed in life even if they remain on the periphery of the mainstream. Many blacks in the ghetto are living proof of that. Racism should not be used as an excuse for not trying to do the best you can in life.

But that does not mean that people should be blind to reality and ignore the existence of racism which impedes progress in the black community and is responsible for the destruction of many lives. This, and many other issues, are some of the subjects discussed in this book whose analysis is also based on first-hand knowledge derived from my life and experience in the inner city

9

and in the black community in the United States in the course of three decades.

Introduction

This is a racist society, and it will be for a long time to come.
- Roger Wilkins[1]

ROGER WILKINS, a veteran of many civil rights battles throughout his adult life, is not a man of hyperbole.

Nephew of the late NAACP leader Roy Wilkins, he served as Assistant Attorney-General of the United States during the Kennedy-Johnson Administration and has experienced racism throughout his life as almost all blacks have. While growing up, he attended Creston High School in Grand Rapids, Michigan, where he was the only black student at that school - as he told William F. Buckley Jr., on the American national public television (PBS) program "Firing Line" - in a conservative mid-western city and Republican stronghold.

The view he expresses that "this is a racist society" is not a lone voice in the wilderness. It is shared by millions of people of all races across the United States, according to polls. It is also a view shared by most black Americans,[2] and by ministers of different denominations. According to the United Church of Christ:

Racism permeates most of our institutions....As a result of racial discrimination, all over the U.S. there are quiet riots in the form of unemployment, poverty, social disorganization, family disintegration, housing and school deterioration, and crime.[3]

11

Many different scholars also contend that America is a racist society. According to renowned sociologist Dr. Kenneth B. Clark, "the United States will never rid itself of racism."[4] Professor Harold Cruse, of the University of Michigan, shares the same view:

The United States cannot and never will solve the race problem unless Americans change the economic, political, cultural, and administrative social organization of this country in various sectors....Racial segregation remains a built-in characteristic of American society....The end result can only be racial wars in the United States.[5]

Many students across the United States also maintain that racism is a serious problem. This view was expressed by almost 80 percent of the freshmen at the nation's two-and four-year colleges and universities: "According to the 25th annual survey of college freshmen, conducted by the American Council on Education and the University of California at Los Angeles, 79.4 percent of the freshmen believed that racial discrimination remained a major problem."[6]

And national surveys show that at least 50 percent of white Americans oppose racial integration, and just as many want laws enacted that would legalize racial discrimination in home sales and renting.[7]

This is hardly a revelation. It is only a blunt assessment of America's perennial problem, in spite of the great progress the country has made in terms of race relations and in pursuit of racial equality.

The United States has always been plagued by racism. It was, in fact, founded on racism when it sanctioned slavery and racial injustice across the spectrum. It was not founded on the twin ideals of liberty and equality that are said to be the pillars of the American Republic, the first since Rome. History refutes that claim; so does contemporary experience.

Slavery was going on when the foundations of the republic were being laid - by African slaves - while the founding fathers were at the same time professing liberty and equality. In fact, many of the founding fathers themselves owned slaves. They include George Washington, the first American president, and Thomas Jefferson who wrote the famous Declaration of

Independence proclaiming to the whole world: "We hold these truths to be self-evident that all men are created equal."

For some inexplicable reason, this universal truth did not apply to Africans in bondage on American soil, and even to those in Africa, obviously because they were considered to be members of the lesser breed or a subspecies of mankind at best.

Even as late as the sixties, racist laws still existed and were being enforced in many parts of the union, especially in the southern states. And in spite of all the progress that has been made, which must be acknowledged even by the most ardent critics, the United States seems to have achieved exactly what the National Advisory Commission on Civil Disorders ominously warned about following the sixties' riots:

> Our nation is moving toward two societies, one black, and one white - separate and unequal....Race prejudice has shaped our history decisively; it now threatens to affect our future. White racism is essentially responsible for the explosive mixture, which has been accumulating in our cities since the end of World War II.[8]

More than 40 years after passage of the most comprehensive civil rights legislation in the nation's history, the problem remains as intractable as ever. Segregation still exists in many parts of society, and racism is just as virulent, only in covert form. But in many cases, it remains just as blatant; police brutality against blacks and racial profiling by the authorities and business owners being the most vivid examples.

What happened to the civil rights laws and to the American dream? Not long before he was assassinated, Dr. Martin Luther King Jr., complained about the killings of civil rights workers and bombing of churches in the south, stating that the perpetrators of these heinous crimes were well known to the authorities, yet nothing was done to punish them. They continued to walk around freely and were treated as heroes of the community by many fellow whites.

The celebrated African-American poet Langston Hughes articulated similar sentiments about America's racial dilemma and black America's perennial longing for equality and justice. He wrote a poem, "A Dream Deferred," in which he raised the question:

What happens to a dream deferred?
Does it dry up like a raisin in the sun
or does it fester like a sore
 and then run
or does it sag like a heavy load
or does it explode?[9]

The sixties provided an answer to that question with a loud bang, as many American cities exploded with riots, starting with Watts in 1965, and culminating in the largest urban insurrections in American history in 1968 when more than 120 cities were rocked by violence and other forms of civil strife triggered by the assassination of Dr. Martin Luther King in April the same year.

The same year Watts exploded was also the same year in which Malcolm X was assassinated, on February 21, only a few months before the riots in the summer. As he put it bluntly in one of his speeches before the Watts riots: "I am one who doesn't believe in deluding myself....I don't see any American dream; I see an American nightmare."[10]

It was also around the same time that the Black Panthers emerged on the scene, forming the Black Panther Party in Oakland, California, in October 1966 under the leadership of Huey P. Newton and Bobby Seale, embracing confrontational tactics with the authorities, especially the police, in their quest for racial equality and justice.

But there is another group of blacks, a rare breed although not a freak of nature, that sings a different tune. There is no dream deferred, they say, and no American nightmare, except a beautiful dream. They are called black conservatives, and identify themselves as such, as opposed to their liberal brethren who constitute the vast majority in the black community across the United States.

Not only do black conservatives see a beautiful American dream; they say America is not a racist society, does not even have a serious racial problem, and has, in fact, fulfilled the dream its most downtrodden members, blacks, sought during the civil rights movement in the sixties. Their position is best summed up in their own words: "Our nation has been the most successful on earth with opportunity for all."[11]

Racism is no longer a major problem in the United States. Race relations are excellent. Black people have equal opportunity like everybody else and are their own number one problem, black conservatives contend. Are they right or wrong?

That is the subject of this book. It looks at the black conservative phenomenon in contemporary America which has attracted increasing attention in recent years, especially since the election of Ronald Reagan as president of the United States in 1980.

Most black conservatives supported Reagan and his policies which they felt were therapeutic for black America as a form of shock therapy to galvanize a significant number of blacks into action to be self-reliant by cutting back social programs including welfare.

They also applauded him for his "color-blind" policies and opposition to affirmative action, setting themselves apart from the majority of blacks who supported and continue to support race-conscious policies, including affirmative action, in order to fight racial injustice.

Other Republican and conservative leaders besides Reagan have enjoyed support as well, among black conservatives, while triggering the opposite reaction among most blacks for their indifference and sometimes hostility towards black America.

The first chapter examines the views and perspectives black conservatives share across the spectrum, and how they differ with their liberal counterparts. It is a comprehensive survey, in telescopic form, of almost all the subjects on which black conservatives have kindled the ire among their brethren across black America; issues which have also served as a lightning rod among many black voters, resulting in overwhelming support of Democratic candidates against their Republican opponents. The issues include affirmative action, self-reliance, welfare, and racism, among others.

Yet, despite the unanimity among black conservatives on those issues, there are significant differences among them on some fundamental subjects which constitute the core of the conservative philosophy.

The chapter addresses this contentious subject which also raises the question: What is really a black conservative? And it attempts to answer the question whose focus on the nature of black conservatives is further addressed in the second chapter, but not exclusively so.

The second chapter examines the relationship between the Republican party and black America, and its policies towards racial minorities especially blacks.

This relationship has been profoundly affected by what many blacks consider to be indifference towards their plight and well-being in a white-dominated society which still remains racist; and sometimes outright hostility towards them by a party that is seen as a bastion of white supremacy, defending and promoting white interests at the expense of blacks more than anybody else.

The chapter also is an examination of what black United States Supreme Court Justice Clarence Thomas calls "the loneliness of the black conservative."

Black conservatives are members of a party that doesn't care about blacks, and which doesn't even want them as members despite professions to the contrary by its leaders. They are also rejected and even despised by their own people in the black community who see them as traitors and puppets for whites.

And their membership in a party that is known for its opposition to civil rights and affirmative action has not helped their cause; earning them the unenviable distinction as "black Judas." As NAACP President Kweisi Mfume stated at the organization's annual convention in Philadelphia, Pennsylvania, on July 12, 2004, as reported by *The Washington Times*, black conservative groups are nothing but mouthpieces of the ultra-conservative movement formed and funded by white Republicans to attack and destroy blacks. As he put it:

"When the ultraconservative right-wing attacker has run out of attack strategy, he goes and gets someone that looks like you and me to continue the attacks. And like the ventriloquist's dummies, they sit there in the puppet master's voice, but we can see whose lips are moving, and we can hear his money talk....

They can't deal with the leaders we choose for ourselves, so they manufacture, promote and hire new ones....(Our enemies tell them that) we are whining, that we are too liberal, that we are using the scapegoat of victimization and that we are even unpatriotic....

They want to do away with many of our rights and much of the legacy of the NAACP....But those days are over and we aren't going back, so run your little right-wing media. Put a whisper here and an innuendo there. It won't work."

Such is the incendiary nature of the black conservative phenomenon across Black America, drawing furious responses from many blacks including those who are not even ideologically inclined towards the Democratic party but who know what it means to be black in a predominantly white society. And it has sometimes even led to intemperate remarks among some blacks.

But the significance of such remarks can only be understood when you put them in their proper context; instead of dismissing them as emotional outbursts which amount to nothing. The answer lies in history and contemporary treatment of black Americans at the hands of the white majority who remain essentially racist.

The third chapter takes a look at a broad spectrum of perspectives on the black conservative phenomenon, within and outside the Republican party and the conservative movement, including individuals who have undergone ideological conversion but not necessarily by becoming liberals. It is also an examination of the other, or darker, side of the Republican party, as a haven for white supremacists, despite professions to the   contrary.

The fourth chapter is a critical analysis of the position articulated by some black conservatives who contend that the criminal justice system favors blacks; and that whites who are victimized by blacks are ignored by the media, while blacks who are victims of crime committed by whites get media attention sometimes out of proportion to the crimes perpetrated against them.

They cite the O.J. Simpson case as a typical example of this; the kind of attitude they claim has poisoned race relations and which has even led many whites to ignore crimes, including church bombings in the 1990s by white racists, committed against blacks.

The chapter also looks at the history of racism against blacks in the United States, and of the crimes committed against them, to refute this argument.

It is also an examination of racism against blacks in the judicial system, and of what many blacks consider to be the callous indifference of black conservatives towards black victims of racism and their denial of racism as a serious problem not only in the dispensation of justice but in all areas of the American society, including the intellectual arena about which we learn more in the next chapter.

Are blacks less intelligent than whites and members of other races? Are there genetic differences among the races which account for the difference in intelligence especially between blacks and whites as well as members of other races who are also considered to be more intelligent than black people?

These are some of the highly explosive issues examined in chapter five, and of the position taken by a number of leading conservatives, black and white, who contend that "there is something there," as Thomas Sowell put it, which explains the difference in IQ between blacks and whites as well as members of other races; an oblique reference to genetic differences as the determining factor and which some conservatives, unlike Sowell, have clearly cited as the main - if not the only - explanation for the difference in intelligence among the races.

The chapter also is an in-depth analysis and critique of *The Bell Curve*, a monumental study by two prominent white conservatives and scholars in which they contend that blacks are indeed less intelligent than whites and members of other races because of genetic differences; an incendiary thesis that continues to fuel debate as much as it did when the book was first published in March 1994 and became an instant best seller among whites, many of whom obviously felt they had been vindicated in their belief that they are indeed more intelligent than blacks; while rubbing their hands with satsifaction, gleefully saying, "See? I told you so!"

Probably the biggest criticism against black conservatives by other blacks is that they ignore racism as a serious problem in the American society. Some black conservatives dismiss racism outright as immaterial in the lives of black people. As Larry Elder bluntly put it: "Race relations are excellent. We all get along just fine."

Is racism no longer a serious problem in the American society? Are race relations really that good, so good that racism no longer plays a major role in the lives of black people as many black conservatives contend?

Chapter six, which is the last chapter, attempts to answer those questions and many others, and concludes this work by saying that black conservatives are dead wrong. Racism is an enduring phenomenon in the American society and its virulence through the centuries since the founding of America has been a fundamental reality of life across the spectrum. And that will continue to be the case for a long time to come. As Professor Nathan Glazer states in his book *We Are All Multiculturalists Now*, the fundamental problem "is the refusal of other Americans to accept blacks."[12]

Chapter One:

Black Conservatives

BLACK CONSERVATIVES are probably some of the most vilified individuals in the black community across the United States. They have the right to differ with liberal orthodoxy, and should be accorded that right. Yet they are treated as traitors to their own people and are expected to renounce their ideology and embrace a liberal agenda they don't like.

But there are reasons for this. Black conservatives are in a peculiar position precisely because they are black in a society they contend no longer denies blacks equal opportunity. The majority of their brethren contend otherwise.

Black conservatives say they are trying to help fellow blacks, yet they advocate policies many blacks feel do more harm than good in a society that has always been hostile to them, and which remains divided by race even if not rigidly so as it used to be.

The role black conservatives play is similar to what Moise Tshombe did to Patrice Lumumba and to the Congolese people in general and to the entire African continent in the sixties. As Dr. Kwame Nkrumah wrote to Tshombe in a letter dated August 12, 1960: "You have assembled in your support the foremost advocates of imperialism and colonialism in Africa and the most determined opponents of African freedom. How can you, as an African, do this?"[1]

That is the same question many African-Americans ask black conservatives: "You have teamed up with some of the worst opponents of racial equality for blacks: white conservatives and others. How can you, as blacks, do this to your own people?"

As an integral part of the black community, black conservatives don't always speak *only* for themselves anymore than black liberals do. They speak as *a part* of that community, not just as individuals or some kind of fraternity of black rightwing ideologues.

And one of the subjects on which they have inflamed passions and continue to fan flames in the black community is race, especially as an insignificant factor in black American lives and in society in general where, they contend, black people have almost equal opportunity to succeed in life just like whites and members of other races do. Thus, when Professor Cornel West, a well-known black liberal and philosopher, says "race matters,"[2] which is also the title of his best-selling book first published in 1993, Dr. Thomas Sowell, former professor of economics and probably the most prominent black conservative, denounces him by saying, "He seems so transparently a hustler."[3]

Yet it is difficult for many blacks, almost of whom are victims of racism only in varying degrees - including black conservatives themselves despite their denials - to believe that people like Sowell really care about their well-being. As the late Carl Rowan, a leading black columnist, bluntly put it: "Vidkun Quisling, in collaboration with the Nazis, surely did not do as much damage to Norwegians as Sowell is doing to the most helpless of black Americans."[4]

And when it was reported that President Ronald Reagan was going to appoint Sowell chairman of the Council of Economic Advisers, a cabinet-level post Sowell reportedly turned down, Thomas Atkins who was then the NAACP general counsel had the following to say: "He would play the same kind of role which historically the house niggers played for the plantation owners."[5]

None of that should not be difficult to comprehend. Sowell has taken a position on a number of issues that is patently hostile and inimical to the interests of the black community and its poorest members, and has done it for years since the late sixties.

He is still doing today, and people listen to him; not just because he expresses views that are unpopular among most blacks; and not because he forcefully articulates a conservative

21

position - many prominent white conservatives do that all time; people pay attention to him mainly because he is black and conservative, and one of the most influential conservatives in the United States regardless of his racial identity; yet who gained such prominence precisely because he's black.

During the seventies, Professor Sowell testified before Congress against raising the minimum wage contrary to what most blacks wanted.6 He also wants welfare and affirmative action abolished, not just mended, again contrary to what most blacks want.

The campaign to abolish both has been led by white conservatives who virtually succeeded in abolishing the federal welfare program in 1996-1997, and have made significant progress in abolishing affirmative action in a number of areas across the United States with the full backing of conservative judges on the federal bench.

But Sowell is not alone in this offensive and what many blacks perceive to be a vicious campaign against them by some of their own. Other black conservatives share his position. For example, Walter Williams, another prominent economics professor, also wants minimum wage, welfare, and affirmative action abolished, as he has explictly stated in different forums through the years and in one of his books, *The State Against Blacks*.8

These are just some of the areas in which black conservatives inflame passions across black America. Poverty is another area. Professor Williams contends, "As a group, blacks have made the greatest advance in human history...unprecedented progress."9 Yet the poverty rate among blacks is three times that of whites, and the unemployment rate twice the national average consistently through the years.

If we look at the progress blacks have made during the past 40 years or so, we can perhaps try to understand what Williams means when he says blacks have made more progress than anybody else in the history of mankind. As Tom Wicker states in his best-selling book, *Tragic Failure: Racial Integration in America*: "African-Americans are not unaware that three times as many blacks as whites were living in poverty in 1959 and...three times as many blacks as whites still were living in poverty in 1989."10

22

The figures were about the same in the mid-1990s and beyond. According to the Census Bureau, the poverty rate in 1996 among whites was 11.7 percent, and among blacks 30.6 percent.[11] That means the poverty rate among blacks was 2.6 times that of whites; not very much different from what it was in 1959 and all the years before 1989, and even thereafter into the nineties.

That is what Professor Williams calls the greatest progress made by blacks in the history of mankind; in spite of the fact that the black poverty rate has remained virtually consistent through the decades, an argument hardly convincing to most blacks that conservatives care about them. It is true that black people in the United States have made great progress since slavery. But it is highly debatable that they "have made the greatest advance in human history," as Williams contends.

Perhaps no issue is as controversial as affirmative action in the debate between black conservatives and other members of the black community.

Black conservatives are opposed to racial preferences to fight racial injustice. They contend it is racism in reverse; it compromises excellence by lowering standards; it stifles individual initiative; and it confirms stereotypes about blacks that they are intellectually inferior and cannot compete with whites and members of other races purely on the basis of merit. These are strong arguments and emotionally appealing.

But they do not correspond to reality, considering the history and experience of blacks as victims of racial discrimination by law and custom, until very recently in the sixties when laws were passed outlawing segregation and other forms of discrimination. Therefore they did not, and still don't, have equal opportunity like whites who have been beneficiaries of preferential treatment at the expense of blacks since slavery. And they need some help to catch up with them.

That is the rationale for affirmative action black conservatives have failed to refute convincingly with empirical evidence.

One of the most prominent blacks in the campaign against affirmative action was Ward Connerly who spearheaded the California Civil Rights Initiative (CCRI) in 1996 to abolish the program in that state. The people of California, most of whom are white, voted in 1996 to abolish it.

Yet strangely enough, one of the arguments Connerly used to oppose affirmative action is the same strong argument his opponents used to support it. He took special umbrage at what Colin Powell said in support of affirmative action: "Some people say we have a level playing field, but we don't yet."[12] Jesse Jackson, whom Connerly has consistently criticized on other issues as well, concurs: "All the evidence I know says there's not a level playing field."[13] And what does Connerly say?: "You argue that the playing field is not level....But what playing field has ever been completely level?"[14]

If there is no level playing field as Connerly himself admits, why is he against affirmative action which is intended to level the field after race-neutral principles have failed to do so? Yet he criticizes Colin Powell and Jesse Jackson for using the same argument he is using. That is the argument for affirmative action because there is no level playing field as he concedes. So why is it wrong for Powell and Reverend Jackson to say that but right for him to make the same argument?

It is easy to understand why black conservatives don't get the support or the following they seek from the black community. As Errol Smith, a black conservative himself, admits in his article, "Time to Repackage Black Conservatism":

> Significant political and social influence has still eluded black conservatives. The black right has demonstrated precious little ability to profoundly influence politics within the black community, or to mobilize black Americans behind a generally conservative agenda....Next to the so-called 'N' (Nigger) word, no other label is so despised and emotionally charged as black conservatives.[15]

That is because many members of the black community see black conservatives as traitors. Therefore it is impossible for black conservatives, hence black Republicans, to represent the black community. That is equivalent to asking the Ku Klux Klan, the American Nazis, Skinheads, the Aryan Nations, the National Alliance once led by the late Dr. William Pierce, former physics professor at Oregon State University who also campaigned for George Wallace, and other organized white supremacist groups to protect blacks. The skin color of black conservatives does not make them any less dangerous than it did Tshombe.

The programs individual white racists and hate groups oppose are also the very same programs black conservatives vehemently oppose: affirmative action; welfare and other forms of government assistance to the poor, a disproportionately large number of whom are black - hence the strong opposition to such programs among many whites; reparations; new congressional districts for blacks, and much more. For example, what Klansman wasn't thrilled when Gary Franks, the black Republican congressman from Connecticut, introduced a bill in Congress in 1993 to abolish black-majority congressional districts?

And what Klansman wasn't delighted when the same black congressman also testified for white plaintiffs in a lawsuit they filed to eliminate black Democratic representative Cynthia McKinney's black-majority congressional district in Georgia? He was greeted outside the courtroom by picketers carrying signs with slogans such as "Gary Franks is an Uncle Tom."

As he was leaving the courtroom, Representative McKinney's husband reached out and shook his hand, and then started screaming in his ear, "Did you have fun selling out the brothers? What did they give you, you nigger? You're a black Judas."[16]

In his book, *Searching for the Promised Land: An African-American's Optimistic Odyssey*, Franks says Democratic congressman Bill Clay of Missouri wrote him a letter saying that as a black conservative, he had no business being a member of the Congressional Black Caucus (CBC). He goes on to say that Clay asked him to get out, because it was an organization that existed "to fight to protect the rights of black people. I offer [this letter] in the hope of jarring your psyche to the reality that black is black and white is white and never the twain shall meet."[17]

Clay's criticism is validated by experience. If black conservatives promote the interests of the black community as they claim, why is it that blacks don't want to elect them as their representatives?

All black Republicans who ran for Congress in the 1990s and beyond, and even before then, in predominantly black districts lost; including Gary Franks himself who lost in 1996 although in a predominantly white district. But even there he lost to a Democrat, James Maloney, a white politician.

Not one predominantly black congressional district in the

United States has ever elected a black conservative or Republican as its representative in Congress. Why do black conservatives keep on losing elections, especially in black constituencies? It is not because black voters don't understand or get their message as black conservatives contend.

The voters hear and understand what black conservatives say whey they campaign for office, both at the local and the national levels. Still, black voters reject them. They don't want them. Black voters wouldn't reject black conservatives if they felt that black conservatives really care about them and want to protect and promote the interests of the black community.

When black conservatives oppose programs such as affirmative action, a higher minimum wage, and government assistance to provide jobs and promote economic development in the inner cities which most blacks support; they are not protecting or promoting the interests of the black community anymore than David Duke is. And when they ignore racism in a society that still has a serious racial problem, they deliberately harm their own people they claim they care about.

In fact, some blacks don't even consider black conservatives to be black anymore. As Roger Wilkins states: "For black Americans who live in a society where racism exists, it is legitimate to set parameters...There is some political and intellectual behavior in which you engage that keeps you from being a black person. Every oppressed community has drawn lines and says certain behavior puts you outside the community."[18]

Wilkin's argument must be read in its proper historical and contemporary context. Its validity is determined by the American experience which shows that blacks are still victims of racism, and by the admission of the majority of whites themselves who say racism remains a significant problem.[19] Therefore it is not just blacks who say that, although that alone would be enough to justify Wilkins' argument even if all whites denied the existence of racism.

In the face of such overwhelming evidence of racism, even if mostly in covert form, it is not difficult to understand why black conservatives are called traitors and not even considered black when they ignore such racial injustice, as Professor Walter Williams does when he contends: "The major problems blacks face have little or nothing to do with racial discrimination and are not solvable through civil rights strategy."[20]

What about segregation? Is that not a major problem when a disproportionately large number of blacks are stuck in the ghetto, and when even those who can afford to move out of poor, congested and crime-ridden neighborhoods in the inner cities are blocked from moving into white neighborhoods simply because they are black? How do you solve this problem without enforcing the 1968 Open Housing Act if the major problems black people face "are not solvable through civil rights strategy," as Williams claims?

And what about employment discrimination against blacks which is consistently twice the national average, translating into an even higher poverty rate among blacks which is three times that of whites?

How do you fight such discrimination and other racial injustices without invoking the 1964 Civil Rights Act which banned such discrimination, if enforcing civil rights laws cannot solve some of the major problems black people face?

But to Professor Williams and other black conservatives, those are not major problems except "illegitimacy, family breakdown, crime, school dropout and drugs."[21] Even these problems have to do with racism, although in varying degrees, depending on the situation in different cases.

The destruction of the black family and social disorganization in the inner cities - where blacks are concentrated - have to do with limited opportunities for blacks more than anybody else because of racism in all areas in life. There is not one aspect of life that is not affected by racism. That is because the larger society discriminates against blacks, and all the problems black people face - without a single exception, yes, including crime, drugs, and illegitimacy - can be explained in terms of racism, only in varying degrees.

Racism is an ubiquitous phenomenon, yet one which black conservatives would rather ignore, pretending that it is not a serious problem if it is one at all. And that is what has triggered such vitriolic condemnation of black conservatives by many blacks, such as Alphonso Pinkney who says black conservatives "are not unlike government officials in South Vietnam who supported American aggression against their own people."[22] It is not a far-fetched analogy.

Racism is aggression. There is nothing benign or pacifist about it. When black conservatives like Walter Williams say racism is no longer a major problem, they are condoning and supporting racism by exonerating racists. And that is an act of aggression by black conservatives against the black community, even if by proxy, condoning - hence supporting - racist conduct among many whites. Just ignore it. It is not a serious problem, they claim.

In that sense, black conservatives are serving as an advance party for racial terrorists. They are storm troopers for racists since, as "blacks," they attack from within to destroy the black community they claim to be helping. For example, when Gary Franks introduced a bill in Congress to dismantle black-majority congressional districts and testified in Atlanta, Georgia, for white plaintiffs to eliminate those districts, he committed an act of aggression against his own people.

His action was the same nefarious deed committed by traitor Tshombe when he teamed up with Western powers, led by Belgium and the United States, to dismember the Congo and kill Lumumba.

Why did Franks introduce such a bill? Why did he take the lead in sponsoring such legislation if he was not just being used by white conservatives and other racists who couldn't care less if all blacks - including himself - disappeared from the face of the United States today, not just from Congress?

Why did he allow himself to be used if the intention was not to get fellow black members out of Congress by testifying against other black representatives in court, knowing full well that had it not been for the creation of black-majority districts which made it possible for them to be elected, they could not and probably would never have been elected and thus got the opportunity to demonstrate their ability as leaders of members of all races?

Why were they or other blacks not elected before if racism was not the main factor? They had the same ability then, and there were other blacks with just as much ability to be congressmen and congresswomen. But the majority of the white voters did not care about them or give them the chance to prove themselves.

It was not until after black-majority districts were created that

28

those elected got the attention of the voters and the opportunity to demonstrate their competence as representatives of all the people in their districts, not just blacks.

It was mainly black voters who first sent them to Congress because they did not have to contend with racism from the black electorate. More whites voted for their re-election only *after* they proved themselves in office to be worthy representatives. That is the only reason they were re-elected: incumbency and demonstrated ability. Before then, they were no more than Ralph Ellison's *Invisible Man*,[23] and James Baldwin's character in *Nobody Knows My Name*.[24]

By introducing a bill in Congress to dismantle those districts and testifying for the white plaintiffs who wanted to eliminate the predominantly black districts, Franks wanted the black members of Congress who were elected from those districts to have remained "nvisible" and be "nobody".

It was that kind of conduct which prompted black Democratic congressman William Clay of Missouri to say that Franks, just after he failed to win a fourth congressional term, was a "Negro Dr. Kevorkian, a pariah, who gleefully assists in suicidal conduct to destroy his own race by supporting conservative legislation that is not in the interest of black people....The goal of this group of Negro wanderers is to maim and kill other blacks for the glorification and entertainment of ultra-conservative white racists."[25]

Strong language indeed, only matched by the perfidy of black conservatives whom Clay also calls a "new Negro cabal." It is a Negro cabal which includes Supreme Court Justice Clarence Thomas, radio talk show host Armstrong Williams, both of whom he named, and others who deliberately undermine efforts by African-Americans to improve their communities and economic development through government programs.[26] Black conservatives are vehemently opposed to those programs as a way of helping promote economic development in the black community because they say such assistance fosters and perpetuates a dependence mentality among blacks, and robs them of the incentive to work hard and be self-reliant.

Yet they ignore the fact that the black community, with few resources of its own, needs some government help, not to be perpetually dependent but to launch different projects to achieve economic independence because of the huge difference in accumulated wealth between blacks and whites due to racism. That is why whites don't need that kind of help as much as blacks do.

Whites have more money per capita and in terms of accumulated wealth. As Professor Henry Louis Gates Jr., head of the African-American Studies Center at Harvard University, pointed out in the late 1990s, only 40 percent of the African-American population belong to the middle class, while a staggering 30 percent are trapped in the underclass.

The rest fall in-between, going back and forth between the two groups.[27] That means 60 percent of black people are poor.

No other ethnic group is so loaded at the bottom, with the exception of Native Americans who seem to have given up after they lost their land and wealth to the white man. Where are all those poor blacks going to get the money to start businesses, buy property, and create jobs in the black community without government help that black conservatives are so much opposed to?

One reason why whites are comparatively much better off than blacks is that the majority of them own homes. Home ownership is a major source of wealth even for blacks in the ghetto who own the homes they live in. And that includes some on welfare.

But because of racial discrimination in mortgage lending, far fewer blacks in terms of proportion own homes than whites do. As Tom Wicker noted: "Discriminatory mortgage funding, one of the mainstays of housing segregation, results in fewer black than white home owners. That's a major reason why, in the mid-eighties, white families typically had eleven times the wealth of black families. Equity in a home is the main source of wealth for most   people."[28]

How do you narrow, let alone close, such yawning gap without federal assistance to blacks? The assistance black conservatives are opposed to is the same kind of help white conservatives and racists are adamantly opposed to for poor blacks, telling them to pull themselves up with their own bootstraps. Where are the boots, let alone the straps?

White conservatives are not very much worried about whites.

That is because the majority of them are financially secure contrasted with blacks. In the late 1990s, only 11.7 percent of whites were poor.[29]

But even whites who are financially secure get loans, while in many cases blacks with even better credit and business record don't.[30] And rich whites don't hesitate to ask for bigger tax breaks for themselves to accumulate even more wealth, while denying blacks much-needed help.

For some inexplicable reason, black conservatives can't see that. But they could not have missed the flaunting of wealth by their white ideological mentors during the 1996 Republican convention in San Diego, California, which earned them a place in the history of political conventions. As Jason Epstein stated in "White Mischief" in *The New York Review of Books*:

> At the Republican convention, one delegate out of five was said to be a millionaire and convention officials struggled to prevent television crews from filming the great nobles alighting from their private jets at the San Diego airport where they had come to demand still lower taxes on their mighty incomes....Greed and fear of blacks, of 'socialism,' and so on, hold the radical right together.[31]

Yet black conservatives don't oppose huge tax cuts for the rich but, ironically, resolutely denounce assistance to poor blacks - they claim they care about - as a waste of taxpayers' money. They contend that such programs for the poor are a form of "socialism" that undermines America's capitalist system. They downplay racism to the delight of white conservatives and other whites while ignoring the fact that "fear of blacks," as Epstein points out, is one of the indissoluble bonds that "hold the radical right together."

In fact, it is more than just fear but also hatred for blacks that unites white conservatives more than anything else. Black conservatives, as the ideological offspring of white conservatives, internalize this hatred as demonstrated by their hostility toward blacks in terms of opposition to affirmative action and other programs intended to help the black community, as well as in terms of their denial of racism as a major problem blacks face everyday.

Black conservatives parrot everything their ideological

31

godfathers say. Yet what they say has very little substance in terms of ideological merit, since American conservatism is driven by racism more than anything else. It is a bankrupt ideology. It would not have as much appeal as it does today - and as much as it has throughout American history - had there been no blacks in the United States and whose oppression has been used to justify the white man's twisted sense of superiority.

It is this twisted sense of superiority that fuels the white man's morbid fear of the very people he oppresses and exploits. And it bolsters his irrational commitment to maintaining the status quo to the detriment of blacks who are perpetually kept at the bottom.

And because black conservatives do not generate their own ideas, they cannot claim to be conceptual thinkers or dissenters within the black community, let alone in the larger society. They do what white conservatives tell them to do, not what they should be doing for blacks. They have ceased to be black. As Professor Martin Kilson states: "It is a clear distortion of the term dissenter to apply it to black conservatives. [They are] akin to client or satellite states...who do the ideological bidding of the WASP establishment."[32]

Malcolm X articulated a similar position years earlier about blacks who do anything for whites: "You bark, when the white man says bark. You bite, when the white man says bite. You bleed, when the white man says bleed."[33]

Black conservatives have been doing a lot of barking and biting as exemplified by the United States Supreme Court Justice Clarence Thomas, probably the most prominent hard-line black conservative besides Dr. Thomas Sowell and Professor Walter Williams. Thomas' hostility toward fellow blacks and liberals in general is maliciously inexorable.

Some have attributed his vindictiveness to the grueling televised confirmation hearings he was subjected to by liberals. As he himself put it: "From my standpoint as a black American, it [the senate confirmation hearing] is high-tech lynching for uppity blacks who in an way deign to think for themselves, to do for themselves, to have different ideas. No job is worth what I've been through - no job. No horror in my life has been so debilitating."[34]

But even if Clarence Thomas had not gone through the Senate interrogation which he compared to a lynching, he still would have been what he is. And that a right-wing conservative like Bary Goldwater and Ronald Reagan, Goldwater's protege. Thomas' malevolent implacability only fueled his hostility toward blacks.

His malevolence is so typical of black conservatives who are particularly hostile to poor blacks in the ghetto whom they say are in the condition they are in because of their own fault: they are the problem; their own number one problem, and not white America or the larger society.

Cavalierly, they ignore the plight of poor blacks, complaining that society is trying to do too much for them, instead of letting them fend for themselves so that they can learn the hard way through shock therapy by denying them help. Don't feel sorry for them: "Each to his own. I got mine, get yours." This is their attitude, reflecting the cruelty of their conservative philosophy. As Jeffrey Toobin stated in his article about Clarence Thomas in *The New Yorker*:

> His Supreme Court record attests that Thomas is still an angry man....Thomas's rage on the subject of his confirmation hearings is evergreen....His votes on the Supreme Court - and his public life as a Justice - have reflected, with great precision, the grievance that simmers inside him...his jurisprudential philosophy, as reflected in his votes and opinions, appears to be more than simply conservative: he looks well on his way to being ranked as one of the most conservative Justices of the late-twentieth century.[35]

Thomas can also look forward to being one of the most hostile jurists towards blacks, having ceased to be black himself even before he went to the Supreme Court. He also recalls with pride that when he was attending a black college in his home state of Georgia, wearing an Afro-hair style did not impress him at all.[36] As political scientist Manning Marable states: "Ethnically, Thomas has ceased to be an African American" in his lifestyle and thought pattern.[37]

Thomas' hostility to blacks has been demonstrated in many ways on and off the bench, including his opinion involving a black inmate in Louisiana that even surprised the other conservative justices on the Court:

> Other former Supreme Court clerks say Landau drafted the opinion in the case for which Thomas remains best known - that of *Hudson v. McMillian*, in

which Keith Hudson, a black inmate of a Louisiana prison, sued his guards for a 1983 beating they had inflicted on him while he was shackled. Seven Justices felt that Hudson had been subjected to cruel and unusual punishment,...and that the eight hundred-dollar damage award (a paltry sum) he won in the trial court should be upheld. Thomas believed that Hudson was entitled to nothing, because he had not suffered "significant injury."[38]

In spite of the evidence, Thomas not only ignored the injuries Hudson suffered but expressed his opinion in a way that left no doubt that he was being deliberately provocative and hostile. Probably the only people who were thrilled with Thomas' ruling were the racists who don't care when blacks are abused, tortured and killed in or out of prison:

The dissenting opinion that Landau drafted for Thomas in the Hudson case is as notable for its airy, dismissive tone as for its harsh conclusion. Thomas's entire description of the injuries suffered by Hudson was that they were minor. According to the judge who tried the case, he [Hudson] had suffered bruises and swelling in the face, mouth, lip, loosened teeth, and a cracked dental plate....One former clerk says of the opinion, "It was such a phenomenally aggressive position for him to be taking so early in his tenure. When that opinion came out, people were sitting there with their mouths hanging open." That may well have been the point. Thomas's Hudson dissent reads like a deliberate provocation - a thumb in the eye of the liberal establishment.[39]

And he thumbed it pretty good as shown by the response from many liberal quarters that were uniform in their condemnation of the opinion.

What was especially remarkable about the opinion, besides its unfathomable hostility, was that even the other conservative judges on the Supreme Court, including the hard-line conservative Chief Justice Rehnquist, disagreed with Thomas. Retired Justice Blackmun put it best from a liberal perspective on how many people were outraged by Thomas' opinion. As Toobin stated:

Justice Blackmun expressed his distress by writing an impassioned opinion concurring with the majority.

He noted that, in Thomas's interpretation, prison officials might not be constrained from "lashing prisoners with leather straps, whipping them with rubber hoses, beating them with naked fists, shocking them with electric currents, asphyxiating them short of death, intentionally exposing them to undue heat or cold, or forcibly injecting them with psychosis-inducing drugs' as long as these punishments were 'ingeniously designed to cause pain but without a telltale 'significant injury.'"

A *Times* editorial [was] entitled "The Youngest, Cruelest Justice"....In their columns, Mary McGrory called the dissent "disgusting," and William Raspberry labeled it "bizarre." But Thomas, far from being discouraged by the reaction to the opinion, didn't seem to mind at all.[40]

As a right-winger for years, Thomas' insensitivity towards the black community can be understood in an ideological context. Bary Goldwater and Ronald Reagan were his ideological mentors. And being a right-winger and caring about blacks at the same time is a contradiction in terms. One good example is Barry Goldwater, a life member of the NAACP for exactly the opposite reason.

Starting with his 1964 presidential campaign in which he whipped up racist sentiments against blacks with his highly inflammatory rhetoric, Goldwater paved the way for the rise of the racist conservative movement and helped thrust into prominence some of the most ultra-rightwing politicians in American history, including George Wallace and Ronald Reagan.

He opposed the entire civil rights legislation - the 1964 Civil Rights Act, the 1965 Voting Rights Act, and the 1968 Open Housing Act - as much as his ideological twin and protege, Ronald Reagan, did; in fact, it was Reagan who gave the opening speech and introduced Barry Goldwater at the 1964 Republican convention when Goldwater won the nomination as the GOP presidential candidate.

And Wallace's stand is well known, of course, from his immortal words when he blocked the entrance at the University of Alabama to stop black students from integrating the school - "I say segregation now, segregation tomorrow, segregation forever" - to his defiance on the anticipated passage of the Civil Rights Bill when he publicly warned President John F. Kennedy: "You will have to bring the troops back from Berlin if you pass that bill."

Those were Clarence Thomas' ideological godfathers as ultra-rightwingers. And when Thomas himself worked in the Reagan and the Bush administrations, he did his best to compile his right-wing credentials, as Toobin noted:

In the Reagan and Bush Administration, Thomas portrayed himself in his speeches as a zealot of the hard right....[On the Court] he has worn his ideological convictions like a full-length parka. Perhaps more than any other person who might have been named to the Court, Thomas repudiates everything that his predecessor, Thurgood Marshall, stood for. Thomas's every vote - even his public utterance, written or spoken - seems designed to outrage the liberal establishment that so venerated Marshall....His jurisprudence seems guided to an unusual degree by raw anger.[41]

That is not justice. That is malice, and unwarranted vindictiveness not only against liberals who were opposed to his nomination as Supreme Court Justice but against the entire black community simply because it enjoys the support of liberals and is therefore equally "guilty" of "opposing" his nomination to the highest court in the land.

It is this kind of hostility which draws strong criticism from many blacks, such as the late syndicated columnist Carl Rowan who wrote: "If you give Thomas a little flour on his face, you'd think you had David Duke."[42]

Thomas, of course, defended his position in a much larger context in order to deflect charges of malicious vindictiveness when he said: "The jugular of the dissenter [is] vengefully slashed at. Does a man instantaneously become insensitive or a dupe or an Uncle Tom because he happens to disagree with the policy of affirmative action?"[43]

The contradiction is obvious. Thomas did not speak out against affirmative action when it benefited him but took a firm stand against the program when it benefited *other* blacks and *other* minorities.

That is a double standard regardless of how black conservatives look at it through their ideological blinders. And it confirms the widespread suspicion, especially across black America, that they are deliberately endangering the black community by opposing programs which help blacks the same way they helped black conservatives themselves as minorities and members of the black community.

They are doing that to impress their ideological mentors, white conservatives, prompting critics like black historian John Henrik Clarke to say: "Black conservatives are really frustrated slaves crawling back to the plantation."[44]

There is no question that Clarence Thomas, whom black congressman Bill Clay called "a snake," was a beneficiary of affirmative action despite his vitriolic condemnation of the program. And he loved it. In accepting his appointment to the

36

Supreme Court, he inadvertently conceded not only the need but the legitimacy of affirmative action. Not once did he comment on his own situation.

Since he insists so much on race-neutral criteria based strictly on merit, why didn't he turn down the job when President George H. W. Bush appointed him a federal judge, or later when he was appointed to the Supreme Court? If merit were the sole criteria for such an appointment, without taking into account other legitimate factors, such as diversity in his case, which conservatives oppose so much, he would not be sitting on the Supreme Court today.

He would not even have been appointed to the Circuit Court of Appeals in Washington, D.C., before moving to the supreme bench. And the reason is simple. Clarence Thomas, never recognized as being among the best and most qualified lawyers in the country, was promoted because he is black. Race played a central in his appointment, whether or not he wants to admit it.

He filled a racial quota that he now loudly condemns and claims to despise, thus despising himself. If it's good for him, it's good for others. And if it's not good for them, it's not good for him. So what's he doing up there?

President Bush appointed Clarence Thomas first to a federal judgeship, and later to the Supreme Court, not because he was the best legal mind available, but because he is black and rigidly conservative. Being conservative was not enough. President Bush could very easily have found a far better qualified white conservative to fill the vacancy; a person who then might have hired Thomas as one his clerks, for diversity, on the president's recommendation.

If mastery of the law, judicial experience, and a first-rate legal mind - all of which collectively constitute merit - were the sole criteria for appointment to the Supreme Court, all the justices on the United States Supreme Court would be white men.

There would be no black and no women sitting on the Court today; not because of their mediocre mental caliber, but because of one reason: white male lawyers are the most experienced in law and constitute the largest pool of the best lawyers to select from. And people who are in a position to appoint anyone to any court are also white men; not blacks or other minorities or even white women. White men dominate America across the spectrum, all sectors of society, the mainstream and the periphery.

While many blacks and women have first-rate legal minds and know the law as well as white male lawyers do, and in many cases even better, they don't have as much experience on the bench as white male lawyers. That is because white men have dominated the bench and the legal profession for centuries, as they have all other fields fields with other white men.

So, for that reason alone, diversity is essential; not only to reflect America and its demographic composition but to achieve justice for all groups and individual who constitute the American society. You can't have justice when some groups are under-represented or excluded from the society or denied rights as equal participants.

Therefore without laws assuring and ensuring diversity, whose significance for some inexplicable reason eludes black conservatives, a black, Clarence Thomas in this case, and two women including a Jew, would *not* be sitting on the bench today. None of them, including Thomas himself, would be on the Supreme Court if Thomas and other conservatives had their way and had abolished affirmative action or had succeeded in stopping this compensatory program from being instituted.

Clarence Thomas was even admitted into college, Holy Cross, because of affirmative action. His admission into Yale Law School, which put him on a fast-track towards a lucrative career because of Yale's reputation as probably the best law school in the United States, was also a result of affirmative action.

And he knows it, as many others do, on how he got into both schools, and how he got high-profile jobs in two Republican - hence conservative - administrations under a party hostile to racial equality as clearly demonstrated by President George W. Bush who unequivocally opposed affirmative action and even had his administration support - in the United States Supreme Court - a white student who sued the University of Michigan for implementing affirmation action in its selection and admission of minority students in order to provide them with opportunities as well as achieve and maintain diversity in the student body reflective of the American society at large.

President Bush, together with black conservatives and their ideological compatriots on the Right, were impressed by none of this; forgetting or ignoring that black conservatives themselves have been some of the greatest beneficiaries of affirmative action they oppose so much.

Even when some black conservatives admit that affirmative action benefited them, a rare concession, they continue to oppose the program for the very same reason that they accepted it in the first place.

Now that they have reaped the benefits, they are determined to make certain that no other blacks get the same opportunity to succeed in life and use the same program that black conservatives used to achieve their goals. For example, black conservative Los Angeles radio talk show host and former practicing attorney Larry Elder, who likes calling himself a libertarian, admits that he would never have had the opportunity to attend Brown University, and later the University of Michigan Law School, had it not been for affirmative action; a program both schools endorsed and implemented through the years and which the University of Michigan defended before the United States Supreme Court in 2003 when a white student sued the school saying she was denied admission into law school because of affirmative action which favored black students although she had higher grades than they did. As Elder conceded:

What it [affirmative action] did for me was to kick me from one level into another level. Without it [affirmative action], I wouldn't have gone to Brown (an Ivy League school) - I probably would've gone to a Big Ten school....I think it is likely that my resume would've looked different if I was subject to the same standards as everybody else....I am prepared to admit that I benefited from affirmative action.[45]

Now Larry Elder disingenuously wants to abolish affirmative action and deny other blacks the same opportunity he seized to succeed in life under a program the federal government instituted to open up doors for blacks and other minorities - including white women, the greatest beneficiaries of affirmative action - who were kept out and denied equal opportunity in a country which has always been dominated by white men and favored whites in general as the dominant race.

It was all right for Larry Elder and other black conservatives to take advantage of affirmative action, but, according to these black rightwing ideologues, no one else should have the same opportunity. And they have not been able to reconcile the two conflicting perspectives. Many of Elder's ilk face the same dilemma when they enunciate their conservative ideology in different forums, and none of them has been able to resolve it.

Although black conservatives articulate the same position on a number of issues fundamental to their conservative philosophy, there are also contradictions in their position showing that much of what they say about blacks is not validated by the American experience, past or present. Even unanimity in their position in some areas is more apparent than real, except their hostility towards other blacks they euphemistically call "tough love" while deliberately inflicting pain on their brethren they claim to love so much.

When Shelby Steele, a leading black conservative scholar and author of *The Content of Our Character: A New Vision of Race in America*, contends that President Ronald Reagan had much to offer black people, he deliberately ignores how much the conservative president hurt black people when he administered shock therapy to them.

Reagan's disenfranchisement of black people (like Bush's in Florida during the 2000 presidential election he would have lost had tens of thousands of black and Jewish votes not been destroyed) cancelled out what limited opportunities and benefits he offered them. Yet Professor Steele contends in his book:

I believe there was much that Reagan had to offer blacks. His emphasis on traditional American values - individual initiative, self-sufficiency, strong families - offered what I think is the most enduring solution to the demoralization and poverty that continues to widen the gap between blacks and whites in America.[46]

Ronald Reagan offered blacks nothing new. And blacks got nothing new from Reagan. Reagan and other conservatives are not the only people who cherish those values, as Shelby Steele implies. In fact, white conservatives with their "holier-than-thou" attitude are some of the most racist people around. They are busy quoting the Bible while at the same time they are denying blacks equal opportunity and don't even mind starving them and other poor people.

They are the ones, not liberals, who deserve the title of a book by Dr. Thomas Sowell, probably America's most prominent black conservative, appropriately entitled if applied to conservatives: *The Vision of the Anointed: Self-Congratulation as a Basis for Social Policy*. For example, the fundamentalism of the Religious Right is inextricably linked with racism.

This is graphically demonstrated by its support for segregated schools through the years since the 1954 *Brown v. The Board of Education* decision to desegregate schools. And it was odiously apparent during its violent, vocal opposition to the civil rights movement in the sixties, and in the seventies and eighties, and even today in the second millennium.[47] It is people like that including Reagan whom black conservatives claim help and care about blacks.

The values Shelby Steele says Reagan instilled in black people have always been cherished by liberal leaders and their followers: from Dr. Martin Luther King, Jr., Andrew Young and Malcolm X to Jesse Jackson, Julian Bond, Kweisi Mfume and many others. They have always preached self-reliance, not dependence on welfare. And they have always taught about the imperative need for strong families and individual initiative.

That is how blacks survived even during slavery, strong families and hard work, and always have through the centuries since they were brought to America in chains from Africa.

And it is the same values, conducive to achievement, black churches have always taught throughout the black community. And millions of blacks, in fact the vast majority, implement those values. That is why most blacks work. They are not on welfare or begging the government to take care of them. Why not, then, since they don't cherish values conducive to achievement as conservatives and many others claim? Most blacks would be begging the government to take care of them, feed them, and clothe them.

Black people did not learn the values of self-reliance, strong families, and individual initiative from Reagan or from other conservatives, black or white. Conservatives just claim more credit than they deserve. And they deserve nothing in terms of helping black people. They have done more to destroy black people, including denying them civil rights and equal opportunity, than they have done to help them.

And the record speaks for itself, as Senator Trent Lott clearly showed with his "off-the-cuff" remark in 2002 when - on Senator Strom Thurmond's 100th birthday - he publicly stated that had Thurmond won the 1948 presidential election (he campaigned as a staunch segregationist), the country would have been better off; it would not have had "all these problems," his euphemism for black claims to racial equality and integration. As he put it:

We're proud of it [Mississippi, Trent Lott's home state, voting for Thurmond in 1948] . And if the rest of the country had followed our lead, we wouldn't have all these problems over the years.

During the 1948 presidential campaign, Thurmond bluntly stated: "All the laws of Washington and all the bayonets of the Army cannot force the Negroes into our homes, our schools, our churches." And Trent Lott, as a typical white conservative who wanted to maintain the status quo and fought against integration, was nostalgic about all that.

He and other white national conservative leaders including congressmen, such as Bob Barr of Georgia, and Attorney General John Ashcroft, have also - even in the 1990s and beyond - been known to associate with white supremacist groups such as the Council of Conservative Citizens, which is more than just a conservative organization but a mainstream platform for racists, and others including the American Enterprise Institute which sponsored Dinesh D'Souza's virulently anti-black best-selling book *The End of Racism*, and the American Renaissance. They have also attended and addressed their meetings. And these are the kind of people black conservatives say care about blacks.

When Shelby Steele and other black conservatives give Ronald Reagan credit for instilling in blacks values black people already had and have always cherished, why don't they also talk about what Reagan did for the rich at the expense of the poor, a disproportionately large number of whom are black because of racism? Why don't they talk about his civil rights record?

Reagan came into office saying he was going to help the poor as never before by relieving the American people of what he called "the punitive tax burden." Instead, he introduced tax cuts that only benefited the rich, while the national debt skyrocketed.

As Michael Lind, hardly a liberal by any definition, states in his book *Up From Conservatism: Why the Right is Wrong for America*, during the Ford and Carter administrations, the federal debt increased by $450 billion.

By glaring contrast, under Reagan, the Republican president who slashed taxes for the rich by 25 percent in three years, and under Bush who raised them marginally, the debt skyrocketed to an astronomical $3.5 trillion,[48] an unconscionable burden on the current and several future generations. As Jason Epstein points out in "White Mischief":

> While the federal debt was rising, the proceeds of Reagan's reckless tax cut were distributed not to garage mechanics in Georgia (or to black workers in the ghettos of Detroit and elsewhere) but in grotesque disproportion to the very rich. According to Gary Wills, citing Reagan's biographer, Lou Cannon, income for the bottom 10 percent fell by 10.5 percent from 1977 to 1986 while the top 10 percent gained 24.4 percent and the top 1 percent gained 74.2 percent, a disparity exacerbated by a sharp increase in the regrssive social security tax.[49]

Reagan's trickle-down theory of economics, which his own Vice President George Bush labelled "voodoo economics" when he himself ran for president against Reagan in 1980, did not produce even a trickle for millions of poor and ordinary working people, contrary to what conservatives say.

The rich got richer; and, if you were rich during the Reagan era of greed, the more benefits you reaped in disproportionately large amounts, without sweat, and at the expense of the poor.

Michael Lind cites even more disturbing statistics, showing that between 1977 and 1980, "a mere 1 percent of families in the United States received 79 percent of all the income generated...with much of that bonanza going to the top tenth of that 1 percent."[50] Admittedly, all those were not Reagan years; he came into office in January 1981.

Still, the income disparity was largest during his presidency of eight years, which was very little comfort to blacks in the inner cities and other poor areas. Yet, in spite of all that evidence, black conservatives say Reagan helped blacks. Further evidence shows otherwise. As Tom Wicker states in his best-selling book *Tragic Failure: Racial Integration in America*:

By 1987, the nation's wealth and income had been more narrowly concentrated: one half of 1 percent held 26.9 of the wealth. Not many of them were black. The top 10 percent of households controlled about 60 percent of the wealth, but not many of them were black either. Reagan's "supply-side" tax rate cuts of 1981...was one good reason: [the tax rate cuts] reduced the "effective overall, combined federal tax rate paid by the top 1 percent of Americans" - who numbered few, if any, blacks - from 30.9 percent in 1977 to 23.1 percent in 1984. In contrast, the percentage of total money income received by the poorest fifth of the population dropped through Reagan years: from 5.1 in 1980 to 4.6 in 1988. That fifth did include lots of African-Americans.[51]

The majority of blacks were, and still are, in that poorest fifth of the American population for one simple reason. Sixty percent of all blacks are poor, and the majority of the poor blacks are among the poorest of the poor, a fact difficult to reconcile with black conservative claims that Reagan helped poor blacks when the poor got poorer, blacks being the hardest hit. The fate of poor blacks is exactly the opposite of that of the rich even in terms of statistics:

In the same years the percentage of money income by the wealthiest fifth of the population rose from 41.6 to 44 percent....Federal Reserve figures from 1989 when Reagan left office show that the richest 1 percent of American households in that year held 39 percent of the nation's wealth, leaving only 61 percent of the national wealth for all the other 99 percent of the people, which included virtually all African-Americans. Annual income levels...were also badly skewed; the top 20 percent of income earning households had taken 55 percent of all after-tax income in 1989, while the lowest 20 percent, in which most blacks were found, received only 5.7 percent of after-tax income...[These] wealth disparities...underline economic and political policies - not least Reagan's - that favor the well-off over the poor and thus have a disproportionate racial effect.[52]

In spite of such huge disparities, increased phenomenally by Reagan's economic policies and tax cuts deliberately favoring the rich and having a disproportionately negative impact on blacks, Shelby Steele and other black conservatives including Dr. Thomas Sowell and Walter Williams, an economics professor like Sowell, still say Reagan helped blacks, instead of admitting that he hurt blacks and impeded black progress.

Reagan's civil rights record was no better than his economic policies for blacks. He refused to extend and strengthen the Voting Rights Act of 1965 until he was forced to do so. Instead, he did everything he could to try and weaken it. By doing so, he probably neutralized the Act by refusing to condemn those who refused to implement it, and by his own firm stand against its extension; thus encouraging defiance among many whites who never supported it in the first place, especially when he said the 1965 Voting Rights Act "humiliated the South"; meaning white southerners who were totally opposed to racial equality including integration and black people's right to vote other Americans took for granted.

At no time did he admit that denial of racial equality and civil rights deeply offended and humiliated the victims, black people in the southern states who were not even allowed to drink at water fountains or use toilets and other facilities used by whites and others, let alone allowed to vote.

It difficult to describe such a leader as someone who helped and cared about blacks. It is also difficult, based on his attitude and on what he did and said, to say he was not a racist or did not condone racism.

During the 1980 presidential campaign in which he became the Republican standard-bearer after he won the party's nomination, the Republican agenda included a proposal to give tax exemptions to segregated private schools.

After Reagan won the election and became president because of the Republican party's racist platform wrapped in coded language to appeal to white sentiments and attack blacks, he "reversed the policy of the Internal Revenue Service that denied federal tax exemption to private schools practicing racial discrimination....He sought to show his doubts about school integration by protecting new forms of segregated education and, not so incidentally, to repay southern political supporters."[54]

Among those schools were South Carolina's Bob Jones University, a third-rate academic institution also notorious for its racist practices including its ban on inter-racial dating claiming such a ban is sanctioned by the Bible, and other bastions of organized hate towards blacks.

But all that is hardly surprising for a leader who launched his presidential campaign in the small town of Philadelphia in Neshoba County, Mississippi, which is very close to the place where three civil rights workers were brutally murdered by the Ku

45

Klux Klan in 1963.

He did not say a word to condemn those murders or racism in general. Instead, he talked about "state rights", code word for racism and for "no rights at all for blacks," southern states invoked in the sixties to perpetuate racial inequalities and brutalize blacks. He was nostalgic about those "good old days" for whites, which were equivalent to time spent in hell for blacks. As Malcolm X said, "A white man's heaven is a black man's hell."

Reagan's thinly disguised racism was also clearly evident when he opposed attempts to make Dr. Martin Luther King's birthday a federal holiday.[55] In addition to his own opposition to the holiday, his own negative feelings about the holiday and racial equality in general were shared my millions other whites across the country. He read the mood of the country well and knew he was standing on solid ground when he opposed the proposed holiday to honor Dr. King and the campaign for racial equality he led at the cost of his life.

Millions of white voters were equally opposed to the holiday, therefore to remembrance of Dr. King as a leader of the campaign for racial equality. And they still are.[56] For example, the state of Arizona under Republican Governor Evan Mecham refused to commemorate Dr. King's birthday and continued to treat it as just another day.

The state of new Hampshire, another Republican stronghold like Arizona, was also strongly opposed to the holiday as were a number of prominent national Republican leaders such as Senator Jesse Helms of North Carolina, a known racist with a track record of opposing racial equality for many years. There was also strong opposition to the holiday among many whites, including Democrats not just Republicans, in different parts of the country.

As president, Reagan was also opposed to affirmative action. This was clearly demonstrated when he appointed a hard-line black conservative Clarence Thomas as director of the Equal Employment Opportunity Commission (EEOC). Thomas, as a hatchet man for Reagan and other conservatives hardly any of whom care about blacks, went on to neutralize the affirmative action program and slow down racial discrimination lawsuits by delaying the litigation process as much as possible to the delight of his ideological mentors and other racists.

Not once did Thomas admit, even obliquely, that President Reagan appointed him to the post in order to insulate his Republican administration from charges of racism. Not only did he do a wonderful job for his racist bosses; he was also handsomely rewarded by the next president, George H.W. Bush, who offered him a federal judgeship in Washington, D.c., and finally a seat on the nation's highest court.

President Reagan compiled his anti-civil rights record without the slightest compunction throughout his two terms. With his assistant attorney general for civil rights, William Bradford Reynolds, an inflexible right-winger, Reagan worked against school integration and tried to block implementing school desegregation plans already approved by the courts.

Using draconian measures designed by Reynolds, Reagan succeeded in doing so in Norfolk, Virginia. Encouraged by this success and with the blessings of President Reagan himself, Reynolds led the fight and launched other court battles against equal opportunity in education. As Tom Wicker stated about the indefatigable Reynolds in his book *Tragic Failure: Racial Integration in America*:

Reynolds, who failed to win Senate confirmation when Reagan tried to make him deputy attorney general, once was described by Benjamin Hooks, then the executive director of the NAACP, as a "latter-day Bilbo." Theodore Bilbo had been an unabashed racist senator from Mississippi.[57]

Reagan also refused to impose economic sanctions on apartheid South Africa and even went so far as to say at a news conference in Washington D.C., that there was no more racism in South Africa, at a time when the apartheid regime was still in power and brutalizing blacks and other non-whites as well as other opponents of its diabolical policies of white supremacy.

Like President Richard Nixon, Reagan also refused to meet with members of the Congressional Black Caucus (CBC) despite several requests by the black congressmen for a meeting with him. And when a meeting on drug abuse was held in the White House, the Reagan Administration did not even invite a renowned congressional authority on the subject, black Democratic congressman Charles Rangel of Harlem, New York, to the meeting. The administration also gave the reason for not inviting

Rangel. "A spokesman lamely explained that 'no chair' was available for Rangel at the White House!"[58] As Jesse Jackson assessed Reagan's civil rights record:

From Philadelphia [Mississippi], where civil rights workers - Chaney, Goodman, and Schwerner - were killed in 1963, the same city where Reagan launched his 1980 presidential campaign but without even saying a word about the murders, to the Bitburg cemetery, to the vote on sanctions against South Africa, it's one unbroken ideological line.[59]

What is even more tragic and terrifying is that Reagan, in addition to his own beliefs on the matter, took such a hostile position on civil rights for blacks because he had the full backing of the majority of whites - and knew it.

He didn't have to worry about what blacks thought or what they had to say. Whites Americans counted, black Americans simply didn't count, in his calculations; be it election strategy, policy formulation, whatnot.

Black people were simply not part of the mainstream, according to him. They were "just here." And as many blacks say about their minority status and lack of power in a predominantly white nation which they feel ignores them most of the time: "We are just here"; implying they are not a factor to be reckoned with. Reagan validated that. As Tom Wicker pointed out:

The anti-civil rights record Reagan accumulated was so lengthy and substantial that he could not have compiled it without the acquiescence and support of white Americans....No president could have compiled such a record in the face of vigorous public support for further measures of racial integration....

Even before his speech at Philadelphia (Mississippi), Reagan had openly opposed the Civil Rights Act of 1964, the Voting Rights Act of 1965, the Open Housing Act of 1968 and in numerous other ways had demonstrated his fundamental opposition to the fact, if not the concept, of integration. And by the time he sought the presidency - nearly winning the Republican nomination in 1976, taking it easily in 1980 - neither his clear anti-integration record nor even his appearance in Mississippi was a political liability.

It was, in fact, largely because of these that Ronald Reagan was elected to the White House....[After he became president, Reagan] sometimes subtle, sometimes open anti-integration approach was sufficiently in accord with the public mood that he apparently profited politically, as demonstrated by his landslide reelection in 1984 and his continuing popularity.[60]

Black conservatives refuse to admit that. Or they just can't see it for some inexplicable reason. The contend that Reagan did "a lot of good" for blacks, as Shelby Steele argues:

> The tragedy of black power in America today [is that it is perceived] primarily as a victim's power, grounded too deeply in the entitlement derived from past injustice....Since the social victim has been oppressed by society, he comes to feel that his individual life will be improved by more changes in society than by his own initiative....He makes society rather than himself the agent of change.[61]

Steele commends Reagan for helping blacks in spite of his tragic civil rights record and economic policies which were blatantly racist in their disproportionate impact on black people. He bemoans black suffering *in the past tense*, contending that "past racial injustice" does not justify entitlement, and totally ignores the fact that such racial injustice is still practiced today. If entitlement can be justified on grounds of racial injustice, then black people are definitely not living in the past when they claim such entitlement as a remedy: affirmative action being the principal one, but which Steele opposes.

And that inexorably leads him to use phrases such as "since the social victim [read, 'black'] has been oppressed by society," without coupling it with "and is still being oppressed today." He also says that the victim "makes society rather than himself the agent of social change." Why does he exonerate society not only from making amends for its injustices but also from being a catalyst for change?

It is true that the victim, black in this context, also has to help himself. But aren't his options limited in a racist society? If they are, is there not a need for society, since it is the perpetrator of injustice, to play an active role as the main agent for change to help improve his condition?

Black people, except for a few you find in every race, are not saying society should do everything for them as black conservatives imply and sometimes even explicitly say, which is very insulting to the entire race. But society *does* have an obligation to help, especially when it is not fair to all of its members, as the racial predicament of African-Americans clearly demonstrates. Yet, black conservatives like Shelby Steele say, no, society has no such obligation.

They deliberately ignore the devastating impact of racism on blacks, a callous attitude which leads Steele and other black conservatives to compliment Reagan for "helping" blacks in spite of his unabashed racist record.

It is this kind of attitude and policies advocated by black conservatives that read like a Ku Klux Klan manifesto which invite ridicule and contempt from many blacks. As Nikki Giovanni said: "The Thomas Sowells, Shelby Steeles and Clarence Thomases...are trying to justify the gross neglect of the needs of black America. We know that such conservatives have no character. They are in opportunistic service."[62]

Nothing black conservatives say has helped to change the perception many blacks have that they are "traitors," "turncoats," "Uncle Toms," "phonies," "opportunists" and all the other names they have been called which cannot be printed here. To get a better understanding of the black conservative phenomenon in the United States, we must look at another aspect beyond a common ideology that unites them, raising serious questions about their true identity. This can be discerned from what they say.

Willie Richardson, publisher of the black conservative monthly *Headway* (formerly *National Minority Politics*) now defunct because it couldn't sell well among blacks - its intended audience - because they saw it as nothing but trash, made this sweeping statement in one of the editions of this intellectually shallow publication: "In their view [of the black elite], blacks will remain perpetual victims. They will never be able to compete on a level playing field, as long as white Americans outnumber them....[Clarence] Thomas rejects the notion that, in all things intellectual and economic, black Americans are simply outgunned at every turn. I join Thomas in rejecting that notion."[63]

Yet, Colin Powell, another prominent black conservative, says exactly the opposite on an issue so fundamental to the black conservative philosophy, raising the question: What is really a black conservative?

Powell argues more reasonably, probably than most of his ideological brethren, when he contends: "The notion that affirmative action should be completely stripped away is ridiculous. Anyone who would suggest that racism is a thing of the past is wrong."[64] He articulates a position identical to liberal Jesse Jackson's, a position another black conservative, Thomas Sowell, calls "the Jesse Jackson rhyme"[65] of mending and not ending preferential treatment for blacks who live in a society where there is no level playing   field.

That one of the foremost black conservatives, Colin Powell, and one of the most prominent black liberals, Jesse Jackson, say exactly the same thing on an issue that sets liberals and conservatives apart does not provide much comfort to black conservatives who try to create the illusion that much as they differ on peripheral issues, there is at least unanimity - as, indeed, there should be - on fundamentals that constitute the core of the conservative philosophy. One of those principles is the employment of race-neutral criteria, hence opposition to affirmative action.

Another black conservative, John Doggett, a classmate of Clarence Thomas at Yale Law School and who testified on his behalf during his Senate confirmation hearing, wrote in the black conservative journal *National Minority Politics*:

> Before Thomas was nominated to the Supreme Court, Democrats had successfully painted the Republican party as an anti-black and racist party. The Democrats had also painted black Republican conservatives as 'right-wing nuts' who were 'traitors to their race'....Thomas is a black Republican and his very existence threatens the underpinnings of American liberalism - the need for black victims, white saviors, and a multi-ethnic array of program pimps....Far too many of our 'black leaders' have lost sight of the importance of being the best in everything. They have decided that it is easier to make excuses, to blame others for our failings, to demand a permanent second class 'set-aside' world.[66]

Doggett articulated a typical conservative position shared by white conservatives. Both black and white conservatives maintain that affirmative action programs helping blacks and other minorities including white women were wrong from the the beginning.[67] Yet only a few months later, Doggett stated: "The Nixon Administration created affirmative action programs in the early 1970s to give black Americans a fair and impartial opportunity to compete for federal jobs. Affirmative action was a rational and totally appropriate response to the systematic and legal exclusion of blacks from every possible opportunity in this country."[68]

This is not the position of black conservatives, of whom Doggett is one. As Sowell says: "Among so-called 'black conservatives,' it is virtually impossible to find anyone who wants to go back to anything, this group being opposed to both the racial discrimination policies of the past and the racial preference policies that came after them."[69] Doggett shares this typical conservative position, as he unequivocally states in the first quotation.

Yet, next, he says "affirmative action was a rational and totally appropriate response to the systematic and legal exclusion of blacks from every possible opportunity in this country."

If affirmative action was necessary to open doors for blacks excluded "from every possible opportunity in this country," as Doggett himself concedes, what about today? Has such exclusion or discrimination stopped? Do blacks have equal opportunity? Doggett admits that blacks even today are still trying to "succeed in the face of vicious racism."[70] So why shouldn't affirmative action programs be necessary today as they were back then, since the same problem that exists today existed in the 1970s when, as Doggett himself admits, "it justified the creation" of those programs?

Doggett says racism still exists and calls it "vicious." Yet in the same breath he argues that affirmative action, which was necessary to deal with this very same problem back then, is not necessary to deal with the same problem today. If affirmative action programs are not necessary today, they were not necessary during the seventies when he says they were "a rational and totally appropriate response to the systematic and legal exclusion of blacks from every possible opportunity in this country...to give black Americans a fair and impartial opportunity to compete."[71]

You can't have "fair and impartial opportunity" in a society where, as Doggett himself admits, "vicious racism" still exists. How does he reconcile the two conflicting positions? His answer is platitudinous: "The issue is equal opportunity, not race." That is true, but only when race is not a factor, which it is, in a society where racism still is a serious problem as Doggett concedes.

Therefore, the issue is also support for affirmative action even to a prominent white conservative such as Robert Dole who was the 1996 Republican presidential candidate. He was opposed to preferential treatment programs for women and minorities since the beginning of his political career but changed his position later and supported affirmative action.

Many people probably dismissed Dole's change of position on this highly controversial issue as a political tactic in an election year to capture white female voters - since blacks, both male and female, hardly vote Republican - and lure Colin Powell to the Republican ticket as his vice presidential candidate. Had he succeeded in doing so, he may have been able to draw a substantial number of black voters away from Democratic President Bill Clinton. As Dole stated: "I told him [Powell], I've been for affirmative action [but] I think there are some changes that should be made."[73]

Dole was talking about mending, not ending, affirmative action. Leading black conservative Thomas Sowell derisively dismissed Dole's declaration as some liberal rhyme without any substance: "Supporters of affirmative action have revealed jjst how bankrupt their position is. They have already prepared their fallback position: 'Mend it, don't end it.' This is the Jesse Jackson rhyme, now echoed by Bill Clinton."[74]

But it is also the black conservative rhyme some prominent black conservatives echo. They include Gwen Daye Richardson, editor of the now-defunct black conservative journal *Headway*. It does not, however, resonate throughout the black conservative community.

Another hot issue for black conservatives is welfare. Thomas Sowell and Walter Williams, both distinguished professors of economics, have earned a reputation as some of the staunchest opponents of welfare and probably the most vocal. Their stand places them in the same league with Charles Murray, a prominent white conservative who, in his 1984 book, *Losing Ground*,[75] contended that welfare should be abolished.

For decades, Murray campaigned for the elimination of welfare, a position shared by Sowell and Williams. Other black conservatives have been equally outspoken. As Deroy Murdock, although an intellectual lightweight in conservative circles, bluntly put it: "The benighted poor, too feeble to fend for themselves, must be nursed for life by Uncle Sugar in order to survive. This very type of paternalism or perhaps maternalism...has fueled welfare that virtually has loved poor Americans to death."[76]

By remarkable contrast, *Headway* stated in its plitical philosophy: "Compassionate conservatism: While stressing the importance of free enterprise and limited government, we must recognize our responsibility as a society to help those who help themselves, or who are unable to help themselves through no fault of their own."[77] But also, almost all black conservatives contend that the welfare system destroys blacks and that too many of them are on welfare in disproportionately large numbers compared to whites. As Joseph Brown states:

In September 1994, an article in the *Wall Street Journal* noted that according to the Department of Health and Human Services: 'The number of whites on welfare comprise 38.9 percent of Aid to families with Dependent Children (ADC) recipients, slightly above the 37.2 percent recipients who are black. But because blacks make up just about 12.1 percent of the overall American population, the share of the black population on welfare easily outstrips the white share by well over 8 to 1.' That is the bitter truth and there is no need in trying to deny it....This destructive system impacts black Americans disproportionately.[78]

Black conservatives seem to have plenty of ammunition in their arsenal to wage war against their the welfare system, as demonstrated by the evidence cited above by Joseph Brown, a leading black conservative journalist. And they *are* horrifying statistics, especially the 8 to 1 ratio, black versus white on the welfare treadmill.

The main reason blacks are on welfare in such disproportionately large numbers, black conservatives contend, is because they see themselves as perennial victims of white America in a nation where racism has considerably "declined," as Shelby Steele describes the situation; a bold assertion contradicted by the black American experience in what is supposed to be the citadel of democracy built on the twin ideals of liberty and equality. As Steele states in his award-winning book *The Content of Our Character*:

With the decline in racism the margin of black choice has greatly expanded. But anything [the psychology of victimization] that prevents us from exploiting our new freedom to the fullest is now as serious a barrier to us as

54

racism once was.[79]

When he says, "as racism once was," he makes it clear that racism is no longer a serious problem in America today. However, Doggett, another black conservative who is also a lawyer, admits "vicious racism" still exists; a confession rare among black conservatives. Another black conservative who has denied, then has admitted, and then has again denied the seriousness of racism is radio talk show host Armstrong Williams. In a rare confession, he had this to say:

> Even today, 30 years after the civil rights movement many whites still harbor racist attitudes. Of course, discrimination against black people by white people still is a serious problem in our society....America has a long way to go toward racial healing and the problem continues to grow....
>
> In fact, recently there seems to have been a surge in racially motivated crimes. For instance, in North Carolina, at a military institution, a black corporal was killed by three white cadets apparently for no reason other than that he was black. Also, in Kentucky a black family was 'discouraged' from moving into a white neighborhood because it was feared that the presence of a black family would bring down the property value of other homes....
>
> We must understand, however, that the problem is not white-versus-black...the problem is conflict itself.[80]

After conceding the seriousness of racism even today, comes the characteristic conservative denial of the problem. If 'the problem is not white-versus-black," as Williams contends, what is racism then? Conflict between whom? Doggett denies, then concedes the viciousness of racism. Williams also flip-flops and tries to land on both sides of the issue at the same time after doing a little semantic boogie. So do others, yet they are all black conservatives.

On hearing such conflicting statements on an issue so fundamental to their philosophy that downplays and even denies the existence of racism, one can't help but wonder: What is really a black conservative?

Are critics right when they say black conservatives are nothing but traitors, opportunists, and puppets - marionettes of white conservatives? Black conservative writings and speeches, and their support of conservative policies hostile toward blacks, confirm that.

Shelby Steele dismisses claims of racism as a form of self-victimization many blacks use to dodge individual responsibility, a position articulated by other black conservatives such as Larry Elder, a nationally syndicated controversial radio talk show host who routinely clashes with fellow blacks because of his outlandish views.

What black conservatives are also saying, in other words, is that self-victimization is equally a kind of an extortion scheme - Dinesh D'Souza, a conservative Indian immigrant calls affirmative action "mugging" by blacks - black people use to extract concessions from guilt-ridden whites who feel they must help blacks because they have oppressed and exploited them for so long and continue to do so.

As Shelby Steele states, blacks who complain about racism "justify or camouflage [their] fears, weaknesses, and inadequacies....The race-holder whines, or complains indiscriminately, not because he seeks redress but because he seeks the status of victim....A victim is not responsible for his condition, and by claiming a victim's status the race-holder gives up the sense of personal responsibility he needs to better his condition. His purpose is to hide rather than fight....The price he pays for the false comfort of his victim's status is a kind of impotence."[81]

There are indeed those who use racism as an excuse. But there are probably even more whose lives have been ruined by racism. That is what Steele refuses to admit because, to him, racism has "declined." "With the decline of racism," as he puts it, there is no need for affirmative action that only encourages the psychology of victimization: "Affirmative action encourages blacks to exploit their own past victimization as a source of power and privilege....Racial preferences send us the message that there is more power in our past suffering than our present achievements."[82]

Because racial victimization is all in the past in most cases, according to Steele, there is therefore only one reason why blacks lag behind other racial and ethnic groups: black people themselves are the reason - they are their own number one problem. And he is not alone in saying so. Most black conservatives say the same thing: Don't blame anybody else for your condition but yourself. As Joseph Brown argues:

Louis Farrakhan and Jesse Jackson feel it's necessary to keep the grievance system alive to further their respective causes....Farrakhan referred to Jews, Koreans, Vietnamese and Arabs as 'blodsuckers' of the black community....People like Farrakhan need enemies, and the immigrants who have come to this country and prospered in the nation's black communities are convenient scapegoats....

These outsiders are simply filling a void that black Americans seem reluctant to fill. They are providing goods and services that must be necessary since many of them do well. In many instances, if the so-called outsiders hadn't stepped in, the buildings housing the businesses would have been boarded shut....To Farrakhan, I say, yes, the black community does have some bloodsuckers. Sadly, many of them look a lot like you and me....Drug dealers are the true bloodsuckers of black America.[83]

Brown ignores racism as most black conservatives do. Banks and other lending institutions discriminate against blacks when they apply for loans as several studies have shown.[84] That is why it is easier for Jews, Koreans, Vietnamese and others than it is for blacks to open businesses in the inner cities; not because blacks are reluctant to do so. Non-blacks get loans while blacks don't. That explains why "the buildings housing the businesses in black communities would have been boarded shut hadn't so-called outsiders stepped in."

Concerning black drug dealers, it is true that they are a major problem in black communities across the United States as Brown says. But that is not why blacks are economically behind other ethnic groups. Most blacks are not drug dealers or users or alcoholics; if they were, black America - in its entirety - would have been pulverized from within. Racism is the primary reason blacks are behind other groups because they are denied equal opportunity, contrary to what black conservatives say.

Brown goes on to say that drug dealers should rot in prison because they wreak havoc across the black community. He criticizes Jesse Jackson for taking the criminal justice system to task because of the stiffer sentences imposed on black drug dealers than those given to whites.

His argument would have merit if the scales of justice were balanced across the color line; which they are not; and if police brutality in the inner cities - which are predominantly black - was not a factor; which it is. Many people including other prominent leaders besides Jesse Jackson have criticized the judicial system for the disparity in sentences given to drug dealers that reflect an unmistakable racial bias against blacks. As New York congressman Charles Rangel argued in "Crack Law Is Biased and Flawed" in *The Wall Street Journal*:

The mandatory federal crack-cocaine sentencing-law [is] unjust due to its disproportionate application to African-American defendants, who represent almost 90 percent of the defendants in these cases. Current law mandates that persons convicted of possessing five grams of crack cocaine receive the same sentence - five years - as those convicted of possessing 500 grams of powder cocaine.

Since enactment of this law, the 100 - 1 quantity ratio has had a devastating and disproportionate impact on the African-American community. The evidence is indisputable. Almost 97 percent of all crack defendants are black or Latino despite the fact that these groups represent less than 50 percent of all crack users and less than 25 percent of the general population.

In Los Angeles, from 1988 to 1991, the U.S. Attorney's Office prosecuted no white suspects on federal crack cocaine charges, while hundreds of white suspects moved through the state court system. In 1992, this two-track system was repeated in 17 states....

Small-time, street-level crack dealers fill our jails and face kingpin sentences with possession of as little as $50 worth of crack cocaine [while the most serious traffickers of powder cocaine, most of whom are white, walk free]....The 14th Amendment requires equal treeatment under the law.[85]

Jesse Jackson and others are justified in criticizing the judicial system for its bias, contrary to what Joseph Brown says. Sentencing disparities cannot be justified when race is the prime determinant in the dispensation of justice. And it can't be but that in a racist society, something that black conservatives don't want to admit in spite of all the evidence showing that the United States is indeed a racist country; hence the persistence of racism in all areas of the American society, even if not always in its most virulent form.

Regarding Louis Farrakhan, the controversial black Nation of Islam leader has been severely criticized by many black conservatives such as Shelby Steele who blame the American society for sustaining what they contemptuously call the grievance industry maintained by blacks. As Steele contends:

Something larger than Mr. Farrakhan must be repudiated, and many more of us must do the repudiating. [That something is] the pattern of social reform that America has offered its former victims [blacks are no longer victims of racism] for 25 years, [specifically] entitlements like affirmative action and diversity programs. [Such a pattern] brings out the Farrakhans in every group so that they can be used as wedges in the group's negotiations with the larger society....

If you are seeking entitlements on the basis of oppression, you must have your Farrakhans or your ACT-UP or your radical feminists....[The Farrakhans and their admirers] embody the alienation and anger that could become manifest in the entire group if the entitlements are not forthcoming.[86]

Steele does not address one fundamental question, and that is, what produced the Farrakhans in the first place. There would have been no need for Louis Farrakhan, Jesse Jackson, Malcolm X, Stokely Carmichael, Huey P. Newton, H. Rap Brown, Eldridge Cleaver, Bobby Seale, the Black Panthers and Black Muslims, and even for Dr. Martin Luther King, Jr. and the entire civil rights movement, had it not been for racism against black people in the United States.

It is white America that made it necessary for all those leaders to emerge on the American political scene. Otherwise we probably would never even have heard of them. And it is white racism that is responsible for the anger in the black community and for the need for affirmative action. it is anger against racial injustice.

There would have been no need for affirmative action if whites did not victimize blacks; in fact, it is whites themselves - some liberal white leaders, including some conservatives such as President Richard Nixon - who started affirmative action, thus conceding the obvious. And there would have been no culture wars and multiculturalism had white people accepted blacks as equal citizens as much as they have accepted other groups.

Blacks are the most despised and least welcome in the United States. Yet they came to the New World before the *Mayflower* dropped anchor at Pymouth Rock, and have been on American soil longer than most whites and other Americans except Native Americans, the so-called American Indians. As Malcolm X said: "We did not land at Plymouth Rock, Plymouth Rock landed on us." Black people are the most American of all Americans yet, paradoxically, the "least" American, because of racism: strangers in their own land. Instead, Steele blames the victims - blacks - and society for fulfilling some of their demands for racial justice.

As an ardent critic of affirmative action, he has yet to explain what affirmative action is going to be replaced with, once it is eliminated in a society where race-neutral principles have failed to produce the desired results of correcting racial injustice. Employment of race-neutral criteria is an unrealistic expectation in a racist society. Why would a racist society implement race-neutral policies to redress racial imbalances when they go against its very nature?

In fact, throughout American history, racism has been so pervasive, and so embedded in the nation's social and moral fabric, that it has become part of the nation's soul. And racists don't fight racism. Ask the Ku Klux Klan. If race-neutral principles provide the answer, then why does racial discrimination still exist across the spectrum in the American society? It is a fact of life which even millions of white admit. Yet, black conservatives insist on color-blindness in a color-conscious society. They are blind to reality or simply don't want to face it.

Racism shows no signs of declining, contrary to what Shelby Steele and other black conservatives contend. What they define as "declining" racism is simply malignancy of the same illness in covert form. And in just as many cases, racism is practiced openly. Steele talks about *The Content of Our Character* - which is also the title of his book - as the solution to black America's problems. But he has used that honorable phrase totally out of context.

The good character of many slaves, and many of them had that, did not free them from slavery. Good character did not protect many blacks from being lynched or their homes and churches from being bombed. Nor did it protect them from Bull Connor and his dogs. Many blacks who suffered and died at the hands of white racists had good character.

And most blacks have good character even today. Yet they are stuck in the ghetto with their good character. They can't get jobs with their good character and skills, and can't get loans with their good character and good credit. Good character of millions of blacks has not ended segregation and racial discrimination.

Good character didn't save Dr. Martin Luther King's life - in fact it helped to get him killed. That is because the problem America faces is bigger than some people think it is. And it has no respect for good character, absolutely none. The problem is white, not black America. Even if all blacks were saints, the problem would remain the same. That is how big the problem of racism is.

Dr. Martin Luther King spoke of his dream, a dream "deeply rooted in the American dream," when people of all races including "my four little children will...live in a nation where they will not be judged by the color of their skin but by the content of theix character. I have a dream today!"[87]

Dr. King's dream has not yet been realized. He knew character was important. But he also knew that character was not enough to fight racism - otherwise you are going to wait forever for people to change and start treating you as an equal. That is why Dr. King supported legislation to make whites "willing" to extend racial equality to blacks. And that is why affirmative action is necessary to make whites open doors to businesses, housing, education and all the benefits whites enjoy and take for granted but from which blacks have been locked out because of racism.

Yet black conservatives say character is enough without programs to help blacks fight racism. No, it is not enough, and never will be enough. The refusal by black conservatives to admit that racism *still* is a major problem, and their opposition to programs intended to help blacks fight racism and catch up with whites and other groups, makes them willing executioners of their own people whose only capital offense is that they are black in a predominantly white society that still has a serious racial problem.

In fact, many blacks - not just militant ones like Louis Farrakhan and his supporters but moderate ones like former U.S. Assistant Attorney-General and civil rights leader Roger Wilkins, now a history professor, Cornel West, also a professor, as well as many others - and some whites such as Professor Andrew Hacker, say America still is a racist society, and not one that just has a serious racial problem.

And they provide empirical evidence to prove it. And conservatives, with their policies and indifference and even hostility toward blacks, have done a very good job to help them prove their case; as have millions of whites who don't want to accept blacks as equals.

Chapter Two:

Black Conservatives and the Republican Party

THE REPUBLICAN PARTY has had a special relationship with African Americans for a long time since slavery.

It was the Republican party that freed the slaves. And it was the Republican party that first led the struggle against racial injustice after the end of slavery.

Yet only a few years after the Emancipation Proclamation of 1863, and after the 13th Amendment to the Constitution in December 1865 which legally ended slavery, and once it was secure in the northern states, the party of Lincoln and Frederick Douglass abandoned the newly freed slaves when federal troops were withdrawn from the last southern states in 1877.

The withdrawal of federal troops left blacks at the mercy of the Ku Klux Klan and other racist organizations determined to deny blacks equality, and ended the era of Reconstruction during which black people, relatively speaking, made significant progress in many areas of life in so short a time.

After Union troops withdrew, the last Republican governments in the south collapsed and Reconstruction was over. Black Codes, laws enacted by the southern states after the Civil War - allegedly intended to facilitate black Americans' transition from slavery to freedom - were, in fact, a thinly veiled device to deny real equality to the newly-freed blacks. They for all practical purposes reintroduced slavery only in another guise.

Those notorious codes persisted into the twentieth century. Yet

Republicans, who have been in control of the White House and Congress most of the time since the Civil War - and through most of the twentieth century with the exception of a few Democratic Administrations - did nothing to repeal those infamous codes. In fact, it was only recently, on "March 21, 1995, [that] the state of Mississippi ratified the Thirteenth Amendment to the United States Constitution abolishing slavery."[1]

It was Lincoln's Republican party that secured full citizenship for blacks under the Fourteenth and Fifteenth Amendments to the Constitution, passing these critical, essential riders in 1868 and 1870, respectively. Ironically, Abraham Lincoln himself did not believe in racial equality and upheld the doctrine of white supremacy - as he clearly stated in one of his speeches in Springfield, Illinois, and on other occasions - and fought the Civil war to save the Union, not to free the slaves. He ended slavery to deprive the Confederacy of its economic base in order to force it to surrender, and not out of humanitarian concern for the well-being of Africans held in bondage.

And tragically, the citizenship these Amendments heralded was quickly diluted with unchecked intimidation, lynching, literacy tests and a poll tax deliberately intended to deny blacks racial equality. As these atrocities became more common and more brutal, the Republican party did nothing to help blacks; nor did the Democratic party which was then unabashedly racist.

However, unlike the Democratic party since the presidency of Franklin Delano Roosevelt, the Republican party does not want to have anything to do with African Americans. Because of such experiences with the Republican party, many blacks cannot see it as a political organization that best represents their interests.

They see it as an instrument of white domination exclusively intended to secure the interests of the white majority. And no leader in modern times embodied, forcefully articulated, and fostered such sentiments among whites as President Ronald Reagan did.

When the former president died on June 5, 2004, at the age of 93, there was an outpouring of emotions that transcended party lines, with white Democratic leaders - and many whites in general - virtually competing with their counterparts in the Republican party to eulogize the fallen giant and torch bearer of the conservative movement in contemporary America. He epitomized the best, and the worst, the Republican party had to offer.

Noticeably absent from all this drama, and with deafening silence, were black leaders and other blacks. But there were those who, although without fanfare, publicly articulated the collective sentiment of black America toward a leader most of them saw as their nemesis during his presidency. One of them was Professor Ronald Walters who, among other works, is also the author of *White Nationalism, Black Interests: Conservative Public Policy and the Black Community*.2

He contends in his book that the conservative movement - which is predominantly white - has had a very negative impact on the American political system and its institutions for more than twenty years, coincidentally since Reagan became president, and that hostility toward blacks has played a critical role in the formulation of policies by conservative leaders.

He analyzes a phenomenon he calls a new White Nationalism and shows how it provides momentum to the conservative ideology across the spectrum leading to policies whose immediate and ultimate objective is to preserve, protect and promote the interests of whites at the expense of blacks and other minority groups, but mainly blacks, the primary target of racial hatred even among some non-whites; although Walters does not go that far blaming other nonwhites for discriminating against blacks.

Reagan knew exactly how the majority of whites felt, having been in the trenches himself with some of the most virulent opponents of racial equality for blacks, and launched his campaign for presidency along those lines, becoming probably the most articulate spokesman of the Republican party in recent times. While the nation mourned his death, black America also mourned, but also for another reason, and had been mourning since Reagan was first elected president in 1980.

His presidency witnessed the slow and painful death of civil rights for blacks under one of the most conservative administrations in American history. As Joe Davidson, not long after the former president died, stated in his commentary, "Reagan: A Contrary View," on American television MSNBC on June 7, 2004:

It's customary to say good things about the dead. Ronald Reagan appointed the first woman to the Supreme Court. He (reluctantly) signed legislation for a national holiday honoring Martin Luther King. He thawed relations with the Soviet Union and signed a nuclear weapons treaty (although it should be remembered that he almost pushed the world to the brink of nuclear war with the Soviets). He was warm and amiable and had a good sense of humor. He liked horses.

Now let's talk about what he did to black people.

After taking office in 1981, Reagan began a sustained attack on the government's civil apparatus, opened an assault on affirmative action and social welfare programs, embraced white racist leaders of then-apartheid South Africa and waged war on a tiny, black Caribbean nation.

So thorough was Reagan's attack on programs of importance to African Americans, that the Citizens Commission on Civil Rights, an organization formed in the wake of Reagan's attempt to neuter the official U.S. Commission on Civil Rights, said he caused 'an across-the-board breakdown in the machinery constructed by six previous administrations to protect civil rights.'

America's move to the political right

During his two terms in office, Reagan captured, solidified and came to personify America's move to the political right. His greatest legacy is as leader of that swing in the American political spectrum. That shift made 'liberal' a dirty word and Democrats cower. What had been conservative became moderate. What was moderate was pushed to the left wing. The shift was so pronounced and profound that black America giddily embraced Bill Clinton despite his promotion of programs, criminal justice and welfare policies in particular, that would have been called racist and reactionary under Reagan.

'Ronald Reagan, it is fair to say, was really an anathema to the entire civil rights community and the civil rights agenda,' Ronald W. Walters, a professor of government and politics at the University of Maryland, told BET (Black Entertainment).com just a few hours after Reagan died, at age 93, on Saturday (June 5).

Walters, in his book *White Nationalism, Black Interests: Conservative Public Policy and the Black Community*, argues that George W. Bush's (stolen) election in 2000 secured the domination of American politics 'by the radical conservative wing of the Republican party, a project begun when Ronald Reagan was elected to the White House in 1980.'

His overwhelming defeat of incumbent Jimmy Carter that year brought a new spirit to America, at least white America. The United States was still reeling in self-doubt after being run out of Vietnam. National shame was raw because 52 Americans had been held hostage by Iran from November 1979 until after Reagan's election.

In 1984, he successfully campaigned for re-election on a 'Morning in America' theme. But his presidency was a long and dreary night for African Americans. Consider this record. Reagan:

• Appointed conservative judges, like Supreme Court Justice Antonin Scalia, who continue to issue rulings to the detriment of African Americans. Walters notes that just 2 percent of Reagan's judicial appointments were black.

• Began his 1980 presidential campaign in Philadelphia, Mississippi, near the site where three civil rights were murdered in 1964.

• Supported racism with remarks like those that characterized poor, black women as 'welfare queens.'

• Fired U.S. Commission on Civil Rights members who were critical of his civil rights policies, including his strong opposition to affirmative action programs. One of the commissioners, Mary Frances Berry, who now chairs the Commission, recalls that the judge who overturned the dismissal did so because 'you can't fire a watchdog for biting.'

• Sought to limit and gut the Voting Rights Act.

• Slashed important programs like the Comprehensive Employment and Training Act (CETA) that provided needed assistance to black people.

• Appointed people like Clarence Thomas, who later became a horrible Supreme Court Justice, to the Equal Opportunity Commission (EOC); William Bradford Reynolds, as assistant attorney general for civil rights; and others who implemented policies that hurt black people.

• Doubted the integrity of civil irghts leaders, saying, 'Sometimes I wonder if they really mean what they say, because some of those leaders are doing very well leading organizations based on keeping alive the feeling that they're victims of prejudice.'

• Tried to get a tax exemption for Bob Jones University, which was then a segregated college in South Carolina.

Defended former Senator Jesse Helms' 'sincerity' when that arch villain of black interest questioned Martin Luther King's loyalty.

The federal budget during the Reagan years tells the tale in stark, dollar terms. According to the Center on Budget and Policy Priorities, as reported by *The Los Angeles Times* as Reagan left office in 1989, programs that helped black America suffered greatly during his tenure....

Frustration with African Americans

Despite this record, Reagan expressed frustration, during a 1989 CBS interview, about his relations with African Americans. 'One of the great things I have suffered is this feeling,' he said, 'that somehow I'm on the other side' of the civil rights movement.

He also was on the wrong side of international issues important to African Americans. Reagan crushed the government of Grenada in 1983 because he felt it had fallen too far into the orbit of Cuba's Fidel Castro. Grenada is a tiny place, smaller in size than Philadelphia, with fewer people than Peoria (Illinois, where Reagan was born and raised). His trumped-up excuse was American medical students on the Caribbean island nation were threatened by government officials he called 'a brutal group of leftist thugs.'

He outraged African Americans and others by relating to apartheid South Africa as a friend and ally. His program of constructive engagement amounted

66

to a go-slow policy under which apartheid was criticized but essentially tolerated. It was a policy that delayed the independence of Namibia, then controlled by South Africa, blocked United Nations' condemnations of South African attacks on nearby African countries and permitted American corporate support for the racist regime. He was loyal to South Africa because, as he told CBS during an interview early in 1981, it was 'a country that has stood by us in every war we've ever fought, a country that, strategically, is essential to the free world in its production of minerals.'

Even as the majority of the American people came to oppose South Africa's racist oppression, Reagan stood by his friend. Pushed by black leaders and organizations, Congress passed sanctions against South Africa. Reagan, on the wrong side of history, vetoed the bill. Congress, to Reagan's shame, overrode the veto.

The gushy tributes to Reagan might be understandable eulogies, but they are also a testament to the persistence of two Americas, one black and one white. The two don't see things the same and the reaction to Reagan is just one more example.[3]

In spite of all what Reagan did to black people, and how much he hurt them, black conservatives embraced him as an icon of liberation for the souls of black folk mired in the fetid swamp of moral bankruptcy whose redemption could be achieved only through shock therapy as administered by this man who coasted into the White House on a wave of anti-black sentiments among the vast majority of white voters; and whose party, the Republican party, embodied virtually everything blacks feared about a predominantly white racist society. The Republican party, especially under Reagan, became synonymous with white America.

Administration of such shock therapy inevitably entailed dispensing a high dosage of cruelty, as a vital component, to ensure success in addressing a myriad problems so typical of the ghetto and the black community as a whole, at least according to conservatives, both black and white, and whites in general.

The problems are: family disintegration characterized by matrifocal households and high illegitimate birth rates in the inner cities that are predominantly black; lack of values conducive to achievement leading to chronic dependence on welfare and high unemployment rates - twice the national average; high dropout rates especially among high school students in the ghetto and elsewhere; poor academic performance among black students in general from elementary school to college level; high crime rates, drug addiction being one of the main factors; and much more.

The Republican party uses coded language to mobilize white voters who know right away what white conservative leaders mean when they say, "crime," welfare," "poverty," and so on, terms synonymous with "black" in the lexicon of white America. They see blacks as a burden on white America, living off the sweat of white workers as if most blacks don't work or are on welfare.

Naturally, of course, a question then arises concerning whites and the Republican party: If, indeed, the Republican party is the party for white America, or for whites, why don't all whites, then, belong to this party? The answer is as simple, or as profound, as the question itself. All whites, or most whites, don't belong to the Republican party for the same reason that all white people don't belong to the Ku Klux Klan, even if an unknown high number of some of them sympathize with this notoriously racist organization and others.

Now, simply because all whites don't belong to the Ku Klux Klan does *not* mean that that the KKK is not dedicated to preserving and advancing white supremacy, or that the Republican party is not a bastion of white power even if millions of whites disagree with the policies of these two right-wing organizations, one of them blatantly racist.

Many white conservatives have been adept at mobilizing white sentiments against perceived "threats" coming from non-whites, especially blacks, in order to build the Republican party into a white national movement, one that is more than just a political party. As Dinesh D'Souza, an Indian immigrant in the United States but who is a conservative himself, concedes:

As the rhetoric of leading politicians like Robert Dole, Pete Wilson, and Phil Gramm suggests, the Republican party hopes to make white opposition to racial preferences a catalyst for massive voter defections from the Democrats. As the *de facto* party of whites, the GOP seems increasingly responsive to growing majority concerns about high levels of nonwhite immigration....Unlike in the past, most immigrants do not come from Europe, but from Asia, Africa, and most of all, Latin America....

Many whites are acutely uncomfortable about what one observer has called 'the browning of America'...[and] insist that owing to their high birth rates, immigrants [and American blacks] are out-breeding other Americans. 'Those with their pants up are going to to be caught by those with their pants down'....

In 1994, white backlash found scholarly support in Richard Herrnstein and Charles Murray's controversial book *The Bell Curve*. It asserts that blacks and Hispanics were, on average, less intelligent than Caucasians and Asians - deficiencies alleged to be possibly inherited....The book became a runaway best-seller, attracting hundreds of thousands of readers....Could it be that Herrnstein and Murray were articulating truths that many whites privately believe?[4]

That indeed seems to be the case. And it explains why *The Bell Curve* became an instant best seller. Most whites, including many liberals to be brutally frank although they are supposed to be friends of blacks, did not buy the book out of sympathy for blacks. If that is why they bought the book, why has there been no universal condemnation of its highly inflammatory arguments construed by many people to be racist?

The Bell Curve fueled white racist sentiments and emboldened many whites to freely assert that blacks are genetically inferior to them and to members of other races. And many of those who argue this way are conservative and belong to the Republican party.

They have also taken the lead in mobilizing other whites to rally around the flag, and erect stockades:

Reflecting a newly emboldened racial consciousness, conservative columnist Samuel Francis in a recent article urges that whites begin a 'reconquest of the United States' by deporting all illegal aliens 'and perhaps many recent immigrants,' repealing all civil rights protections for minorities, using forced birth control on welfare mothers, and incentives for whites to have more children and minorities to stop....

[All that] appears to be solidifying what sociologist Robert Blauner terms 'a dominant white racial identity.' White backlash is now a political juggernaut that threatens to reverse the liberal immigration and civil rights policies of the past generation, and to further polarize the races in this country.[5]

The Republican-dominated Congress did just that when, in the mid-nineties, it passed sweeping legislation virtually abolishing welfare and other social programs for the poor, a disproportionately large number of whom are black; and a tough immigration law which many lawyers described as draconian and the most inhumane anti-immigration legislation in the history of the country, earning the legislative body distinction as "an anti-immigrant Congress." And it remained that way under Republican control, promising more drastic measures in the future, to sanitize America and keep it "white."

It is the Republican party that is the party of the white backlash that threatens to roll back the gains blacks have garnered since the sixties during the civil rights movement. And most blacks know that any black who identifies himself, or herself, with the Republican party is considered to be a traitor or someone who doesn't care about the well-being of fellow blacks in a white-dominated society.

Even some blacks themselves in the Republican party know that they are totally out of place in such a "lily white" environment. As. J.C. Watts, the black Republican congressman from Oklahoma who became one of the national leaders of the party but who was frustrated in his position because many white leaders in the party did not listen to him, conceded even before his disenchantment with the party's white leadership and his decision in 2002 not to run again for his congressional seat: "Many believe that it is just hard to imagine that a minority would be a Republican."[6]

Still, that has not dissuaded a number of blacks from joining the Republican party where, as Malcolm X put it, they "look like a fly in a cup of milk."[7] Malcolm X was talking about blacks who are zealous to be around whites, "begging" them to be their "friends," people who don't want to be bothered and see such blacks as just imposing on them.

His assessment has been validated in the Republican context where blacks are simply tolerated and seen as pests. For example, during the 1996 Republican convention in San Diego, California, only 52 delegates out of nearly 2,000 - which was a mere 2.6 percent of all the Republican delegates - were black, "the second lowest percentage since the Goldwater debacle of 1964."[8] Why, if the Republican party is really interested in having blacks as members, as black conservatives contend?

Prospects for improvement are dim due to Republican leadership's lack of interest to recruit black members. As Faye Anderson, president of the black Douglass Policy Institute, an education and research group in Washington, D.C., lamented in August 1996: "I wish Republican strategists would stop running away from African-Americans."[9]

About four years later, she left the Republican party, in disgust, because of its indifference toward blacks and its unwillingness to recruit them as members. As she stated in her article in *The New York Times* in July 2000, during the same time the Republican National Convention was being held in New York City to nominate George W. Bush as its presidential candidate, the Republican party was a party of "master illusionists [who produced] a parade of African-American and Hispanic speakers [during the convention who have] taken center stage, made-for-television illusion of inclusion....Earlier this year, I made a noisy exit from the Republican party in an effort to send a message to party leaders."[10]

Her message was simple: the Republican party is racist. But she did not join the Democratic party. She remained independent.

Few blacks, and even whites, would disagree with that. As *The Washington Post* chief political correspondent Terry Neal stated:

I'm black and I spend a lot of time with black folks, so I have some idea of what I'm talking about....White conservatives...don't have deep roots in the black community....[Even] most of the blacks who have moved into the middle and upper classes, still feel that the GOP is on the wrong side of the track on social justice issues. For instance, many of them feel that they got to where they did based in part - I said, IN PART - because of affirmative action, which Republicans rail against incessantly. And I think that even among many of those who 'have made it' there's still a sense that the GOP represents a slice of America that they can never be a part of, nor they particularly want to be a part of.[11]

Prominent whites who have publicly stated that white Republicans and conservatives are racist - playing the race card - include United States Senator Hillary Clinton; a point also underscored by her husband, former President Bill Clinton, who has also said or implied that Republicans use race as a weapon against blacks and other minorities to advance their agenda.

Faye Anderson articulated a position shared by other black Republicans when she said the Republican party was not interested in having blacks as members. All these black Republicans are conservative themselves, like their white counterparts, in a conservative party. As Vincent Watkins, a black Republican and president of a political consulting firm in Atlanta, Georgia, stated:

71

Across this country from one coast to the other, black conservative candidates, at all levels - local, state, and federal - tell of how they receive little to no support from the [Republican] party. Often they receive absolutely no financial support, very few in-kind services, incomplete and/or outdated telephone and mailing lists, and at best, token volunteer assistance, and the list goes on.[12]

And the answer is simple: Black conservatives are not welcome in the Republican party.

White Republicans see black conservatives as presumptuous, just begging to be around people who couldn't care less if all blacks - including conservatives among them - vanished from the face of the earth. Black conservatives have placed their racial pride on the Republican auction block in hopes for a few crumbs. To them, self-respect and black community consciousness is irrelevant. Not accepted by whites, and not respected by fellow blacks, they are caught in a dilemma U.S. Supreme Court Justice Clarence Thomas has describes as "the loneliness of the black conservative."[13]

Even many whites see the Republican party as white and insensitive to minorities, although some of them would probably not go as far as George McGovern did when he said during the 1972 presidential campaign that it was worse than the Ku Klux Klan. As Jonathan Aiken states in his book *Nixon: A Life*: "Nixon was compared to Adolph Hitler in three McGovern's speeches, and accused of leading a party worse than the Ku Klux Klan."[14]

The collective sentiment of millions of blacks towards the Republican party has been expressed many times by many people, including Robert Franklin in these terms: "Many of the Democrats who were against passage of the 1964 Civil Rights Bill later switched to the Republican party, and the party made room for those with segregationist attitudes....For the past three decades, the GOP has gone out of its way to distance itself from black voters and to scapegoat them for the nation's problems. Their recent attacks on affirmative action have also not helped....A lot of people have come to the conclusion, through the words and deeds of the GOP, that civil rights are not the party's priority. Black voters want to know what Republicans have done for them lately, and the answer invariably comes back, 'not much.'"[15]

It is rare for Republicans to admit that their party uses blacks as a scapegoat for the nation's problems and that it does not want them as members. But United States Senator Richard Lugar of Indiana, who was a 1996 presidential contender, is one such Republican. As he stated in an interview with the black conservative journal *National Minority Politics*:

"I have said frequently that the Republican party must strive to be inclusive. In particular, I have argued that minorities should not be made scapegoats for [the nation's] economic problems....Communities can come across together racial lines to address problems of the whole community [and we] should promote such cooperation on a national level."[16]

The Republican party is not doing that, and has no interest in doing it, as its record clearly shows, and as some black conservatives themselves - including prominent ones such as JC Watts - admit. If the party is genuinely interested in racial harmony and in drawing blacks into its ranks as equal participants and not just as supplicants and spectators, it would be making a concerted effort to go into black communities, explaining its policies and listening to blacks in order to enroll them as members.

Even black conservatives themselves cannot explain what the Republican party has done for them when they say it is the best party for blacks. Frustrated for lack of an answer, some black Republicans are forced to admit that the Grand Old Party (GOP) has indeed done very little for blacks. As Jerry T. Burley explained how black voters perceive the Republican party:

While running for Congress in Texas' 18th congressional district...African Americans said they would not vote for me simply because I was a Republican. I received a call from a preacher late one night at the campaign headquarters....When I told him that I was a Republican, it was as if I had let all the air out of a baloon. He started to explain how in all his 83 years he had not voted for a Republican and that he could not see himself doing it this time [even for a fellow black]....I was told by a [black] woman who said she was a Christian and loved the Lord, that if Jesus himself came to Earth and ran as a Republican, she could not vote for him. It was her belief that the [Republican] party was evil.[17]

In his article, "GOP Displays Uncompromising Harshness Toward the Poor," Burley admits the Republican party has not done much for blacks and that most blacks are not attracted to the party. So what is he and other blacks like him doing in a political party that does not care about black people? One answer is that they may be trying to prod the party into doing something for African Americans.

But even when they look to the party's leadership for guidance and assistance, they don't get it. Republican party leaders, from the grassroots level all the way up to the national level, don't seem to be interested at all in recruiting blacks as members of a political party which even many white Republicans themselves consider to be a private club exclusively for whites similar to country clubs for white golf players and other whites.

Had this not been the case, they would have launched a sustained campaign, not just during election time, to try and get blacks into the party as they always have done among whites. As Oklahoma's black congressman J.C. Watts stated: "The Republican party will never become the majority party until we regain our legacy as a party for minority Americans. We put forth no organized effort on outreach, none."[18]

White Republicans just don't want blacks in their party. Blacks are just begging them to be part of "one big happy family." But whites are impressed by none of that. Blacks in the Republican party have always remained "the black sheep" of the family. The attitude of white Republicans, although not expressed openly but nonetheless confirmed by their deeds in ignoring blacks, was best summed up by one major contender for the Republican presidential nomination during the 1996 campaign who bluntly stated: "I don't have a plan to involve blacks in my campaign."[19]

It is comments like that which have many people, black and white, wondering why black conservatives are so eager to be members of a party that doesn't care about them, and doesn't even want them to be seriously involved in any party activities except as mere spectators staring from the sidelines.

The statement by the Republican presidential candidate that he had no plans to involve blacks in his campaign applies to all blacks, *including* black conservatives already in the Republican party - and not just to blacks who don't belong to the party as some black conservatives want to believe. They are only deluding themselves. As another leader, a state chairman of the Republican party in one southern state emphatically stated during the same 1996 presidential campaign: "We don't need   blacks!"[20]

He said it loud and clear. And he was talking about *all* blacks, including black Republicans. Not only was he blunt about it, he made the statement at a conference attended by black Republican political strategists who had requested a meeting with white Republican party leaders to see what they can do for the party during the campaign and thereafter. He addressed the blacks directly at that meeting and others elsewhere, baiting them to pass on his message to their people in the black community: the Republican party has no interest in black people.

And as Nancy Reagan also reportedly said to her husband Ronald Reagan on the telephone during the 1980 presidential campaign at a meeting of Republicans in New Hampshire but which he, although the leading contender, did not attend since he was somewhere else during that time: he would love to see how many white people were there.[21] Reporters said she thought her microphone was turned off and did not expect to be caught off-guard making such a remark, with all that it implies.

The dilemma, or predicament, black conservatives are caught in is analogous to that of black American intellectuals Professor Harold Cruse has explored in his magnum opus, *The Crisis of the Negro Intellectual.*[22] In spite of their achievement, they are not fully accepted by white America; nor do they fully identify themselves with their brethren, the poor and less educated, trapped in the ghetto. Still, black conservatives have not stopped pursuing white Republicans, dying to be a part of them. And white Republicans keep on erecting stockades.

It is easy to understand why black conservatives are so lonely. Whites don't want them. And most blacks don't want them, either. That is why the vast majority of blacks don't vote for black conservatives. For example, J.C. Watts represented a predominantly white district, not a black one; so did Gary Franks - who lost his Connecticut congressional seat in the 1996 election when he tried to win a fourth term - and was one of only two black Republicans, together with Watts, in Congress. In 1994, 25 black Republicans ran for Congress in predominantly black districts. They all lost.

In 1996, no fewer than 25 ran. They all lost, as have the rest in subsequent elections. And they get no help, not even sympathy, from the Republican party, the very party they are literally slaving for.[23]

The reason the white Republican party does not want blacks, which for some inexplicable reason black conservatives fail to grasp, is simple, in fact very simple. It is because they are black. As simple as that, no matter how you look at it. Black conservatives can continue to delude themselves into believing that is not the case. But that does *not* change reality. And it is a harsh reality. The reality is racism.

Racism is a major problem black people face in the United States, the citadel of democracy. Yet black conservatives contend otherwise. As one leading black conservative, Robert Woodson, put it: "Racism is not the most important problem that confronts our nation today."[24]

Why not?

Racism is the main reason blacks lag behind other ethnic groups, including new arrivals such as the Vietnamese and Cambodians who emigrated to the United States towards and after the end of the Vietnam war. As Jesse Jackson said, they have been riding on the backs of blacks who fought and died in the trenches fighting against racism during the civil rights movement and even after that; blacks planted the seeds, others are reaping the harvest; they won the war for racial equality - in terms of legislation - only to be relegated to the bottom. That is racism. Why this still eludes black conservatives defies explanation.

Racism is deeply entrenched in the American society. According to *The New York Times*:

A new survey shows that a majority of Americans are pessimistic that blacks and whites will ever get along....According to the survey, 55 percent of both blacks and whites believe that relations between whites and blacks will 'always be a problem' in the United States....In one sharp difference, whites generally opposed and African-Americans supported increased governmental efforts like affirmative action to lift black achievement....

The poll surveyed a far larger proportion of the total number of people surveyed than is usually included in such a poll. Among the more intriguing findings of the survey was the amount of pessimism among African-Americans.

The poll indicated that 76 percent of black college graduates said race relations would always be troublesome for the country, while 56 percent of blacks who have not earned a college degree felt that way....

Conversely, 48 percent of white college graduates voiced such a pessimistic view, while 56 percent of whites without a college degree felt no solution to animus between the races would ever be found.[25]

In spite of such overwhelming evidence of racism and the intractable nature of the problem, black conservatives say things are just fine. Not only are race relations good, and even excellent according to some black conservatives, but black people can succeed and climb as high as whites in all fields and areas of life. As Frederick Robinson, a prominent black conservative, stated: "The American dream is alive for any American willing to work hard....Personal responsibility, discipline, hard work and drive can indeed make the difference in America - regardless of a person's background."[26]

Yet, a few months earlier, Robinson took fellow conservative Dinesh D'Souza to task for making simplistic and outlandish statements about the insignificance of racism in the United States when he reviewed D'Souza's book appropriately titled - at least according to conservatives - *The End of Racism*. Robinson took exception, contending:

An East Indian immigrant who has only been an American citizen for four years, many will certainly question D'Souza's analysis of a complex issue like race in America....Unfortunately, unoriginality isn't the book's only weakness. In many cases, D'Souza passes ivory tower intellectualization off as genuine, real-world-tested analysis....For example, he argues that black deviancy is what perpetuates racism. Amazing! In other words, if black people get their act together, white racism will go away. Nonsense....

While it is true that black pathology fuels racism, it's folly to think that black problems provide the only grist for the bigotry mills....Too, the chapter on slavery is an oversimplification. His suggestion that slavery was not as brutal as popularly portrayed and his assertion that as a system it was not as savage as the Jewish holocaust is dead wrong. No doubt, the enslavement and legal disenfranchisement of blacks was one of the most tragic episodes in human history. As James Baldwin said, there are worse things you can do to a man than kill him. Enslaving him is one of them.[27]

The contradiction is obvious. One moment he says racism still is a serious problem, as one can deduce from the preceding quotation, next he says it is not, as he contends in the first quotation. It is a stark flip-flop typical of black conservatives.

If hard work is all it takes to succeed in America, as Robinson and other black conservatives contend, then racism is no longer a problem. Yet, that is in a nation where the majority of whites themselves say they don't want racial integration, and want laws passed to give them the legal right not to sell or rent their property to a person because of his race.[28]

If hard work is all it takes to succeed in the land of "milk and honey," why is the unemployment rate among blacks twice the national average consistently through the years, decade after decade? Are all those blacks lazy and uneducated? Why is the poverty rate among blacks three times that of whites - the same as it was in 1959?[29]

When does racism come into the picture?

If racism exists, which it does and is a big problem according to the majority of whites millions of whom are openly racist, does it not affect the lives of black people, impeding progress among them and reducing their life chances? If millions of whites are undoubtedly racist and therefore admit that racism exists, as do millions of other whites, why is it impossible for black conservatives to see that? They may be color-blind, unlike millions of whites, but that does not mean that the United States is a color-blind society. As Professor Cornel West bluntly stated: "This society is chronically racist."[30]

It is even hard to believe that black conservatives are really black when they deny all that. Being black is more than skin deep, as is being white. As Harold E. Ford, a black Democratic congressman from Tennessee, put it, a black person in Congress who articulates a conservative position is "not a black congressman."[31]

Because of the insensitivity of the Republican party toward blacks, it is almost impossible for a Republican - black or white - to represent blacks, a view shared by black law professor, Lani Guinier, and others including a significant number of whites not all of whom are liberal. As Paul Craig Roberts and Lawrence Stratton, two prominent white conservatives state in their book, *The New Color Line*, concerning Lani Guinier and others who share her position:

University of Pennsylvania law professor Lani Guinier argues for black solidarity to counter 'legislative dilution.' She goes so far as to doubt that a black Republican representative could qualify as a black representative....

Guinier's view is standard fare among Critical Theorists, who argue that color blindness is 'cultural genocide' for blacks.[32]

Naturally, since black conservatives have ceased to be black because of their hostile views and policies shared by racists such as Ku Klux Klan leader David Duke who is a prominent Republican and almost won the governorship of his home state of Louisiana in the early nineties, coming in second in terms of votes from millions of whites in that southern state, there is no question that they will continue to be members of the Republican party - even if they are not welcome - and do harm to the black community they were once a part of, until they lost their identity. In fact, that is why they belong to the Republican party.

Jerry T. Burley is one of the few black conservatives who have admitted the shortcomings and mean-spiritedness of the Republican party that barely tolerates him as a member no more than it does other black Republicans all of whom are seen as interlopers. As he explicitly states:

Many in the Republican party cannot picture themselves downtrodden and seem to display an uncompromising harshness toward the poor....For those who feel that they pulled themselves up by their bootstraps, I have not found anyone who has become a success in a vacuum. There is always some person or persons who are responsible for helping us become successful.[33]

The Republican party's opposition to affirmative action and lack of compassion for the poor only confirms that it lives up to its reputation as a mean-spirited club of the rich and the citadel of white supremacy that couldn't care less about blacks. Black people are very aware of that, a point also made by Burley who has seen both worlds as a member of the Republican party and the black community. As he states from experience:

The prevailing attitude in the African American community is that the Republican party does not care about them....The leadership of the party cannot continue to dismantle programs designed to assist those less fortunate, while at the same time appearing to increase subsidies which will benefit the wealthy.[34]

He sounds like a Democrat, not a Republican. It is very rare that you hear a black Republican or conservative speak out against tax cuts for the rich, or against of elimination of social programs for the poor.

Yet black Republicans are quick to call for elimination of programs for the poor just like their white counterparts do. They are also quick to blame other blacks for their condition while ignoring the racism that is responsible for most of that condition, just like the Republican party does. For example, in their *Agenda for America: A Republican Direction for the Future*,35 not once do Republicans, throughout their 318-page book, address the problem of racism by whites against blacks; with poverty in general - and only in oblique references - getting only peripheral mention and in a perfunctory manner. Instead, they vehemently criticize affirmative action.

And it is obvious why. That is what whites complain about and efforts are being made to abolish the program. What about white racism blacks complain about? Programs such as affirmative action were started exactly for that purpose: to fight racism. The quest for racial justice is not on the Republican agenda for one simple reason. The Republican party represents whites, not blacks. It is dedicated to maintaining white domination, not achieving racial equality. Otherwise it would have embraced blacks the way the Democratic party has and continues to do.

Even in 2004, when a "compassionate" conservative George W. Bush was running for a second term as president of the United States, there still was a great amount skepticism over Republican attempts to win the hearts and minds of black voters. And such skepticism came from a number of Black Republicans themselves including prominent ones on the national scene.

One of them was Arthur Fletcher, Jr., former assistant secretary of labor in the Nixon Administration. As he put it:

Nixon won the White House without a black vote two times, Reagan won the White House without a black vote two times. Bush won the White House without a black vote one time. Bush junior has won it without a black vote....I'm not sure they're going to make a bona fide effort to attract blacks.[36]

Another prominent black Republican, former United States Senator Edward Brooke from Massachusetts who was the first black elected to the senate since Reconstruction, hence the first to be elected in the 20th century and who served in the senate from 1967 - 1979, was also unimpressed by Republican efforts, if any, to appeal to black voters and address issues that are fundamental to their well-being. As he stated:

I saw some hope in Ed Gillespie as the new chairman of the Republican party that he would recognize the need to make the Republican party inclusive and open up its doors to black voters and organizations. But in order to achieve that goal, they've got to, from the very beginning, make it known to black voters that they stand for issues that affect the lives of black people. The Republican party should be far more representative of the entire population. And it doesn't have that.[37]

During the presidential campaign in 2004, Gillespie had been going around the country trying to win black support for the Republican party's agenda which most black voters consider to be hostile to their interests. And in what amounted to some kind of joke, he enlisted the help of black boxing promoter Don King and travelled with him to boost his chances of winning support in black communities across the United States.

Why he took with him on the campaign trail a black person whose expertise is boxing, and not electoral politics, defies rational explanation, besides the stereotypical view about blacks as a people who just love and only excel in sports, and dancing of course, and would therefore be impressed by Don King and flock in "multitudes" to the Republican party; which would be quite a spectacle, better than a circus let alone a boxing match.

This reminds me of the time when Muhammed Ali was sent to Africa on a diplomatic mission concerning the volatile situation in southern Africa when white minority regimes were oppressing blacks and other non-whites.

President Julius Nyerere of Tanzania, chairman of the frontline states fighting apartheid and other minority regimes including Rhodesia, felt insulted and refused to meet Ali to discuss the matter with him. Prominent African American columnist Carl Rowan was highly impressed by Nyerere's stand and supported him, saying it was an insult to African leaders to send a boxer, Muhammed Ali, to discuss weighty issues of international diplomacy and politics with them.

And he was right. When did American leaders send golf and tennis players to represent them at meetings with European leaders to discuss major issues of international diplomacy? They send the Kissingers.

The parallels are almost exact, with Republicans not taking blacks seriously and asking a boxing promoter, Don King, simply because he's black, to explain to them why the Republican party is good, not just for white America, but for black America as well. Being black was not enough for him and for the Republican party to win the hearts and minds of African Americans; if anything, many of them may have have felt insulted as much as President Nyerere and other African leaders were when Muhammed Ali - instead of the American secretary of state or some other high ranking official - was sent to Africa to discuss important issues of southern Africa with them.

Also, the Republican party's condescending attitude toward blacks could not escape the attention of Democrats who have a long and solid record of supporting black people in their quest for racial justice since the civil rights movements, and of helping them alleviate their economic plight through a number of federal programs when they are in control of the White House and Congress. As Democratic national chairman Terry McAuliffe stated:

> The Republicans, it's all a photo op. If they think going out with Don King is somehow going to get young African-Americans (who love boxing!) to vote for - Don King - it's laughable. When I travel, I travel with (U.S.) Representatives John Lewis, Stephanie Tubbs-Jones, I go out with African-American leaders who have fought their entire lives for rights; not Don King.[38]

And prospects are bleak the Republican party will make inroads into black communities even if it makes a concerted effort to reach out to them. Its policies are hostile toward blacks and the poor. And it does not intend to change those policies. As Hazel Trice Edney, NNPA Washington correspondent, stated in "Black Republicans Question Party's Commitment' in *The Grand Rapids Times*:

> Bush (junior, like his father) opposes affirmative action, a major issue for many African-Americans. He opposed an affirmative action program involving the University of Michigan Law School last year (2003) that the Supreme Court upheld. He announced his opposition on Dr. Martin Luther King Jr.'s birthday. He has further alienated blacks with appointment of far-right judges and his pledge to fill any Supreme Court vacancies with judges similar to Clarence

Thomas and Antonin Scalia, the two most conservative members of the court.[39]

As the 2004 presidential election gained momentum, skepticism also mounted among many blacks including black Republicans themselves that black people would be no better represented at the Republican National Convention that year - to nominate Bush as the party's candidate for his second and last term as president - and in other Republican forums than they had been in the past whenever the Republican party was involved.

And the same publicity stunts were expected at the convention from a party that had been known for its lack of substance when it comes to dealing with blacks and their well-being, besides deliberately hurting them. As former Senator Edward Brooke stated: "You will find - and I dare say, I hope it won't be true, but, I'm almost positive that it will - that there won't be many black Republican delegates at the national convention. And that's sad."[40]

He was vindicated by history.

Lack of representation of blacks in significant numbers at Republican party meetings only underscores what many people, black and white, have know all along: the party does not represent blacks. It does not even represent poor whites, most of whom belong to the Democratic party. And the fact that blacks are not well-represented, if at all, at Republican party meetings does not bother white Republicans at all.

Therefore no genuine effort is made to get them involved in the party, at any level, and for whatever reason, even if it is just for fund raising to help the party spread its message to blacks and other minorities. Yet, white Republicans raise funds all the time to spread their message to white voters.

And black Republican delegates to the Republican National Convention are no more than a front - window dressing - for the party for publicity purposes for its "color-blind" agenda which, in fact, is very white for all intents and purposes, with absolutely nothing for blacks. As Hazel Edney stated:

At the Republican convention in Philadelphia four years ago (in 2000), the GOP hired many black entertainers and attempted to showcase Colin Powell and Condoleezza Rice, who became the two most prominent blacks in the Bush administration. According to the Joint Center for Political and Economic

83

Studies, there were only 85 African-Americans among the 2,066 delegates, or 4.1 percent....By contrast, there were 872 black delegates - 20.1 percent - at the 2000 Democratic National Convention, a figure that is expected to increase this year in Boston.[41]

And it did.

The tendency among white Republicans to ignore blacks is not only a product of racism; it also has to do with inequity of power. Had whites not been the dominant race, they would not have been able to win elections without forging alliances with members of other racial groups including despised blacks.

And Republicans, together with members of white supremacist groups most of whose members such as David Duke are also members of the Republican party, have been the most brazen - unlike white Democrats - in flexing their muscles to demonstrate power as members of the dominant race; but more often than not expressed in ideological terms - although also quite often to the far right of the ideological spectrum - rather than explicitly and crudely in terms of race; hence their use of coded language - "crime," "welfare," drugs," and so forth - when they talk about blacks to galvanize white voters into supporting conservative candidates and policies hostile toward blacks.

And tragically, racist assumptions and stereotypes about blacks among whites are taught and learnt from the very beginning, since childhood, reinforced by the dominant position of whites from which even the poorest and least educated whites derive satisfaction, hence power, as members of the ruling race dominating blacks and other non-whites. As Professor Manning Marable, also director of the Institute for Social Research in African American Studies at Columbia University, states:

Racism is accepted and unchallenged by the majority of whites....Whites, beginning at a very early age, are thoroughly socialized to uncritically accept racial inequality....American educators generally believe that children are mostly unaware of racial categories or racism, until they are taught to think and act consciously in ways that reproduce race....What is most remarkable is that white children generally insist that an individual's lack of ability or ability is race-specific, even in the face of evidence that disproves or contradicts what what they are observing.

Another way for educators to think about how children help to reproduce racism is to recall the findings of Kenneth and Mamie Clark in the 1940s, whose research found that racial segregation reproduced negative self concepts among black children as early as the age of three....

If the African-American child, as scholars have long documented, has the ability to recognize and understand what discrimination is, to realize that his or her place in society is unequal and inferior, then it is not unreasonable to assume that young whites also have the ability to code and interpret racial categories.

'Whiteness,' that is, the state of being white, is reproduced and lived in daily life, in both conscious and unconscious ways. Certain benefits or privileges exist and are created and enjoyed simply by being white. That recognition or desire to become white, that is, to be 'privileged,' can be observed and understood even by children. The racial system in America is something that people, including children, repeatedly and constantly encounter, and frequently find pressing against them.

Most whites and African Americans in the United States still live in essentially parallel racial universes. The majority of white Americans remain in deep denial about this.

The impact of racism on the lives of most people of color, however, is continuous and very real. Whites and blacks as groups generally have strikingly divergent opinions about political issues. Our children notice all of this, and it directly affects them permanently.[42]

But after you grow up, the question is whether or not you should judge people solely - if at all - on the basis of race. Sadly, many people use race as the sole determinant or criterion for judging others. Again, in the political arena, it is white Republicans who have been adept at employing this standard of judgment to advance their agenda for white America.

For whatever reason, which has nothing to do with genetics in terms of intelligence as many racists believe about black people, blacks in the Republican party find it difficult to fathom the depth of such commitment by their white counterparts to this agenda. Yet even some whites in the Republican party, although only a handful, concede that their party is indeed handicapped by racism within its ranks. As former Illinois congresswoman Lynn Martin who also served as secretary of labor under President George H.W. Bush (1989 - 1992) stated:

Is the Republican party doing enough to win the votes of African Americans? No, it is not. Racism is still too prevalent in America. Republicans must battle this evil. We must put ourselves and our party on the line to include the working men and women of the African-American community.[43]

Lynn Martin and Senator Lugar are some of the white

85

Republicans who admit that the Republican party has not actively recruited black members mainly because of racism more than anything else. Yet, with twisted logic although not necessarily twisted minds, black conservatives contend that it is the Democrats - black and white - who accuse Republicans of racism and who have labelled the Republican party as anti-black and racist; this, despite admission by some of its own white members, including prominent ones such as Senator Lugar and former Labor Secretary Lynn Martin, that their party is indeed hobbled with racism.

And the Republican party continues to compile its record of corporate greed, providing welfare to the rich, denying help to the poor, and disenfranchising minorities - especially blacks - as happened during the 2000 presidential election in Florida where thousands of black votes (Democratic) were declared invalid to help George W. Bush "win" the election with the help of his brother Jeb Bush who was then governor of that state.

Also some defections from the Republican party lend credibility to the argument that the party is indeed racist and does not care about the poor. For example Leon Panetta, former chief of staff in the Democratic Administration of President Bill Clinton, said he left the Republican party because of its policies toward minorities and opposition to civil rights. According to *The Washington Post*: "Panetta's conscientious performance [as head of] the civil rights enforcement office [in] the department of health, education and welfare,...conflicted with [President] Nixon's 'Southern Strategy' [of appeasing southern racists by ignoring civil rights for blacks] and drew the wrath of Attorney-General John Mitchell. Panetta quit in protest."[44]

But that was not the end of his political career. He simply couldn't do what he wanted to do within the Republican party: "Disillusioned with the Republicans, he ran for the House in 1976 as a Democrat and served there until 1993....Recalling the reason he quit the Nixon Administration, I asked Panetta how he felt about going back to a state [California, his home state] that had just approved Proposition 209 - eliminating all affirmative action programs [in a campaign led by Republican Governor Pete Wilson]. 'I think,' he said, 'the country now has to make the same fundamental decision it had to make in the middle of the civil rights enforcement battle in the Nixon Administration....Are we going to retreat? Or are we going to try to continue going forward?...Any time somebody wants to use the race card as a scapegoat [Panetta did not pander to the white majority that passed Proposition 209]...the politics of division can still be used....We've got to reach out and provide equal opportunity to people who have not had those opportunities in the past."[45]

Interestingly enough, black conservatives say there is no need to do that since black people have equal opportunity in the United States, and have had that since the end of the civil rights movement which reached its peak in 1968, the same year Dr. Martin Luther King was assassinated. However, a few, in fact very few black conservatives, see it in a different light, somewhat, although not like most blacks do.

One of these few black conservatives is Robert Woodson, despite the fact that he still maintains that racism is not the nation's major problem, as cited earlier. Yet he has much to say about white conservatives, hence white Republicans: "Conservatives got their reputation the old-fashioned way - they earned it. Their record on battling racial discrimination has been short of stellar."[46]

That is why when Ronald Reagan became president, he tried to dilute and even repeal the Voting Rights Act of 1965, supported tax exemption for segregated schools, opposed affirmative action, and implied Dr. Martin Luther King was a communist - "We will find out in 50 years, won't we?," he said at a press conference in the early eighties in response to a question on whether or not he thought Dr. King was indeed a communist. And the 50 years was in reference to the time when classified documents by the FBI on Dr. King will be made available to the public.

Reagan also tried in many ways to reverse the gains garnered by blacks since the civil rights movement and blocked a number of civil rights initiatives launched during his tenure by Democrats and civil rights groups. Internationally, his anti-black policies gained prominence when he supported the apartheid regime of South Africa and even had the audacity to say in public at a press conference in Washington D.C. that apartheid and racism against blacks in South Africa "no longer exists the way we knew it here in the South." Bishop Desmond Tutu also said he got nowhere with Reagan, and with Patrick Buchanan, on apartheid when he met the president at the White House.

Yet, in spite of their denial of racism as a major problem in the United States, Republicans have now and then had a rude awakening to harsh realties when some of their own people differ with them, especially in public. As U.S. Supreme Court Justice Sandra O'Connor, an Arizona conservative and Reagan appointee, wrote in the *Adarand Constructors v. Pena* decision on affirmative action that the Republican party opposes so much:

> The unhappy persistence of both the practice and the lingering effects of racial discrimination against minority groups in this country is an unfortunate reality, and government is not disqualified from acting in response to it.[47]

Although many black conservatives may admit racism still exists, they don't see it as serious problem that profoundly affects the lives of most blacks and hope, may be even pray, that their party, the Republican party - which doesn't even want them - will make a genuine effort to sell itself to African Americans. But they are frustrated by the lack of interest in such a move throughout the rank and file of the Grand Old Party (GOP), an assessment made by another leading black conservative, Willie Richardson, publisher of the black conservative journal *Headway*, now defunct because of lack of interest in the publication in the black community; many saw it as "trash," and an organ for the white conservative movement hostile to their interests and well-being. As Richardson states:

> While the gender gap has received a lot of attention, the Republican's race gap has hardly been mentioned. In fact, the race gap is so large that it is more like a canyon. Unfortunately, GOP leaders seem to be either unconcerned about their race gap or have conceded this vote to the Democratic party *ad infinitum*. Has it escaped GOP leaders' attention that 1960 was the last year a Republican presidential candidate received more than 15 percent of the black vote?[48]

No, it has not. They just don't want - You! And they don't need the black vote. Otherwise they would be stomping the ghetto to get the black vote. Has it escaped the black conservatives' attention that the Republican party and its white members have time and again through the years made their position clear, abundantly clear, on how they feel about blacks, and that they don't want them or need them? They don't care. So why do black conservatives keep on begging them?

Gwen Daye Richardson, editor of the black conservative publication *National Minority Politics*, renamed *Headway* although that did not help it to make any headway into the black community, explained how she and her editorial staff - all black - were ignored by the 1996 Republican presidential candidate Robert Dole and his team whom they asked probing questions about the Republican party and its relationship with blacks. As she stated:

In mid-August [1995], we contacted each of the [Republican] campaign press offices to request answers to five specific questions. We gave each of them adequate time, about 45 days, to submit their replies. We called each campaign three times prior to the deadline, to be sure they had received the questionnaires and to request photos. The manner in which they responded, or failed to respond, was instructive....

Senator Robert Dole of Kansas was the last candidate to submit his, after about 25 calls were made to his office over a period of a month-and-a-half. The day before the absolute deadline, a member of his press team told us, 'We probably should have *never* agreed to do this in the first place'....45 days is more than enough time to answer five questions, even for someone as busy as front-runner Dole.[49]

It had nothing to do with not having enough time, as Gwen Daye Richardson and her fellow blacks at their black conservative journal realized. It had to do with them being black. As simple as that; no way around it, ifs or buts. Presidential candidates, however busy they are, answer questions almost everyday from the media, especially from reporters on their campaign trail. It just happens that most of those reporters are white, like the candidates themselves, and their audience is predominantly white; which is the primary constituency of all white Republican candidates and of the Republican party itself. And that is the truth, plain and simple, but a bitter pill for black conservatives to swallow.

Senator Bob Dole and his staff were just blunt about it, and about whom Gwen Richardson noted:

When they finally did submit responses, obviously in a hurried fashion, all the questions were answered in the third person, such as 'Bob Dole believes one of the most important issues that must be addressed....' For months, we have heard rumors about the arrogance of Dole's staff....

What did the candidates say about America's future? Two questions stand out. The first question we asked was, 'What will be your top priority if you are elected president? In other words, what, in your view, is the most important problem Americans face?'.... The final question was, 'What factors do you believe are responsible for the dearth of minority voters who support the Republican party?' Most of the candidates either dodged this question, seemed to be in denial that such a 'dearth' exists, or, in the case of black voters, are comfortable with the single-digit support the GOP is currently receiving nationally.'[50]

Dole, the leading Republican candidate, did not even personally answer the questions submitted to him, his staff stating in no uncertain terms that they shouldn't even have accepted the questions in the first place. But the fact that even the other Republican candidates did not care to explain or find out why so few blacks vote for Republicans shows how much white Republicans really care about black people.

Yet all those were presidential candidates who were supposed to be concerned about all American citizens, *including blacks*; the most American of all Americans. They came before the Mayflower. The first African slaves arrived in Virginia in August 1619, while the Pilgrims on the Mayflower landed at Plymouth Rock in Massachusetts in November 1620. Yet, in spite of having been in America all this time, longer than most whites, they still are not accorded full citizenship rights. As Malcolm X said, "We did not land on Plymouth Rock, Plymouth Rock landed on us."[51]

The racism Malcolm X was talking about is the same kind of racism you find in the Republican party: ignore blacks, oppress them, exploit them, deny them their rights, deny them help and, if possible, even get them out of here: "Go back to Africa!," as some whites say now and then. And as Malcolm X said: "They just don't want us here."[52] Yet, in spite of all this, and in spite of the fact that it's plain as day and night that white Republicans don't want blacks in their party, some of these very same people, white Republicans, have the gall to ask why black Americans don't support the Republican party and Republican candidates and their policies; and why they complain about racism. They know the answer.

The Republican party's silence, deafening silence, on matters of race and racism speaks volumes about its attitude and policies

90

toward blacks. Republicans just don't want to be bothered - even if questions about the Republican party and blacks come from Republicans who "just happen" to be black. Gwen Daye Richardson and her colleagues learned the hard way. So did Faye Anderson, a lawyer, who left the party, disgusted, as we learnt earlier.

Other blacks in the party have had the same rude awakening even if some of them don't want to admit it. Just because they are Republican does not mean that they are no longer black, at least to whites in the party, even if they are no longer black mentally.

Blacks are seen as one people not because they are a monolithic whole or because they think alike; they are seen as one people because they are black, and they are oppressed collectively, not individually, as blacks. To racists, there is absolutely no difference between black liberals in the Democratic party and black conservatives in the Republican party. They are still black, first and foremost, and are headed for the noose just as fast if they run into the Klan somewhere out there.

Ask the Ku Klux Klan and other racist groups most of whose members are either Republicans or support Republican policies and politicians. Go and tell them, "I am a black conservative," and see if they will say you are different from other blacks who are not conservative or Republican.

They are impressed by none of that. You are just another "nigger" to them.

Even though Gwen Richardson and her colleagues are conservatives, they are no more accepted in the Republican party, and by whites who don't like blacks, anymore than other blacks are. That's the bottom line, black, the common denominator that unites all blacks regardless of ideology. When they are oppressed collectively because they are black, they must respond to such oppression collectively as black, and not respond individually simply as Americans *just* like other Americans. They are *not* treated just like other Americans. As Professor Nathan Glazer states in his book, *We Are All Multiculturalists Now*, the fundamental problem is "the refusal of other Americans to accept blacks."[53]

Even in the Democratic party, they are not fully accepted as equals, but much better than they are in the Republican party. And they really have no other choice besides completely staying out of the political arena; which they can't since America is their country too, and they have the right, natural right, to have a say on policies and other matters that affect their lives.

Black conservatives, of course, try to explain to their longed-for constituency, black America, that liberalism - the Democratic party's ideology - has failed them, and that conservative policies of the Republican party are the best alternative to the "bankrupt" and "paternalistic" policies of the Democratic party which pampers them as if they were infants; not out of genuine concern for blacks but out of guilt over centuries of racial oppression of black people in the United States since they brought to the "promised land" in chains from their African motherland.

Yet black conservatives have not been able to convince blacks to embrace Republican policies let alone abandon the Democratic party which has a track record fighting for their rights especially since the sixties during the civil rights movement.

Unfortunately, the Democratic party lost support among most whites in the southern states, battle ground for civil rights, because of its stand against racial injustice, prompting Democratic President Lyndon Johnson to say the party had lost the south from then on. Since then the south has become a Republican stronghold and a bastion of white nationalism in the Republican party the same way it was in the Democratic party when the majority of southern whites - who were then Democrats - strongly opposed racial equality for blacks.

But that does not mean the north is a bastion of true liberalism embracing blacks. There is an ambivalence toward blacks among many northern whites: whether they should accept them as equals or treat them as inferior.

It is a dilemma many of them have not been able to resolve, prompting many blacks to feel that whites in northern states are just as racist as their southern counterparts, only in a disguised way by publicly supporting blacks in their struggle for racial equality. And the struggle continues, in the south and in the north, more than 40 years after the civil movement. As Janice Rhodes, a black teacher in Grand Rapids, Michigan, where this author once lived, stated as recently as 2004: "In the South, at least you know where you stand, whereas in the North, you're trying to figure out where you stand."[54]

She was one of the blacks who wanted to migrate south, a migratory trend that has been a significant demographic shift since the seventies, with many blacks returning home in the south in search for a better life especially after the success of the civil rights movement that won civil rights for blacks even in some of the most virulently racist states in the southern part of the United States.

The racial dilemma in the north also has been a factor in this reverse migration, and played a role in Janice Rhodes' decision, as it has in many other cases, to move back down south, where her roots are, although she changed her mind for financial reasons. According to *The Grand Rapids Press*:

Janice Rhodes gave serious thought to moving to the South a few years ago, looking for a change in culture. She knows others who did so for job opportunities and warmer climes. Ultimately, the retired Grand Rapids teacher changed her mind when she saw how low the pay was - $5,000 a year less than she earned teaching English at Grand Rapids Ottawa Hills High School.

But she said she does get weary of dealing with the ambiguities of race relations in Michigan, one of the reasons she considered moving. 'In the South, at least you know where you stand, whereas in the North, you're trying to figure out where you stand,' said Rhodes, a retired state employee who runs a day-care center in Grand Rapids.

Subtle racial tensions in the North, an improved racial climate in the South - along with greater job opportunities there - may be driving forces causing a drift of blacks to the South.

From 1985 to 2000, more than 31,000 blacks migrated from Michigan to southern states. Most of those left Detroit....

Donald Williams, a former dean of minority affairs at Grand Valley State University, said many blacks have mixed feelings about staying in the north to face subtle racism. 'The South has been more honest with their dislike for African Americans than the North,' Williams said. 'The South is a comfortable place to be. The racism is blatant, but you know where you stand. In the North, so many people pretend they like you when they really have disdain.'

The racism is 'never more evident' in Grand Rapids than in disputes over honoring civil rights leaders, he said. The city became divided along racial lines in an effort to rename Franklin Street for slain civil rights leader Martin Luther King earlier this year. The city was equally divided over the naming of Rosa Parks Circle in 2001.[55]

Some black conservatives have tried to capitalize on that, saying the Democratic party doesn't care about blacks, either, but takes them for granted since they vote *en masse* for Democratic candidates; although they also go too far when they claim that it is the Republican party, instead, that cares about them or that has solutions to their problems.

But History proves otherwise, as does contemporary experience with the Republican party and its policies among blacks, a downtrodden minority. Compounding the problem for black conservatives in their quest for black support is their contention that black people can pull themselves up by their own bootstraps just like whites and everybody else who has done so.

The problem with this argument is that even black conservatives themselves know that many people, of all races not just black, have neither the boots nor the straps to pull themselves up with; it's just that blacks are hit the hardest, more than anybody else, because of racism. As Gwen Daye Richardson, a leading black conservative herself conceded: "The Republican party is viewed as being too heavily weighted toward balancing the budget and too little on compassion; in other words, out of balance....In many regions bumper stickers proclaim, 'Clinton! At least He Cares'....The public perception [is] that Republicans are mean-spirited."56

And the record speaks for itself. It is the Republicans who, more than anybody else, have opposed social programs for the poor through the years. Yet they have always been generous to the rich rewarding them with big tax cuts while cutting back financial or social help for the poor. It is also the Republicans who have been least sensitive to the plight of blacks as victims of racism. And it the Republicans who are up in arms when a white person loses a job to a black person, while maintaining stone-silence when a black person is dismissed and a white is hired for the now-vacant position.

The Republican party is saddled with what has been called compassion deficit, and which Walley Naylor, an outspoken black conservative and Republican, strongly criticized in the following terms: "We have a moral obligation to get our financial house in order, as well as respond with compassion to those who are less fortunate. But present-day Republican ideology says it is impossible to live up to both obligations. The newly minted welcome mat for minorities at the GOP has been replaced by one that reads, 'Welcome - sometimes'....I also know that a black Republican candidate will probably never gain broad support against a white Democrat; and that very little effort is spent to get minority voters to identify with and vote for Republican candidates...[and] minorities are still being taken for granted and shut out from party decision-making meetings."[57]

What Naylor has written about black Republican candidates losing to white Democrats happened in Michigan when Ronald Reagan, the most popular conservative leader in modern times, was president of the United States. Bill Lucas a black and Wayne County sheriff, was the Republican candidate for governor in the eighties.

A former FBI agent, Lucas had a reputation as a tough law-and-order Republican, a quality hailed by conservatives as almost exclusively theirs, while accusing Democrats of being soft on crime and criminals, especially black criminals who "commit all that crime," as the saying goes, so stereotypical of blacks. He was even publicly endorsed by President Reagan.

Yet Bill Blanchard, a white Democrat and well-known liberal, trounced him in the general election although Lucas had solid conservative credentials in a conservative state whose governorship has been dominated by Republicans for decades. Michigan even voted for the notorious racist George Wallace during the 1972 presidential campaign, the only northern state to do so.[58]

Still with all his conservative credentials, Lucas lacked one essential attribute: He was not white. As a simple as that. And he lost. Blanchard coasted to victory on a wave of white sentiment, only to be tossed out later by John Engler, a white Republican and solid conservative who also gained national attention when he abolished welfare for single men and women in 1991 when he was governor.

Michigan became the first state in the nation to do so and set the tone for the Republican "revolution" that came only a few years later when the Republican-dominated Congress abolished welfare nationwide in 1996, a program for the poor that had existed for 60 years, first launched during the Great Depression in the 1930s by liberal Democratic President Franklin D. Roosevelt.

Had Blanchard faced another black Republican candidate, he

would have been re-elected. White is virtually synonymous with power, and money, in this world. Those are just simple facts of life. Color is immaterial, but it carries a lot of weight. And white conservatives, especially, have through the years used it very effectively as a weapon against blacks to keep them down, at "the bottom of the well," as black legal scholar Derrick Bell put it.[59]

Even some black conservatives have conceded that much, with conservatism also being another synonym for racism. As Robert Woodson, a black conservative we encountered earlier, stated:

> In the '60s, I, like many blacks, equated conservatism with racism....Conservatives were the most strident opponents of our efforts to promote civil rights. Conservatives have not taken the time to show how their policies can stimulate the economic and social revitalization of low-income communities, nor clearly explain the reason that underlies their agenda....Conservatism continues to be perceived as adversarial to the interests of blacks.
>
> Many conservative leaders remained silent in the face of vicious racially motivated crimes, such as a series of church-burnings in the South [during the 1990s], but they rolled into action when a disgruntled white fireman complained of reverse discrimination. The silence of conservatives confronted with compelling instances of discrimination against blacks speaks volumes about their public image.[60]

It is interesting that some black conservatives complain about racism among white conservatives and in the Republican party when such racism frustrates their political goals and ambitions but ignore it when many blacks complain about it. Woodson himself is one such black conservative. He even says racism is not a major problem in the United States, contrary to what even the majority of whites themselves, not just blacks, say.

Clarence Carter, another black conservative, also admits: "Conservatism is popularly characterized as mean-spirited, divisive, exclusive, racist...'wanting to starve children, abuse the elderly and neglect the poor'....These ugly portrayals would not take hold in the minds of the American public if there was not a prevalent negative image of conservatism....The Republican party has failed to develop a long-term strategy to recruit black men and women."[61]

The frustration of black conservatives within the Republican party - where even they themselves, although not all, admit they are not quite welcome - is brought into sharper focus when one takes into account the fact that even other blacks outside the GOP who identify themselves as conservatives on a number of issues, mainly social issues such as combating crime and fostering family values, do not want to join the Republican party.

Instead, they remain securely anchored in the Democratic party where, together with liberal blacks, they constitute a formidable 81.1 percent of all blacks who identify themselves as Democrats.[62] For example, John McWhorter, a black professor of linguistics at the University of California, Berkeley, and author of highly controversial books such as *Losing the Race: Self-Sabotage in Black America*[63] and *Authentically Black: Essays for the Black Silent Majority*[64] in which he lays the blame at the doorsteps of black America for the failure of many black people to succeed and excel in many areas in the American society, was asked on national television - during the reading of his book *Losing the Race* - if he was a Republican.

He said he still was a Democrat and voted Democratic, in spite of his mainstream conservative views which kindled the ire among many blacks whom he says complain too much about racism, segregate themselves from the larger society, and don't value education as much as they should, if they do at all.

One wonders why people like him wouldn't feel "safe" in the Republican party where they would find comfortable accommodation for their conservative views, some virulently anti-black. The only place they feel "safe" and welcome is the Democratic party.

Even the Republican party has not made significant progress or any serious attempt to recruit them as members. For example, the Heritage Foundation, a conservative Washington-based think tank says only 8.7 percent of all blacks identify themselves as Republicans; and 5.5 percent as independents.[65] As Adam Meyerson, editor of the mainstream conservative journal *Policy Review* stated: "Sometimes before the end of this (20th) century, a very substantial minority of African Americans are going to begin identifying themselves with political conservatism rather than political liberalism. This cataclysm will not necessarily benefit the Republican party, because many of the most articulate voices of the new black conservatism will be Democrats."[66]

If that is the case, as Meyerson argues, why are the emerging black conservatives avoiding the Republican party, the flagship of the conservative movement? Why won't they become Republican? The answer is simple. Black conservatives within the Democratic party, and those who consider themselves to be independent, do not trust the Republican party which has been the home for racist groups and individuals espousing virulently anti-black views.

It was the Republican party that welcomed segregationists such as Senator Strom Thurmond who left the Democratic party in the sixties when the Democrats championed civil rights for blacks; Thurmond left in 1964 and quickly became a prominent leader of right-wing Republicans opposed to racial equality fore blacks.

Even today, it is the same Republican party where hate groups and racist leaders such as David Duke have found comfortable accommodation as they did in the past even before Barry Goldwater tried to elevate racism to a lofty status during the 1964 presidential campaign when he was the Republican candidate and won all six southern states, the hotbed of racism, against the Democratic presidential candidate Lyndon Johnson. He appealed to white supremacists using coded language against blacks. Johnson, on the other hand, supported civil rights for blacks and won the election.

But it was a victory that was also a loss to the Democratic party in the south from which it has never recovered. Because of racism, white voters in the south flocked to the Republican party in large numbers after the 1964 general election, turning the south into a bastion of white nationalism and a Republican stronghold that has played a critical role in every congressional and presidential election for Republicans since Richard Nixon won the presidency in 1968 by adopting the Southern strategy to appease white racist voters.

And black conservatives know that, even if they pretend not to. Gwen Daye Richardson is one of those who don't deny it. With unusual candor among black conservatives on the subject of race, she has the following to say about the conservative movement, hence the Republican party, and its image:

There are extreme elements which have latched onto the conservative movement....David Duke is a good example who hides behind conservatism to

98

disguise genuine racism toward blacks and others he considers to be unworthy of equal protection under the law.

Then there are militia groups, like the Freemen of Montana....There are others who claim to advocate a color-blind society and equality of opportunity, yet they only protest discrimination when it occurs against white males, not against blacks, women or members of minority groups....These extreme elements abound within the conservative movement [led and represented by the Republican party]."[67]

What is it that is attracting all these hate groups and other racists into the Republican party as opposed to the Democratic party? Even the Ku Klux Klan (KKK) and other racist groups openly endorsed Ronald Reagan when he first ran for president in 1980, an endorsement that attracted media attention when he was campaigning in Pulaski, Tennessee, where the KKK was founded on Christmas Day in 1865 under the leadership of an uneducated although not illiterate Confederate General Nathan Bedford Forrest.

The leadership was first offered to General Robert Lee, the commander of the Confederate forces which fought the Union army led by General Sherman during the civil war, but he turned down the invitation because of his age and told the founders of the KKK to choose a younger leader to lead the organization, not because he was opposed to its hatred of blacks. They chose General Forrest.

Many of the Republicans today are lineal descendants - in terms of racist beliefs, and even genealogically - of those early racists, prompting Democratic presidential candidate George McGovern during the 1972 presidential campaign to say that Richard Nixon, the Republican candidate, was leading a party that was worse than the Ku Klux Klan.

Reagan's endorsement by the KKK and other hate groups prompted Democratic presidential candidate, and incumbent, Jimmy Carter to publicly say on national television, "There is no room for racism in this country,"[68] in pointed reference to Reagan for his endorsement by hate groups. Another Republican, Pat Buchanan who also worked as communications director for President Reagan, got similar endorsement when he ran for president in the 1990s and in 2000, with racists and hate groups publicly stating that "he's our candidate."

Before Reagan, was Barry Goldwater, also endorsed by hate groups during his presidential campaign in 1964. And it was Reagan who gave the nomination speech at the Republican National Convention in San Francisco when Goldwater was formally nominated as the Republican presidential candidate and the standard-bearer of the Republican party and the conservative movement in the United States.

An arch-conservative, Goldwater was the darling of ultra-rightists in the Republican party and in other groups such as the John Birch Society and the White Citizens' Council. At the Republican National Convention in 1964 where he was endorsed by acclamation as the Republican presidential candidate, he openly whipped up racist sentiments - as he had done before throughout the campaign - by appealing to white extremist groups, stating:

Extremism in the defense of liberty is no vice; and moderation in the pursuit of justice is no virtue.[69]

Therefore it is not the desire to balance the budget, or trimming the bureaucracy to have smaller government and lower taxes, issues Republicans talk so much about, that is attracting white extremists into the Republican party. Preaching hate against blacks has nothing to do with balancing the budget or having smaller smaller government and lower taxes.

Opposition to civil rights by white conservatives during the sixties had nothing to do with balancing the budget, having smaller government, or lowering taxes; nor does it have anything to do with fostering *family values*, another buzz-term the radical right confabulates, when white Republicans embrace and welcome other segregationists into the folds of the Republican party.

South Carolina U.S. Senator Strom Thurmond and others left the Democratic party, angry, precisely because it championed civil rights and racial equality for blacks. There was no other reason than that, why they left the party, or why they became Republicans.

Had they simply liked Republican policies, they would have joined the party before.

It was not until the civil rights movement gained momentum in the sixties with the support of white liberals in the Democratic party that they left this party and were warmly embraced by fellow racists in the Republican party.

Even conservatives themselves, both black and white, admit that conservatism has a bad image and that the Republican party has a bad track record even today with regard to blacks, many of whom believe that it wouldn't even mind starving them to death. And little has changed in terms of perception and reality concerning the Republican party among the vast majority of African Americans. As David Bositis, a senior researcher at the Joint Center for Political and Economic Studies in Washington, D.C., states in his paper, "African Americans and the Republican Party":

Black elected Republicans remain something of an anomaly. At the present time, with over 8,000 black elected officials in the United States, fewer than 80 are Republicans elected to partisan office [Republican versus Democratic]....There are presently 550 black state legislators in the country, of whom just 10 are Republicans including one party switcher from North Carolina....

From the perspective of congressional races [where there are hardly any black Republicans who win the party's nomination to run for Congress, since whites are chosen as candidates almost all the time except in extremely rare cases] we can only conclude that no change as yet has taken place in the relationship between African Americans and the Republican party.

[And] the level of participation of African Americans in Republican party organizations has never been strong, and the prospects for improvement appear dim....Black involvement in internal party affairs has been very limited.

Of the 153 members on the Republican National Committee (RNC) from the U.S., just one member is black - Harry Singleton, the national committeeman from the District of Columbia....

The likelihood of any significant increase in black membership on the RNC or as delegates to the Republican National Conventions [where they choose presidential candidates] is small....In sum, there has been no significant change in the role of African Americans in internal Republican party affairs, and...there is little reason to expect any change.

Black identification with the Republican party is weak and has remained unchanged....In January 1996, in a Joint Center for Political and Economic Studies National Opinion Survey of African Americans, 8.7 percent identified themselves as either Republicans (4 percent) or leaning toward the Republican party (4.7 percent). This was unchanged from 1992....Some young African Americans [less than 20 percent] 'try on' a Republican identity while they are young, but as they move through their twenties and into their thirties, they move toward the Democratic party....[And] a large majority of African Americans continue to support affirmative action [so strongly opposed by Republicans]....The black Republican vote for president and Congress has hovered around 10 percent....

The only clear conclusion that can be drawn is that little has changed in the fundamental relationship [between African Americans and the Republican party].[70]

And the reason is simple. That is because the Republican party is racist or simply doesn't care about blacks. And its ideology of conservatism is synonymous with racism and raw bigotry as it always has been. Since the end of Reconstruction, the Republican party has been as racist as it is today. Its policies and attitude toward blacks prove it.

It has no interest in recruiting black members because its constituency is white. It is the hub, the nerve center, of the white oppressive machinery that keeps blacks in bondage as second-class citizens. It is the mused and sometimes articulated credo of today's Republican party that the party remain that way. The pleas and petitions, wails and tears, of black Republicans to prod the party's leadership into embracing blacks have fallen on deaf ears and continue to do so. As black Republican U.S. Senator Edward Brooke of Massachusetts stated way back in the sixties:

The Republican party must, by person-to-person contact, work with people who live in America's cities and demonstrate to them a genuine and sincere concern for their problems and aspirations....

Since the advent of Franklin D. Roosevelt, members of minority groups have, rightly or wrongly, believed that the Democratic party would best serve their interests. Because of this, the composition of the Republican party has lacked that pluralistic quality which has benefited the Democratic party so much.

The voices of these groups have not been heard in Republican party councils. We learn about their problems second-hand. We have not had the advantage of their thinking or their suggestions for solutions to their problems. Worse, they have not been present as participants to influence the direction in which the Republican party should move.[71]

More than 40 years later, after the black senator took his party to task for its failure and unwillingness to attract minorities into its ranks, the Grand Old Party (GOP) has yet to take up the challenge. The reason is simple, and clear, as black and white.

White Republicans don't want to be bothered. They don't want, they don't need, or allow, blacks into their ranks, neighborhoods, occupations, schools, or social circles, simply because they are black.

Why that eludes black conservatives remains inexplicable to the rational mind. As Ed Vaughn, a Democratic state legislator representing a predominantly black Detroit constituency in the Republican-controlled Michigan state legislature states:

> The issue of race in this country. Many times when people like myself, and you, advocate for the population that's underserved for the most part, African-Americans, many times white Americans assume that this is something just for us, and I tell all of my colleagues in Michigan, my white colleagues, that I don't know how in the world anyone could vote Republican because every bill that comes through is designed to help rich people. And I don't know too many rich ones around there. Unless you live in Grosse Pointe or Okemos, in Michigan.
>
> And the whole issue of welfare. When the word welfare is mentioned, they always think of blacks - when more people on welfare are white, than are black. Somehow we have to get through this racial divide....I'm concerned about the racial divide....Racism is so deep in this country.[72]

With their racial politics of exclusion, appealing only to white voters and supporters, Republicans have played a critical role in dividing the country along racial lines as if the problem were not serious enough already. Racism is deeply entrenched because of such divisive tactics and politics.

Yet black conservatives can't see that. They continue to beg white Republicans in their desperate attempt to inch their way into areas - political and social enclaves - where they are not wanted or respected as if they don't even have respect for themselves as human beings, except as puppets manipulated at will by racists who use them whenever they want to do so. They have never learned from history. And they probably never will. Only a few of them have, as we learn next.

Chapter Three:

The Other Voices Within and Without

IT MAY NOT BE many of them, but disillusionment with the Republican party has forced some blacks to renounce their membership in a party they feel best represents their interests and those of black America articulated from a conservative perspective.

Yet to most blacks, the core of the conservative philosophy that has found forceful expression in policies formulated and implemented by the Republican party is at variance with what they perceive to be their best interests, contrary to what black conservatives contend, as we have learned in the preceding chapters.

Some of the black conservatives who have made a dramatic exit from the GOP include Faye Anderson, a lawyer and political activist of some "prominence" within the Republican party although the role she played has been dismissed as peripheral by a number of Republicans themselves including her detractors who may consider her to be an apostate or simply a liberal infiltrator. As she said about the Republican party and its warm embrace of racists while at the same time saying it wanted minorities as members:

You can't get the Republican leaders to listen. This is an issue that is of keen concern to me and a lot of people. You can't talk about inclusion when under that tent are people who'd just as soon see us hanging from a tree.[1]

Her remarks came after a report in *The Washington Post* in December 1998 said that United States Senate Republican majority leader Trent Lott of Mississippi, U.S. Senator Jesse Helms of North Carolina, Congressman Bob Barr of Georgia, and other leading white Republicans - including former governors Guy Hunt of Alabama and Kirk Fordice of Mississippi - were affiliated with the Council of Conservative Citizens (CCC), a far-right wing organization founded in Atlanta, Georgia, in 1985 but now based in St. Louis, Missouri, and which is the reincarnation of the notoriously racist White Citizens' Council which terrorized and killed blacks and civil rights workers, including whites, in Mississippi and other parts of the south in the fifties and sixties.

It was established by former activists in the segregationist White Citizens' Council and preaches white supremacy and separatism. Its leader, attorney Gordon Lee Baum, was an organizer and field director for the White Citizens' Council and established the Council of Conservative Citizens largely by contacting and recruiting old members of the White Citizens' Council from the council's old mailing list.

Faye Anderson's departure from the Republican party inevitably came after some soul searching led her to conclude that she was a member a party that couldn't care less about blacks and other minorities. And as Michael Tomasky stated in his article in *National Interest*, which was also published in *New York Magazine*:

> For all their talk of a big tent, most Republicans still don't get it about race - as witness the Senate majority leader's disinclination to renounce white supremacists.[2]

In fact, even the national chairman of the Republican party, Jim Nicholson, denounced the Council of Conservative Citizens as "racist" and called on anyone with ties to the organization to sever them. And a number of congressmen sponsored a resolution in the House to "condemn the racism and bigotry" of the organization.

But out of more than 120 co-sponsors of the resolution, only nine were Republicans, further confirming fears among blacks that the Republican party was racist and did not care about them.

And the resolution was killed even before it got to the House floor, blocked by Republican leaders in a Republican-dominated Congress.

Trent Lott said he would not support a resolution condemning the Council of Conservative Citizens, and added, "if they start on one group or one kind, I don't think that's wise." Yet he did not hesitate to vote for a similar resolution in Congress in 1994 denouncing Black Nation of Islam leader Khalid Muhammad for his anti-Semitic remarks. Trent's ties to the Council of Conservative Citizens drew national attention when it was revealed that he was a regular attendant at the council's events and addressed its members several times.

The organization's literature and web sites, and its activities in other forums, consistently promote the genetic and intellectual superiority of whites over blacks and other non-whites. Therefore it is not surprising that it fully endorsed Richard Herrnstein and Charles Murray's highly inflammatory book, *The Bell Curve*, in which the authors contend that black people have lower IQs than whites for genetic reasons.

In fact, the founder of the White Citizens' Council, Robert B. Patterson who established the first White Citizens' Council in Indianola, Mississippi, in July 1954, became a founding member of the Council of Conservative Citizens (CCC) and even today continues to write racist articles about blacks in publications of the CCC.

Within two years, by August 1956, the White Citizens' Council had chapters in 30 states. And like its predecessor, the Council of Conservative Citizens also has nationwide membership and strongly supports Republican candidates and policies.

As the founders of the Council of Conservatives Citizens clearly stated when they first met in Atlanta, Georgia, in 1985, they were opposed to government "giveaway programs, special preferences and quotas, crack-related crime and single mothers and third-generation welfare mothers dependent on government checks and food stamps," in pointed reference to blacks, as the coded language they used clearly shows.

That also is a typical Republican agenda - and strategy of appealing to white voters - black conservatives support as if being black means absolutely nothing to them, although it does to whites in the Republican party, to which black conservatives belong, and elsewhere across the country.

And not surprisingly, many of the Council of Conservative Citizens (CCC) members are Republicans or support the Republican party. Democratic state legislators from Mississippi and elsewhere have also spoken at the organization's meetings, and some of them are members, although their party, the Democratic party, is seen by many whites as being too sympathetic toward blacks and other minorities at their expense.

The only difference is that while Republican leaders of national stature have addressed members of the CCC at their meetings, Democratic national leaders have not; for example, Bob Barr, a prominent Republican congressman and former prosecutor, spoke at the organization's national board meeting in Charleston, South Carolina in 1998.

David Duke, a well-known white supremacist and member of the Republican party, is also one of the people who have addressed members of the the Council of Conservative Citizens at its meetings at the invitation of the organization's leadership. Others include leaders of the Christian Identity and several other white supremacist organizations, including Richard Butler of the Aryan Nation.

Jared Taylor, editor of the racist publication *American Renaissance*, has also spoken at the CCC meetings. His organization, American Renaissance, contends that blacks are genetically inferior to whites. And when David Duke addressed a meeting of the South Carolina chapter of the CCC at Clemson University, he publicly urged its members to fight for their "white genes."

Among the CCC members and supporters are many Republican leaders although they have been described as low-level in the Republican party (GOP). Still, that does little to shed the GOP's racist image among many people, especially blacks, when it has some of its people - including leaders - as members and sympathizers of a racist organization such as the Council of Conservative Citizens.

And when Trent Lott spoke at the council's meeting, he explicitly told its members that they represent "the right ideals and the right philosophy," and also told them, "we need more meetings like this...The people in this room stand for the right principles and the right philosophy. Let's take it in the right direction and our children will be the beneficiaries,"[3] knowing full well that it was a racist organization.

His intention was obvious, and he showed his true colors and exactly where he stood on the subject of race, as he clearly demonstrated later when he spoke with nostalgia about the good ol' days of Senator Strom Thurmond when the South Carolina senator was an avowed segregationist, paying him the highest compliment by saying had Thurmond won the presidency, "we would not have all these problems we have today," meaning integration and racial equality, with blacks having the right to be treated as equal citizens and even take whites to court.

In all its ideological essentials, and the tactics it uses to appeal to white sentiments against blacks and other minorities, the Council of Conservative Citizens is an advanced version of the Republican party in its purest form. It is white, while the Republican party which has a sprinkling of blacks and other minorities is considered even by whites themselves to be a party for whites that best protects their interests against blacks and other non-whites.

And the similarities in the political manifestos of the two organizations are striking, although the Republican party is not openy racist but is adept at sending subliminal messages to whites using coded language to mobilize them against minority interests of blacks and other non-whites. As the Anti-Defamation League which investigates hate groups and compiles reports on them states in its assessment of the Council of Conservative Citizens:

Since its inception in the mid-1980s, the Council of Conservative Citizens (CCC) has cloaked itself in the mantle of mainstream conservatism to mask its underlying racist agenda. The CCC bills itself as a 'grassroots' organization working on issues of concern to conservatives, such as opposition to affirmative action, 'big' government, gun control, and increased immigration.

The CCC co-opts both the language and issues of conservative causes to camouflage the true aim of the organization, which is to regain what it sees as the lost power base of the white population of the United States....A pro-white and anti-minority stance is at the heart of every CCC chapter.

A racist political group, the Council of Conservative Citizens (CCC), has been making waves in the national media ever since it became known that mainstream politicians such as Senator Trent Lott (Republican-Mississippi) and Representative Bob Barr (Republican-Georgia) were keynote speakers at CCC conferences. According to the CEO of the CCC, Gordon Lee Baum, Senator Lott has addressed the group a number of times, and Representative Barr made an appearance in front of the group in 1998....

In a recent interview in *The Washington Post*, Gordon Baum reportedly said, 'Do we have a few members who might have been in the Klan? Probably - but so what? None are leaders.' Mr. Baum is once again masking the truth - various heads of CCC chapters are well plugged in to the extremist network of groups whose philosophy meshes with that of the Klan....

Considerably more polished than traditional extremist groups, the Council of Conservative Citizens propounds its bigotry in the guise of hot-button conservative advocacy. Striking hard-right positions on such contentious issues as...affirmative action, the organization has insinuated itself into the mainstream successfully enough to attract a number of prominent conservative politicians to its gatherings....

An examination of the origins, membership and publications of CCC suggests that it remains...squarely within Southern racist traditions. While not every CCC chapter may be equally extreme, all are founded on anti-minority bigotry. The roots of the CCC rest in white opposition to integration during the civil rights movement....

The beliefs of the CCC fall within the racially charged tradition of its predecessor (White Citizens' Council) but reflect contemporary fears of its constituency....CCC members focus on issues like interracial marriage, which the group calls 'mongrelization of the races'; black-on-white violence; and the demise of white Southern pride and culture, best exemplified n the debate about the Confederate flag....

Both on its national and chapter Web sites and its primary publication, *The Citizens Informer*, CCC's belief in white superiority and its derision of of nonwhites, particularly African Americans, are delineated without apology....*The Citizens Informer* is edited by Sam Francis, formerly a controversial *Washington Times* columnist who was eventually dismissed for defending slavery....

By appealing to widespread resentments (against minorities, especially blacks) and successfully attracting prominent conservatives, the Council of Conservative Citizens has been able to recruit numbers of relatively moderate individuals into an organization that maintains strong connections with extremists.

Its record demonstrates that CCC has not tried to break away from its racist antecedents. Instead, it has adopted not only its predecessor's racial attitudes but also its strategies, deriving from them the tools to advance a racist agenda from the grassroots to the senior levels of government.[4]

That is why some of its members and supporters are prominent national leaders, especially Republicans. In essence, the Council of Conservative Citizens is the Republican party itself in its crudest form, although the GOP, unlike the CCC, does not use overtly racist language. But its use of race to mobilize white support for the Republican agenda hostile toward minority interests is no different from what the Council of Conservative Citizens does.

And the policies it advocates - for example against affirmative action, immigration and 'big' government - are the same policies advocated by the Council of Conservative Citizens. So is the exclusion of blacks from the two organizations although, here again, the Republican party does not openly say it does not want blacks as its members. But its unwillingness to reach out to blacks and recruit them into the GOP achieves exactly the same objective.

It must also be emphasized that white extremist groups support the Republican party and its policies for very good reasons, as much as Barry Goldwater appealed to these very same groups during his 1964 presidential campaign enabling him to win all six southern states where opposition to civil rights for blacks was strongest.

That is why even the Ku Klux Klan and other hate groups endorsed Ronald Reagan when he first ran for president in 1980. And that is why white supremacists such as David Duke and others as well as their followers are members of the Republican party. They know what they have in common: hostility toward blacks more than anybody else.

These are some of the reasons *why* some blacks have left the Republican party or have simply stopped to actively participate in its activities even if they have not formally renounced their membership in the GOP; they should have known, of course, even before they joined the party what the party was all about just like the majority of blacks know. Some, of course, like Faye Anderson, have left the Republican party with a lot of noise, complaining about the racism within the party and toward blacks. She made that clear when she left the GOP.

And a few years later when commenting on the forthcoming 2004 general election, she said "Republicans have a race problem. The white swing voters will not support a party that appears harsh, so they use black and brown faces to appeal to white voters, not to take care of those voters."[5]

Another defector who may also have gained notoriety in conservative circles for being a turncoat is Oklahoma journalist and columnist Richard Dixon. Neither of them - he or Faye Anderson - may have been a political heavyweight even among fellow black conservatives in the Republican party, let alone in the party itself where they don't even "exist" according to many white Republicans who simply tolerate them. But the defection of both or of any other blacks from the party, if their departure can be called a defection at all or simply a rude awakening to reality, dramatizes the plight blacks face not only within the Republican party but in the country as a whole at the hands of Republicans especially when they are in power.

Blacks constitute only a small percentage of the Republican party membership. Therefore, even if all of them left the party, it would not be an exodus, but only a trickle that went in, and that is now flowing out. It hasn't happened, of course. But it is important to know what some of the black conservatives who have left the party have to say about their black ideological compatriots. As Richard Dixon, who describes himself as "a former black conservative," stated in his article in *Black Oklahoma Today*:

Black conservatism finds its roots in White conservatism. Its elements are a total belligerency to present day black leadership, an indifferent attitude to the historic struggle of the African-American experience, an elitist view of the urban poor, and a total disconnection with the black populace in general....

It is from a white elitist perspective that black conservatives like Walter Williams, Thomas Sowell, and Shelby Steele derive their notions about the state of Black America in this country. They harbor, embrace, and validate these notions to the detriment of African-Americans and add fuel to a widening racial polarization.[6]

Whatever credibility black conservatives may have had in the black community, and that's highly questionable, has been eroded, compromised or impaired, not by their lack of ideological clarity - other blacks know exactly what they are saying - but by their ideological bankruptcy since they have nothing new to offer and have not come up with any innovative solutions to address the problems of black America in a race-conscious society where the majority of whites put a premium on race as they continue to harbor racist attitudes, and attitudes of superiority, toward blacks even if they are not overtly racist.

Such criticism of black conservatives does *not* come only from liberals, black and white, but also from some black Republicans themselves. They include John Wilks, a prominent black Republican who served in the Nixon and Ford administrations, and who dismisses the claim that black conservatives have generated new ideas and have become prominent in the media and in other forums on merit and for their ideological contribution.

He had this to say about black conservatives, as quoted by *The New York Times*: "They merely say they're conservative, say they're opposed to affirmative action and are immediately picked up by a right-wing white sponsor."[7]

Their emphasis on self-reliance is nothing new to blacks. Black people have been self-reliant since slavery. They are survivors. They have survived the worst. And they continue to survive, and thrive, without being lectured by whites, liberal or conservative. Black conservatives' blistering attack on welfare dependency among blacks, as if most blacks are on welfare, is also misleading, even if valid in a limited context.

Most blacks, even the poorest of the poor, work. They are not on welfare. Yet when many whites hear black conservatives talk the way they do, they feel vindicated in their stereotypical view of "all" blacks as lazy, nursed on the welfare tit.

And their attack on affirmative action - contending, as white conservatives and many other whites do, that it is racism in reverse - has no rhetorical or substantive appeal to the majority of blacks who, from cumulative and daily experience, know that racism is an enduring phenomenon in a country where they are not fully accepted by whites as equal citizens for no reason other than that they are black descended from slaves who were brought to America in chains to work for whites.

Little has changed in this asymmetrical relationship between blacks and whites in terms of perceptions: master versus slave or servant; hence Derrick Bell's description of blacks as "faces at the bottom of the well," and Cornel West's "race matters," and much more. Racial justice is an ideal that has yet to be attained. Black conservatives contend otherwise, setting them apart from their brethren in the inner cities and elsewhere.

Even their attempts to claim some renowned black leaders as fellow conservatives have not been very successful, if at all. For example, they claim that Malcolm X was a conservative like them because he taught self-reliance. Yet they forget that he identified himself with the masses, the grassroots, the poor, while they don't. They are detached from their own people. He was not. They are elitist. Malcolm X was not. They dismiss racism, saying it is not a serious problem in the lives of black people. Malcolm X said it was. He took it very seriously and never believed that white people will *ever* accept blacks as equals. He was down-to-earth, with the poorest of the poor in the ghetto. He never forgot his roots. That's why he said, in one of his speeches, "I like small people."

The kind of conservatism black conservatives ascribe to leaders such as Malcolm X, and even Dr.W.E.B. DuBois and Booker T. Washington, simply because they taught self-reliance, is political conservatism which ignores race as a fundamental reality in the lives of black people; something these leaders never did.

They contend that black people have always been conservative; which is true in some respects. But they are social conservatives, supporting strong family values as clearly demonstrated by their strong ties to the church among other things, and the work ethic they have always upheld and cherished since slavery. They are *not* political conservatives of the red-neck type like black conservatives are.

And because of their bitter experience at the hands of racists who wanted to uphold states' rights, so that they can do whatever they want to do to blacks in their own states without federal intervention, the majority of blacks believe the federal government has an important role to play to guarantee their rights as equal citizens in a country where they have yet to be accorded full status as fellow Americans by millions of whites who don't consider them to be full human beings or as their equal.

Therefore, much as black conservatives talk about self-reliance, they are seen by many other blacks as mere puppets of white racists who couldn't care less if all blacks vanished from the face of the earth today. As Professor Sherri Smith of the University of Alabama in Huntsville who, apprehensive of the black conservative phenomenon, studied black conservatives for two years stated in "Blacks Wary of New Black 'Conservatives'":

Many so-called 'black conservatives' receive the label simply because they believe in self-help. They don't say the system or the government should take care of everyone. Thus, Malcolm X, Frederick Douglass, Martin Luther King, Jr., and others are erroneously labeled black conservatives....The problem many African-Americans have with these 'conservatives' is that they appear to air the problems of the black community to the entire nation without offering any real solutions.[8]

Perhaps no one exemplifies the anomalous position of black conservatives, in relation to black America, as Glenn Loury. A professor of economics at Boston University, formerly at Harvard, he was one of America's most well-known black conservatives whose role as a leading public intellectual - he calls the term public intellectual "oxymoronic" - included testifying before Congress offering solutions to Black America's perennial problems.

He left the conservative movement and became "a progressive," as he put it; neither liberal nor conservative, although he began to articulate views acceptable to liberals and, in fact, sounded like one, thus incurring the wrath of his former colleagues in the conservative movement.

As a conservative, he was against affirmative action and even worked for the Reagan administration. After his ideological change, he wrote a book, *The Anatomy of Racial Inequality*,[9] in which he says the problem black people face is not just racial discrimination but a much more complex problem of what he calls "racial stigma" because of the kind of image whites have of African Americans as unequal. And this perception has a profound impact on policy far more than what blacks themselves really are.

Unlike in his previous years when he was a conservative, he now says in his book that color-blind policies cannot solve the problem of racial inequalities because they do not take into account the harm caused to blacks as an oppressed minority throughout their history in the United States when their mistreatment was an accepted way of life. And it still is, in many fundamental respects.

The way whites view blacks only makes matters worse, reinforcing the stigma associated with being black - the racial identity of a people who have always been considered inferior - thus justifying discrimination against them.

Therefore being black is a problem by itself. Loury now

contends that the problems of black America will not be fully addressed without taking race into account; a repudiation of his earlier position when he was a conservative. It also amounts to acceptance of liberal orthodoxy which has always embraced race as part of the solution to America's racial dilemma, a democratic nation yet which has not fully accepted blacks as equal citizens.

He has undergone quite a transformation from what he was before. He even supported the University of Michigan in its pro-affirmative action case which went all the way to the US Supreme Court.

He may not call himself a liberal, but he now supports liberal policies on a number of issues including racial preferences, in school admissions, for example, in spite of lower grades of the minority applicants; which explains why his former colleagues in the conservative movement have been so harsh in their criticism of him and his new ideological position.

His reassessment of his earlier political beliefs, and the indifference of conservatives toward the plight of black America especially the underclass, have led him to examine the attitudes of whites and the social patterns which reinforce negative stereotypes of blacks as a people not worthy of trust and membership on equal basis in the American society. They are "the other America," to use Michael Harrington's term - also the title of his book[10] - in a slightly different context; Harrington used the term to embrace all poor people across racial lines.

Loury says some people - whites in this context - see the problems of some groups - read, black people - face are part of their nature. Therefore nothing can be done about them. Just ignore them. And that is one of the major problems blacks face: society's unwillingness to help them solve their problems by providing them with opportunities including remedial measures to correct racial injustice or mitigate its effects; hence the need for affirmative action and other race-conscious solutions to the perennial problems of race in America.

It is a radical departure from his past. He says over the past 50 years, the United States has repudiated white racism; he obviously starts with the *Brown vs. Board of Education* US Supreme Court ruling in 1954 that outlawed segregation. But such repudiation has been limited to overt racism without addressing a deeper problem:

assumptions about the nature of blacks which shape white attitudes toward African Americans as an inferior group. And that stigmatizes blacks, limiting opportunities for them. He also concedes that he himself has been subjected to indignities because of his racial identity as an African American.

His departure from the conservative movement occurred in the mid-1990s following publication of three books by conservatives which he found to be deeply flawed intellectually. The first one was *The Bell Curve*11 by Richard Herrnstein and Charles Murray; Dinesh D'Souza's *End of Racism*,12 and *America in Black and White: One Nation, Indivisible*13 by Stephan Thernstrom and Abigail Thernstrom; the last book was published in 1999.

It was actually *The Bell Curve*, published in 1994, and *The End of Racism*, published in 1996, which prompted his departure from the conservative movement, with the Thernstroms' work only adding fuel to the fire a few years later. Publication of *The End of Racism* led to Loury's resignation from the conservative American Enterprise Institute which sponsored D'Souza's book. And he was highly critical of *The Bell Curve* which he said was full of errors and contained "sweeping conclusions based on poor science." Finally, he said he was disturbed by what he regarded as intellectual lapses and racist content of *America in Black and White* by the Thernstroms.

On a personal level, his re-examination of conservatism was profoundly influenced by one of his relatives, Uncle Fred, an elderly figure on the South Side of Chicago where Glenn Loury grew up in the black community. One day he said he visited his uncle who was very uncomfortable with Loury's political orientation and conservative philosophy. The uncle said to him: "I don't see us in anything you do. It's like we're the whipping boy for you, like you're exploiting your insider status as a black to give comfort to all these people who hate us. Why are you doing that?"14

Although his break with fellow conservatives may have been prompted by the publication of anti-black books in the mid-1990s, Loury said he had for many years been troubled by the position articulated by his fellow conservatives on a number of issues involving race. Why he remained within the conservative movement, with such doubts, is not fully explained. He says he did not have the courage to fully state his position, although he did when left the conservative movement. Some people may feel that a plausible explanation is that he did not leave before because he was still a conservative at heart despite his disagreements with fellow conservatives on race.

Yet, despite his ideological re-orientation away fom conservatism, Loury says his new position on race does not contradict his previous analysis of the problems of race, personal responsibility and other issues, stating: "I still believe in taking personal responsibility, in blacks dealing with the dysfunctional behaviors in their communities." But he also concedes that there were "flaws in my earlier arguments."[15]

His admission that there were flaws in his previous ideological position has drawn some of the sharpest responses from his former colleagues in the conservative movement in which he was considered to be a leading black conservative intellectual. As Richard Higgins stated in "Breaking Ranks: Glenn Loury's Change of Heart and Mind": "That explanation does not wash with most black conservatives, some of whom have savaged Loury for his defection. In its review of *The Anatomy of Racial Inequality*, *The Wall Street Journal* accused Loury of 'trashing his former black colleagues' and called the book a 'turgid 226-page effort to intellectualize 'blame-whitey' explanations for the state of black America.'"[16]

Loury turned to neo-conservatism because he was disillusioned with the civil rights movement. But he did not find a comfortable home in the conservatism movement because he still cared about the poor in the inner cities and the racial predicament all blacks are trapped in, because of the unwillingness of the white majority to live up to the ideals of liberty and equality for all, also embracing African Americans who are still considered to be outcasts in their own country and the only one they have known as home. As Paul Krugman, in trying to explain Loury's dilemma - trapped between the dogmatic left and the dogmatic right - states in his article, "Glenn Loury's Round Trip: The Travails and Temptations of A Black Intellectual":

The dogmatic rigidity, left and right, that has left Loury without an ideological home is also why this nation has such a hard time talking honestly about race.

Reading Loury's dissertation today, 22 years after he wrote it (in 1976), is a depressing experience - precisely because the essays were so good and remain so relevant. In the first few pages, he stated the central dilemma of race policy in modern America. He was willing to give American society the benefit of the doubt, to assume that in the future, racism - direct economic discrimination - would no longer be a major force holding African-Americans back. But he argued that this probably would not be enough; therein lay the dilemma.

On one hand, we all believe that individuals deserve to be judged on their own merits, not by who their parents were or what group they belong to. On the other hand, anyone who imagines that a child growing up in the South Bronx has the same chance to make it as an equally talented child growing up in Scardsdale is living in a fantasy world. So merely eliminating *current* racial discrimination might very well fail to eliminate the effects of past discrimination.

Indeed, Loury argued persuasively that even a world of 'equal opportunity' might 'perpetuate into the indefinite future the consequences of ethically unacceptable historical practices.' If you find that prospect unacceptable, you must support some form of social engineering - which ultimately, no matter how you package it, means giving some people special consideration based on the color of their skin as well as on the content of their character.

In a better world, Loury would have spent the last 22 years devising policies - working with other well-intentioned people to come as close as possible to squaring this circle, finding ways to eliminate the legacy of past racism with as little intrusion as possible on the colorblind ideal. But he has basically never been able to get off square one - because at no point over the past two decades has he been able to find allies who are even willing to accept the reality of the dilemma.[17]

Loury's identification with conservatism started after the end of the civil rights movement when he felt that the problems blacks faced also had to do with what was going on in the black community itself. Racism could not be blamed for everything; nor could the past be blamed for one's failure to succeed in life. As he explicitly stated in 1990, in his book *One by One from the Inside Out* when he was still affiliated with conservative organizations and think tanks, "[we blacks] must let go of the past and take responsibility for our future."[18] And that contradicted liberal orthodoxy:

You can't ignore the past. The present is the product of the past. Racism exists now as it did then and is an omnipresent phenomenon, liberals contend. It penetrates every fibre of the American social fabric. Conservatives contend otherwise: racism is not what it used to be. And where it exists, it does not impede progress because of equal opportunity now available to blacks.

That's a contradiction, of course. You can't have equal opportunity where racism exists. And if you insist that black people have equal opportunity, you're saying racism no longer exists; or if it does, it is not a serious problem, if it's one at all. That is the black conservative position. It is also the same position mainstream conservatives, that is white conservatives and others on the ideological right, forcefully articulate, leaving them open to the charge that they are indifferent to the plight of blacks people or simply don't care.

Ironically, it was a black liberal scholar, Professor William Julius Wilson at Harvard University, a sociologist, who challenged liberal orthodoxy on race without being excommunicated from the liberal camp, mainly because he continued to embrace liberal policies on many fundamental issues, including race itself.

In his book, *The Declining Significance of Race*,[19] written when Glenn Loury was still studying for his Ph.D. in economics at MIT, Wilson contends that class is more important than race in the destiny of blacks in the United States; a position equally and forcefully articulated by conservatives and Marxists, strange bedfellows. As a true liberal of course, Wilson favors federal intervention in helping to alleviate the plight of the poor, unlike conservatives including Loury when he was in the conservative camp.

Coincidentally, Thomas Sowell's *Race and Economics*[20] was published around the same time Wilson's book was, advancing similar arguments. In his book, published in 1975, Sowell, a prominent black economics professor, contends that market forces, not race, are the critical factor.

But whereas Sowell as a true conservative rules out race - for example, his contention in his book that employers hire people on the basis of need and skills and not on the basis of race, thus levelling the playing field for blacks - Wilson still sees race as a factor, but playing not significant a role as it once did; a thesis that comes pretty close to what conservatives say. And that was Loury's position when came to be identified as a conservative, although with nuances to his argument about race many people did not understand or simply ignored because he was in the conservative camp.

When Loury became a part of the mainstream conservative movement, many fellow blacks accused him of not caring about the condition of his people trapped in poverty in the ghetto because of racism. Yet his conservatism was not of the color-blind type even from the beginning when he moved to the right on the ideological spectrum; a point underscored by Krugman:

Loury's problems began with the left. Although his dissertation was written only a dozen years after passage of the (1964) Civil Rights Act, he saw clearly that the problems facing African-Americans had changed. The biggest barrier to progress was no longer active racism of whites but internal social problems of the black community. But black leaders, and to a lesser extent liberalism as a whole, flatly refused even to contemplate that possibility. He also found powerful pressures - 'loyalty tests' - operating against any black intellectual who tried to challenge the orthodxy.

To Loury's credit, he did not give in to these pressures. He said what he thought. In doing so, he found himself labeled a 'black conservative' - and thereby exposed to new and dangerous seductions. Let's face it: Any articulate minority intellectual who reliably espouses conservative positions is automatically offered a ticket to a very nice lifestyle.

No more rejections from picky academic journals or grubbing for sabbatical time. Instead there are cushy fellowships at Hoover, guest editorials in *The Wall Street Journal*, and invited articles in *Commentary* - maybe even a regular column in *Forbes* - and a steady stream of invitations to plush conferences in nice places. All this and more lay before a bona fide academic star such as Loury. Until personal problems temporarily derailed him in 1987, he was well on his way to high political office and all the rewards that brings in later life.

But at some point Loury made the discovery that eventually confronts every honest intellectual who gets drawn into the political arena. The enemies of your enemies are not necessarily your friends. The Glenn Loury who wrote that 1976 thesis was not a conservative. He criticized the simplistic anti-racism of the liberal establishment because he wanted society to tackle the real problems, not because he wanted it to stand aside.

His seeming allies on the right, however, turned out to be interested only in the critique, not in the next step. According to Loury, 'When I told one gathering of conservatives that their seeming hostility to every social program smacks of indifference to the poor, I was told that a surgeon cannot properly be said to have no concern for a terminally ill patient simply because he had moved on to the next case.' Loury found out that the apparent regard for his ideas by conservative intellectuals was entirely conditional. Any questioning of conservative orthodoxy was viewed as an act of betrayal, giving aid and comfort to the liberal enemy. It was the loyalty test all over again.

The final straw was surely the grotesque affair of Richard Herrnstein and Charles Murray's *The Bell Curve: Intelligence and Class Structure in American*

Life. This book came close to claiming that, given your genes, it makes no difference to your economic success whether you grew up in Scarsdale or the South Bronx. The implied subtext was that this absolves society from any responsibility to do something for children growing up in the South Bronx.

Since *The Bell Curve* was published, it has become clear that almost everything about it was inexcusably wrong: suspect data, mistakes in statistical procedures that would have flunked a sophomore - Murray (Herrnstein is deceased) clearly does not understand what a correlation coefficient means; deliberate suppression of contrary evidence, you name it. Yet conservative publications such as *Commentary*, which was always happy to publish Loury when he criticized liberal evasions, would not grant him space to critique *The Bell Curve*.

So Loury is now on his own, or rather, at the head of a small movement of like-minded people, centered on his new Institute on Race and Social Division: rejected by the black political elite, which still wants to blame everything on white racism, and equally rejected by a conservatism that wants to do precisely nothing about continuing racial inequality. And the dilemma Loury identified so clearly 22 years ago remains not only unsolved but also unconfronted.[21]

With his dramatic shift to the liberal camp on fundamental issues of race, poverty, employment and education, to name a few, one would assume that Loury would be fully embraced by liberals.

But there seems to be no such thing as accepting the return of the prodigal son probably among a significant number of them because they don't feel that he has fully embraced liberal policies on *all* problems the way they have, especially on race. As he stated in "Leadership Failure and the Loyalty Trap" in his book, *One by One from the Inside Out*, published in 1995 after his acrimonious debate with his fellow conservatives the previous year following the publication of *The Bell Curve* which they defended, despite its intellectually and scientifically indefensible thesis that black people are less intelligent than whites and members of others races because they have weak genes, a conflict that led to his departure from the conservative movement:

They [black leaders] are fearful of engaging in a candid, critical appraisal of the condition of our people because they do not want to appear to be disloyal to the race. But this rhetorical reticence has serious negative consequences for the ability of blacks as a group to grapple with the real problems that confront us.

Moreover, it represents a failure of nerve in the face of adversity that may be more accurately characterized as intellectual treason than racial fealty. After all, what more important obligation can the privileged class of black elites have

121

than to tell the truth to their own people?[22]

Still, despite such vitriolic condemnation of black leadership, which is mostly liberal, even after he left the conservative movement, Loury is no longer the outcast he once was, and even made a dramatic re-entry into the liberal camp, at least in public, at a place considered to be one of the main centers of liberalism, Harvard University, which also has a highly influential institute of African American studies staffed by some of the most renowned black liberal scholars in the nation.

He was invited by Professor Henry Louis Gates, Jr., head of the African-American Studies Center at Harvard, in 2000 to deliver the W.E.B. DuBois Lectures which were published by Harvard Universy Press as a book, *The Anatomy of Racial Inequality*, which has become one of Loury's most influential works.

After his ideological shift, Loury conceded that the conservative analytical framework ignores the history of racism in the United States, including contemporary racism. As he states: "Contemporary American society has inherited a racial hierarchy - the remnant of a system of racial domination that has been supported by an array of symbols and meanings deleterious to the reputation and self-image of blacks."[23]

But why did it take him so long to realize that? He contends that nothing that he says or does now contradicts his earlier position. That is a contradiction since he also says he has re-evaluated some of the things he said in the past and has found flaws in some of his arguments, especially about race.

He obviously knew all along about the devastating impact racist white America has had on black America but still believed that individuals, hence the title of his book *One by One from the Inside Out*, would by sheer effort be able to climb out of the quagmire of misery and poverty in the ghetto, from deep inside, in spite of racism.

That is probably why in 1990, as a true conservative, he testified before Congress against proposed civil rights legislation that sought to introduce stronger legal measures against employment discrimination.

The proposed legislation did not even address the issue of the underclass in the ghetto, yet Loury linked the two, arguing that such legislation would not solve "the real problem" which has to do with "drugs, criminal violence, educational failure, homelessness, and family instability."[24]

But after his ideological conversion, he now states in *The Anatomy of Racial Inequality*: "The 'conservative line' on race in America today is simplistic. [S]uch 'pathological' behavior by these most marginal of Americans is deeply rooted in American history....[W]hile there may be a grain of truth in the insistence by conservatives that cultural differences lie at the root of racial disparity in the United States, the deeper truth is that, for some three centuries now, political, social, and economic institutions that by any measure must be seen as racially oppressive have distorted the communal experience of the slaves and their descendants."[25]

Although he does not unequivocally state that he has embraced liberalism, some of the positions he has now taken after his break with the ideological right are within the liberal tradition he once rejected and perhaps even despised because of the intellectual myopia of its proponents, black and white, whom he then felt did not fully address, confront or understand the problems of the underclass - a loaded, and often disparaging term preferred by conservatives - in the ghetto, and of black people in general in a white-dominated society.

What he also probably did not understand was the irrelevancy of black conservatives and their solutions - including his when he was in the conservative camp as a leading black conservative intellectual - to the problems of black America then and now.

The refusal of blacks to vote for black Republican candidates - not one has ever won a congressional seat from a predominantly black district - is just one example of the pariah status of black conservatives in the black community. They are an anomaly. And their opposition to affirmative action and other programs supported by the majority of blacks sets them even farther apart from their own people, while they remain anchored at the far end of the ideological spectrum characterized by right-wing ideology insensitive to the interests of blacks and other minorities and the poor.

Even black conservative publications such as *Headway*,

formerly *National Minority Politics*, which drew a clear conservative ideological line have never gained wide readership in the black community. Obviously, many blacks see them as "trash" or nothing but propaganda by right-wing ideologues who don't care about blacks and simply use black conservatives to try and destroy their own people.

That is one of the reasons, if not the main reason, *why* the black conservative journal *Headway* ceased publication. If black people don't want to buy it, why continue publishing it?

Black conservatives have offered nothing new to black America. Self-reliance, which they preach so much and which is probably their only rallying point for black support for their conservative agenda, has not helped them to win support in the black community for one simple reason: most blacks are self-reliant, and they don't need to be taught self-reliance since this virtue is deeply rooted in black American history since slavery. Besides their irrelevancy to the black community, if they have any hidden agenda, it is no longer hidden. The majority of blacks see them as being insensitive to the racial problems black America faces.

They also see them only as puppets, being used by white racists as attack dogs to insulate whites from charges of racism, make their own people look bad by harping on "lack of values" in the inner cities, and blame the victims - blacks - for all their problems including racism. The Republican policies they advocate are anathema to black America. They have, in fact, condemned themselves to irrelevancy. And as Professor Cornel West states in "Unmasking the Black Conservatives":

The publication of Thomas Sowell's *Race and Economics* in 1975 marked the rise of an aggressive and widely visible black conservative assault on the traditional liberal leadership of blacks in the United States. The promotion of conservative ideas is not new in Afro-American history. George S. Schuyler, for example, published a witty and acerbic column in an influential black newspaper, the *Pittsburgh Courier*, for decades, and his book *Black and Conservative* is a minor classic in Afro-American letters. And Zora Neale Hurston, one of the most renowned Afro-American woman writers, wrote reactionary essays - some of which appeared in the *Reader's Digest* - and gavce her allegiance to the Republican party - facts overlooked by her contemporary feminist followers. Yet the bid for conservative hegemony in black political and intellectual leadership that was initiated by Sowell's book represents a new development in the post-civil rights era.

The bid is as yet highly unsuccessful, though it has generated much attention from the American media. Besides Sowell, a senior fellow at the Hoover Institution on War, Revolution and Peace at Stanford University, other prominent figures in the black conservative movement are Glenn C. Loury, a professor at Harvard's Kennedy School of Government; Walter E. Williams, a professor of economics at George Mason University; I.A. Parker, president of the Lincoln Institute for Research and Education, Inc.; Robert Woodson, president of the National Association of Neighborhood Enterprises; and Joseph Perkins, editorial writer for *The Wall Street Journal*. Though there are minor differences among these people, they all support the basic policies of the Reagan administration, including the major foreign policies, the opposition to affirmative action, the efforts to abolish the minimum wage, the proposals for enterprise zones in the inner cities, and the vast cutbacks in social programs for the poor.

These publicists are aware of the irony of their position - that their own upward social mobility was, in large part, made possible by the struggles of those in the civil rights movement and the more radical black activists they now scorn. But they also realize that black liberalism is in a deep crisis. It is this crisis, exemplified by the rise of Reaganism and the decline of progressive politics, that has created the intellectual space that the black conservative voices - along with the non-black ones - now occupy.

The crisis of black liberalism and the emergence of the new black conservatives can best be understood in light of three fundamental events in American society and culture since 1973: the eclipse of U.S. economic and military predominance in the world; the structural transformation of the American economy; and the moral breakdown of communities throughout the country, especially among the black working poor and underclass.

The symbolic events in the decline of American economic and military hegemony were the oil crisis, which resulted principally from the solidarity of the OPEC nations, and the military defeat in Vietnam. Increasing economic competition from Japan, West Germany and other nations ended the era of unquestioned U.S. economic power. The resultant slump in the American economy undermined the Keynesian foundation of postwar American liberalism: economic growth accompanied by state regulation and intervention on behalf of disadvantaged citizens.

The impact of the economic recession on Afro-Americans was immense. Not surprisingly, it more deeply affected the black working poor and the underclass than the expanding black middle class. Issues of sheer survival loomed large for the former, while the latter continued to seize opportunities in education, business and politics. Most middle-class blacks consistently supported the emergent black political class - the black officials elected at the national, state and local levels - primarily to ensure black upward social mobility. But a few began to feel uncomfortable about how their white middle-class peers viewed them. Mobility by means of affirmative action breeds tenuous self-respect and and questionable peer acceptance for many middle-class blacks. The new black conservatives voiced these feelings in the form of

125

attacks on affirmative action programs, ignoring the fact that they had achieved their positions by means of such programs.

The importance of this quest for middle-class respectability based on merit rather than politics cannot be overestimated in the new black conservatism. The need of black conservatives to gain the respect of their white peers deeply shapes certain elements of their conservatism. In this regard, they simply want what most Americans want - to be judged by the quality of their skills, not the color of their skin. But surprisingly, the black conservatives overlook the fact that affirmative action policies were political responses to the pervasive refusal of most white Americans to judge blacks on that basis.

The new black conservatives assume that without affirmative action programs, white Americans will make choices on merit rather than race. Yet they have adduced absolutely no evidence for this: Hence, they are either politically naive or simply unconcerned about black mobility. Most Americans realize that job-hiring choices are made both on reasons of merit *and* on personal grounds. And it is this personal dimension that is often influenced by racist perceptions.

Therefore the pertinent debate regarding black hiring is never 'merit vs. race' but whether hiring decisions will be based on merit, influenced by race-bias against blacks, or on merit, influenced by race-bias, but with special consideration for minorities as mandated by law. in light of actual employment practices, the black conservative rhetoric about race-free hiring criteria - usually coupled with a call for dismantling affirmative action mechanisms - does no more than justify actual practices of racial discrimination. Their claims about self-respect should not obscure this fact, nor should they be regarded as different from the normal self-doubts and insecurities of new arrivals in the American middle class.

It is worth noting that most of the new black conservatives are first-generation middleclass persons, who offer themselves as examples of how well the system works for those willing to sacrifice and work hard. Yet, in familiar American fashion, genuine peer acceptance still seems to escape them. In this regard, they are still influenced by white racism.

The eclipse of U.S. hegemony in the world is also an important factor for understanding black conservatives' views on foreign policy. Although most of the press attention they receive has to do with their provocative views on domestic issues, I would suggest that the widespread support black conservatives receive from Reaganite conservatives and Jewish neoconservatives has much to do with their views on U.S. foreign policies. Though black conservatives rightly call attention to the butchery of the bureaucratic elites in Africa, who rule in the name of a variety of ideologies, they reserve most of their energies for supporting U.S. intervention in Central America and the U.S. alliance with Israel. Their relative silence regarding U.S. policy of 'constructive engagement' with [apartheid] South Africa is also revealing.

The black conservatives' stance is significant in light of the glacial shift that has occurred in black America regarding America's role in the world. A consequence of the civil rights movement and the Black Power ideology of the

'60s was a growing identification of black Americans with other oppressed peoples around the world. This has had less to do with a common skin color and more to do with shared social and political experience.

Many blacks sympathize with Polish workers [in communist Poland]and Northern Irish Catholics [in Northern Ireland] - despite problematic Polish-black and Irish-black relations in places like Chicago and Boston - and more and more blacks are cognizant of how South Africa oppresses its native peoples, how Chile and South Korea repress their citizens, and how Israel mistreats the Palestinians.

This latter identification especially worries conservatives. In fact, the radical consequences for domestic issues of this growing black international consciousness - usually dubbed anti-Americanism by the vulgar right - frightens the new black conservatives, who find themselves viewed in many black communities as mere apologists for pernicious U.S. policies.

The new black conservatives have rightly perceived that the black liberal leadership has not addressed these changes in the economy. Obviously, the idea that racial discrimination is the sole cause of the predicament of the black working poor and underclass is specious. And the idea that the courts and government can significantly alleviate the plight of blacks by enforcing laws already on the books is even more spurious. White racism, though pernicious and potent, cannot fully explain the socioeconomic position of the majority of black Americans.

The crisis of black liberalism is the result of its failure to put forward a realistic response to the changes in the economy. The new black conservatives have highlighted this crisis by trying to discredit the black liberal leadership, arguing that the NAACP, the National Urban League, the Congressional Black Caucus and most black mayors are guided by outdated and ineffective viewpoints. The overriding aim of the new black conservatives is to undermine the position of black liberals and replace them with black Republicans, who downplay governmental regulation and stress market mechanisms and success-oriented values in black communities.

Yet the new black conservatives have been unable to convince black Americans that conservative ideology and Reaganite policies are morally acceptable and politically advantageous. The vast depoliticization and electoral disengagement of blacks suggests that they are indeed disenchanted with black liberals and distrustful of American political processes; and a downtrodden and degraded people with limited options may be ready to try any initiative. Nevertheless, black Americans have systematically rejected the arguments of the new conservatives.

This is not because blacks are duped by liberal black politicians nor because blacks worship the Democratic party. Rather, it is because most blacks conclude that while racial discrimination is not the sole cause of their plight, it certainly is one cause. Thus, most black Americans view the new black conservative assault on the black liberal leadership as a step backward rather than forward. Black liberalism indeed is inadequate, but black conservatism is unacceptable.

This negative reaction to black conservatives by most blacks partly explains the reluctance of the new black conservatives to engage in public debates in the black community, and their contrasting eagerness to do so in the media, where a few go so far as to portray themselves as courageous, embattled critics of a black liberal establishment - while their salaries, honorariums and travel expenses are paid by well-endowed conservative foundations and corporations.

The new black conservatives have had their most salutary effect on public discourse by highlighting the breakdown of the moral fabric in the country and especially in black working poor and underclass communities. Black organizations like Jesse Jackson's PUSH have focused on this issue in the past, but the new black conservatives have been obsessed by it, and thereby given it national attention. Unfortunately, they view this urgent set of problems in strictly individualistic terms, and ignore the historical background and social context of the current crisis.

The black conservatives claim that the decline of values such as patience, hard work, deferred gratification and self-reliance have resulted in the high crime rates, the increasing number of unwed mothers, and the relatively uncompetitive academic performances of black youth. And certainly these sad realities must be candidly confronted. But nowhere in their writings do the new black conservatives examine the pervasiveness of sexual and military images used by the mass media and deployed by the advertising industry in order to entice and titillate consumers.

Since the end of the postwar economic boom, new strategies have been used to stimulate consumption - especially strategies aimed at American youth that project sexual activity as instant fulfillment and violence as the locus of machismo identity. This market activity has contributed greatly to the disorientation and confusion of American youth, and those with less education and fewer opportunities bear the brunt of this cultural chaos.

Ought we to be surprised that black youths isolated from the labor market, marginalized by decrepit urban schools, devalued by alienating ideals of beauty and targeted by an unprecedented drug invasion exhibit high rates of crime and teenage pregnancy?

My aim is not to provide excuses for black behavior or to absolve blacks of personal responsibility. But when the new black conservatives accent black behavior and responsibility in such a way that the cultural realities of black people are ignored, they are playing a deceptive and dangerous intellectual game with the lives and fortunes of disadvantaged people. We indeed must criticize and condemn immoral acts of black people, but we must do so cognizant of the circumstances into which people are born and under which they live. By overlooking this, the new black conservatives fall into the trap of blaming black people for their predicament.

The ideological blinders of the new black conservatives are clearly evident in their attempt to link the moral breakdown of poor black communities to the expansion of the welfare state. For them, the only structural element of political-economic life relevant to the plight of the black poor is the negativce role of the state and the positive role of the market. An appropriate question to these descendants of slaves sold at the auction block is, Can the market do any

128

wrong?

They claim that transfer payments to the black needy engender a mentality of dependency which undercuts values of self-reliance and the solidity of the black poor family. The new black conservatives fail to see that the welfare state was the historic compromise between progressive forces seeking broad subsistence rights and conservative forces arguing for unregulated markets. Therefore it should come as no surprise that the welfare state possesses many flaws.

I do believe that the reinforcing of 'dependent mentalities' and the undermining of the family are two such flaws. But simply to point out these rather obvious shortcomings does not justify cutbacks in the welfare state. In the face of high black unemployment, these cuts will not promote self-reliance or strong black families but will only produce even more black cultural disorientation and more devastated households.

Yet even effective job programs do not fully address the cultural decay and moral disintegration of poor black communities. Like America itself, these communities are in need of cultural revitalization and moral regeneration. There is widespread agreement on this need by all sectors of black leadership, but neither black liberals nor the new black conservatives adequately speak to this need.

At present, the major institutional bulwarks against the meaninglessness and despair rampant in Afro-America are Christian churches and Muslim mosques. These churches and mosques are indeed fighting an uphill battle; they cannot totally counter the pervasive influence on black people, especially black youths, of the sexual and violent images purveyed by the mass media.

Yet I am convinced that the prophetic black churches - the churches that have rich cultural and moral resources and a progressive politics - do possess the kind of strategy it takes to meet the crisis of black culture. That is, churches like Jeremiah Wright's Trinity United Church of Christ in Chicago, Herbert Daughtry's House of the Lord Pentecostal Church in Brooklyn, Charles Adam's Hartford Memorial Baptist Church in Detroit, and Frank Reid's Ward African Methodist Episcopal Church in Los Angeles are able to affirm the humanity of poor black people, accent their capacities, and foster the character and excellence requisite for productive citizenship. Unfortunately, there are not enough of these institutions to overcome the cultural and moral crisis.

What then are we to make of the new black conservatives? First, I would argue that the narrowness of their viewpoints reflects the narrowness of the liberal perspective with which they are obsessed. In fact, a lack of vision and analysis, and a refusal to acknowledge the crucial structural features of the black poor situation, characterizes both black liberals and conservatives. The positions of both groups reflect a fight within the black middle-class elite. This parochialism is itself a function of the highly limited alternatives available in contemporary American politics.

Second, the emergence of the new black conservatives signifies a healthy development to the degree that it calls attention to the failures of black liberalism and thereby encourages black politicians and activists to entertain more progressive solutions to the problems of social injustice. Finally, I would predict that the next area for black conservative attacks on the black liberal leadership will be that of U.S. foreign policy.

The visible role of the NAACP and black elected officials in the antiapartheid movement will probably come under a heavier ideological assault. This attack can only intensify as black liberal leaders find it more and more difficult to pass the conservative litmus tests for pro-Americanism in foreign affairs: uncritical support for U.S. policy toward Israel and U.S. intervention in Central America.

Perhaps the widening of the split between black liberal leaders and black conservative critics will lead to a more principled and passionate political discourse in and about black America. I am confident that with more rational debates among conservative, liberal and leftist voices, the truth about the black poor can be more easily ascertained. The few valuable insights of the new black conservatives can be incorporated into a larger progressive perspective that utterly rejects their unwarranted conclusions and repugnant policies.

I suspect that such a dialogue would unmask the new black conservatives as renegades from the critics of black liberalism who have seen some of the limits of this liberalism, but are themselves highly rewarded and status-hungry ideologues unwilling to question the nature of their own illiberalism.[26]

Society, white society, must accept its share of the blame for the plight of black America. And it must be willing to help and even sacrifice in order to solve the problem.

Black America must also accept its share of the blame. Absolving society of the blame, as black conservatives do, is not going to help solve black America's problems but will only exacerbate the condition leading to increased racial polarization. Nor will self-neglect by blacks themselves in their own communities help improve their condition by expecting to extract concessions, and may be even unconditional help, from white America guilty of past and contemporary racial oppression.

Millions of whites *don't* feel guilty. And even some of those who do, don't even think about helping black America. Therefore blacks must continue to play their part, helping themselves, as they always have done. But they still need help from white America because of the magnitude of the problems they face.

The message of black conservatives has not resonated well across black America for obvious reasons. And it probably never will, unless they fully address racism, *including* ingrained stereotypical attitudes toward blacks among most whites, and exhort society to play its role in helping black America solve its problems.

Racism is a perennial problem. And it is a major one. It is impossible to have equal opportunity where racism exists. Why this eludes black conservatives, who are black themselves, defies rational explanation.

Chapter Four:

Racial Injustice Against Whites: A Black Conservative Perspective

THROUGHOUT American history, more whites than blacks have been the perpetrators of racial injustice and have in most cases been protected by the judicial system instituted and dominated by members of their race.

Today, some people argue that it is blacks, not whites, who are protected by the judicial system as they get away with murder and "all that crime" perpetrated against whites, and that black racism is condoned while white racism is condemned.[1]

Professor Walter Williams, one of the most outspoken black conservatives today, blames blacks, not whites, for the deterioration of race relations in the United States today, especially since the end of the civil rights movement which brought about fundamental change in terms of legislation guaranteeing civil rights for blacks. He cites crime statistics and slanted justice "in favor" of blacks to bolster his case. As he states in his article, "Souring Racial Relationships":

> The seemingly racially motivated - seemingly because two suspects charged were black - arson against black churches ought to be roundly

condemned....

There isn't the national moral outrage against today's black church burnings as there was against church burnings and bombings during the 1960s civil rights movement. Increasing numbers of white people are becoming insensitive toward acts of violence of this sort. While most white people wouldn't torch or condone torching of a black church, they may see it as a kind of comeuppance.[2]

If the burning of black churches by white racists is a punishment well-deserved, as Williams claims most whites believe and which they probably do, why do they feel that way?

He justifies their attitude and offers a classic defense of racism that has earned black conservatives a reputation as "lap dogs" of white conservatives who couldn't care less about the problems of black America, many of them caused by racism. He frames his argument in this context: "Let's look at just a few things that may create such an attitude. According to the U.S. Justice Department's 1993 report 'Highlights From 20 Years of Surveying Crime Victims,' 99 percent of the victims of crimes are white. Blacks murder whites at 18 times the rate that whites murder blacks. Black-on-white assaults are 21 times the rate of white-on-black assaults. Blacks are 64 times more likely to rape a white woman than whites are to rape a black woman. If [that] is not enough to sour race relations, there's court sanction and pockets of vocal black support of black criminals."[3]

Williams' finding that courts favor blacks over whites is a startling revelation. One wonders how the courts, dominated by whites, cannot be racist against blacks in a society where even the majority of whites admit they don't like blacks.[4] Such hate is nothing but racism. Racism cannot be explained any other way; it is hate, and this is not an ingenious way of defining it. If racism is not hate, what is it? When the majority of whites say they don't like blacks, what makes them not racist? In fact, according to polls cited earlier in this work, the majority of them don't even want to integrate with blacks.

Even some of the people who run the judicial system admit that blacks don't always get justice simply because they are black. One such critic of the judicial system is Bruce Wright, a retired black judge who sat on the New York State Supreme Court, and author of a book, *Black Robes, White Justice: Why Our Legal*

*System Doesn't Work for Blacks.*₅ The high incarceration rate of blacks, as opposed to whites, is a clear example of that. Capital punishment is another example of judicial bias against blacks. A black person is 4.5 times more likely to receive the death penalty for killing a white person than a white is for killing a black.₆ As Tom Wicker points out in his book, *Tragic Failure: Racial Integration in America*:

> 'Getting tough' imprisonment is what Americans have chosen...to do about the children of the ghetto.... A destructive side effect of an aggressive imprisonment policy is that it sustains many African-Americans' strong - if by no means irrational - sense that the criminal justice system is biased against their race....
>
> Anti-black bias is everywhere in the criminal justice system. In New York State young African-Americans are *twenty-three times* more likely to be imprisoned than white men are. Three times more young whites are on probation than are in New York prisons, but for blacks the opposite is true.[7]

That is the judicial system Professor Williams and other black conservatives say favors blacks over whites. And it goes on everywhere, not just in the state of New York. The videotaped beating of Rodney King by the police in Los Angeles; the murder of Amadou Diallo, an immigrant from Guinea, West Africa, by the police in New York City where he was shot at 41 times, and hit 19 times; the torture of Haitian immigrant Abna Louima at a police station in New York City where a white police officer, with the connivance of his colleagues, rammed a broom stick into his rectum; another videotaped beating of a black youth in Los Angeles whose head was repeatedly banged against the hood of a police cruiser while he was at the same time being punched by several other police officers; yet another videotaped beating of a black "car-thief" by the police in Los Angeles, in spite of the fact that he had surrendered and was lying on the ground as he continued to sustain repeated blows from a policeman's flashlight while other policemen pinned down the suspect and even delivered their own blows as well; the shooting deaths of blacks in Cincinnati, Ohio, in Detroit, Michigan, by white police officers, and elsewhere; these are only a few cases, and examples, of police brutality perpetrated against blacks, day in, day out, across the United States by the police, for no other reason than that the people targeted are black.

How many whites, and even other people such as Hispanics and Asians, do you see being shot or beaten up by the police the way blacks are? Hardly any. It's always blacks, at least most of the time. Why? Because of racism. They are the primary target.

The disparity in sentencing for black and white drug dealers across the nation is another example of racial bias against blacks under the criminal justice system black conservatives such as Walter Williams claim favors blacks, in spite of all the evidence to the contrary.[8] Even incontrovertible evidence of police brutality, televised nationwide, has not been enough to get white policemen who brutalize blacks convicted.

The policemen who brutalized the teenager in Los Angeles, punching him and trying to smash his head on the hood of a police car, were not punished or convicted of the crime. The white officers who beat up Rodney King walked away free from the first trial. Many blacks, even some whites, knew the white officers would be acquitted simply because they were white.

That is something blacks expect from the white American judicial system in many cases. And they were proven right, a point underscored by Tom Wicker in his searing indictment of the racist judicial system, and of the racist American society in general, in his book, *Tragic Failure: Racial Integration in America*:

> Shortly before the first [Rodney] King trial in Los Angeles, an associate professor of government at Harvard named Katherine Tate placed a telephone call to her mother, who lives in the South. The daughter...was sure the white officers who had beaten King would be convicted. Their actions had been videotaped and widely televised, and she thought their guilt could not be doubted.
>
> Tate therefore was surprised to hear her mother, whom she described as a rather traditional African-American who had never been an activist, express the quiet conviction that the white officers would be acquitted. Her mother, Ms. Tate concluded, had a 'visceral feeling' that black people never get justice in white America....
>
> The first King verdict - not guilty - can only have deepened that 'visceral feeling.' Katherine Tate herself asked me in tones of hurt and bewilderment: 'Why are white people like they are?' Her mother had good reason to doubt the outcome of the King case because anti-black bias is everywhere in the criminal justice system.[9]

Walter Williams and other black conservatives contend

otherwise. As Larry Elder, a lawyer and radio talk show host in Los Angeles who is also one of the most outspoken black conservatives, bluntly stated in an interview with *Reason*, a conservative magazine, people like Jesse Jackson are just looking for a great white oppressor who doesn't even exist.[10] Yet it is difficult to see how the judicial system - let alone the whole white-dominated society - is biased in favor of blacks who always "play the race card", as Larry Elder said in a television interview in 2004 in the case involving Michael Jackson who was accused of child molestation, when there is overwhelming evidence showing that blacks are, indeed, perennial victims of racism.

Here are the facts, in a nutshell: White police officers are rarely punished for brutalizing blacks, a common experience in the inner cities across the nation. Blacks are more likely than whites to be executed. Blacks receive longer sentences for less serious crimes than whites do for more serious crimes such as cocaine manufacturing and trafficking. And laws, such as those dealing with drugs, are unabashedly biased against blacks. There is evidence to prove it all:

> The death penalty is notorious for racial bias, and not just in the Deep South. Under the 1988 drug kingpin law, the Justice Department was empowered to seek death for drug-related murders by big narcotics operators and their associates.
>
> At the time of writing, execution had been sought for forty-two defendants, thirty-seven of them African-Americans. *But three fourths of all drug-trafficking defendants are white.* Nor was this a hangover from the Reagan and Bush administrations; in 1993, Bill Clinton's attorney-general, Janet Reno, sought ten death penalties under the 1988 law, and all ten defendants were black.[11]

Why were all of the *defendants* black, when the biggest drug dealers are white? How did the whites escape the death sentence if the system is not biased against blacks?

The law explicitly states that the Justice Department *may* - and not that it *must* - seek the death penalty for such offenders. Instead, the department targeted blacks in pursuit of a twisted, distorted justice that is unmistakably racially biased against them, sparing whites. Smaller drug dealers in the inner cities are targeted just as much. Being poor is bad enough, but being black compounds the felony:

Differing federal penalties for possession and use of powdered cocaine and crack cocaine show the same pattern of racial bias....A nonviolent first offender convicted in federal court of possessing five grams of crack receives a mandatory sentence of five years in prison. Possession of five grams of powdered cocaine, on the other hand, is only a misdemeanor, punishable at worst by a year in prison. Crack defendants, however, are much more likely to be black because crack is cheaper and easily available in underclass neighborhoods.

Only about 4 percent of crack defendants are white, although in 1993 a national survey found that 46 percent of crack smokers were white. And since federal law treats a gram of crack as the equivalent of one hundred grams of powdered cocaine, minor - mostly black - street peddlers of crack can and do get long, harsh sentences mandated for major - often white - dealers in powdered cocaine.[12]

This grim assessment is corroborated by other reports, such as *Harper's* telescoped telegraphically:

•Mandatory minimum jail sentence, in years, for possession of five grams of crack: 5.
•Chances that an American sentenced for crack-related offenses is white: 1 in 25.
•Mandatory minimum sentence for possession of five grams of cocaine: 0.
Chances that an American sentenced for cocaine possession is white: 1 in 3.[13]

Yet Professor Walter Williams says America's courts favor blacks, as do other black conservatives. If such disparity in sentencing is not judicial bias against blacks, what is it? Instead, black conservatives such as Joseph Brown, Ezola Foster, and Larry Elder say let all those blacks rot in prison, and dismiss Jesse Jackson as a demagogue when he criticizes the criminal justice system for sentencing disparity in drug cases.[14]

Why do they ignore racial bias in sentencing, if justice is indeed color-blind? Ezola Foster even defended the white police officers[15] who savagely beat up Rodney King in spite of the the fact that such brutality was even videotaped and televised worldwide.[16]

137

Another black conservative, radio talk-show host Armstrong Williams, is also well-known for his views about blacks "getting away with murder," implying the judicial system does, indeed, favor blacks; a point underscored by Ezola Foster's blistering attack on Rodney King as a criminal who got what he deserved from "law-abiding" white police officers who almost killed him when they brutalized him.[17]

When white policemen are acquitted in spite of overwhelming evidence of brutality committed by them against blacks, and it happens time and again across the United States, how can the government, whites and other people expect blacks to have confidence in the criminal justice system?

When racial profiling goes on, with black motorists and even pedestrians being stopped by the police more than anybody else, blacks are told the policemen are just doing their job. Even when racist law enforcement officers such as Sheriff Harry Lee of Jefferson parish in Louisiana, although he is Chinese, imply by their words and deeds that "all" blacks are criminals, black people are still told that these officers are simply doing their job.

In the late eighties, Harry Lee got media attention when he gave orders that all blacks driving through his parish should be stopped because "they are up to no good."[18] That's any black driving through that parish. Similar incidents have been reported through the years in Texas, Maryland, and elsewhere. Yet, the police officers are simply doing their job because blacks "commit all that crime," as the saying goes.

It has sometimes taken riots, ignited by racial prejudice and injustice, to remind white America that blacks don't always get justice in the citadel of democracy. Because of this injustice, the attitude of a significant number of blacks, especially the youth, when they are mistreated, is "See you in the next riot." And this should not, in any way, be misconstrued as defiance of the law by blacks; it is failure of the law to protect them, and this is only one way of dramatizing their plight when everything else fails.

A few high-profile cases only serve to strengthen their conviction that for them justice is "served" only when they are locked up, beaten up, shot and killed even if they are innocent. When they win, law enforcement officers who arrested them feel that they have been defeated and humiliated, instead of saying

138

justice has won. The beating death of Johnny Gammage in Pittsburgh, Pennsylvania, the cousin of a well-known football player, Pittsburgh Steelers defensive lineman Ray Seals, was just one of the cases, besides Rodney King's, showing blacks that they don't get justice under the criminal justice system dominated by whites, many of them racist:

Three policemen were indicted...in the killing of a black motorist who was asphyxiated after they pulled him over in the Pittsburgh suburb of Baldwin on October 12. Allegheny County District Attorney Bob Colville brought charges of third-degree murder (*not* first- or second-degree) and involuntary manslaughter against Lieutenant Milton Mulholland and Patrolman John Vojtas of the Brentwood police, and one count of involuntary manslaughter against Michael Albert of the Bladwin police. All three are white....

The victim, 31-year-old Johnny Gammage,...was driving Seals' Jaguar at the time he was stopped by police. A total of five cops eventually joined in a struggle in which Gammage was beaten with flashlights and pinned to the ground, as several officers applied chokeholds. Two of the police officers were not charged, and one of them is to testify for as a prosecution witness....District Attorney Colville rejected the recommendation of a coroner's jury that the police be charged with criminal homicide.[18]

In spite of all the evidence against them, they were acquitted:

Thousands of people from throughout Allegheny County, both black and white, came to Pittsburgh on November 16 (1996) to protest the acquittal of police in the death of black motorist Johnny Gammage. Gammage was killed October 12, 1995, by five police officers after a routine traffic stop....Two other officers who took part in the beating of Gammage, Whitehall Sgt. Keith Henderson and patrolman Shawn Patterson, were never charged.

Gammage was killed after his car was pulled over in the early morning hours of October 12, 1995, along a deserted section of Route 51. The county coroner ruled Gammage died of asphyxiation due to compression of his neck and chest. At the time of his death, four officers were attacking Gammage, who was lying face down on the roadway.

Patrolman Patterson said earlier in the year that he had been instructed by Vojtas to place his foot on Gammage's neck. Prosecutors never called Patterson to testify in the trial.

The police maintain they were simply attempting to subdue Gammage, who they claim was violently resisting them. A tow truck driver who witnessed the murder contradicted the police version. He testified that police started beating Gammage, hitting him from behind with their night sticks, and continued to beat him while he lay face down on the pavement.

Paramedics who were called to the scene initially treated Vojtas for an injured thumb, only attending to Gammage after they realized he was no longer breathing.

The acquittal was almost a foregone conclusion. A coroner's jury recommended murder charges against all five police. The prosecution, however, filed lesser charges of involuntary manslaughter against three....No charges were filed against Henderson or Patterson. All-white juries for the cases were brought in from Chester and Lancaster counties, two of the wealthiest counties, located in the eastern part of the state.

The *Pittsburgh Post-Gazette* and local television stations in anticipation of rioting placed reporters in Brentwood. The November 15 issue of the newspaper contained the provocative front-page headline, 'Gammage Partly Responsible for His Own Death.' The article quoted a juror who justified the verdict on the grounds that Gammage got out of his car holding a cellular phone and address book, in violation of Vojtas' order that he get out of the car empty-handed.[19]

How many whites are beaten up or killed simply because they have cell phones or address books in their hands the way Gammage did?

Another black, a girl, who was known to have epileptic seizures, was shot dead in California by white police officers simply because she was using her cell phone in her parked car; they claimed they thought she had a gun. How many white girls, and boys, have been shot this way, or have been approached by the police suspecting them of being criminals simply because they are sitting in their cars or using their cell phones? Obviously, many have been approached. But are they treated the same way blacks are?

In Philadelphia, when white police officers on a routine check approached young white boys who were not supposed to be on the streets late at night because they were too young to be out that late, they told the boys, "Your dad will get you for this," or "We will report you to your dad."

But when they approached black boys, of the same age, they arrested them. Some black police officers complained about this, saying, "Black boys have fathers too!" So why didn't the white officers tell the black boys the same thing they told the white boys that "We'll tell your dad," or "Your dad will get you for this?," if justice is, indeed, color-blind in a color-conscious society?

In Detroit, the brutal murder of a black motorist Malice Green who was beaten to death by the police elicited more sympathy from whites for the white police officers who killed him than his murder did. "The two white cops, Walter Budzyn and Larry Nevers,...broke Green's skull with a rain of blows from their long-handled flashlights after stopping him on a traffic charge in southwest Detroit."[20]

Around the same time, Lee F. Berry, another black, was shot to death by the police in Detroit after a traffic violation.[21] The police officer followed Berry all the way to his house on West Outer Drive, a black middle-class neighborhood, just to kill him, and even used profanity before shooting him. Berry was unarmed. He was 26 years old and had graduated from Wayne State University with a bachelor's degree in journalism just the year before he was killed.

Yet another black, Errol Shaw, a mentally ill deaf-mute, was shot dead by a white police officer who claimed the victim threatened him and the other officers at the scene with a garden rake.[22] The other officers were black. They did not draw their guns; only the white officer did, and pulled the trigger. He was acquitted of all charges by a predominantly white jury.

Earlier, the same white officer had threatened a black motorist on the highway, threatening to blow his brains out and called him a "nigger." The case involving this white officer and his use of a racial slur, was featured on NBC national television in 2004 in a one-hour special program, *Inside Edition*, exclusively devoted to the shooting death of Errol Shaw. As in Shaw's case, the police officer who killed Berry was never punished either. In both cases, Berry's and Shaw's, the city of Detroit agreed to pay the victims' families millions of dollars for the "innocence" of their police officers who were simply "doing their job."

Yet another black, Dwight Turner, was shot dead by the police in Detroit on September 8, 2000. According to Larry Roberts, in his report, "Detroit Police Kill Again": "Turner was shot in the chest while standing on his front porch. Before police arrived he had fired his legally licensed handgun at a stray dog that was terrorizing the neighborhood. Turner had repeatedly called city authorities to capture the dog, but his calls went unanswered.."

And as usual, the police claimed they shot Turner in self-defense because he ignored their demands to drop the gun and instead pointed his gun at them. But neighbors and friends strongly disputed the police version. Their account was

141

corroborated by the Wayne County medical examiner who said the fatal bullet entered Turner's body in a downward angle, even though Turner was standing on the porch three feet above the officer who shot him. And that indicated that Turner was bending to put down the gun - just as his neighbors said - when the police officer shot him, killing him in cold blood.

The *Detroit News* described the Detroit police department, at least some of its officers, as "out of control." And investigative reports by the *Detroit Free Press* and the *Detroit News* showed that between 1993 and 1998, members of the city's police department killed 40 people. They were all shot. Yet, 35 officers involved in the killings were exonerated following internal investigations, protected by the blue wall of silence, and four were convicted of only misdemeanors. The investigative reports also revealed a pattern of police frame-ups: planting illegal drugs and other evidence on victims and shooting people in the back.

Even black children, 11-year-olds and others, have been shot and killed, or severely beaten by racist white police officers in Detroit and elsewhere across the country.

How many whites are treated this way? How many whites are killed this way? How many whites are beaten up the way blacks are, often, and so brutally that they sometimes suffer permanent damage including severe brain injury, are crippled and paralyzed, and even killed? The killing of blacks nationwide - it's open season - prompted Joe Davidson, a black journalist, to ask, "Have police declared war on blacks?" That was also the title of his article in the black news magazine *Emerge* in which he went on to say:

Police brutality is a national problem that seldom gets the attention of the Rodney King incident in Los Angeles. Black men are frequent victims, and...white cops are often the assailants....

The abuse [of power] is not limited to injuring the victim. When the public's protectors become villains, the fundamental premise that binds citizenry to its government, the legitimacy it conveys to its leadership, is undermined. When that bond deteriorates, cooperation between the community and the police lessens, weakening the fight against crime. Unpoliced police are just a few goose steps away from committing assault, battery and murder in the name of the law.

In more practical terms, the cost of police abuse is great. Hubert Williams, president of the Police Foundation, points to the urban rebellions that have generally resulted from incidents of police brutality. 'Excessive use of force is at the heart of most of the civil disorders that have afflicted this country,' he says. 'There is no single offense that creates the level of violence, the trauma, the economic drain as does this issue.'

In two particularly disturbing examples of black men being victimized by white cops, the black men were cops, too. Two white officers were fired in Nashville, Tennessee, for the December 14 beating of a black-on-duty undercover cop who worked in the same police station and on the same shift as those who did the beating. 'I feel I was treated like a piece of meat thrown out to a pack of dogs,' said officer Reggie Miller, who suffered a groin injury.

In a New York subway station, undercover transit officer Derwin Pannell was gunned down last November by fellow officers he recognized as he attempted to arrest a farebeater. Two white cops showered Pannell, an African American, with gunfire that left him seriously injured. *Newsday* reported that prosecutors struck a deal with the two shooters and two other officers on the scene, making prosecution unlikely. The prosecutors agreed not to use the officers' statements against them - just the opposite of the warning given given to suspects, that anything they say may be used against them.

Pannell said his gun was in its holster when his colleagues fired 21 shots - three hit - without warning. He had collared one suspect and was looking out for another he feared might return to help the one he was holding. His relief upon first seeing his colleagues turned to shock, as he observed them 'at point-blank range, in a combat stance, with their guns pointed directly at me. I covered my vitals, went into a fetal position, and was shot,' he said.

Police brutality often goes unpunished, even when a civil judgment - which provides an independent assessment of the facts - or settlement results in a significant payment to the victim or to the survivors. A nationwide study by Gannett News Service last year showed that cops accused of brutality get promoted more often than punished.[23]

And they are mostly white. Yet, black conservatives don't see racism in any of this but, instead, blame the black victims for not obeying the law even when they have done nothing wrong.

But even if they have broken the law, is this the way to treat them? Does the law say brutalize them, and even kill them? If the law if fair, why is it that white suspects and criminals don't get the same treatment blacks get from white police officers in the name of justice? And when some blacks riot, the authorities don't even think about addressing the fundamental cause of such civil unrest, as happened in Los Angeles in 1992, and in Benton Harbor, Michigan, in 2003, when a black motorcyclist was killed in an unjustified chase by white police officers, triggering a riot by blacks.

It is a tragedy that society, the white-dominated society, is sometimes forced to respond only when blacks riot, in a feigned effort to calm them down to avoid future eruptions, and not because it wants to treat them fairly.

There is no question that riots are wrong and should not be condoned in any way, even by the most oppressed members of society, blacks. But they are also only a manifestation of a deeper problem deeply rooted in American history and in the national psyche.

Even when racial injustice has been exposed in an ugly and violent way, the judicial system *still* finds it necessary to tip the scales of justice against blacks as occurred in California after the 1992 Los Angeles riots, some of the worst in American history:

> As a result of the Los Angeles riots of 1992, it took two trials before two of the four police officers videotaped beating Rodney King were sentenced to thirty months in prison. But a little later a white judge sentenced Damian Williams, an African-American, to the maximum prison term of ten years for the brutal beating of three men, one a white truck driver, during the riots. At sentencing John J. Ouderkirk told Williams that it was 'intolerable in this society to attack and maim people because of their race.'
>
> After the beating of Rodney King, which seemed 'intolerable' to many Americans, white and black, and the light sentencing of only half of the white men - policemen at that - who manhandled him, Judge Ouderkirk's ten-year sentence against a black civilian for a similar offense, as well as his ringing lecture, angered African-Americans.
>
> The Reverend Cecil Murray of the First AME Church of Los Angeles observed that 'contextually, this says to blacks that the pattern of history continues.' And Ray Evans, who heads a work furlough program for juvenile offenders, called Williams' sentence 'an excellent example of the kind of dual system we have...,one for blacks and one for whites.[24]

A racist society naturally is going to have a dual judicial system, in practice, even if not in the legal sense. In many cases, it is impossible for those who are racially oppressed to get justice under such a system because, by its very nature as an integral part of a racist society, its function is predicated on the maintenance of the privileged position of the dominant racial group: whites in the American context.

It also happened in apartheid South Africa. It happened in Nazi Germany and in the Soviet Union against the Jews. It happened in colonial Africa where the system was both racist and imperial to the detriment of the "natives." And it continues to happen today in Rwanda and Burundi, in Africa, where the Tutsi continue to dominate and oppress the Hutu majority whom they have held in virtual servitude since they conquered them 400 yeard ago.

And it always has had dire consequences wherever it has been practised. This includes the United States where blacks as an oppressed minority naturally *cannot* trust those who control the dual judicial system; a point underscored by Tom Wicker in his poignant study of the tragic failure of racial integration in America:

> This black perception of dual systems of justice may well have been a major factor in late 1995 in the acquittal of the football star and movie actor O.J. Simpson, in his celebrated trial on charges of murdering his former wife Nicole and her friend Ronald Goldman.
>
> Most whites, every indicator showed, believed Simpson had been proved guilty by the evidence. A jury with seven black members nevertheless found him not guilty. One reason appeared to have been that the jury believed some evidence provided by the Los Angeles Police Department had been faked or planted, particularly by Detective Mark Fuhrman, and should have been inadmissible. Testimony in the trial showed Fuhrman to hold virulent racist views, and blacks - particularly residents of Los Angeles - almost universally consider the LAPD racist and corrupt.
>
> Many blacks celebrated Simpson's acquittal perhaps because in some cases they saw it as a racial victory over an anti-black justice system. The contrast between this view and and the white expectation of a guilt verdict appears to have shocked the white community, at least temporarily, into realization of the nation's deep-seated racial division.[25]

This deep-seated racial division has divided the United States into what Professor Andrew Hacker calls, "Two Nations: Black and White, Separate, Hostile, Unequal,"[26] which is also the title of his book on the same subject. And that is exactly what the U.S. Riot Commission that investigated the riots of the sixties warned about almost 40 years ago.

The fact is that the United States, even back then in the sixties, was already divided along racial lines into two hostile camps, one black and one white, which could clash anytime. And they did. They still do, now and then. And it has been that way throughout the nation's history which began with the outright enslavement of millions of Africans taken in chains to "the land of the free."

The adjectives Professor Hacker uses can aptly be used to describe the judicial system as one that is white, separate, hostile, and unequal for blacks; an assessment validated by the black

American experience.

In his book, *Black Bourgeoisie*, published in 1957, the renowned black sociologist E. Franklin Frazier described black Americans as "a nation within a nation"[27] precisely because they had not been accepted by whites as equal citizens and lived in their own world, segregated by and from white society, confined to the periphery of the mainstream.

Today, almost 50 years later since he wrote the book and made that assessment, little has changed for the majority of blacks - in terms of status - in spite of all the civil rights laws passed in the sixties. Blacks remain "a nation within a nation," strangers in their own land at the mercy of the white majority who remain hostile to them. As Professor George Fredrickson states in his book *Black Liberation*:

> African-Americans remain at the mercy of a white majority that remains racist...denying the palpable fact that blacks as a group suffer from real disadvantages in American society and will continue to do so unless radical action is taken....Whites dominate the electorate, as well as the economy, and 'the politics of race' is a fact of life pushing government social policy in a conservative direction.[28]

Given the nature of conservative politics and its hostility to black interests as has been demonstrated throughout American history, that rules out any prospects for fundamental change to improve race relations. Andrew Hacker shares this assessment in his bleak portrayal of the black American predicament when he states: "Legal slavery may be in the past, but segregation and subordination have been allowed to persist....A huge racial chasm remains, and there are few signs that the coming century will see it closed."[29]

Although black conservatives may dismiss that as paranoia or hysterical hyperbole by liberals, not every one of them dismisses racism lightly and treats it as just another minor social problem, no more than a nuisance now and then. Most contend that racism is not the number one problem black people face; it is blacks themselves who are their own number one problem more than anybody else, a statement that comes pretty close to declaring racists as saints.

But there are those, rare among black conservatives, who see

146

racism as a major problem, even if not *the* major problem blacks face in the United States. And there are those, of course, who say racism will always exist - so what? You can still excel in life just like anybody else; there are plenty of opportunities for most blacks to do that, black conservatives maintain.

One of the black conservatives who didn't dismiss racism lightly was Bill Hardman from Grand Rapids, Michigan, a city in which I used to live; he was actually from Kentwood, a suburb of Grand Rapids having a status of its own as an administrative entity under its own jurisdiction and political leaders including representation in the Michigan state legislature.

Grand Rapids is located in southwestern Michigan, a Republican stronghold for decades just like the city itself, the second largest in Michigan after Detroit, and one of the 100 largest cities in the United States. All the state representatives from Grand Rapids, and the congressmen, were Republican, as they had been for years. Gerald Ford, who later became president of the United States and who grew up in Grand Rapids, was one such congressman when he represented the Grand Rapids area in Congress.

Bill Hardman was, at this writing, a state representative, representing Kentwood as a Republican in the Michigan state legislature which itself was dominated by Republicans. He was the only black Republican in the 148-member legislature. Like the city of Grand Rapids itself, Kentwood, his constituency, is overwhelmingly white.

Although he was a black Republican, hence a black conservative, he had the following to say about racial diversity to which most of the people in his party, black and white, are strongly opposed since they claim it amounts to reverse discrimination when you start giving opportunities to blacks simply because they are black, and not as individuals who should be given opportunity purely on the basis of merit. He also had something to say about racism in his article, "Diversity Has Much to Offer," in *The Grand Rapids Press*:

It had been a wonderful evening. My wife and I had just attended one of the gala events at the Grand Center [in Grand Rapids]. The speaker had been inspiring, the cause noble, and the atmosphere truly uplifting.
Because it was a formal 'black-tie' event, hundreds of women expressed

their individuality by donning beautiful gowns and dresses. My wife, Clova, looked exceptionally good. Like the other men attending the affair, I wore my tuxedo. Although I'm sure we all looked nice, we all seemed to look the same.

As hundreds of people exited the Grand Center, Clova and I stopped to talk with a few friends. A well-dressed couple approached us. The stylish, young, upper-middle-class-looking woman politely but firmly interrupted our conversation with 'Excuse me.' I turned around, and looked at her with a friendly smile and responded, 'Yes?'

'We need some water,' she stated.

'Oh, you thought I worked here. I am a guest as well,' I replied.

'Oh,' she blushed. 'How was I to know? I assumed you worked here. We've got to find a waiter,' she said as she rushed off.

A moment of awkwardness chased away the excitement we had just been feeling. My friend seemed to be more offended that I was perhaps because I'm used to people assuming. Out of hundreds of men in look-alike tuxedos, she had picked me out, the only black man, and assumed.

Assumptions like that have not been unusual for me. These unpleasant assumptions have taken many forms, ranging from being stopped by law enforcement officers for driving in the wrong area, to being followed by sales personnel in a department store. Yet these irritations pale in comparison to people still being denied jobs or promotions or other economic opportunities because of the color of their skin.

The assumption that I was an employee at the event instead of a guest is not an issue. Clova and I have gotten to know some of the wait staff, and we consider them friends. That the assumption was based upon my skin color, however, is the issue.

Racial prejudice and institutional racism have been problems in America from its inception. We've tried to eliminate institutional racism with laws and policies, and we've made real progress. Because of these achievements, there is a sentiment that says enough has been done. However, here in Michigan, we've seen firsthand how the discussion on race continues and has the potential to divide us.

Note the reaction to the United States Supreme Court decision on the two University of Michigan admissions lawsuits. A wide range of business and community leaders sided with the university. The decisions touched off a negative reaction elsewhere and, with it, the beginning of a ballot drive that could place the affirmative action question before the voters.

People of diverse races bring unique valuable experiences and qualities that help us live in a racially diverse society. I support a policy that allows us to work toward racial diversity in our universities, and our businesses and relationships as well. As long as our universities can base admissions on factors such as home residence, 'legacy' admissions because of a relative's earlier attendance, income level or athletic talent, they should be able to take the race of a prospective student into account. Surely, universities should have the ability to admit students to create an educational environment reflective of society as a whole.

Regardless of our beliefs about public issues like admissions policies or affirmative action, our most important discussion is within our personal lives and our own hearts. I ask each one of us to search his or her own heart. Even with good intentions, we can easily slip into hasty pre-judging of others.

This also was brought home to me recently. While out in public, I encountered a young man. His hair, plaid shirt and initial manner all communicated to me 'redneck.' It was easy for me to imagine his truck with a confederate flag on the back and a rifle on the seat. Instead, his warm greeting and conversation dispelled this negative stereotype, and I later reflected that he was the friendliest person I had met all day. I was embarrassed by my prejudice. I had pre-judged him by his own outward appearance.[30]

As a black man, he knew what all that meant. That is how blacks in general are pre-judged by society, dominated whites, and collectively branded as "criminals," prone to violence, and much more. And that is how the judicial system treats them, as much as police officers do as Bill Hardman like many other blacks can testify, having been stopped by the police himself for being black in the "wrong neighborhood" where only whites are welcome.

And just as he said universities should be inclusive to reflect the racial and ethnic composition of the American society, so should the judicial system which is still dominated by whites in disproportionately large numbers, leaving out blacks in many cases or assigning them peripheral roles.

Contrary to what black conservatives such as Professor Walter Williams say, racial bias in the judicial system is probably the most glaring example of racism perpetrated against blacks. And it has nothing to do with the high crime rate in the ghetto.

Most blacks even in the ghetto itself are not criminals. They are hard-working, law-abiding citizens. As Stokely Carmichael said, "We are the hardest working and least paid," cleaning up your floors, taking care of your children, and doing all the dirty work - the other jobs nobody else wants to take because it's too dirty, too demeaning, too hard, or pays too little. But that's not what you hear in court or among whites in general; it's about blacks "committing all that crime"; hence the high incarceration rate, the stiff punishment, and "three strikes you're out."

Racial bias in the dispensation of justice has been amply demonstrated. It is a pervasive phenomenon whose prevalence has been validated by both ideological camps, liberal and conservative, although more by the former than the latter. Yet, in spite of all the proof showing blacks face racial discrimination in the administration of justice, Walter Williams is bold enough to assert that the legal system not only works for blacks but tips scales in their favor even when there is damning evidence against them.

All that, he contends, justifies the lack of concern among most whites about the burning of black churches by white racists. There is a lack of proportional perspective on his part in all this, or he deliberately omits some facts from his assessment to justify his ideological position. For example, he ignores the fact that there was incontrovertible evidence against the white officers in the brutal beating of Rodney King. Yet, in the first trial, they were found "Not Guilty" under a system he says favors blacks. Instead, he cites cases of judicial "favoritism" for blacks and the enthusiastic response such unfairness toward whites evokes from blacks to prove that the system does, indeed, favor them. As he states:

> The most visible of these was the O.J. Simpson acquittal and the televised glee of many black people and black 'spokesmen.'
> There's the failure of the national media to report black hate crimes. Little mention was made of the hate crime against Michael Westerman of Guthrie, Kentucky, murdered by a carload of blacks who were offended by his flying a Confederate flag on his pickup truck; or Mark Belmore, a white student at Northeastern University stabbed to death by four black men who made a pact to kill the first white person they saw; or Melissa McLaughlin, murdered by six black men in Charleston, South Carolina, several of whom told the police they made a sort of New Year's resolution to kidnap a white woman, rape her and then kill her.[31]

In the Simpson case, Williams ignores the fact that the racism of the Los Angeles Police Department, especially of Detective Mark Fuhrman, made it impossible for the black jurors to believe the evidence brought against a black defendant, however compelling it may have been; although it may not have been in Simpson's case. For example, the wool cap and the gloves the police claimed he wore when he allegedly committed the crime, didn't fit Simpson, prompting his lead defense attorney, Johnny Cochran, a renowned black lawyer, to make an oft-quoted statement in his closing argument, "If the glove doesn't fit, you must acquit."

Would you trust a Klansman, a Skinhead, or a Nazi testifying against a black? Fuhrman's hostility toward Simpson was a foregone conclusion, making it impossible for such a racist not to present evidence biased against a black defendant. To make things worse, Simpson was once married to a white woman, the murder victim, which made made Furham "sick," as all racists - including the notoriously racist country music singer and writer David Allan Coe - feel about black men married to or going with white women.

In other words, even if Simpson was guilty, it was the racist judicial system, of which the police are an integral part, and not the black jurors, that was responsible for his acquittal. Yet the black jurors are blamed for being on guard against racism in the courtroom and in the police department.

Regarding racially motivated attacks on whites by blacks, since the national media fails to report hate crimes by blacks against whites as Williams contends, how did he and the rest of the country hear about all those brutal murders if the media didn't report them? Was it not because local papers, television and radio carried those stories and transmitted them nationwide through a network of local affiliates?

All that should be reported, as it indeed was, otherwise we would not have known about it; and should be condemned no less than cases involving the murder of blacks by whites. And the murders of these whites were condemned by blacks as well, something Professor Williams should know if he did his homework on this.

Professor Williams also speaks strongly against black hate crimes. What about hate crimes committed by whites against blacks? Why doesn't he talk about that just as much? He doesn't even mention it; he should, if he is really interested in fairness. Instead, he ignores the fact that there are racially motivated murders of blacks which have gone unreported for years. As Gordon Parks, a black and formerly a photojournalist for *Life*, discovered when he covered the civil rights movement: "Too many of us are still unaccounted for in the terror-ridden swamplands of the South."[32]

Much as Williams talks about hate crimes committed by blacks against whites, citing Department of Justice statistics and media reports to build his case, one can't help but wonder how he could have missed statistics from the same source about crimes of hate committed by white people against blacks.

The statistics show that whites commit more hate crimes, numerically and proportionately, than blacks do. Professor Williams did his study, published in August 1996, after all those statistics had been published. Yet, he does not, even once in any context, cite them to provide a balanced picture - even if he had to try to refute their validity with some other evidence.

The Department of Justice statistics show that whites commit twice as many crimes of hate as those commited by blacks, an unpalatable fact deliberately ignored by black conservatives such as Walter Williams, Larry Elder, Armstrong Williams, Joseph Brown, Ezola Foster and others. Professor Williams deliberately ignored the Department of Justice's "Uniform Crime Reports," for hate crimes committed in 1994, which, in part, reads:

Bias-motivated crime is a phenomenon that touches all segments of society....Preliminary figures show 5,852 hate crime incidents were reported to the FBI during 1994.

The incidents were reported by more than 7,200 law enforcement agencies in 43 states and the District of Columbia (D.C.). Participating agencies covered 58 percent of the U.S. population. Sixty percent of the incidents were motivated by racial bias....

The 5,852 incidents involved 7,144 separate offenses, 7,187 victims, and 6,189 known offenders. Crimes against persons accounted for 72 percent of hate crime offenses reported....Thirteen persons were murdered in hate-motivated incidents. As in previous years, hate crimes in 1994 were most frequently directed at individuals. Individuals comprised 84 percent of all reported bias crime victims for the year....

Law enforcement agencies reported the number of known offenders for 61 percent of hate crimes coming to their attention in 1994. Among the 6,189 known offenders reported to be associated with hate crime incidents, 57 percent were white, and 30 percent were black.[33]

That is almost twice the number of black offenders. And as everyone knows, those were not the only hate crimes committed. Most of them go unreported, and the perpetrators, black and white, walk free.

But the disparity in the commission of those crimes, twice as many by whites, cannot be ignored. It is critical to debunking the myth that blacks commit "all crimes" including hate crimes. And it is a myth deeply embedded in the national psyche and sours race relations probably more than Professor Williams and other black conservatives realize - especially when Williams says that hate crimes by blacks against whites go unreported.

He leaves the unmistakable impression among most whites, which they have always had but which he helps to fortify, that black people - because of their "bestial" nature - commit more hate crimes than whites do. And he has done nothing to correct that impression.

For every murder cited by Williams that was committed by a black, there is an unprovoked murder of a black like the ones he mentioned. It is not just whites who are victims of unprovoked murders; more blacks have been victims and continue to be victims of such attacks, since they are the primary target in a society dominated by whites, the majority of whom are racist, with a significant number among them being virulently hostile toward blacks whom they consider to be inferior to whites; a sub-species of mankind at best.

True and sadly enough, Michael Westerman was murdered by blacks, shot from a passing car as he drove his pickup truck, with his wife in it, that had a Confederate flag on the eve (January 14, 1995) of Martin Luther King Day, as it obviously did on other days. The blacks in the car saw that as an insult, and thought the driver was a racist because of the flag on his truck, although they had no right - none whatsoever - to kill him even if he was indeed a racist.

I read about the case in the media - including *The Nashville Banner*, a paper also read in Westerman's hometown of Guthrie, Kentucky - which Williams says don't cover hate crimes committed by blacks. It was also reported on local television, then carried by other media in different parts of the country, of which Williams was unaware or simply chose to ignore this fact.

The Associated Press (AP), the oldest and largest news agency in the world, also carried the story, saying Westerman "was a friend" of his attackers and that his death was apparently a mistake because his truck had tinted windows through which the gunman fired at an unidentified target, believing it to be a group of white racists. The headline in *The Nashville Banner*, January 20, 1995, said: "Youths Thought Targets Were Racists."[34] It is a tragedy that could have been avoided.

There is also a "subtle" distinction - which in no way justifies murder - between the victim in this case and those targeted by white racists in general.

The blacks who killed him thought he was a white racist or the truck had white racists in it. Would they have attacked him, or "them," if they thought they were not racist? If their intention was simply to attack or kill a white person, they could have attacked any white in their hometown or anywhere else, and on any day and not just on Martin Luther King Day, whether he had a Confederate or not.

By contrast, whites racists don't target just black militants, the New Black Panthers or the Luis Farrakhans and other blacks who are ready to engage them in combat if they have to, in self-defense; they attack *any* blacks, whether they are militant or not, racist or not.

Still nothing, including contemporary let alone historial racial oppression, justifies what those young blacks did to Michael Westerman. But white racism did play a part, twisting their minds, and prompting them to engage in "retaliatory" violence against perceived white racists. As if to confirm their fears, cross burnings by white racists immediately followed after Westerman was killed, to create an atmosphere of terror against blacks in general.

But in nearly identical fashion, even more gruesome, Christopher Wilson, a 31-year-old black man, was abducted, robbed and set on fire - turned into a fleeing human torch - in 1993 by two white men in Florida who shouted racial slurs peppered with scatological language. As flames were consuming him, and had him screaming for help, his white abductors cheered, amused by the spectacle and thrilled by his agony.35

During the same year - and around the same time Professor Walter Williams cited cases of hate crime by blacks against whites - Morris Dees of the Southern Poverty law Center reported terrifying hate crimes committed against blacks by whites. One involved two white men who put a noose around a black man's neck, burned a cross and threatened to lynch him. A second one involved several skinheads who tortured and almost beat a black man to death. A third case involved a skinhead who beat a black

154

man to death in St. Louis, Missouri.[36] Many other incidents were just as terrifying. And many more went unreported, as happens all the time, including those involving whites as the victims.

It is true, as Williams says, four black men stabbed a white student, Mark Belmore, to death in Massachusetts. But so was a black, stabbed to death, by white racists elsewhere.

In June 1995, Timothy Welch and Gary Cox beat and stabbed a retarded black man in South Carolina, the same month when the two white men burned down two black churches in the same state. During their trial for torching the black churches, they admitted to having been members of the Ku Klux Klan, and one of them had a Klan membership card in his pocket when he was arrested.[37]

And in 1991, the Southern Poverty Law Center represented an Ethiopian student who was clubbed to death by skinheads for no other reason than that he was black.[38]

In 1998, James Byrd, Jr., a black man, was dragged to death behind a pickup truck by three white men in Jaspers, Texas; a case that made international headlines because of the gruesome nature of the crime.

Not coincidentally, it was around the same time that a black man was also dragged to death by a white man in South Africa in a country that had just emerged from apartheid. Yet apartheid is still very much alive in many ways in South Africa as much as vicious racism is in the United States.

Ironically, in the United States, the laws that were passed to protect blacks and other victims of hate crime are the very same ones that are being used to persecute them under a judicial system Walter Williams and other black conservatives claim favors black people. Although blacks commit fewer hate crimes than whites, they are arrested more than whites. As Jon Dougherty stated in *WorldNet Daily*:

Although 'hate-crime' legislation has been championed by minority groups in hopes it would discourage racially motivated crime, a recently released FBI crime report reveals that a higher percentage of blacks than whites are charged with race-biased 'hate crimes.'

The FBI's 'Hate Crime Statistics' for 1999 show that 2,030 whites were arrested that year for 'hate crimes' against blacks, compared to 524 blacks who were arrested and charged with a 'hate crime' against whites.

According to the U.S. Census Bureau, blacks make up 12.8 percent of the population - or about 34.5 million of the country's 280 million people - so, given the arrest rate versus population percentage, the data indicates that blacks are one-and-a-half times more likely to be arrested for a 'hate crime' than whites.

The Census Bureau's November 2000 statistics listed the nation's white population at 226.8 million, or 82.2 percent of the total....

'Unfortunately, hate crime laws have boomeranged on blacks,' Steve Dasbach, the national director of the Libertarian Party, said in a recent statement. 'African-Americans thought that hate crime legislation would protect them, but instead they're being used as another legal weapon to prosecute them.'

Dasbach also said the FBI study indicated that another 87 blacks were arrested for hate crimes against other blacks. 'Hate crimes aren't just for KKK members anymore. They're now being applied even to same-race crimes...apparently giving racist police, prosecutors or judges another weapon to use against African-Americans,' Dasbach said....

'Hate crimes' legislation is written in such a way that authorities often have too much arbitrary power to decide whether a crime had a racial undertone.

Many believe that 'hate crime' laws, now in 45 states, have hit poor and minority communities the worst. 'It is demonstrable that these laws hit the poor and minorities hardest. It wasn't meant that way, but that's the way it is,' said Christopher Plourd, a criminal defense lawyer who has represented a number of clients charged with 'hate crimes.'

'In the same way that [police] don't go on white college campuses trying to enforce drug laws, but come to the 'hood, they'll use these new hate crime laws against the NAACP's own constituents,' Van Jones, director of the Ella Baker Center for Human Rights, told columnist Arianna Huffington in an interview....

The FBI said there were a total of 7,876 'bias motivation' incidents in 1999. Anti-white incidents accounted for 781 of those, while anti-black incidents numbered 2,958. Anti-Hispanic incidents accounted for 466 of 829 ethnicity/national origin-related incidents.[39]

If even hate-crime laws that were intended to protect blacks cannot protect them but are, instead, used against them by racist police officers, prosecutors and judges, what better proof do you need to show that the criminal justice system is biased against them?

And with all this proof, what makes black conservatives really believe that the judicial system coddles blacks or is lenient towards them as opposed to whites - who control it - and others?

No one in his right mind would say black people don't commit hate crimes or have never commited hate crimes. People are people regardless of race.

Hate crime knows no race or color, gender or ethnicity, class or national origin. People of all races are capable of committing hate crimes and the some of the most despicable acts. They have done so, and they continue to do so.

Six black men in Charleston, South Carolina, as Professor Williams states, murdered Melissa McLaughlin, a white woman. But so was a black woman murdered by whites in another state around the same time. In 1994, three white men belonging to a hate group known as the White Brotherhood, killed a black woman in South Bend, Indiana, simply because she was black; no other reason than that.[40]

Numerous white supremacist organizations - no fewer than 500 by the late 1990s according to the Southern Poverty Law Center - and their lock-step-thinking members pollute the entire nation. And proof of their evil, expanding, encompassing existence is clear.

Also, at least one out of every six white Americans believe blacks are genetically inferior to whites. And at least half of all whites don't want racial integration, and just as many say they should have the legal right to discriminate against blacks since it is a matter of personal preference whom they want to deal with; be it in housing, employment, and many other areas of life, not just social. And there are statistics to prove that, documented by national surveys.[41]

All these are indisputable elements of the doctrine of white supremacy. Millions of white supremacists, not just a few thousands, exist in America today, capitalizing on irrational fear of blacks as some kind of monsters or simply inferior beings who absolutely have no right to be around whites let alone mingle with them. Some of this "niggerphobia" has even infected the judicial system, police departments and other law enforcement agencies, the same agencies Professor Williams and other black conservatives say favor blacks or are simply too easy on black criminals, obviously out of guilt for three hundred years of oppression of black people by whites in the United States since they brought them to the promised land in bondage from Africa.

Why would racists be everywhere else except in the judicial system? In fact, the system itself has even condemned itself because of its racial bias against blacks as evidence clearly shows.

And many of white supremacists belong to various organizations that publish racist literature to spread their message and pollute other minds, especially of young white boys and girls, across the nation. They also use the Internet, virtually penetrating every household across the nation, 24 hours a day, seven days a week, with many whites digesting the message, accepting it or rejecting it, in the privacy of their homes without any need for them - for those who are accept the message - to attend any meetings held by racist merchants to be recruited.

They can simply use the computer to join any hate group they want to join. They even invoke Scriptures to spread their message of hate, as clearly demonstrated by the Ku Klux Klan, the Christian Identity movement, the Aryan Nation and others, and by hate-filled publications such as the *Fiery Cross*. Some of them even have their cars and pickups sporting threatening stickers, "Nigger Hunting License,"[42] "Coon Hunter" and much more.

What is behind all this? Black racism and courts favoring blacks? There was racism against black people even before some of them started killing whites. America was founded and thrived on racism, and not on the twin ideals of liberty and equality as it is claimed. Otherwise Africans who were taken to America would not have been bound in chains, and they would have been free from the moment they landed on American soil. Its founders deliberately chose to buy and enslave blacks - not Europeans, and not even Arabs in North Africa - in the quest for a free supply of labor, fuelled by unparalleled greed for riches, infused with a dose of racism.

This is not to justify the killing of whites by blacks. But whites have played a major role in promoting racism and turning other people against them. It is a historical fact that whites chose to enslave blacks for economic reasons and religiously-inspired racism rooted in the belief that white people have the mandate to rule members of the "lesser breed," blacks and people of other "inferior" races. That is what Rudyard Kipling called "the white man's burden."

It is an erroneous belief and the worst form of superstition that has caused incalculable damage and poisoned race relations for centuries. And it continues to do so, not only in the United States but in Africa as well, the black man's homeland, and everywhere else where the white man has conquered and subjugated other people in fulfillment of his "divine mandate" to rule the world.

From racist theology to racial terrorism, whites started torturing and killing blacks purely for sport, and institutionalized the custom of lynching in the United States, while at the same time quoting the Bible as true Christians to justify their evil deeds.

From toddlers on up, including ministers of the Gospel, whites travelled for miles to attend lynching parties complete with refreshments and other forms of entertainment including singing and dancing, while at the same time cheering when a black man was strung up a tree or even roasted alive; prompting Elijah Muhammad, leader of the Black Nation of Islam, to say that he had seen enough evil of the white man to last him 26,000 years.

When he was growing up in Sandersville, Georgia, he saw a black man being lynched, an incident that left an indelible mark on his mind, as did another incident on Malcolm X when he was growing up in Lansing, Michigan.

Malcolm X's father, a Baptist preacher like Elijah Muhammad's father who also had been a slave, was killed by the Ku Klux Klan who dumped his body on the railway tracks to be run over by a train. His father also had a store in Lansing. But it was burned down by racists. When the firemen came, they just stood there and did nothing to put out the fire. Years later, Malcolm X recalled with bitterness saying they did not put "one drop of water" on the house, and added, "The same fire that burnt my father's house still burns my soul." That is the kind of treatment blacks have had at the hands of white racists. Yet you still have some people wondering why they are angry when they continue to be mistreated even when they go to court to seek justice.

This is in a country that is known worldwide as the citadel of democracy whose founding fathers proclaimed, "We hold these truths to be self-evident that all men are created equal," while owning slaves.

During their time and even after the end of slavery, the life of a black person meant absolutely nothing. He was no more than a beast of burden to be flogged, mutilated, and killed at will by his master or by any other white person.

Even newspapers carried lead stories, and advertisements, to let white people know when and where the next lynching party would take place, so that they should be ready to attend the "festival" reminiscent of the carnival atmosphere at the coloseum in imperial Rome. They rode horses, took trains, even walked, and later drove cars to witness lynchings and enjoy themselves, thrilled by the spectacle of a black man begging for his life, or watching him flogged and mutilated to death.

Bodies of black men, even of black women many times, decorated trees like Christmas ornaments throughout the south. They hanged from ropes like baubles before their gruesome deaths. Many were suffocated, a slow painful death. Only a few found comfort in their neck breaking quickly, thus ending their pain if they died immediately, as children and grownups thrust knives and other sharp objects into the body, celebrating. They even cut off body parts and took them home as souvenirs. It is this kind of organized terror that helped fuel the growth of racist groups across the country.

White hate groups have existed since slavery. Did blacks start those groups? Did "favoritism" of blacks by the system motivate whites to form these groups? Were slaves favored? Were blacks after the end of slavery favored? Why did Reconstruction end if black people were adored and coddled by whites?

Why do white racist groups exist today, and why are new ones added? There are more than 500 today. Why?

Most people probably know about the Ku Klux Klan (KKK) more than any other hate group because of its long history of savagery and notoriety through the years. During the first two decades in the 20th century, millions of whites including U.S. senators, congressmen and governors, belonged to the Klan. Even more were sympathetic to its goals, waffling only on becoming members.

But the KKK was not the only organization that was founded after the civil war to terrorize and murder blacks at will. First organized during Reconstruction, the Klan was - and still is - virulently anti-black and vowed to maintain white supremacy. Other white supremacist groups, besides the Klan, included Men of Justice, the Pale Faces, the Constitutional Union Guards, the White Brotherhood, the Order of the White Rose, and the Knights of the White Camellia.

At one time, the Knights of the White Camellia, founded in Louisiana in 1867, were reputed to have had even more members than the Ku Klux Klan. But the Klan has been the dominant group - absorbing others - throughout American history since the end of the civil war. For example, today there is a group called White Camelia of the Ku Klux Klan, obviously a lineal descendant of the Knights of the White Camellia, and even maintains a web site to propagate its racist views and ideology. It is a Texas Klan group led by Charles Lee. Other hate groups also have web sites to spread their message and recruit members, targeting the youth.

In the 1990s, a resurgence of the Klan was clearly evident in the support of David Duke of Louisiana, a prominent white supremacist leader with followers and supporters in many parts of the country. He was able to mobilize Klan followers across the nation into a potent political force which, together with white racism in general, played a critical role in his campaign for governor of Louisiana in 1994.

He almost won the election, coming in a strong second. He also ran for president in 1992 but his campaign for the White House fizzled, galvanizing his supporters and sympathizers to come out in full swing for the gubernatorial campaign in Louisiana two years later.

For such an openly racist person to come close to winning the governorship of a state, that just shows you how many racists there are, ready to swing into action to push their white supremacist agenda. Many are out in the open and don't even try to hide their feelings about blacks, as millions of them clearly showed in Louisiana when they openly supported and voted for David Duke to be their governor.

There are those who would claim that the Ku Klux Klan, the racism of David Duke and his followers, and the increase in the number of hate groups among whites has to do with blacks attacking whites and with the judicial system favoring blacks, letting them go free when they attack and kill whites or giving them light sentence that's no more than a slap on the wrist. They are dead wrong or simply not telling the truth.

The Ku Klux Klan, the radical religious right and their ministers such as Jerry Falwell who called Bishop Desmond Tutu "a phony" in the early 1980s when Tutu was campaigning against apartheid - Falwell said this on ABC national television's program *Nightline* in an interview with Ted Koppel; as well as other rightwingers including another minister, Pat Robertson, and a number of his colleagues in different churches who are also busy preaching the Gospel while harboring and fostering white supremacist sentiments, and hate groups such as the Aryan Nation and the Christian Identity movement; they are all the very heart of raw-naked bigotry and unconscionable hate that has its own momentum fueled from within. Blacks have nothing to do with it, except as victims.

Such hate, and racism, has always existed even when blacks had no rights, none whatsoever "in the land of the free and the home of the brave." Nor does white supremacy or any other form of racism have anything to do with the media coddling black criminals. Yet, that is the kind of ammunition black conservatives use to justify white indifference toward black plight, including attacks by white racists on blacks. As Professor Walter Williams states:

The same week Melissa McLaughlin was raped and murdered, a few hundred miles away in Tallahassee, Florida, a black man was set on fire by two white youths. That incident made the national media, and President Clinton mentioned it in his address as an example of continuing racism in America.

Neither Clinton nor the national press mentioned the racially motivated murder of Melissa McLaughlin. Maybe they accepted the counsel of South Carolina's State Senator Robert Ford who said he doubted Melissa's murder was an act of racial hate....Americans are stacking piles of combustible societal kindling, in the form of quotas, false reporting [covering up for black criminals] and implicit sanctioning of interracial crimes [by blacks against whites], waiting to be set ablaze by racial arsonists.[43]

Much as Williams condemns interracial crimes, he dismisses lightly the racially motivated burning of a few - out of 73 - black churches as "seemingly motivated." He made his outlandish estimate, of only a few black churches burnt by racists, because two suspects charged were black; ignoring observations by federal authorities that most of the arson incidents, even if not all, were indeed racially motivated. In fact, it turned out later that not all of them were racially inspired, but most were.

At the time Professor Williams passed his characteristic judgment, he did not even make a marginal attempt to present a balanced picture by making an objective statement that racism could not be entirely ruled out in some of those infernos and may

162

indeed have played a major part. Why didn't he say that when the investigation was still going on, an inquiry that later confirmed that some of the fires had not only been deliberately set but were, in fact, set by white racists?

Instead, he makes the cavalier statement that the arson attacks were "seemingly racially motivated," conveying the unmistakable impression that he denies the plausibility of the claim by blacks and others - including many whites, especially liberals - that at least some of the black churches, if not a significant number of them, were indeed burned down by white racists.

The tragedy that is the inevitable result of this line of reasoning pursued by Walter Williams is that it justifies arson and other hate crimes perpetrated by white racists against blacks. It condones them, even if not deliberately, and it glosses over some of the most despicable acts committed by white supremacists who claim to have a mandate derived from heaven to dominate, oppress, and even kill blacks because they are simply not fit to live.

I seriously doubt that is his intention, not only because he is black but because he is just a human being with a conscience. Much as many of us may disagree with him and with other black conservatives on a number of fundamental issues, he and his ideological compatriots are not the incarnation of evil anymore than their opponents are a paragon of virtue. But it is sad that he took a position on the arson cases that exonerated white supremacists and their sympathizers, and could be misconstrued as sanctioning hate crimes against blacks.

He did not wait for the results of the investigation before saying, or at least implying, that most of the fires were *not* set by white racists. And no matter how one looks at it, such reasoning amounts to sanctioning racial crimes by whites against blacks, however inadvertently.

Williams contends that lack of concern among whites about the burning of black churches is a justified reaction to all the crimes committed by blacks against whites, and to the coddling of black criminals by the courts and the media. Facts do not support his position, given the amount of evidence that has been compiled through the years on racism against blacks in the courts and in the media.

And what about crimes committed by whites against blacks? What about police brutality against blacks, and media bias against blacks portraying virtually all blacks as criminals? Even one of the leading black conservatives, Gwen Daye Richardson, concedes that much, although such an admission is rare among black conservatives. As she states:

> Media too often makes generalizations about black Americans, which tend toward stereotypes. They too comfortably and quickly reduce blacks to the lowest common denominator - neighborhoods full of crime, drugs, illegitimacy and death....
>
> Yes, black males are disproportionately victims of gunshot wounds, and, yes, too many young black males are involved in the criminal justice system. But the vast majority, 75 percent by recent estimates, are law-abiding citizens. Blacks comprise the only ethnic group which is defined by its worst elements.[44]

Yet, that is the same media that Walter Williams claims covers up crimes committed by blacks against whites; the same media that - known for sensational journalism - through the years has done a very good job portraying blacks as criminals more than anybody else, reinforcing racial stereotypes whites already have about black people - who snatch all the purses, steal all the cars, rob all the banks and party stores, and routinely empty cash registers at gas stations on their way home from work, or wherever, before they hit the highway, and so on.

Still, he's quick to notice the media's "bias" against white people whom it simply ignores when they are attacked and victimized by blacks. Why he fails to notice the media's bias against blacks, eludes me, and I'm sure many other people and not just blacks. He does not even say the media is biased, period, against both whites and blacks. He is firm on saying it is biased against whites.

One can go on and on, *ad infinitum*, documenting cases of media bias against blacks, as Ishmael Reed and others have done. As Reed stated in his article, "Stats, Lies and Videotape," in the black news magazine *Emerge*:

> When I read an article announcing that the NBC television network was going to produce a special week dealing with violence in America, I prepared myself for a frenzy of African-Americans being scapegoated for America's

social problems.

NBC is gaining a reputation for enriching its stockholders by producing violence, especially involving Blacks and sometimes Latinos, as its No. 1 product. In March 1993, the network had to apologize for staging an explosion scene in a report critical of GM trucks.

Unlike the African-Americans, and Latinos, whom the networks constantly malign, GM had the means to fight back. Michael Gartner, then president of NBC News, was forced to resign.

Last December, NBC had to defend itself against charges made by Senator Kent Conad (Democrat - North Dakota), who accused the network of 'seeking to raise ratings by showing a television movie with a gratuitously violent scene of execution.'

I watched the first two installments of NBC's *America, the Violent*. Predictably, the people shown perpetrating violence were African-Americans, or code phrases were used to implicate them. The lessons of the Republicans' infamous Willie Horton campaign weren't lost on the black pathology merchandisers at NBC, and so on Monday, January 24, a white woman was featured. She was shot while driving through a 'high-crime' area. The next night, the case of a black teenager who had been convicted of murdering white women was featured.

From the efforts of NBC and network news in general, you wouldn't know that 70 percent of the people arrested in this country are whites, while they constitute less than 50 percent of those who are incarcerated.

You also wouldn't know that the majority of violent crimes against whites are committed by other whites, just as the majority of violent crimes against blacks are committed by other blacks. The same holds true for yellows and browns, but the featuring of the rare assault on whites by blacks, especially white women, is obviously done to attract the perverted to an inflammatory product....

As someone who has monitored networks for three years as chairperson of P.E.N. (Poets, Essayists and Novelists) Oakland media committee,...my monitoring, for example, reveals that NBC network news depicts violence as an inner-city problem in an America that's otherwise placid and wonderful....

On December 10, Tom Brokaw told an ABC *Nightline* audience that he and his crew were hanging about inner-city Los Angeles because - are you ready for this? - he was concerned about black people who adhere to traditional values being hemmed in by drive-by shootings. Brokaw wants us to believe that he and his crew had noble aims, instead of behaving like predators, lusting after some ratings-boosting mayhem to break out.

Appearing before the Radio and Television News Directors Association, Dan Rather accused commercial television of 'putting good ratings ahead of responsible journalism. They've got us putting more and more fuzz and wuzz on the air, cop-shop stuff, so as to compete not with other news programs but with entertainment programs, including those posing as news programs, for dead bodies, mayhem and lurid tales.'

Rather's accusation is similar to the town madame taking to the pulpit to preach against prostitution. Not only does CBS network news offer a steady

165

video of blood to its viewers, but it, like its counterparts, seems to subscribe to a theory, held by David Duke and New York's Upper West Side intelligentsia, that all of America's social problems are traceable to the actions of an 'underclass.'

Underclass apparently means black because when columnist Sam Roberts of *The New York Times* wrote about 'the propensity among African-Americans for violence,' he didn't distinguish between the black underclass, overclass, middle class, people with a lot of class and those with no class. He meant *all* blacks.

Dan Rather anchored the notorious *48 Hours on Crack Street*, which nailed blacks as being responsible for the crack epidemic, even though, according to a newspaper survey, the typical crack addict is a white male. Last September 16, Rather anchored a report about the failure of the drug interdiction program, during which all of the consumers of drugs pictured were black when, according to statistics, nearly 80 percent of the consumers are white.

Also, Rather was unduly harsh in his tacit criticisms of tabloid television shows, because shows such as *A Current Affair, Inside Edition, Unsolved Mysteries, Hard Copy* and the various afternoon talk shows such as *The Oprah Winfrey Show*, provide a more balanced picture of the United States' social problems than television news.

When CNN initially covered the Spur Posse case, named for a white California suburban gang that awarded notches for each times a member had sex with a girl, the identities of the white middle-class youngsters, at first, were protected by the camera. Inexplicably, the footage was spliced with pictures of black youngsters' comments about rape. They had nothing to do with the story, and there was no attempt to conceal their identities. By contrast, *Hard Copy* provided an in-depth look at this suburban crime, s well as a follow-up about the outcome of the case.

When it comes to merchandising black pathology, PBS is always willing to show that it can get down like the rest of them.

During the network's own black pathology week, Charlayne Hunter-Gault interviewed Latonya Hunter, a young writer whose diary was reproduced by a New York publisher. It's full of some of the grim pictures of inner-city life that we get elsewhere. This talented young woman, who now lives in the suburbs, which one would think, from network news, are oases of civility, recited the usual stories about drive-by shootings and violence that occurred in her Bronx neighborhood.

The appearance of such an articulate young person on television is rare. More and more the reporters from the Jim Crow communications industry, which only includes about 8 percent of minority reporters and editorial writers. are engaging in video/audio child molestation.

Young members of gangs are guided by reporters through a recitation of their ugly crimes for the titillation of upscale audiences such as those devoted to National Public Radio (NPR).

NPR's Phyllis Crockett, an African-American, accused white NPR reporters of using teenagers to reinforce their 'preconceived' notions about black life after an especially nasty piece by David Isay called 'Ghetto Life 101.' He provided some black children with tape recorders, whereupon they wandered through neighborhoods and engaged in antisocial activities.

These children were clever enough to know what was expected of them. Isay pleaded innocent to protestations of some black NPR staffers, and Howard Kurtz, writing for *The Washington Post*, favored the position of some NPR's white staffers who accused their black colleagues of engaging in political correctness.

Also during black pathology week, Spencer Michels of PBS's KQED in San Francisco coached a black teenager to recite some of his crimes - stealing cars and selling drugs - for the amusement of the same white suburban audience that gets its kick from gangster rap.

Television networks attempt to conceal their lurid intentions by ending such stories with the teenage informant entering a rehabilitation program. Though both a black and a white male run the Omega Boy's Club, the San Francisco club of which the black teen is a member, the MacNeil/Lehrer producers showed the white male admonishing the youth.

Giving whites the credit for rehabilitating blacks is a typical network practice. Though there are thousands upon thousands of blacks working with black youth throughout the country, whites are usually shown on television guiding black youth, or posing as experts in these stories.

During my monitoring of black pathology week, I also watched CNN's series on violence. In one segment, called 'Kids and Guns,' all of the pictures shown were black children, even though guns are just as available to suburban and rural children as they are to those in inner-city neighborhoods.

It was CNN that offered the lowest moment in black pathology week. On the same Friday morning during which Charles Jaco promoted the usual propaganda against black people, CNN showed a line of blacks seeking earthquake relief in Los Angeles. The audio covering this picture was about how some people were engaged in the illegal trafficking of food stamps, essentially indicting every black person in the line with a crime without any substantiation whatsoever. This is another vile practice of the networks: using pictures of anonymous blacks to go with crime commentaries [thereby implicating *all* blacks in crime].

I can't imagine the kind of psychological agony black reporters and news anchors must feel when the networks they work for push such vicious stereotypes. During black pathology week, CNN's Bernard Shaw seemed to wince as a segment on violence, featuring black suspects, was shown. A smart columnist such as Clarence Page of the *Chicago Tribune*, must feel hamstrung when he is called upon by the producers of NPR's *Weekend Edition* to condemn so-called black anti-Semitism.

Its comments were broadcast Sunday, January 30, toward the end of the network's offensive, all because one black man made a wild speech at a New Jersey college. Page was not prompted to criticize the anti-black attitudes of some Jewish Americans, including those at NPR who had a hand in producing "Ghetto Life 101." Clarence Page also told the anchorwoman, Liane Hansen, that up to now, black-on-black violence has been a taboo subject in the black community. I don't know where he's been. I wrote about black-on-black

167

violence in my book, *Shrovetide In Old New Orleans*, published in 1978, and *Ebony* magazine did a feature on the subject nearly a decade ago.

One of the few commentators who consistently knocks down the racist myths perpetrated by his white colleagues is Carl Rowan (he died in September 2000), who came up with that memorable comment about the media's decade-long assault upon black Americans, 'We have been out-propagandized.'

President Clinton also made his I-Know-How-To-Handle-Blacks State of the Union Speech during black pathology week. Every time an issue such as crime or welfare was mentioned, the CNN producer would zoom in on the faces of black representatives [in Congress] so often it became a sinister game. Maybe this producer isn't aware of the facts, but I know that Clinton knows the majority of people on welfare are white women.

The president has learned what the networks have learned. When you point the finger at blacks as responsible for the sins of society, your poll numbers jump and your ratings soar.

Clinton didn't mention blacks while proposing tough crime legislation, but it was clear to CNN whom Clinton had in mind. At the end of black pathology week, CNN presented on this *Week In Review*, Clinton's remarks about crime. All of the pictures in the report were of black youth being handcuffed, chased or lying on the ground, under arrest. This report, narrated by Dick Wilson, was followed immediately by a story about Michael Jackson's out-of-court settlement with a youth who accused him of molestation. All of those invited by CNN to comment about Jackson's predicament were middle-aged white males.

In the black pathology business, a story about anonymous black criminal suspects, followed by one having to do with the possible criminal behavior of a black celebrity is what I would call a black pathology double feature.[45]

This is the media - print and electronic - which black conservatives, although not all, say favors blacks. Yet the standard fare, and staple diet, it feeds to the public on the "true nature" of blacks, how they live and what type of people they are, is - "all that crime," committed by, you know who. And this is the media whose reporters are said to be liberal, hence sympathetic to black people, unlike conservatives.

Most reporters - like professors in colleges and universities - are said to be liberal. And even they themselves say so, according to surveys. What they say also shows that they are, indeed, liberal. This is what prompted Malcolm X to say there's no difference between a Republican wolf and a Democratic fox.

And even when news reporters report many incidents in which blacks are brutalized by racist police officers, and are attacked by members of hate groups and other racists, it does *not* mean that

168

they favor blacks. That's simply reality. They are reporting what's going on.

Now, contrast that with the portrayal of blacks by the same media as "criminals," committing "all that crime" as biased reporting clearly shows, amply documented by Ishmael Reed and others. You'll then really know how much the media "favors" blacks over whites and other people. And that shows how pervasive racism is in the American society where blacks have never been fully been accepted as equals.

Way back in 1963, Malcolm X warned that white people will *never* accept blacks as equals. More than forty years later, what he said is as valid as it was back then although there has been significant progress in terms of economic prosperity and social mobility for a significant numbers of blacks since the civil rights movements.

But they are mainly middle-class blacks. Their brethren in the lower class have not made much progress because of the *same* problem, racism. Just go to the ghetto. Millions are stuck in the same condition, with the same low income, and the same social problems, no matter who is in office, Democrat or Republican. They were no better off under Jimmy Carter when he was president than they were under Ronald Reagan when he was president; no better off under Bill Clinton than they were under senior Bush and junior Bush as president. They suffered the same racism at the hands of racists; they were brutalized just as much by racist cops; and they earned just as little or just as much as they did under Democrats and Republicans.

The problem is power. That is what makes racism vicious. Whites are on top, and they will always be on top, because they have *the power* black people don't have. As simple as that. And that is the harsh reality of racism in the American context where blacks are at the mercy of whites, many of whom couldn't care less what happens to black people and about the problems they face because of racism; be it in the ghetto, with the police, at work, in housing or anywhere else in society.

Black conservatives may claim racism is not serious a problem as it once was and as many blacks claim it still is in their lives; or they may even pretend it does not exist at all in the lives of many blacks, since some may claim they have never had any racial

169

problems in their lives, or they have had only minor "skirmishes."

But that does not change reality. And it includes media indifference and even hostility toward black plight, a reality Professor Walter Williams and other black conservatives fail to grasp or deliberately ignore to fortify their conservatives perspective on a number of fundamental issues critical to black America. For example, Williams took President Clinton and the national media to task for not mentioning the racially motivated murder of Melissa McLughlin, but never mentioned how biased the media was against blacks in many respects when he said it ignores crimes committed by blacks against whites.

Also his charge against the media raises questions as to how he heard about the murder in the first place. He would probably say he got it from the local media, not the from the national media. But if the local media carried the story, which it did, it was with the full knowledge and understanding - by newspaper and television reporters in South Carolina - that it would get out and go beyond South Carolina where the murder took place and would be picked up by other newspapers and television stations, as it obviously was, and would not be suppressed. And it was *not* suppressed. Also anyone who contacts the Southern Poverty Law Center will get a long list of black victims beaten, raped, tortured, mutilated and killed by whites, and unreported in the press through the years.

There are also cases of jury nullification by white jurors who don't want to convict white perpetrators of hate crimes against blacks, and of the authorities who don't want to classify many of those crimes as hate crimes which are sometimes dismissed as misdemeanors as happened in Grand Rapids, Michigan, in 2003. In this case, involving a black motorist and his black girlfriend who were attacked by two whites who also hurled racial slurs at the black driver, the prosecutor contended that it was a hate crime. The white jury disagreed, as did the white judge, and the case was dismissed as a misdemeanor; and after appealing, it was the same result.

Both blacks and whites must look at the kind of society they live in and the environment that encourages such brutal acts of violence by both and against each other. It has to do with the racist nature of the American society, regardless of how much the country has done to address the problem.

The problem still exists, even if it is not as bad as it was before in some respects. White America, not black America, is responsible for racism that has permeated the American society and virtually every fiber of its fabric. It spawns acts of random racial violence from a number of black individuals directed against whites. And we blacks must admit that if we want to be fair. But these acts of violence are nowhere close to organized hate, systematic white terrorism that is the hallmark of the Ku Klux Klan, the American Nazi, or the skinhead variety. Nor is it comparable to the numerous racial incidents by individual whites against blacks even if black violence against whites is not triggered by specific racial incidents.

White racism in America has the same effect on blacks and on society as a whole as much as apartheid still has on blacks in South Africa because of what it did to them for hundreds of years; in both cases for more than 300 years of oppression and exploitation by whites.

It is bound to trigger acts of retaliatory violence by blacks against whites in South Africa one day, especially if the ruling African National Congress (ANC) fails to improve economic and social conditions of the black majority, reducing the huge income gap between blacks and whites.

Like blacks in South Africa, black people in the United States were treated for centuries as nothing by whites. In both cases, in the United States and in South Africa, blacks were enslaved, and the life of a black person meant absolutely nothing to the white majority. As Dr. Martin Luther King summed up the situation in the American context following the murder of civil rights workers in the south during the sixties:

If Stokely Carmichael now says that nonviolence is irrelevant, it is because he, as a dedicated veteran of many battles, has seen with his own eyes the most brutal white violence against Negroes and white civil rights workers, and he has seen it go unpunished.

Even when blacks and whites die together in the cause of justice, the death of the white person gets more attention and concern than the death of a black person.

Stokely and his colleagues from SNNC were with us in Alabama when Jimmy Lee Jackson, a brave young Negro man, was killed and James Reeb, a committed Unitarian white minister, was fatally clubbed to the ground. They

171

remember how President Johnson sent flowers to the gallant Mrs. Reeb, and in his eloquent 'We Shall Overcome' speech paused to mention that one person, James Reeb, had already died in the struggle.

Somehow the president forgot to mention Jimmy, who died first. The parents and sister of Jimmy received no flowers from the president. The students felt this keenly. Not that they felt that the death of James Reeb was less than tragic, but because they felt that the failure to mention Jimmy Jackson only reinforced the impression that to white America the life of a Negro is insignificant and meaningless.[46]

The life of a black person still means nothing to many whites - it can't when racism is so prevalent, since racism is, in essence, the diminution of life.

If the media and the president of the United States focus their attention on racially motivated attacks and killings of blacks, it is not because the murder of whites by blacks for racist reasons is any less tragic. It is to emphasize one ugly truth: white racism, more than black racism, is responsible for racial hostility and polarization across America today as much as it has been throughout the nation's history; only in covert form in many cases nowadays. To contend otherwise, as black conservatives do, is rank dishonesty. Racism is a malignant tumor draining the life of the American body politic. It is a cancer deeply embedded in the national psyche.

Was the failure by President Clinton and the national media, as Walter Williams claims, to mention the murder of Melissa McLaughlin justified? No. The life of a white person is no less valuable than that of a black person, and the life of a black person is less valuable than that of a white person. But in order to place all racially motivated murders - black and white as well as others - in their proper context, people of all races, but especially whites, must acknowledge the damage white racism has done and continues to do to race relations. It is a context that cannot be comprehended without understanding the forces that shaped it.

The devastating impact that white domination and oppression has inflicted on blacks and on the nation as a whole is enormous. And it will be a long time before, if ever, the great divide between black and white is bridged, let alone closed. Apportion guilt accordingly. As Whitney Young, president of the Urban League, said, to equate "anti-white feelings [among blacks with white racism would be] to equate the bitterness of the victim with the evil that oppresses him."[47]

What causes their bitterness? Do they, as victims, have to be blamed for being bitter about being oppressed by whites? And as Malcolm X put it, "the white man is in no moral position to accuse anyone else of hate."[48]

Much as Walter Williams sympathizes with white victims of black racially motivated violence, there is no reason why he shouldn't sympathize with millions of blacks who are victims of white racism. White racism ranges from outright discrimination in employment and housing and daily insults to lack of sympathy for black victims of white terrorist acts.

May be Williams does sympathize with fellow blacks as well, only in a guarded manner and does not want to show his true feelings as if he's "whining" like other blacks do, that's the common talk, when blacks complain, as if they're infants who want to be pampered.

Still, one wonders how much sympathy he has for fellow blacks since he believes, as other black conservatives do, that black people are favored at the expense of whites in many areas of life, and not just by the criminal justice system. The concern about his position is justified especially when one hears what he says: "The major problems blacks face have little or nothing to do with racial discrimination and are not solvable through civil rights strategy."[49]

He's wrong, dead wrong, about that. Racism is the major problem blacks face today as they always have. It drives everything else. Almost every major problem blacks face - from segregation to unemployment and family disintegration - has to do with racism one way or another.

But how often do you hear black conservatives condemn it? Usually they are silent, like the Klan. Williams, of course, and other conservatives such as Robert Woodson dismiss racism lightly as no more than just a minor problem, if it is one at all. Larry Elder goes even further than that.

He says black people are more racist than whites, the NAACP is more dangerous than the Ku Klux Klan, America's biggest problem is *not* racism but illegitimacy - by blacks, of course, and much more, as he bluntly states in his book, *The Ten Things You*

*Can't Say in America.*50

White racism didn't just start, and it didn't end with the civil rights movement as black conservatives like to believe; nor does it continue to exist because of black "pathological" behavior as many whites and conservatives claim. Racism needs no justification - or diagnosis. It is there, it is real, like Mount Rushmore: large, imposing, solid, and visible.

Even if all blacks were John the Baptist or Mother Theresa, or became saints overnight, racism would *still* exist for one simple reason: the majority of whites don't like black people. As simple as that. They accept Asians, Hispanics and others more than they do blacks. Even Asians and Hispanics know that. And even they, in general, don't like black people, and make fun of them as much as white racists do.

Many whites - and others, of course - say they avoid blacks because black people commit "all that crime." Don't whites commit crime, a lot of crime, mostly in white communities? Do other whites in those communities discriminate against them? Don't whites steal? They admit they do, but "you guys steal more than we do. Hey, you could win an Oscar for that," is their attitude toward blacks.

Are all blacks criminals? If it's simply a matter of class, why is it that many whites even in suburbs don't want blacks as neighbors? They are middle-class themselves. They moved out of the inner cities for the same reasons whites also move out of white neighborhoods in search of better life. Yet as soon as blacks move in, many whites move out. Who is responsible for white flight from suburban areas when blacks move in? Black crime or white racism?

If whites avoid blacks because of "all that crime," is that why they don't hire blacks? Do they discriminate against white criminals? They accept the riff-raff among them more than they do middle-class blacks. Why? Because of raw-naked racism. Whites are "our problem," is their attitude. And blacks? "Scum of the earth," obviously, no matter what class, middle or upper. As long as you are black, you're out. You're not welcome. Case closed.

You can call it whatever you want to call it - personal preference, whatever. That does not change its nature. It is still

174

racism.

What has been the justification for racism by whites through the centuries since the founding of America when blacks were not committing "all that crime," and were not killing whites? America was founded and thrived on racism. What makes it different today from what it has always been? Racism is racism. What is the difference between racially motivated bombings and burnings of black churches in the south in the fifties and sixties and the racially motivated burnings of black churches during the nineties?

Professor Walter Williams and other black conservatives obviously see a difference between the two. Interestingly enough, the difference these ideological compatriots see is between white racism - *and* white racism. And they don't have any blind-folders on.

Even white racists are mystified by that. They wonder what the KKK and all their other organizations are all about. They also wonder why millions of other whites don't like blacks - that's why about 50 percent of them don't want racial integration, as national surveys show. So does empirical evidence. Segregation is everywhere.

Still, black conservatives maintain there is a difference between white racism - and white racism. The burning of black churches by white racists in the nineties is different from the burning of black churches by white racists in the fifties and sixties. Segregation today is different from segregation back then. The list goes on and on.

That is the logic of black conservatives. Sadly, it does not correspond to reality in a society where race matters. If race didn't matter, racism wouldn't be a major problem today. And that is what sours race relations. Black people don't, contrary to what Professor Walter Williams claims, as do other black conservatives.

Many racial incidents through the years also confirm that racism remains a major problem in the United States, and not because black people are responsible for its continued existence. Attacks by skinheads are some of the most glaring examples of racism, and of who is responsible for what, and why, as the case of Nathan Thill tragically shows.

A skinhead in Denver, Colorado, Thill shot a West African

175

immigrant to death in what was indisputably a racist attack. As Thill himself, a 19-year-old, bluntly told a television interviewer, "[I] walked through town with my gun in my waist, saw the black guy and thought he didn't belong where he was at. How easy it would be to take him out right there. Didn't seem like much to me."51

The slain black man, 38-year-old Oumar Dia who was persecuted in his native country of Mauritania by the Arabs who still enslave blacks and dominate every aspect of life as much as they do in Sudan, was forced to leave his native land because of persecution. He was helped by some human rights groups and sought refuge in the United States, only to die at the hands of other racists.52

What is important to understand here, instead of dismissing the case as an isolated incident and the work of a lone wolf, is that skinhead and other racist attacks on blacks are not only a product of a sick mind; they are also, probably more than anything else, a reflection of the racist mentality of the larger society, however latent and sophisticated the racism may be in many cases nowadays. The attacks would not be taking place had there been no tolerance for such conduct. It is the climate. It is conducive to hate.

Nathan Thill may have pulled the trigger, but society was the gun itself. It is society, a racist society or one that tolerates hate, that fueled his hatred because of its increasing intolerance of minorities especially blacks. And there are many cases to prove that.

Just look at the rollback of affirmative action that has gained momentum across the nation through the years. Look at the vicious attacks on government programs intended to help minorities in the promised land, the land of opportunity. Look at racial profiling, and police brutality, with blacks being targeted more than anybody else. And look at the high incarceration rate among blacks, and the stiff sentences handed out to blacks more than anybody else by the criminal justice system black conservatives say favors blacks or is lenient toward blacks. Also look at the litany of lies about blacks committing "all that crime," and using "all that dope." The list goes on and on.

True enough, Oumar Dia suffered in his native Arab-dominated country of Mauritania where blacks are not only routinely persecuted and enslaved but also killed at will. But Dia was not only persecuted in the United States but brutally murdered in "the land of the free" for exactly the same reason. He was forced out of his country because he was black, and he was killed in the United States because he was black. As *The New York Times* reported:

> Eight years ago, Arab authorities expelled Mr. Dia from his native Mauritania because he was black, his friends said. On Wednesday night, after work as a housekeeper in a downtown Denver hotel, Mr. Dia, a 38-year-old father of three, crossed paths with Mr. Thill, a burly former meat packer who carried a .22 caliber pistol, Celtic tattoos on his forearms, and a visceral hatred of people different than him.
>
> 'Oumar was one of milions of people who came to the United States to improve their circumstances, fascinated by the American dream,' Mohamado Cisse, a friend said. 'For Oumar his dream was shattered....It was not a stray bullet that killed Oumar,' said Mr. Cisse, a Senegalese vendor. 'The murderer knew exactly what he wanted to do: to kill someone who was black.'[53]

The skinhead who shot Dia dead couldn't agree more. Thill saw himself as a soldier in a race war, what white supremacist leader Matt Hale, a lawyer and whose title is Pontifex Maximus of the World Church of the Creator but who was imprisoned in 2004 for threatening to kill a judge, calls RAHOWA: Racial Holy War.

The racist "church," which has its own bible and whose members don't believe in turning the other cheek, is based in Illinois and is one of the fastest-growing white racist groups in the United States. And its members have carried out some of the deadliest attacks on non-whites and Jews.

One of the victims was a black football coach at Northwestern University in Illinois who was shot dead when he was jogging with his two daughters. Matt Hale's followers espouse the same doctrine of white supremacy other racists, including Nathan Thill, do. As Thill put it: "In a war, anybody wearing the enemies' uniform is an enemy and should be taken out," he said of his black victim, who was shot at a bus stop waiting for a bus, and wearing his "uniform," his black skin. He went on to say: "I guess I was kind of thinking about him because he was black....I had the right [to kill him] because he was black."[54]

The words have a familiar ring. Racist groups see skin color as a uniform in a race war. As Mississippi Ku Klux Klan leader Robert Shelton bluntly stated: "The one and only solution is America for the white man. We are at war in America. Look at the color of your skin - that is your uniform."[55]

And any white person who tries to help or is sympathetic to blacks is also fair game, branded as a "race traitor," and a "nigger lover." That is what happened in Denver when Oumar Dia was shot. Skinhead Thill shot a white woman who tried to help Dia. The woman, Jeannie Van Velkinburgh, a 36-year-old single mother of two boys, was shot in the back, the bullet severing her spine. Doctors said she would be paralyzed for life.

Van Velkinburgh, a nurse, responding to press inquiries from her hospital bed, said: "I was trying to help someone who needed help....I would do it again if I thought there was a chance that I could save someone's life."[56] She died in 2002 from complications of her injuries, about five years after she was shot.

Skinheads have been a conspicuous hate-filled phenomenon in different parts of the country, intimidating, beating, and killing blacks. And many skinheads have a reputation for candor, as the Denver case clearly demonstrates. According to *The Boston Globe*: "A white teenager with a shaved head has brazenly admitted that he shot and killed a West African immigrant at a bus stop, saying he didn't want to live in a world with blacks. 'I don't like some blacks. I guess it's a sort of a thing that I love my own people and I'd like to see a place where just we could be,' Nathan Thill, 19, told KUSA-TV in a jail interview."[57]

Denver's mayor, Wellington Webb, a black, responding to the murder, said: "We've had a three-week rash of unanticipated violence by individuals that have been active as skinheads. It is certainly my hope that these are individual incidents."[58]

For black conservatives and others to argue that these are isolated incidents that do not reflect a national pattern is to ignore empirical evidence. Lynda Gorov, of *The Boston Globe*, in trying to explaining the skinhead attacks and other acts of racial violence, put it this way:

No one can explain why racial violence has erupted again in Denver, once a locus for Skinheads. But the reemergence meshes with national trends....

In the 1990s, the Alabama-based Southern Poverty Law Center, which tracks movements...of hate groups, said it uncovered 30 groups nationwide, a number that climbed to 37 last year. And that's only the 'tip of the iceberg,' spokesman Mark Potok said, because most skinheads do not belong to an identifiable organization but only share a fascination with neo-Nazism and whie supremacist views.

Since 1988, 48 [known] murders nationwide have been attributed to skinheads by the center, including the two killings in Denver in November [1997].[59]

What is even more terrifying is that skinheads, like many other hate groups, are well-armed, having some of the latest and deadliest weapons in their arsenal. And they use them. As Gail Gains of the B'nai B'rith Anti-Defamation League stated: "Two weeks ago, we would have said there were no active skinheads in Denver. Now we know there are, and they seem to be armed to the teeth. It's like a fraternity of hate."[60]

And Carl Raschke, professor of religion at the University of Denver, had this this to say: "For 10 to 15 years, they've been talking about starting a revolution, hyping each other with their own rhetoric: 'You talk the walk, but when are you going to walk the walk'? They know the code, and they know when to act. They are the silent brotherhood....But they seem to want a situation where they have to bring out their guns."[61]

Skinheads went on to unleash more terror. Just a few days later after the wanton, senseless murder of Oumar Dia, another black, this time a woman, was attacked. She was ambushed at a convenience store by assailants who boasted that they were skinheads, using a racial slur, calling her a nigger, before beating her "in the latest in a string of apparent race-based crimes in Colorado. Shomie Francis, 26, of Aurora, told police she was jumped by six people as she was getting some food at a 7-Eleven [convenience store] about 2 a.m. on Thanksgiving Day. Paramedics called to the store treated her for cuts and wounds to her face."[62]

Her attackers, who included a Hispanic, ran away but they were caught, arrested, and jailed for investigation of ethnic intimidation and assault. Strangely enough, in spite of all the evidence of the physical injuries the victim sustained, and witnesses at the store, Denver police sergeant Michael O'Neill downplayed the racist attack, saying: "To call it a beating would be an exaggeration."[59]

179

However, Andrew Hudson, a spokesman for Denver Mayor Webb Wellington, called the incident "an atrocious act of violence [and we] are determined to prosecute those involved."[63]

If skinhead activity and terrorism against blacks by other hate groups is not compelling evidence of a deeper problem which is the racist mentality of the larger society that refuses to strongly condemn racist attacks - where is the public outcry? - black conservatives routinely dismiss as an aberration, then the problem is not going to be solved. Races will continue to drift farther and farther apart.

Ignoring the problem as black conservatives do is not going to solve it. Nor is the problem going to disappear simply because it is ignored by society, white-dominated society. Hate crimes are not decreasing, as black conservatives claim. They may be less noticeable because perpetrators try to hide when they commit those crimes, but not fewer. As reported by *The Christian Science Monitor*: "[There has been] a sharp upswing in the 1990s of reported hate crimes and continued racially motivated violence, including widely publicized cases of black men being killed or beaten for associating with white women....'There is evidence of incredible violence [against blacks today],' says Martha Hodes, a historian at New York university."[64]

With all this evidence, and much more as we have shown in this study, it is hard to believe how black conservatives can say race relations are very good, and that racist attacks against blacks are merely isolated incidents. It is even harder to believe that the primary victims of racist attacks - black people - are the ones, Professor Walter Williams contends, who are responsible for souring race relations. What about millions of white racists who outnumber the entire black population?

There are only about 40 million blacks in a nation of more than 280 million people, of whom about 85 percent are white. Are all those whites not racist? Even national surveys show that the majority don't want to have anything to do with blacks. That's why about 50 percent of them don't want racial integration. And that is why there is so much segregation even today, in spite of *all* the integration that has taken place through the years.

Instead of blaming blacks for souring race relations, focus on the cause, the real culprits: white racists; not all whites, but racists.

Otherwise race relations are not going to get any better. And they can, but not by exacerbating racial tensions and blaming the victims for that.

Black people are the primary victims of racism. And you have more blacks than whites who are victims of racism. To contend otherwise is to contradict reality. It is a distortion of the truth and may be even a deliberate misinterpretation of facts, for whatever reasons, including ideological. In this case, such distortion or misrepresentation of facts reflects a perspective on crime so typical of conservatives, including black conservatives.

Chapter Five:

Conservatives and Blacks' Intelligence

THE MENTAL CAPACITY of black people has always been a subject of controversy long before publication of *The Bell Curve*.[1]

What *The Bell Curve* has done is fuel debate on this highly inflammatory subject by claiming to have proven that blacks are mentally deficient, through no fault of their own, because of black - or "Negroid" - genetic inferiority.

This confirms the belief that many whites, in fact the majority according to polls, and others have always had, that non-blacks are intellectually superior to blacks because they have better or stronger genes; as they rub their hands with satisfaction, gleefully saying, "See? I knew it all along; they aren't too swift upstairs, you know who!" Conservatives have played a leading role probably more than anybody else in propagating this myth, and they continue to do so.[2]

In his book *Race and Culture: A World View*, Thomas Sowell, a leading black conservative, discusses, among other things, the explosive subject of race and intelligence. He contends that there are IQ differences between blacks and whites as well as members of other races, an observation even some whites liberals admit is an empirically verifiable fact.[3] But why that is the case is what sets Sowell and others of his ilk apart, fueling the debate on racism between liberals and conservatives.

Solidifying his credentials as a highly controversial figure is his other argument in an equally explosive manner in the same book. He contends that the colonization of Africa was, on balance, a blessing for Africans.4 He implies that black Africans should be grateful Europeans colonized them, an issue that is directly related to black people's intellectual capacity; for, only a fool or mental weakling would like to be colonized, dominated, abused and exploited.

It is a thesis that contradicts what many blacks say, including Dr. Walter Rodney in his internationally acclaimed and well-documented book, *How Europe Underdeveloped Africa*,5 which conversely means how Africa developed Europe through exploitation of the African continent by the imperial powers.

Sowell has incurred the wrath of many blacks and liberals but has won accolades from conservatives for his startling "candor." These plaudits include: "If a white man wrote this book, the liberals would lynch him. When it comes to flouting liberal dogma on race, this courageous book makes Charles Murray's *Bell Curve* look positively restrained. So why has Thomas Sowell been spared the public flogging the liberal elite gave Murray? It's tougher to make the 'racist' label stick to a black man."6

Murray's *Bell Curve*, to which Sowell's *Race and Culture* has been compared, has not only fueled the debate on intelligence but has also, by association, made Sowell even more controversial. As Professor Barbara Bergmann states:

We know what Sowell thinks...from his books and articles, so it didn't surprise me that he would pan my book *In Defense of Affirmative Action* as severely as he did in his April 23 [1996] editorial-page commentary 'Affirmative Action: Logic vs. Sentiment.' But I was surprised that he gave the reader hardly a hint of the substance of my arguments....

My book develops the argument that when a business has never hired anybody but white men for a particular kind of job - a job that plenty of women and African-Americans could do well - that situation deserves to be rectified, and affirmative action is the only practical way to do it....

Mr. Sowell's own logic isn't impeccable. He tells us about racial disparities in Malaysia and the Fiji islands that are supposedly not due to discriminatory exclusion (but due to differences in mental capacity), and wants us to join him in thinking that those examples prove that disparities are never due to discrimination.

It just doesn't follow, and wishing doesn't make it so. Mr. Sowell likens my book to a rotten egg on the grounds of my statement that the theme of *The Bell Curve* is that blacks have poor-quality genes. Maybe I'm wrong there, but many other readers of that book got the same impression I did. I'd love to hear what

Sowell hails *The Bell Curve* as "one of the most sober, responsible, thorough and thoughtful books to be published in years."[8] On IQ differences among the races, Sowell says it is difficult to deny that there must be something going on - "there is something there," as he put in his book *Race and Culture* - even if we don't know exactly what it is. That is easily interpreted as an endorsement of the genetic argument that members of other races are more intelligent than blacks, as Murray and Richard Herrnstein - the co-author who died - contend; a position many people consider to be racist and scientifically specious.

Although the two authors have addressed a subject that has to do with genetics, they are not geneticists by training; a factor that many critics have used to question the authors' credibility in tackling such a highly complex subject that has to do with science. Murray is a sociologist, and Herrnstein, who taught at Harvard University until his death in 1994 in the same year their book *The Bell Curve* was published, was a psychologist.

After Herrnstein's death, it was Murray who was left to face the heat and defend the book's highly controversial thesis. And he is still doing it today.

Murray is not the only one who is frank about that. Some of the leading conservative publications articulate the same position and have endorsed his book. As Professor W. Fitzhugh Brundage of Queen's College in Ontario, Canada,[9] states in his article 'The Return of Respectable Racism" in *The Queen's Quarterly*, the *National Review* (a leading American conservative magazine) is one of those practicing "respectable racism" by endorsing *The Bell Curve*. He goes on to say, "*The National Review* crowed that it [*The Bell Curve*] 'confirms ordinary citizens' reasonable intuition that trying to engineer racial equality in the distribution of occupations and social positions runs against not racial prejudice but nature, which shows no such egalitarian distribution of talent.'"[10]

The National Review conducted a symposium of fourteen distinguished social scientists on the book, some of whom described it as "mischievous,' "deeply flawed," and "a moral and political *cul de sac*."[11] Many other people in and outside academia consider the book to be racist with deep implications in the areas of social policy and race relations. Such apprehension is not without foundation.

There may be some policy makers - not just conservatives but may be even many white liberals - who embrace its even views, even if privately, with dire consequences for the whole nation if they get the opportunity to act on them. And there are millions of whites - across the ideological spectrum - who now feel vindicated in their belief that they are indeed genetically - hence intellectually - superior to blacks because their racist views have been given academic respectability by the devastating indictment of racial equality that is the central theme of *The Bell Curve*. Here is a summary of the book's main arguments, paraphrased and elaborated on accordingly:

•Intelligence - not environment, poverty or education - is at the root of our worst social problems. Intelligence levels differ among identifiable groups in society, especially along racial lines.

•IQ is the most critical factor in determining one's status in life, and is therefore of paramount importance in the formulation of social policy. Years of concealing these facts have only yielded massive social problems - built on the lie that there are no differences in intelligence between blacks and whites.

•People of below-average intelligence find it very difficult - almost impossible - to resist crime or stay married, pathologies so characteristic of black America.

•IQ is inheritable, with the environment and education playing only a minor role as demonstrated by the 15-point difference in IQ scores between blacks and whites that has persisted since World War I (when IQ tests were first given to black and white soldiers) and which has proved impossible to erase. Therefore there is only one explanation left: genetic.

•There is a direct correlation between cognitive ability and middle-class values that are pitifully lacking across black America even among blacks who earn middle-class income.

•There is a direct relationship between IQ levels and crime, illegitimacy, divorce, welfare dependency and unemployment, maladies black Americans are afflicted with - more than members of any other racial group: the lower the IQ, the bigger the problem.

•Those who are chronically unemployed fall exclusively in the lowest quarter of intelligence, a conclusion that justifies the high unemployment rate among blacks and which society can do nothing about since it is directly related to genes.

•Expanding federal programs for any kind of assistance harms those with low IQs, who are mainly black since blacks have the lowest IQs among all racial groups, and blacks are the most dependent on federal assistance. A disproportionately large number of blacks, contrasted with whites and members of other groups, can't even read beyond the fourth-grade level, according to national educational surveys.

•People should be hired on the basis of IQ scores, not interviews, references or even specific-job performance tests; a practice that will exclude blacks from better-paying jobs since they have the lowest IQs.

•IQ tests are not racially or culturally biased. They have an uncanny ability to predict academic achievement and job performance, based on decades of research empirically verified, because they measure general intelligence. Therefore blacks use the cultural-and-racial-bias argument against the validity of IQ tests only as a cover-up for their meager intellect.

•IQ tests fell out of favor with the academic elite - almost all of whom are liberal - in the 1960s because of their misguided belief in equality of ability and talent among the races, ignoring the fact that whites, Asians, Native Americans (Indians), Hispanics and others surpass blacks in both.

•Group traits and differences among the races are inherited; the role of culture and environment being only peripheral.

•Environment and history do not account for the poor performance of blacks in the American society across the spectrum - academic, social and economic - an argument that entirely ignores racial discrimination.

•There are differences between blacks and whites of the same IQ, with whites and members of other races doing better than blacks in school, at work, and in life in general. Genes explain all this.

•Arthur Jensen, William Shockley, and Richard Herrnstein were right when they argued years ago that the difference in intelligence levels between blacks and whites were genetic in origin. They noted that American blacks have higher IQs than African blacks who hardly score above 70 and have the lowest IQs in the world (which explains why black Africa is so backward; an argument Philippe Rushton repeated recently in his article, "IQ: Why Africa is Africa - Haiti Haiti").

•An IQ of 70 is considered retarded.[12] And such "retardation" among black Africans has to do with genes, hence race. Arthur Jensen went so far as to say on American television on the *Phil Donahue Show* in the early eighties that American blacks have higher IQs than "their cousins in Africa," as he put it, because they are racially mixed; implying genes from whites have made them smarter than blacks in Africa, the logical extension of which is: the more white blood you have, the smarter you are; also the lighter you are, the smarter you are. And, of course, the darker you are, the less intelligent you are. If you have a dark skin, you also have a dark mind, in total darkness.[13]

Those are the central arguments of *The Bell Curve*. Sowell's endorsement of this highly controversial work is shared by other black conservatives, some of whom have endorsed similar views espoused by people like Jared Taylor, a white separatist,[14] who condemns racial integration. Professor Walter Williams has endorsed Taylor's book, *Paved with Good Intentions: The Failure of Race Relations in Contemporary America*,[15] in glowing terms: "[It] should be on everybody's shelf. Admittedly, it is tragic reading. But it's far better to know and do something about liberals tearing down our country before it's too late."[16]

Taylor's work is yet another contribution to the debate on race relations in America, giving "credibility" to Herrnstein's and Murray's views on black-white differences in intelligence. *The New York Times* called Murray "the most dangerous conservative" in America, and went on to state: "Over a decade, Charles Murray has gained ground in his crusade to abolish welfare. But now, with his contentious views on IQ, class and race, has he gone too far? Bob Dole and Newt Gingrich may have more power than Murray may, and Rush Limbaugh and Pat Buchanan may have more direct influence. But no other conservative has the ability to make a radical thought seem so reasonable. Where others rant, Murray seduces with mountains of data and assurances of his own fine intentions. He will never be the country's most famous conservative, but he may well be the most dangerous."[17]

Another inflammatory work that has fueled debate on racial differences in intelligence, and has been hailed by conservatives in phosphorescent particulars, is J. Philippe Rushton's *Race, Evolution, and Behavior*.[18] The *National Review* carried this endorsement of Rushton's fiery work: "[It] describes hundreds of studies worldwide that show a consistent pattern of human racial differences." Steven Blinkhorn, with an equally glowing endorsement, wrote in *Nature*: "A frank attempt to rehabilitate the concept of race as a primary descriptive category." Richard Lynn, writing in *The Spectator*, another American conservative magazine, had this to say: "Should, if there is any justice, receive a Nobel Prize." And Chris Brand stated in *Personality and Individual Differences*: "Undoubtedly *Race, Evolution, and Behavior* is the best wide-ranging read in differential psychology since Jensen's (1981) *Straight Talk About Mental Tests*."

Other comments on Rushton's book included those of Malcolm W. Browne who wrote in *The New York Times Book Review*: "An incendiary thesis that separate races of human beings evolved different reproductive strategies to cope with different environments." And Transaction Publishers of Rutgers University remarked: "Why are the races different? How different are they? This book examines genetic theories to overturn the prevailing view that if all people were treated the same, most race differences would disappear. Rushton examines international data on over 60

188

variables, including brain size, intelligence, crime, and sexual behavior, and finds that Asians and Africans average at opposite ends of a continuum with Europeans intermediate."[19]

On Rushton's scale, blacks rank lowest among the races as the most mentally deficient. How valid are the results of IQ tests that show that the average IQ among black Africans is 70, that of American blacks 85, and among whites 100 which is considered to be normal intelligence? We will try to answer that in due course.

In terms of definition, an IQ between 65 and 85 is below normal intelligence, and subjects with IQs ranging from 51 - 70 being classified as morons.[20] The 15-point gap between blacks and whites in the United States, which has existed since World War I, translates into a yawning gap of 30 points in IQ differences between blacks and whites whose IQ is 70 and 100, respectively. If the 15-point gap has proved impossible to erase, what are we to make of attempts to close - let alone erase - the 30-point gap that exists between whites and black Africans?

Undoubtedly, race is a factor in the interpretation of such data, contrary to what conservatives and others say. Racism is an integral part of the universal experience where those who look different always will be different in more than just one way; it is not peculiar to the United States or to the Western world, although Westerners conquered the whole world and, by so doing, propagated the myth of white racial superiority since Europeans, hence whites, had the mandate, divine mandate, to rule members of the lesser breed. That was the logic of imperialism, with the technological theory of imperialism - "Thank God, we have the Gatlin gun, and they have not" - having the biggest impact on a global scale.

But even with racism, empirically verifiable facts remain facts. It is conclusions drawn from those facts that are given a racial twist by warped minds of racists even if they are renowned scholars, and may be even by some blacks who believe that whites are indeed intellectually superior to black people. This is not to even remotely suggest that black conservatives believe that *all* whites are more intelligent than blacks. Professors Thomas Sowell and Walter Williams, highly respected economics professors, probably don't believe all whites are more intelligent than they are. But they cite empirical evidence, for example, to show that whites

189

in general do better in school than blacks do. Sowell's book, *Race and Culture*, even includes a chapter appropriately titled "Race and Intelligence" devoted to the subject of IQ differences among the races, and is documented. But how solid, how exact, and how objective are his sources?

Respect for empirical evidence is a mark of scholarship regardless of who marshals the evidence, including racists. Facts are facts. The intent does not change the content when some people use those facts to serve their own purposes. And it serves no purpose to deny the truth. Thus, you have Jared Taylor, a white separatist, stating in his book *Paved with Good Intentions*:

> It is frequently pointed out that children of wealthy parents get better SAT scores than children of poor parents. The economic advantages of whites are said to give them better access to the culture that is embodied in the test. In fact, white children from families with incomes of $10,000 to $20,000 get better SAT scores than black children from families with incomes of $70,000 or more. Even Asians from poor families, many of whom are new comers to the United States and are from genuinely different cultures, score slightly better than black children from the wealthiest families....
>
> At the best engineering schools, the average SAT math score is 700 or better. In 1983, only 205 blacks in the whole country scored that high (0.28 percent of test takers), while 31,704 whites and 3,015 Asians did (3.3 percent and 8.6 percent, respectively, of all test takers). Engineering schools are constantly criticized for not admitting enough blacks, but what are they to do?[21]

That is not a figment of the imagination or manipulation of facts and figures by a warped racist mind, although Taylor is undoubtedly a racist. He is honest about it; his public statements don't leave any doubt about that, including his appearance on national television, for example, when he got involved in a heated exchange with Phil Donahue - and other guests - on NBC television in 2003 on the subject of racial integration and other issues involving race.[22] The difference in SAT scores between blacks and whites as well as Asians is a matter of public record. As Sowell states:

> Many leading American colleges have student bodies whose average Scholastic Aptitude Test scores - verbal and quantitative combined - add up to 1,200 points or more....There were fewer than 600 black students in the entire country with combined SAT scores of 1,200 in 1983, compared to more than 60,000 whites. There are about a dozen engineering schools in the United States

where the average mathematics score alone on the Scholastic Aptitude Test is over 700 out of a possible 800. There were fewer than 200 black or Mexican students who scored at that mathematics level in 1985, fewer than 100 Puerto Ricans, and fewer than 50 American Indians.[23]

Even at higher levels of education where one might expect better results, the performance by blacks - as well as Hispanics and Native Americans (American Indians) - is just as dismal in terms of racial differences with whites and Asians. Students in post-graduate schools are supposed to have higher IQs in general than the average student body at the undergraduate level. Yet, as tests for admission into post-graduate schools show: "Similar patterns are found in post-graduate education. A score of 650 or above on the quantitative portion of the Graduate Record Examination (GRE) is common at top-rated American graduate schools...but fewer than 150 black students in the entire country met this standard in 1978 - 79. For top American law schools, a common threshold was a score of 600 on the Law School Aptitude Test in the 1970s and a college grade-point average of 3.25. Only 39 black students in the country met those standards in 1976."[24]

Poverty isn't a valid excuse for poor performance across-the-board; nor is culture, which some blacks contend is biased against them. They are Americans themselves, born and raised on American soil. I am black myself and am not trying to provide any excuses. As blacks, we should just face reality, however harsh it is, and wherever we are: in Africa, America, Europe and elsewhere.

If culture and poverty were valid excuses, Asian-American students would not be excelling in school, surpassing practically everybody including whites from a middle- and upper-class "culture" that, supposedly, is responsible for test biases against black students. Not only did Asian students come from a totally different culture, unlike that of black Americans which is as American as apple pie practically in all - not just in fundamental - respects; they also had to learn English as a second language since English is the primary medium of instruction in the United States. Most of them also came to America poor.

Charles Murray, Jared Taylor, Arthur Jensen, William Shockley, Phillipe Rushton and others may be dismissed as racists for pointing out that even some of the poorest Asians do better in school than black students from some of the richest families in the

191

United States, just as poor white students on average score higher than blacks from high-income families. But the evidence is not racist. It is empirical. And there are blacks who concede that. They include Thomas Sowell. As he states:

Asian American students from families with low incomes scored higher on the quantitative portion of the Scholastic Aptitude Test in 1981 than did black American, Mexican American, and American Indian students from families earning several times as much....Asian American students from families with incomes of $6,000 or less scored higher on the mathematics portion of the SAT than black, Mexican American, or American Indian students from families with incomes of $50,000 or more....In the United States, blacks of above-average socio-economic status have not averaged as high IQs as whites from lower socio-economic status.[25]

What are we to make of that, from a black scholar such as Sowell, when he says even blacks from better economic backgrounds have lower IQs than poor whites? It is, undoubtedly, an empirical fact and it should not, out of political correctness, be politicized or distorted to please blacks in spite of their poor performance in general. But is Sowell also saying that whites are genetically superior to blacks - hence their higher IQs - as racists claim?

Sowell puts a premium on cultural capital, which is indeed a principal factor in human progress. It is true that culture can facilitate or impede progress or stunt intellectual growth. But there are other factors that are also critical to the functional utility of culture depending on historical and socio-economic contexts Sowell and other conservatives don't pay much attention to. For example, Eurpoeans and Asians in Africa do better in business than indigenous Africans; an empirical fact. But why? The most common answer is, "because they they work hard." Granted, they work hard. But since they work so hard, and many of them do, why were they not successful where they came from? Why in Africa? Why was their dynamic culture static, in their case, in their original homeland where they also should have excelled? They are the same people, with the same culture.

Their culture, which is the engine of progress, did not change or acquire vitality when they emigrated to Africa. Nor is racial discrimination against Africans during colonial rule, and its lingering effects including negative psychological impact on the "backward, primitive natives" - who include educated Africans in this context as defined by "civilized" Europeans and Asians - taken into account as factors impeding progress, anymore than continuing racial discrimination in the United States is taken into consideration as one of the main obstacles to economic progress among blacks.

Sowell's position is typical of that in both contexts, Africa and America, ignoring other factors critical to the role of culture. As Professor Myron Weiner states in *Foreign Affairs*: "In his extensive writings, Sowell has argued that international experience overwhelmingly demonstrates that differences in skills and cultural values among communities are the principal determinants of advancement, not affirmative action programs or political protest movements (which include the American civil rights movement). His views have been unpopular among African-Americans, but in recent years it has become more acceptable to point to the need for addressing the issue of values and skills."[26]

Conservatives especially, including black conservatives, have been among the most vocal proponents of Sowell's thesis. It has validity in a limited context, but that should not be used to obscure or gloss over other realities such as racism and lack of opportunity for blacks. As Weiner points out:

There is nonetheless much to criticize in Sowell's analysis. Indians and Chinese, for example, have been far more entrepreneurial abroad than at home, at least until recently. Clearly, the structure of the economy mattered, in addition to the culture of the immigrants. Self-selection is also important; the success of migrant communities may reflect the talent of those enterprising few who chose to migrate more than some quality of their culture. Then too, migrant communities that do well in one country do not necessarily do as well in another. Second generation Arabs and Turks appear to be doing better in the United States than they are in France and Germany. Culture in these cases is presumably the same, yet the outcomes differ. The ease with which citizenship is acquired, the acceptance of cultural and religious diversity by the host population, and educational opportunities may be factors in explaining the differences.[27]

One critical test of Sowell's thesis of cultural capital is the success of African immigrants in the United States in spite of the fact that they come from cultures that are supposedly paralyzed by inertia in terms of progress compared to most round the globe. Many conservatives acknowledge the fact that Africans are not only mentally deficient but are also the most backward people in the world.

Yet, somehow, in spite of all that - lack of cultural capital, limited financial resources, and may be even mental deficiency or limited mental capacity many people believe black Africans are known for more than anybody else - black Africans managed to become one of the most successful immigrant groups in the United States. In Britain, they were the most educated group by the 1990s, surpassing the Chinese who earlier topped the list, and other groups including successful Indians and Pakistanis and the native Britons themselves, as reported by the London *Times*.

And in the United States, as pointed out by *The Economist*, African immigrants ranked fourth in terms of median household income among the foreign born, right next to some of the most competitive groups: East Indians who ranked first, followed by Filipinos, the Japanese, and then Africans.[28]

But who would have thought African immigrants would do better than the invincible Orientals - Koreans and Vietnamese in terms of household income, considering the profound cultural differences among those groups, with Africans ranking last in every conceivable way virtually with no cultural capital to invest, according to conventional wisdom? That is without even mentioning their low IQ of 70, on average, which is considered retarded in terms of IQ definition. And since a dynamic culture, so essential to progress, is a product of intelligence, how have Africans - people with meager intellect and static cultures - managed to surpass genetically superior Orientals nd Europeans in median household income in the United States, and in educational achievement in Britain?

What accounts for the economic retardation of African Americans - black Americans - who are a people genetically related to Africans more than anybody else? It can't be low intelligence; untold numbers of American blacks, in spite of racial discrimination, surpass millions of whites in many areas of life: in school, at work, and elsewhere. The evidence is everywhere, with blacks excelling in all fields. And they have been doing so for many years even before affirmative action was instituted in the 1970s. In fact, there was a large middle class among blacks in the United States long before affirmative action. Nor can superior intelligence of whites account for the success of whites when non-whites including immigrants besides Asians surpass them.

Why has white superior intelligence not enabled white people to outperform non-white immigrants in the economic arena where intellectual ability is also critical to success? As reported by *The Economist*: "Among non-refugee immigrants of working age, those between 15 and 64, the percentage on welfare is lower than for the native-born. The same pattern holds true for unemployment....After ten years in America, legal immigrants have higher than average incomes....In general, foreign born Americans [including African immigrants] do extremely well."[29]

Is it because their cultures are superior to that of native-born Americans including whites who constitute the vast majority of the American population? If their cultures are superior, so is their intelligence, including the intelligence of "retarded" Africans, since culture is a product of intelligence. But that is a concession white America will never make, especially regarding Africans who supposedly lack both dynamic culture and intelligence, as much as their black American cousins do.

Conservatives insist that blacks lack culture or values conducive to achievement; which, by logical extension, also means blacks lack intelligence. For, why would intelligent people fail to develop a dynamic culture that will help them cope with their environment and facilitate progress? One might be tempted to conclude, as Sowell has, that "there is something there, whatever its origin might be," as he put it, about the difference in IQs between blacks and whites as well as Asians and members of other races - implying the difference is genetic in origin.

Whether we like it or not, we must face the uncomfortable fact that there is indeed a 15-point difference in IQ scores between blacks and whites that has persisted through the years - for almost 100 years now since World War I - and which so far seems impossible to erase, for whatever reason. Even liberals, black and white, concede that much. It is also true that IQ tests *generally*, but not *specifically*, predict how an individual who has taken the test is going to do in school, contrary to what critics of those tests say, that the scores mean nothing in terms of future academic performance.

But the tests really do *not* and can *not* measure intelligence because they do *not*, and can *not*, measure *all* of it. For example, wisdom is a form of intelligence, compassion is also a form of intelligence, something Herrnstein and Murray as well as others don't acknowledge, or simply deny, since neither can be measured by IQ tests; as much as they deny a host of other abilities including the ability to draw or compose music as forms of intelligence; why Mozart or Beethoven, or Litz who is also said to be the best piano player who ever lived, and others be considered geniuses eludes me, if musical ability is not a form of intelligence. Yet, it can *not* be measured by IQ tests.

Critics say all that is just talent, not intelligence. Yet, one wonders why talent is not a form of intelligence much as its use and expression entails intellectual ability. Is wisdom really just talent? Intuition is also a form of intelligence. Yet, IQ tests, in spite of their alleged comprehensive capability, can *not* measure that anymore than they can measure a person's potential ability to succeed in business, in the professions and in life in general.

All that is intelligence, contrary to what *The Bell Curve* says; so is leadership ability, and so is creativity. Creativity includes the ability to draw and compose music, not just the ability to invent, an area in which black people are considered to be deficient or totally incompetent. Still, it is a critical component of intelligence no one has been able able to even estimate, let alone measure, just as no one has been able to measure patience, compassion, or the ability to lead or get along with people.

We can even employ a linguistic criterion here, to try and understand the scope of human intelligence. In everyday language, from the common man on the street to the people in the professions, we say a person who doesn't know how to get along with people is stupid. He is stupid regardless of how high his IQ is. A stupid person is not an intelligent person. He lacks common sense and other attributes of intelligence including the ability to reason well. Such an individual may be intelligent in some areas, but inarticulate, doltish, or plain "dumb" in others. So is someone who lacks compassion. For example, laughing at the physically or mentally disabled, or the poor, is not a sign of intelligence. But people do that all the time, including those considered to be highly intelligent.

Intelligence tests do not measure intelligence because nobody really knows what intelligence is, especially in terms of its scope and depth. For example, black people in Africa are said to have the lowest IQs in the world - at the retarded level - scoring less than 70 on average. Yet, intelligence experts are unable to explain how these "retarded" black Africans are able to do so well in school including top American and European universities where many of them not only excel academically - far surpassing whites - but crown their careers as university professors in *all* fields including engineering, nuclear physics, mathematics, law, medicine, chemistry, biology, computer science, philosophy and much more.

If you don't believe it, just do a random or systematic search of the faculty members at some of the world's leading universities and other academic and research institutions. Be prepared for a surprise. I know some of them.

Some of my African schoolmates in the United States ended up as professors; others as lawyers, doctors and engineers. For example, when I was a student at Wayne State University in Detroit in the early and mid-seventies, there were only two black students working on their Ph.D's in physics.

Both were black Africans: John Muhanji from Kenya and Emmanuel Sendezera from Malawi. Sendezera ended up as a physics professor, not only in the United States but in South Africa where he also taught physics at the highest-rated English-speaking academic institution, the University of the Witwatersrand, and at other schools. Yet physics is one of those subjects black people supposedly cannot handle well, if at all.

In many countries today, not only are there African professors in all academic disciplines in major universities; they are some of the best. And that includes black American professors who are also African. What are they doing teaching in those institutions of higher learning if they are members of a "retarded" race, with an average IQ of 70 - 85? And if they have high IQs, what kind of IQs did their parents have, or how can parents who belong to a "retarded" race produce children with high IQs, hence high intelligence? What kind of genes do they have that set them apart from their own parents from whom they are supposed to have inherited those genes? And since they are black themselves, why would their genes be so different from those of fellow blacks who are supposed to be retarded?

The argument may be advanced that no one denies there are individual Africans with high IQs. But it is also a fact that retarded people usually have retarded children. And Africans are, on average, considered "retarded." Yet, untold numbers of their offspring are not mental weaklings as demonstrated by their academic performance in Africa and abroad. In pointing out the miserable performance of blacks on IQ tests, Sowell is undoubtedly being cited by racists as proof of an honest black scholar who admits to the mental deficiencies and genetic inferiority of his own people. But it proves nothing of the sort, although such candor has made him a pariah to the civil rights establishment, hence a hero among white conservatives. He is also critical of black leaders for opposing publication of IQ test results. As he states in his book *Race and Culture*:

The concentration of recent and bitter controversies on black-white differences has led to a banning of group IQ tests in some American cities and to widespread reluctance to publish such data. This has occurred at a time when a rising socioeconomic level among black Americans might lead to an expectation of a rise of IQ levels.

The test scores of black students on the Scholastic Aptitude Test have in fact begun to rise and, since standardized test results tend to correlate with one another, an inference might be made about a corresponding rise in black IQs. But the ban on IQ testing, and pressure against publication or discussion of interracial IQ difference, makes it unlikely that this inference can be tested in the near future.

Ironically, black political leaders and spokesmen are among the strongest supporters of this suppression of evidence. The taboo against discussing race and IQ has...had the perverse effect of freezing an existing majority of testing experts in favor of a belief that IQ differences are influenced by genetics.[30]

Sowell says an improvement in the socio-economic status of blacks might also lead to an improvement in their IQ scores. Yet, he concedes that socio-economic factors have not proven to be the prime determinant in IQ differences between blacks and whites. An inference from a corresponding rise in black IQs - due to improved socio-economic status among blacks - cannot be made anymore than it already has.

Tests have consistently shown through the years that whites and Asians from poor families score higher than blacks from high-income families, an empirical observation whose validity he concedes. He cites other cases: "Blacks tend to score lower than whites on a variety of aptitude, academic achievement, and job tests, but even when comparing blacks and whites with the same test scores, the subsequent performance of blacks tends to be lower, whether academically or on the job. This includes academic performance in colleges, law schools, and medical schools, as well as job performance in the civil service and the Air force."[31]

That is even more disturbing, since it goes beyond IQ testing to include not only performance in school but also at work. Blacks lag behind in all those areas, as studies show. But *why* that is the case is an entirely different matter, given the inscrutable ways of nature. There is simply no single explanation, as proponents of the genetic theory such as Arthur Jensen, would have us believe.

It is true, the differences are real. And they cannot be explained or understood by claiming that the differences do not exist. Denial is an implicit admission that blacks are indeed genetically inferior to whites and people of other races.

And the differences wil not go away simply because one denies their existence. As Sowell points out: "When the Chinese tested in Hong Kong, Singapore, Boston, New York, and San Francisco repeatedly show a superior sense of spatial conception, it is difficult to deny that there is something there, whatever its origin might be. Professor Jensen believes that the origin is genetic."[32]

It is findings like that, which imply, although they do not prove, there is a genetic component involved in the superior performance of members of other racial groups that have some blacks worried. This occurs when they see that neither improved standard of living nor passage of time helps them boost their performance on intelligence tests. As Sowell states: "Time in itself guarantees no progress....Black soldiers in World War II scored further behind white soldiers than in World War I."[33]

Nor is such poor performance confined to blacks in the United States, or fully explained in terms of cultural bias against American blacks when it comes to abstract questions that seem to be particularly difficult for black people in general, no matter where they come from:

Questions involving three-dimensional conceptions of space, for example, tend to be especially difficult for African youngsters and also for Jamaicans....In the United States, the Chinese did better than either Jews or blacks on spatial conceptions.

Differences in spatial perceptions have been linked empirically to differences in body chemistry Whether these in turn are linked to genetic differences, and whether these differ significantly by race, are separate questions.

Considering how relatively recently in its long history Western civilization acquired its current conception of three-dimensional perspective, it can hardly be surprising that similar concepts are not uniformly perceived within or between cultures.[34]

That seems to be a plausible explanation for the differences in spatial conceptions and perceptions between Africans and members of other racial groups. But what about American blacks who, although genealogically and historically related - to varying degrees - to Africans, have internalized Western culture and values after being separated from their African cousins for so long? They still *don't* do well on spatial conceptions and perceptions just like their African relatives don't, including their little cousins in Africa - and Jamaica - who did poorly on the test.

The question is *why* they don't do well on those tests. If the question is cultural, as this writer believes it is, it must be narrowed to which particular aspects of culture are responsible for the poor performance of blacks on IQ tests in general. That is because culture, as it is being currently used as an explanation in a comprehensive way, has not provided a complete answer to the mystery; a point underscored by Sowell:

Low overrall test scores for particular groups are often blamed on 'cultural bias' in the tests, and in particular on the use of words or information more likely to be familiar to some groups, such as white, middle-class test takers in the United States....

But most critics who argue this way often fail to ask whether in fact it is these kinds of questions that account for the low overall scores of groups who do poorly. Almost invariably, low-scoring groups do their worst on non-verbal questions, on abstractions that do not require middle-class vocabulary on information....Black-white mental test score differences are likewise greatest on abstract questions.[35]

That is the area in which blacks, in general, are most handicapped. And it may be the reason why black America, like black Africa, has not produced many scientists and inventors, although black people don't lack creative ability critical to invention as demonstrated, for example, by their scientific inventions in many different fields especially in the United States, however limited the contribution to the pool of scientific knowledge. Creative ability also is demonstrated by blacks in music and other areas; for example, it is impossible to have artistic ability without a fully developed creative faculty.

All that mental activity is originality that entails conception of ideas at a high level of abstraction: when one composes music, for example, or creates something entirely from his or her own imagination. Black people do that all the time, despite their alleged low intelligence, as specious IQ authorities claim. Empirical evidence is nonetheless disturbing on IQ scores for blacks round the globe, not just in the United States:

> In Jamaica, where IQs average well below normal, the lowest performance was on the least verbal test....Low-scoring groups tend to do their worst on nonverbal and noninformational - i.e. abstract - questions....West African boys 'obviously became bored' with abstract questions, according to observers, and their scores fell when tested on such items....
>
> American Negro soldiers tested during World War I tended to 'lapse into inattention and almost into sleep' during abstract tests (just like their little cousins in Africa), according to observers....It makes no real difference whether poor performances in abstract thinking are due to neglect or to lack of capacity. In either case it has serious ramifications in a scientific and technological society.[36]

Richard Herrstein and Charles Murray articulate their position from the same perspective Thomas Sowell does, although they have gone further than that in terms of providing data on IQ scores by blacks in the United States and in Africa. As they state in *The Bell Curve*:

> The difference in test scores between African-Americans and European-Americans as measured in dozens of reputable studies has converged on approximately a one standard deviation difference for several decades. Translated into centiles, this means that the average white person tests higher than about 84 percent of the population of blacks and that the average black person tests higher than about 16 percent of the population of whites....(One) line of evidence pointing toward a genetic factor in cognitive ethnic differences is that blacks and whites differ most on the tests that are the best measures of g, or general intelligence....The black mean is commonly given as 85 (almost at the retarded level), and the white mean as 100 (average intelligence), and the standard deviation as 15....

One reason for th(e) reluctance to discuss (IQ) averages is that blacks in Africa, including urbanized blacks with secondary educations, have obtained extremely low scores....The median black African IQ (is) 75 (which is retarded), about ten points lower than the current figure for American blacks (which is slightly above the retarded level)....Where other date are available, the stimates of the black African IQ fall at least that low and, in some instances, even lower.[37]

Low intelligence is a serious problem, of course. Pity to those who have it, is the attitude of many people. Compounding the problem for black people, who generally have "low" intelligence, is their poor performance in abstract thinking as demonstrated by Sowell in his work *Race and Culture*. All that definitely reduces chances of succeeding in life in general. It limits employment opportunities in a technologically advanced society like the United States. It can have a devastating impact on one's overall well-being even in terms of social interaction, although that is not the reason why a disproportionately large number of blacks are unemployed.

They are denied jobs mainly because they are black. Many of the jobs that blacks are told they are not qualified for do not require comprehension or articulation of ideas at a high abstract level as does employment in scientific research. Statistics show that whites who get better jobs than blacks are not necessarily more intelligent or even better qualified than blacks, but are given those jobs simply because they are white.

There is no question that the implications of IQ tests and racial IQ differences are enormous; for example, in terms of social policy formulated to justify group preferences collectively defined as affirmative action, while at the same time society tries to achieve equality purely on the basis of individual merit. If blacks are indeed intellectually inferior to whites and others, then by any objective criterion, they don't deserve equality in education and employment. They should be relegated to the sidelines, discriminated against and segregated from members of superior races - Caucasian and Mongoloid - however objectionable such a policy may be on moral or ontological grounds.

Those are the dire consequences of manipulating IQ tests in life. And that is what *The Bell Curve* is all about. The work has profound implications, and white conservatives and racists knew it when they applauded Richard Herrnstein and Charles Murray soon after their book was published in March 1994.

The racist implications of IQ test results have blacks and others worried, and justifiably so. They don't want them published because publication of such data will, to the delight of racists, conservatives, and partisans of the genetic theory, prove that blacks do indeed have weak genes and are therefore inferior to whites and Asians.

But, to the dismay of the racist-conservative-partisan intellectual fraternity members, if the IQ level among blacks begins to rise, however slowly, they should be willing to publish the results proving that they have been wrong and indeed racist. Or, they should support publication of studies that give a full explanation for the difference in IQ scores even if the 15-point gap persists.

They should answer the question around which the IQ debate revolves: What do the differences in IQ scores really mean, besides their pontificated answers that blacks are less intelligent than members of other races? That is scholarship. And it must be pursued vigorously instead of suppressing evidence of what has been empirically verified.

But right now, there is no full explanation for the difference. Therefore, no conclusion should be drawn from the data currently available, as racists and others have done, until the study is completed. For example, the outstanding performance of inner-city students at the Westside Preparatory School in Chicago founded by Marva Collins, a black woman, is persuasive evidence that the study on black/white differences in intellectual capacity is inconclusive. And that has put many racists on the defensive, a significant number of whom are conservative.

Herrnstein and Murray, of course, don't give credence to reports - even to the evidence - that black students are indeed doing that well at Marva Collins' school or anywhere else in the few schools in the inner-cities where, it has been reported, the academic performance of black students has dramatically improved.[38] And the reason is simple why the two conservatives are skeptical about the reports. They simply refuse to see blacks as intelligent, a belief shared by the majority of whites according to polls.[39] Tom Wicker also gives an example of whites who have such blind faith in their innate ability and intellectual superiority over blacks in his book *Tragic Failure: Racial Integration in America*:

Ronald Ferguson (a black professor at Harvard) recalls an instance at Northwestern University when a white man told Ferguson's classmate Glenn Loury (who is also black and from the inner city in Chicago) that a certain book on mathematics would be over Loury's head.

Loury,[40] now an economics professor at Boston University, quickly demonstrated that the book, to him, was relatively elementary. Ferguson recalls that the surprised white was embarrased - and resented the exposure of his stereotype of a black man who wouldn't understand math.[41]

Some white professors also harbor such racist stereotypes. When black students excel, these professors believe the students cheated by stealing the information or creating crib sheets from which to write their essay exams. When they are presented with evidence to the contrary, they *still* refuse to believe black students are as good as their writing or research demonstrated. Wicker cites one such case:

Vice Chancellor Harold Wallace of the University of North Carolina (UNC) recalls the case of a black student whose white professor had accused her of plagiarism. The woman took her case to Wallace, also an African-American, but the white professor was convinced of her innocence only when presented with examples of outstanding writing she had done in high school and in other UNC courses. The white professor admitted to Wallace that he 'didn't think black students could write like that.'[42]

That is the position of the poisonous writing of Herrnstein and Murray, *The Bell Curve*. They maintain that blacks are locked in place, at the bottom, because of their inferior genes. Any dramatic improvement in their academic performance comparable to whites, as demonstrated by Marva Collins' students, is laughable because nothing of the sort has happened; it's totally out of the question - and against nature, is their position. They dismiss such reports simply as "stories too good to be true," as they put in *The Bell Curve*:

Accounts of phenomenal success stories in education - the inner-city school that suddenly excels as the result of a new program or a new teacher - are a perennial fixture of American journalism. Are they true?....

Claims for long-term academic improvement, let alone increases in cognitive functioning, typically fade as soon as hard questions begin to be

204

asked. A case in point is Chicago's Marva Collins, who gained national attention with claims that her shoestring-budget inner-city school, launched in 1975, was turning out students who blew the lid off standardized tests and were heading to the best universities.

Between the age of 5 and 10, she claimed, her pupils, deemed 'unteachable' in regular schools, were reading Plato, Aristotle, Chaucer, Shakespeare, and Tolstoy, according to stories in the popular media....She was asked by both Presidents Reagan and Clinton to become secretary of education. She continues to train large numbers of teachers in her methods. Are her celebrated anecdotes borne out by data? We do not know. Despite years of publicity about Marva Collins, we can find no hard evidence.[43]

What better evidence than the students themselves, whom she taught, and others she continued to teach? Why would other teachers continue to go to her to learn her methods if her methods were not working? The teachers must have been impressed by the results from other teachers taught by her. That by itself, let alone the students she has taught already, is evidence enough that her methods do work.

Still, with finesse, Herrnstein and Murray give credence to none of that. Their chaffing skepticism is understandable, although unjustified, considering the position they have taken on this controversial subject of the nature of intelligence; and about which, frankly speaking, they know very little since they are not geneticists by training but social scientists: Herrnstein a psychologist, and Murray, a sociologist.

Next we are going to have other social scientists and barbers claiming to know brain surgery. Even geneticists themselves *still* don't know much about the nature of intelligence and intelligence itself.

Yet Herrnstein and Murray remained unpertubed as they pursued their research on intelligence. Theirs is a position that fits their dialectic paradigm. For, why would these invidious investigators believe that black students had, all of a sudden, gone from being dumb to being intelligent, on par with whites, when black students were born with a genetic "lock" keeping them at the bottom of the intellectual gene pool? As the two conservative authors contend in their book, a person's IQ is basically stable throughout his life without dramatic shifts in either direction - unless a catastrophe strikes. Only in the wake of such a denouement is there a plunge. They state in their book:

After about the age of 10, the IQ score is essentially stable....On the comparatively rare occasions when large changes in IQ are observed, there is usually an obvious explanation. The child had been bedridden with a long illness before one of the tests, for example, or there was severe emotional disturbance at the time of one or both of the tests.[44]

What about the other extreme when IQ scores skyrocket? Since a person's IQ is essentially the same throughout his life due to genetics as the two conservative scholars claim in their tome, *The Bell Curve*, that is bound to become a reference text among white racists, how can there be a dramatic improvement in his intelligence without undergoing genetic mutation into an intellectually superior being? When IQ scores go up, as it has been reported in many cases, then a person's IQ is not fixed, or "locked" in place, at the bottom, as the IQ of blacks is supposed to be.

Even if it increases slightly, that also deletes a rigid definition of IQ being stable. There is room for improvement, and improvement *does* occur. While it is generally true that a mature, older person who is short seldom grows late in life, that also is not a fixed rule. It has happened before, and it probably happens more than people realize. So it is with genes. They are indicators, not absolutes.

Genetics is not an infallible science or truth. Genes do not play a dominant role in determining one's intelligence potential or any other potential. IQ standards simply create the illusion that some people are superior or inferior to others. Standards can be modified or formulated to reflect a more realistic assessment of one's potential across the spectrum, unlike IQ tests which are structured in such a way that there is no room for such improvement or modification, especially since there are verifiable reports of increases in IQ scores.

In fact, there are confirmed reports of dramatic increases in IQ scores. Herrnstein and Murray discuss what they call the Flynn effect, named after Professor James Flynn of New Zealand who studied dramatic increases in IQ over several decades throughout the world. The two authors concede in *The Bell Curve* that such increases did occur, but attribute them to environment, not to genes, thus inadvertently undermining their argument on absolute genetics. As they state in their book:

206

The tendency for IQ scores to drift upward as a function of years since standardization has now been substantiated, primarily by Flynn, in many countries and on many IQ tests besides the Stanford-Binet. In some countries, the upward drift since World War II has been as much as a point a year for some spans of years.

The national averages have in fact changed by amounts that are comparable to fifteen or so IQ points separating whites and blacks in America. To put it another way, on average, whites today may differ in IQ from whites, say, two generations ago as much as whites today differ from blacks today. Given their size and speed, the shifts in time necessarily have been due more to changes in the environment than to changes in the genes.[45]

In view of all these dramatic increases in IQ scores by as much as 15 points due to the environment, what makes a person's IQ stable throughout his life as the two authors and others claim? Also, what makes genes the prime determinant in black/white IQ differences? And why would whites today differ in IQ scores from whites two generations ago if genes are, indeed, the absolute judge of intellectual power? Are their genes different? They are all white, aren't they? So, don't they have the same genes as white people who are intellectually superior to blacks?

And since genes determine intelligence, what kind of genes do whites today have which their kith-and-kin didn't have two generations ago? In fact, you are talking about their parents and grandparents as well, including aunts and uncles and other genetically close relatives within that time span.

The genetic argument regarding black/white IQ differences implies that people in industrialized countries - where quantum leaps in IQ scores have taken place - have, somehow, miraculously, been transformed into genetically superior beings. Why not, since IQ is determined primarily by genes as Herrnstein and Murray insist in their book? Yet, they reject that very same argument. No, there have been no changes in genes to account for the phenomenal increase in IQ scores in those countries, they say.

Well, since dramatic improvement in IQ scores can be explained otherwise, and not solely on the basis of genes or as a function of genes, why don't they also reject the genetic argument in the case of black/white IQ differences that they invoke throughout their book as the only valid explanation for the 15-point gap in IQs between blacks and whites?

If people in other countries can boost their IQs by as much as 15 points, because of the environment and not genetic improvement, why not blacks?

Herrnstein and Murray offer a simplistic answer: The reason why blacks can't do that is because they are black. It is a racist argument. Otherwise they would not be hanging on to the genetic argument with bulldog tenacity to explain the 15-point gap in IQ scores between blacks and whites.

In spite of the concession that IQ scores have risen dramatically in the general population of several countries not due to genes but due to environmental factors, Herrnstein and Murray maintain: "The stability of IQ over time in the general population has been studied for decades, and the main findings are not in much dispute among psychometricians."[46] They share that position with the psychometricians.

Yet, they are unable to explain what makes their argument valid in countries where IQ scores have gone up dramatically in recent years, as they themselves admit, due to factors other than genes, while insisting on the universal application of the genetic criterion or argument and at the same time denying it. As Jay Ambrose stated in *The Washington Times*:

Many, while giving lip-service to IQ tests, have nevertheless acted as if they say something definitive and immutable about people, one example being the estimable Charles Murray. In the 1994 book, *The Bell Curve*, the social scientist wrote with another author [Richard Herrnstein] that public policy should take account of IQ-test differences between whites and blacks.

Mr. Murray has now had his comeuppance. His theory has been shattered by something known as the Flynn effect, an extraordinary finding reported this year [1996] that IQ scores in industrialized nations have shot skyward in recent decades.

If intelligence were strictly innate as many psychologists have contended, a rise of this size would not be possible. Geneticists concur on that much, and one conceivable conclusion, then, is that people are being made dramatically smarter by environmental factors. That would mean IQ tests primarily indicate intellectual development at a given moment, as Binet suggested, and not a predetermined learning ability. Or possibly people are getting better at taking the tests and not in the scope and creativity of their intellects, which is a way of saying IQ-test-results should be viewed as meaningless.[47]

Murray and Herrnstein admit: "There are things we do not yet understand about the relation between IQ and intelligence, which may be relevant for comparisons not just across times but also across cultures and races."[48] Why write that kind of book then, and rush to conclusions that blacks are intellectually inferior to whites and members of other races for genetic reasons more than anything else?

Their confession that "there are things we do not yet understand about the relation between IQ and intelligence" is obviously no more than lip service and a preemptive measure to deflect criticism of their pseudo-scientific work as racist. They say the exact opposite throughout the book that intelligence is a function of genes, nothing else. Blacks are dumb, stuck at the bottom. Case closed, no way out.

Yet evidence does, indeed, show that black people are comparable to whites in intelligence, since intelligence is heavily dependent on the environment and other factors for members of all races, although the genetic component also plays a critical role. As Ambrose points out:

> The relatively unpublicized increase in scores, first revealed by a New Zealand academic names James R. Flynn, is a body blow to the supposed science of intelligence measurement....IQ tests are less successful in the professions and business and other non-academic pursuits. Might it be, then, that academic giftedness is but one kind of intelligence?....
>
> What do we ordinarily mean when we say someone is intelligent? Perhaps we want to convey that someone is quick-witted or extremely alert to his surroundings. But we know at the same time that some people come to their conclusions slowly but profoundly. Are they dumb?[49]

Obviously they are considered "dumb." People talk about them being being "slow," implying "they're not too swift upstairs," the same way they talk about the retarded and others of limited intellectual ability or who are considered to be mentally deficient. But that is not a very intelligent judgment. It discounts wisdom as a form of intelligence, and caution as sign of wisdom and intellectual calculation.

You are being wise, hence intelligent, when you take your time, weighing pros and cons, to make a decision you don't have to regret later, had you made it in a hurry. It reduces mental capacity to one dimension: speed. Simply because your are quick, or swift, in giving answers, does not mean that you are also profound in thinking. Intellectual depth has nothing to do with swiftness.

Nor is it very intelligent for intelligence tests and their supporters to give a definitive answer when they cannot measure business acumen or the excellence of a lawyer and success in different professions. For example, IQ tests cannot tell whether or not a student excellent in math and physics is going to be a good let alone an excellent engineer; or whether or not a recent medical school graduate is going to be a good doctor even if he graduated with honors or earned other forms of academic distinction. Nor, on the other hand, can the tests reveal a person who is a failure in school is also going to be a failure in life in other areas outside academic work.

It takes intelligence, *and motivation*, to do all that: to be a successful businessman, an excellent defense lawyer or prosecutor, a skilled doctor, a great house builder or farmer, or parent. The list goes on and on.

Yet, proponents of the genetic theory, putting a premium on IQ scores, remain undaunted as they persevere in propagating the myth of black inferiority. And it is no surprise that a large number of them are conservatives who include academics such as Arthur Jensen, William Shockley, Phillippe Rushton, besides Richard Herrnstein and Charles Murray and others who try to hide their racial prejudice against blacks behind the wall of scholarship that is twisted to justify their racist position.

They use scholarship to win credibility for their racist views many would have dismissed as rubbish. For example, what do anatomical contrasts have to do with intelligence? Rushton excels in that area, delving into "intricate" details about the differences in reproductive organs of blacks - especially of black men - and those of whites and members of other races. He also claims blacks have the smallest brain. They ignore the high number of blacks who excel in their fields and outperform many whites in different intellectually demanding tasks, despite their "small brain" as blacks.

Even they themselves, Herrnstein and Murray, do admit in their book, *The Bell Curve*, that one test alone has shown that there are more than 100,000 blacks in the United States today who have IQs of 125 and above, signifying very high intelligence. They include those with IQs of 140 and above.[50] A score of 140 and

210

above is considered to be genius-level IQ. Yet, in spite of their "small" and "dull" brains, you find many such blacks. And they outperform whites with "bigger" and "sharper" brains.

They also claim blacks, because of their low intelligence, top the charts in terms of reproductivity. What about the Chinese, for example, acclaimed for their high intelligence like the other Orientals? China has the largest population in the world. And it continues to explode despite official government policy limiting the number of babies a couple may have.

Also look at India, Indonesia, and Japan. Their population growth has skyrocketed through the years. And they have an excessive number of people per square mile, far more than what experts consider to be appropriate. The same case may be made for Korea, North and South, and Vietnam. The people of all these countries, with the exception of India, are defined as Oriental. They are also acclaimed as the most intelligent people in the world, besides Jews.

Yet India, a non-Oriental country, equals the citizens of these countries in terms of IQ scores, professional job holders - especially in the telecommunications and medical fields as well as in computer science - and in creativity. How is it that these non-Orientals from the Indian sub-continent have done so well? And how is it that members of African ethnic groups such as the Igbo and the Yoruba are known throughout the West - including the United States - as among the most highly educated people, excelling in all fields and even surpassing many whites, if Africans are indeed not as intelligent as people of other races?

And if the high IQs of Orientals, and Indians, are correlated to population growth - the higher the IQ, the smaller the population - since population control is a function of intelligence as Rushton and others claim it is, why have they failed to control it? And does IQ really determine birth rate, as Herrnstein and Murray claim in their book that blacks - since they have low IQs - multiply faster and far more than whites do, as clearly demonstrated by the high birth rates in the ghetto across the United States?

Now, contrast all that with the "dumb" Africans whose countries are technically underpopulated. Most African countries have fewer than 10 million people. And they have vast expanses of territory with uninhabited arable land. Their low intelligence and

211

abnormal reproductive organs should have produced exactly the opposite.

It is superstition misrepresented as scholarship by these racist conservative scholars, as clearly demonstrated by Herrnstein and Murray when they invoke "scholarship" to defend Rushton:

J. Philippe Rushton, a developmental psychologist at the University of Western Ontario, argues that the differences in the average of intelligence test scores among East Asians, blacks, and whites are not primarily genetic but part of a complex of racial differences that includes such variables as brain size, genital size, rate of sexual maturation, length of menstrual cycle, frequency of sexual intercourse..., hormone levels..., marital stability..., law abidingness, and mental health.

For each variable, Rushton has concluded, the three races - Mongoloid, Caucasoid, and Negroid - fall in a certain order, with the average Caucasoid in the middle and the other two races on one side or the other....Contrary to popular belief, on the proposition whether brain size is correlated with IQ, the evidence strongly favors the pros and cons, even after correcting for stature....

Rushton's work is not that of a crackpot or a bigot, as many of his critics are given to charging. Nor are we sympathetic with Rushton's academic colleagues or the politicians in Ontario who have called for his preemptory dismissal from a tenured professorship. His work is plainly science. As science, there is nothing wrong with Rushton's work in principle.[51]

Herrnstein and Murray also invoke the "infallibility" of science to "prove" that blacks are intellectually inferior to whites because on average blacks score 15 points below whites on IQ tests. Because of that they have triggered an avalanche of criticism from many quarters, especially from the academic community. As reported by *The Economist*: "Enraged academics have spent the past two years producing rebuttals. So far the results are disappointing."[52]

That is not surprising. Given the complex nature of the subject they are addressing, one can expect some of the rebuttals to be disappointing. That is because no one understands the subject of intelligence that well; not Jensen, not Shockley, Herrnstein, Murray, Rushton or anybody else.

The human mind is a universe unto itself, deep, mysterious, and unfathomable. Much of what we know about it, is very little knowledge, and the rest nothing more than sheer speculation. *The Bell Curve* may sound convincing. But that is because it has addressed only one facet of human intelligence: IQ. Yet, even that remains beyond the full grasp of intelligence experts; they know only so much, or, so little. Hence their confession that IQ tests have limitations, and that they are valid only within given contexts.

It is true that the 15-point gap in IQ on average between blacks and whites, is real. *The Bell Curve* goes to great lengths to confirm that as a valid indicator of the difference in intellectual capacity between members of the two races. But it does not mean that the conclusion is valid.

For all their functional utility in predicting performance in school, IQ tests are simply not comprehensive enough to deal with such a complex subject as intelligence in all its facets and have, in fact, never been promoted as comprehensive analytical tools even by some of its strongest proponents. Simply because someone has an outstanding academic record as a law student does not necessarily mean the potential/future attorney will be a good lawyer, let alone an excellent one.

Yet by identifying this future barrister as a top law student, IQ tests imply that he is going to be one. What about the law student who earned lower grades, yet turned out to be a better judicial advocate, and may be even an excellent one? It is the *same* field, law, in which he excelled as a legal practitioner. And it is the same field in which he did not excel in school.

It takes superior intelligence to be an excellent lawyer, not just an excellent student. Yet, intelligence tests do not address that aspect of intelligence: excellence in one's field at work and in the future.

Instead, these examinations are quick to emphasize the difference in intellectual capacity between the races, despite all the evidence to the contrary, at work where blacks excel and even surpass whites in their fields, in life in general, and even in school.

What we are to make of the 15-point difference in IQ between blacks and whites is the central issue, without politicizing it or rushing to conclusions about a phenomenon that mortals have yet to comprehend and probably never will. The essence of intelligence is as elusive as the nature of God. Perhaps Canadian psychologist Donald Hebb put it best when he asked which contributes more to intelligence, heredity or environment: it is like asking which contributes more to the area of a field - its length or its width? "Neither can contribute anything by itself."[53]

But even if one day scientific research will show that the difference in IQ between blacks and whites is genetic, and whites are more "intelligent," the findings will *still* not necessarily be conclusive. In many areas of scientific inquiry, subsequent research has shown that what is science today is superstition tomorrow. Science is not perfect. It cannot and never will be perfect because of the nature of man.

We are mere mortals, with limitations. We are not endowed with infinite capacity for knowledge, especially on a subject such as intelligence whose study is no less than an attempt to probe the essence of our very being, and of life itself. It is a quest that has baffled mankind since the beginning of time. And it will probably never give us the ultimate answer. Life is a mystery - intelligence its very essence.

Perhaps common sense, more than science, will provide a better answer in this case. IQ experts continue to debate group differences in tests between blacks and whites as well as Asians and others, with blacks at the bottom, rock bottom. Yet, these very same acclaimed authorities admit that there are blacks at *all* levels of IQ, except that they are extremely rare at the highest levels; which is, and probably always will be, inexplicable. It is a mystery.

But if race is indeed a factor in group differences, why is it not just as much a factor in IQ differences between blacks and whites as individuals? A black person is no less black, or a white person any less white, simply because he is an individual or is counted as an individual as opposed to being an an integral part of his racial group whose members are collectively assessed in terms of intellectual capacity, hence IQ. What makes race more important between racial groups than between individuals who belong to different races?

To put it another way, why is race less of a factor between individuals than it is between groups of races? It is the same yardstick, race, that is used to measure differences in IQ between blacks and whites. If black people are genetically inferior to whites and members of other races, and are therefore unable to generate and comprehend ideas at a high level of abstraction, there would not be a *single* black person, *not one*, at the highest levels of IQ.

Nor would there be any black capable of understanding mathematics, physics, biology, chemistry, computer science, philosophy, psychiatry, medicine, law, economics, literature and any other academic subjects all of which entail abstract comprehension.

White people, like the one who told Glenn Loury that one of the college math textbooks was above Loury's head, would be confirmed in their belief that they are intellectually - hence genetically - superior to blacks. Their poor-quality genes would make it impossible for blacks to tackle those subjects since they require superior intelligence and comprehension.

It doesn't even have to be many; only *one* black person is enough to vindicate the whole race for one simple reason: he has the same genes his people have. They are all black. Yet you find, not one, or two or three, but untold numbers of blacks who have distinguished themselves in *all* academic disciplines in the United States before affirmative action - multi-talented Paul Robeson being only one of them - as well as in Africa and elsewhere.

What kind of genes do they have? And what kind of genes do their people, as a racial group, have but who are collectively judged to be intellectually inferior to whites and others?

Black people have performed and continue to perform as well as - and in many cases even better than - whites, and are found at the highest IQ levels. If they are intellectually inferior as Herrnstein and Murray and others claim, then they have no business being up there, rare or not, one or twenty. There would be none. What are these extraordinary representatives of the black race doing in the same league with genetically superior beings, whites? Every white person however dumb and ignorant, because of superior genes, would be able to surpass *all* blacks including black professors and scientists, without exception.

There would not be a single black, however intelligent, surpassing any white, in any field, if race is indeed the determining factor in the distribution of intelligence among human beings. It would be against nature for inferior beings, blacks, to outperform their genetic superiors, whites and other non-blacks. This is simple genetic logic, invalidating the genetic argument about race, yet whose simplicity eludes even some of the best minds among racist scientists and scholars.

There are millions of whites in the United States who do not go far in school, not because they do not have the opportunity to do so, but because they failed academically. At the same time, there are many blacks who not only completed school but excelled in all subjects. There are many whites in college today who are surpassed academically by blacks in the United States, Canada, Australia, Britain, and in other European countries where many African students go to school.

It also happened in South Africa when Afrikaners were in power and black Africans were denied equal opportunity in education and other areas. Whites were astounded by the academic performance of some of the African natives who didn't know "A from B", or one plus one, as Nelson Mandela stated in his book *Long Walk to Freedom*:

> On March 14, [1964 during his treason trial] our first witness was not [Chief Albert] Luthuli but Dr. Wilson Conco. Conco was the son of a Zulu cattle farmer from the beautiful Ixopo district of Natal. In addition to being a practicing physician, he had been one of the founders of the Youth League [of the African National Congress, or ANC], an active participant in the Defiance Campaign, and the treasurer of the ANC.
>
> As a preparation for his testimony, he was asked about his brilliant academic record at the University of the Witswatersrand where he graduated first in his medical school class, ahead of all the sons and daughters of white privilege....
>
> At the end of his testimony, when Conco was cited for some medical achievement, Justice Kennedy [also from Natal] said in Zulu, a language in which he was fluent, '*Sinjalo thina maZulu*,' which means, 'We Zulus are like that.' Dr. Conco proved a calm and articulate witness who reaffirmed the ANC's commitment to nonviolence.[54]

You cannot teach a monkey medicine, let alone expect the money to graduate first in medical school surpassing genetically superior beings, whites. This was the attitude of many whites towards black South Africans, also applied to Conco and others. Based on genetic logic used by proponents of the genetic theory of intelligence who contend that whites are intellectually superior to blacks, the "monkey" (Conco) must have superior genes, surpassing the genes of whites.

The response people like Charles Murray would probably give is that they are talking about group differences: that whites in general score higher than blacks on IQ tests, but, not all whites

216

score higher than all blacks.

They only logical assessment that can be made of this is that whites are not more intelligent than blacks; only some whites score higher on IQ tests than some blacks just as some blacks score higher than some whites, regardless of the numerical proportion. The higher proportion of scorers, among whites or blacks, does not validate the genetic argument about intelligence distribution among the races anymore than it invalidates the counter-argument that race has nothing to do with intelligence; only individual ability, regardless of race, does.

What Herrnstein and Murray as well as others fail or refuse to address is not the issue of race but the reality of individual differences regardless of race, and of the historical role people of European origin, hence whites, have *not* played in the advancement of mankind and human civilization. They were *not* the first to make major contributions to the advancement of knowledge.

One wonders what happened to their superior intelligence. The Chinese, for example, had superior talents in printing, coinage, art, and banking, and invented gunpowder among other things, long before Europeans had achieved much on their own and while they were still wallowing in the intellectual backwater. The Arabs were also ahead of Europeans in mathematics and medicine for centuries.

Black Africans were also ahead of Europeans in a number of areas, including philosophical inquiry in which they could match the best European minds, as clearly evident in the philosophical knowledge so characteristic of traditional African societies that are a repository of wisdom. Science, medicine, thermodynamics, hydraulics and a myriad other advances - from the invention of the wheel to cartography, oceanography, calligraphy, among several - came from the Arab world and the Orient. Europeans, with their "superior" intelligence, were obviously not asleep during all that time.

When Europe started to develop, it did not do so *en masse* or as a single unit of a racially homogeneous society. It developed in defined limits. The Germanic states formed the nation of Germany in the late nineteenth century that became one of the leading nations with its universities which were the best in the world until the 1930s. Yet, it also went through upheavals, torn by war and other conflicts. Italy had its glory realized from the fourteenth to the sixteenth century. England emerged after the fall of the House of Lancaster and became a major power after the Industrial Revolution, yet faced stiff competition from its rivals including Germany and France. France was rocked by civil wars, including the French revolution, although it enjoyed high status during the brief period of its celebrated *philosophes* in the eighteenth century. The continent went through turmoil, with its history marked by successes and failures.

And none of these states matched the prolonged period of prosperity, productivity, and power that filled significant time spans in the Orient, in the Arab world, and even in parts of Africa, until much later.

The genetic theory of intelligence implies the exact opposite: Europeans, hence white people, should have blazed the trail and remained ahead in all fields. Even today, predominantly white nations are facing stiff competition from non-white ones in terms of scientific progress and in other areas because of the high level of intelligence among non-whites including blacks.

People who emphasize academic excellence and study hard succeed no matter what race they belong to. Test scores are marginal, and frequently not a cogent indicator. What is interesting is that test-score differences between blacks and whites are greatest on abstract questions.55 The critical question is: Why do some blacks score higher than whites on abstract questions if they are genetically inferior to whites? It should be impossible for them to do that, or soar that high, just as a duck cannot soar as high as an eagle because of their genetic differences.

Dismissing criticism of people like Arthur Jensen, William Shockely, Philippe Rushton, Richard Herrnstein and Charles Muray as liberal paranoia when they produce works that carry a racist message, however subtle, and especially when the authors are known for their racist views, is an unconscionable defense of racism that should not go unchallenged even at the risk of being called paranoid. Conservatives have earned quite a reputation in that area.

Some black conservatives even try to outdo their white ideological mentors in the mainstream media by invoking the aura of scholarship to sanitize those works as harmless pursuits of knowledge. But the content of those essays, which is not always objective in the tradition of genuine scholarship, does not change the intent, which is to consign blacks to a permanent inferior status in the hierarchy of the races.

It would be not only wrong but dangerous for blacks to have the same kind of jobs as whites - for example as doctors, engineers, judges, and professors - if they are less intelligent than whites. That is *exactly* what Charles Murray, endorsed by others of his ilk, intends to do.

And the central thesis of his treatise makes that clear: black people have weak genes; which explains why they have so low IQs, 85 on average in the United States, a score that is defined not only as low intelligence but close to the retarded level.

Otherwise he and Herrnstein would not be advancing the genetic argument in an effort to explain IQ differences between blacks and whites. Yet the two authors concede in their work: "There are things we do yet understand about the relation between IQ and intelligence, which may be relevant for comparisons across cultures and races."[56]

To their credit, that is an important observation critical to objective inquiry of knowledge, although it is not their intention to do so, since - despite their concession - they at the same dismiss it when they emphatically state: "Cognitive ability is substantially heritable...How much is IQ a matter of genes? In fact, IQ is substantially heritable in the population as a whole....Inherited cognitive ability is extremely important. In life's outcomes, it is more a matter of IQ than anything else about circumstances [for example, racism against a black person is far less important than his IQ for him to succeed in life]. High cognitive ability means that the chances of success in life are affected by genes....Ethnic groups differ intellectually....There are genuine cognitive differences between the races."[57]

It is a thesis that has also been forcefully articulated by Philippe Rushton with regard to blacks in Africa and elsewhere. He went to the University of the Witwatersrand in 1998 to conduct some research which fortified his thesis about the intellectual inferiority of black people. As he states in his article "I.Q.: Why Africa is Africa - and Haiti Haiti":

What critics have objected to - very strongly - is the statement that sub-Saharan Africans have an average IQ of 70. This is, indeed, extremely low. in North America, an IQ of 70 suggests bordeline mental retardation.

Critics of the finding that the average African IQ is 70 say that it simply must be wrong. They insist that biased testing procedures must have been used, even though dozens of separate studies have corroborated the results from East, West, Central, and Southern Africa. For example, one 1992 study carried out for the World Bank reported a random sample of 1,639 adolescents in the West African country of Ghana had an average IQ of 60.

in 1998, I went to Johannesburg, South Africa, to initiate a 5-year series of IQ studies in the university system to determine whether such a low IQ was accurate. I, too, wondered how well all the previous data had been collected, if sufficient care were taken in giving instructions, ensuring motivation, having a quiet room for testing, or giving enough time to complete the tests.

First, I contacted psychologists in the Faculty of Education at the University of the Witwatersrand and together we tested hundreds of students of African, East Indian, White, and East Asian backgrounds, along with those of mixed ancestry, under optimal testing procedures, using culture-reduced tests....We used the Raven's Matrices, one of the best known, well researched, and most widely used of all the culture-reduced tests.

Consisting of 60 diagrammatic puzzles, each with a missing part that the test taker attempts to identify from several choices, it is an excellent measure of the non-verbal component of general intelligence.

Typically, the test is so easy for university students that they do it in less than 20 minutes. We set no time limit for the test. All those being tested were allowed to complete   it.

We found African university students averaged an IQ of 84. In some studies, by other researchers, they have scored lower (IQ=77). In still others of our studies, highly-selected engineering students who took math and science courses in high school scored higher (IQ=103).

Assuming that, like university students elsewhere, the African university students on average score 15 points above the general population, the African general population average of about 70 would appear to be corroborated.

One way to comprehend an IQ of 70 is to think in terms of mental age. For example, for adults an IQ of 70 is equivalent to a mental age of 11 years. So the normal range of mental ages in Africa is from 7 to 16 years, with an average at 11 years.

Eleven-year olds, of course, are not retarded. They can drive cars, build houses, and work in factories - if supervised properly. They can also make war.

In terms of mental age then, the Africans who drop out of primary school correspond to 7-year-olds. Those who get to high school correspond to 11-year-olds.

The top university students we tested correspond to 16- and 17-year-olds. Adult whites, by contrast, have mental ages ranginfd from 11- to 24-years, with an average mental age of 16- to 18-years.

This is an astonishing fact....But it seems to be very difficult for people to

220

grasp. One reason put forward by Arthur Jensen in the G Factor (p. 367 - 9): many sub-70 IQ whites are retarded as a result of in utero misfortunes, with visible deficiencies in motor skills and speech. The majority of sub-70 IQ blacks, in contrast, are technically normal. They appear fully functional.[58]

People of low intelligence at the retarded level, in this case black Africans in general with an average IQ of 70 which is classified as retarded, cannot develop countries, of course. They have the mental capacity of 11-year-olds, as Rushton and other IQ experts claim, and are therefore not mature enough or intelligent enough to handle intellectually demanding tasks. As that great humanitarian and benevolent missionary Albert Schweitzer said:

The Negro is a child, and with children nothing can be done without authority. We must, therefore, so arrange the circumstances of daily life that my natural authority can find expression. With regard to the Negro, then, I have coined the formula: 'I am your brother, it is true, but your elder brother.'[59]

That is the logic of the genetic argument of intelligence: No country can develop without a high IQ among the general population, since development is a product of intelligence. And it sounds very convincing. But is that really the reason why African countries are not developed?

Africans have enough intelligence, in fact more than enough to develop their countries as clearly demonstrated in their everyday lives at work, in school, and in the professions where they are found in all fields. High IQ should be taken into account, as general intelligence of the general population critical to national development, but not to the exclusion of other factors.

African countries are capable of producing a critical mass of high-skilled people and much-needed manpower without which a country cannot develop, and they have produced many such highly educated and well-trained people. But many of them have also left their countries because of other factors: lack of opportunities, bad leadership, and bad policies, factors which are responsible for the brain drain. And there is, of course, continued exploitation of Africa by the industrialized nations of the West more than any other. But that is the subject of another book.

Suffice it to say, the alleged mental inferiority of Africans and their cousins in the United States, African Americans, and others elsewhere, is used by racists - including those in academia - to justify discrimination as a function of public policy to deny black people opportunity across the spectrum.

That is why conservatives say racism is no longer a major problem in the United States, with black conservatives only being used and manipulated by the right-wing establishment to propagate views and promote policies that are hostile toward blacks. As John Wilks, a black Republican who served in the Nixon and Ford administrations, said about black conservatives: "They merely say they're conservative, say they're opposed to affirmative action and are immediately picked up by a right-wing white sponsor."[60]

And interestingly enough, *The Black Curve* has also found ready acceptance among some black conservatives who continue to propagate its views about race and intelligence as if it were gospel truth. Publication of *The Bell Curve* has not only fueled, but has brought out into the open, the debate on IQ differences between blacks and whites that Herrnstein and Murray ingeniously have attempted to justify on genetic grounds in order to prove a scientific underpinning to an intellectually untenable doctrine of white supremacy. It is a white supremacist tome. And it has been fully endorsed by Thomas Sowell, a position shared by other black conservatives noted for their intellectual blind-spot to the continued existence and malignancy of racism.

Sowell's endorsement of *The Bell Curve* on grounds of scholarship does not justify his neglect of the work's racist implications. It only gives comfort to racists when they see that a distinguished black scholar and prolific author deliberately avoids pointing out what is obvious to them and practically everybody else; namely, Herrnstein and Murray's contention that black people have inferior genes - they just can't help it[61] - and all that such a devastating racist indictment entails in a society where the majority of whites, according to polls, say they have done enough for blacks,[62] although racism remains a fact of life.

They are contradicting themselves since they are the very same people who discriminate against blacks, while at the same time saying they have done enough for blacks. Why do you keep on practicing racism, then, against blacks if you have done enough to end racism?

Ignoring racist intent in works by conservative scholars is the same position Sowell took earlier when he supported Arthur Jensen who concluded that black/white differences in IQ scores are permanent because they are genetic; blacks will *never* be able to close the gap.

Jensen has maintained the same position since 1969 when he first burst on the international scene with his inflammatory article on the subject. As Sowell himself admits, "Professor Jensen believes that the origin [of black/white IQ differences] is genetic," but chooses to emphasize the fallacious point that Jensen was only interested in finding different types of mental abilities and ways of learning. Therefore, Sowell continues, Jensen "was urging a course of action equally compatible with purely cultural differences in styles of thinking."[63]

That was not Jensen's basic argument. He argued, and still maintains, that blacks are innately intellectually inferior to whites. As simple as that. He explicitly stated in his article, that Sowell discusses in his book *Race and Culture*, that he expected no changes in IQ scores between blacks and whites. His article was titled, "How Much Can We Boost IQ and Scholastic Achievement?," and was published in the *Harvard Educational Review*, winter 1969.[64]

The gap is permanent, he contends. It is hereditary, and hereditary influences, that is genes, far outweigh socio-economic factors blamed for black mental deficiency: inferior education, poor nutrition, scant prenatal care, and IQ tests culturally biased against blacks. All these factors mean very little in determining black academic performance, and blacks use them only as an excuse for their meager intellect. Sowell does not emphasize that. But Jensen does. Yet he has chosen to defend Jensen and, by doing so, is defending Jensen's racist position however inadvertently and regardless of good intentions on his part, not as a black scholar, but simply as a scholar.

Many experts were skeptical about Jensen's published findings when they were first published. His credibility was further eroded - the criticism was dismissed by Herrnstein and Murray in their work *The Bell Curve* - in the 1980s when one of Jensen's "major sources, British psychologist Cyril Burt, was accused by his official biographer of inventing figures and the names of researchers who ha[d] supposedly compiled them."[65] However, that did not end the debate on intelligence.

Jensen's reputation may have been called into question because of these revelations, but the genetic argument over black/white IQ differences has not only persisted but has also gained credibility among a number of scholars through the years. Jensen was blunt about it, while black conservatives are not blunt about his bluntness, or Herrnstein and Murray's.

Sowell is not the only black conservative who deliberately ignores the racist message of white conservatives that traditionally is spread under the guise of scholarship, and even as compassion for the less endowed, although its content as well as its intent is unmistakably clear, however veiled.

Professor Walter Williams is another one who has used his status as a scholar to give credibility to the the twisted logic and racist views of white conservatives in solidarity with his ideological compatriots. One of his most daring moves in this area was his endorsement of Jared Taylor's opprobrious oeuvre, *Paved with Good Intentions: The Failure of Race Relations in Contemporary America*, helping to give credibility to an ominous opus whose central message is that racial integration and equality is downright wrong.

Taylor's message, transmitted under the axiom of erudition, and a searing indictment of race relations during the past 30 years or so, has been hailed by one influential national conservative club as: "The most outspoken book the club has ever offered. And the most painful. Jared Taylor does indeed blow the lid off - but with such relentless factuality that the politically porrect will find it impossible to dismiss him. To be sure, they are trying to ignore him, with honorable exceptions like *Kirkus Reviews*, which dared to speak of Taylor's treatment of 'American's doublespeak on race.' All the braver is Walter Williams, brilliant black economist and syndicated columnist."[66]

Taylor's message is clearly racist. Its racist nature is something Professor Williams does not even mention, let alone discuss, while white conservatives, unlike black ones, don't deny it or gloss over it. This is clearly demonstrated by what they choose to highlight from the book, typical of which is Pete Brimelow's vituperation in the *National Review* in which he smugly observed: "'Was the mugger black?,' asked my wife sympathetically. As a Canadian newly arrived in Manhattan, she honestly didn't know that you must never ask. Her hostess, caught off balance in mid-crime story, admitted that he was. Then she hurriedly covered herself: of course, she said, this meant nothing. Besides, being a Canadian, however, my wife was and still is in some respects invincibly innocent. And now she was really puzzled. 'But aren't most muggers in New York black?' she inquired. Her hostess was outraged. 'I don't believe that,' she snapped."[67]

The message is clear, reminiscent of the Willie Horton case, a typical white conservative strategy to mobilize whites against blacks and against white liberals who are sympathetic to blacks and other minorities. Statistically, in the New York context, that may be true in terms mugging and may be other crimes as Brimelow strongly implies. But even if it is true that most muggers in New York are black, why highlight it? Obviously because it is true, is the most likely response.

What about white crime in New York City and all over the country, including corporate welfare fraud, which is committed mostly by middle- and upper-class whites? What about other crimes, including drug trafficking, whose biggest perpetrators are white, and not black? Who highlights that? How many times do we hear about it in the media? It's *always* about black crime.

And what about racism? Is it not a serious problem? But that is something conservatives, both black and white, hardly talk about, because they see it only as a minor problem, if it is one at all, compared to muggings by blacks. Not that crime committed by blacks is not a serious problem, although numerically, and in many cases proportionally, whites commit more crime than blacks do. But so is racism. It is *not* a minor problem as conservatives contend. It is a major problem, and a very serious problem, although conservatives pretend otherwise and hardly provide a balanced picture that should include what white America is doing to black America to make the lives of many blacks miserable for no other reason than that they are black.

Brimelow is one such typical white conservative, and he has endorsed Taylor's book in glowing terms: "The single greatest strength of Jared Taylor's *Paved with Good Intentions* is its massive and merciless crushing of this type of hysterical denial ('Aren't most muggers in New York black?' 'I don't believe that'), which currently paralyzes all discussion of race relations in America. Considered entirely by itself, this achievement makes his book the most important published on the subject for many years....Taylor documents in immense detail that the U.S., far from suppressing its blacks and poor, in fact subsidizes them, publicly and privately, including more than $2.5 trillion in federal moneys alone since the 1960s....Nearly fifty years later, Myrdal's panacea of integration, equality, and confident social engineering had been followed by disaster. This news could not be more unwelcome. It is hardly surprising that both Left and Right prefer to cling to the myth of a culpable - but therefore at least in theory correctable - white racist America."[68]

Brimelow's assessment is interesting, for it is an assessment that has helped to sell a book that Walter Williams says "should be on everybody's shelf" in spite of its blistering attack on racial equality. He has endorsed a book written by someone who is honest about being a racist, hence his opposition to racial equality and integration as forcefully articulated in his work *Paved with Good Intentions*, thereby implying he is one also.

Taylor himself has also, in other forums,[69] made his feelings known about blacks as a despicable lot because of their alleged genetic inferiority; and has cleverly used his supposedly well-intentioned thesis - hence the title of his work *Paved with Good Intentions* - to promulgate this message by condemning racial integration and equality.[70]

That is the kind of book, and message, that black conservatives like Professor Walter Williams endorse as much as Thomas Sowell and others have Arthur Jensen's, and Richard Herrnstein and Charles Murray's works.

Ignoring and downplaying racism in spite of its persistence and virulence, however covert, is typical of many black conservatives since they don't consider it to be one of the major problems - if it is one at all - that blacks face today in the United States. It is a position that has earned black conservatives the unenviable distinction of being accomplices to those determined to deny blacks full equality in a society that believes it has done enough for black people.

They are also determined to take back whatever society has done for blacks; hence the rollback of affirmative action, among other things. And what *The Bell Curve* says is nothing short of a subliminal message aimed at white racists - and it's millions of them, all over the place -to enable them pursue this goal, with black conservatives acting as their storm troopers in the offensive against black America.

What is the essence of *The Bell Curve*? It is a blueprint for social Darwinism gone wrong. It is an attempt to segregate and channel people into stereotyped closets of superiority and inferiority. It perverts reason, compromises legitimate research, and sanctions racial injustice in the name of democracy and individual merit.

The policies advocated by *The Bell Curve* can be summed up in one phrase: "survival of the fittest," enhanced by its corollary: "might is right," which is white-determined, and white-controlled, in a predominantly white nation. Prominent black conservatives have endorsed the book despite its racist intent because it advocates policies they promote, ignoring its central message.

A closer look at what Herrnstein and Muray say regarding black America raises serious questions as to whether black conservatives who have endorsed the book, and other blacks who subscribe to its premises, best serve the interests of the black community they claim to champion and promote. Excerpts from the book will help us understand the book better.

More than any other segment of the American society, black America is plagued with high unemployment that defies solution in the absence of national will to confront the problem. Even as recently as 2003, almost 40 years after years after the civil rights movement that pushed through Congress legislation for racial equality, blacks were *still* hit hardest by unemployment mainly because of racism. According to *The New York Times*:

> Unemployment among blacks is rising at a faster pace than in any similar period since the mid-1970s, and the jobs lost have been mostly in manufacturing, where the pay for blacks has traditionally been higher than in many other fields....Nearly 90 percent of those lost jobs were in manufacturing, according to government data, with blacks hit disproportionately harder than whites.[71]

Besides Native Americans, blacks are the least successful ethnic group in the United States even when the economy is robust. Why? *The Bell Curve* has an answer: "Success or failure in the American economy, and all that goes with it, are increasingly a matter of genes that people inherit....IQ is substantially heritable....Who becomes poor?....Low intelligence is a stronger precursor of poverty than low socioeconomic background....Poverty is concentrated among those with low cognitive ability. [In 1989] the mean IQ of people below the poverty line was 88. A third of them had IQs under 81. Eighty-two percent had below average IQs....The longer the period of unemployment, the more prevalent is low IQ. Short-term unemployment is not conspicuously characterized by low IQ; long-term unemployment is."[72]

The policy implications of Herrnstein and Murray's analysis are enormous. First, they shift the blame from society and deposit it on black Americans for perennial unemployment problems prevalent in the black community and for their predicament as the least successful ethnic group. The poor are blamed for being poor. The unemployed are chastised for being unemployed, and even for being homeless and hungry. Racism is ignored in all cases.

The two conservative scholars obviously have concluded that the fate of black America is sealed. Nothing can done to solve its problems because of the low IQ of blacks, 85 on average, which is at the retarded level. Therefore African Americans are locked in an inferior position, *vis-a-vis* whites and others, because of their purported weak genes; hence black Americans' low IQ. They just can't help it. Pity the folks.

Herrnstein and Murray ignore the nature of unemployment that bedevils industrialized countries and which would affect the fortunes and misfortunes of black Americans even if there were no racism in the United States as much as it would affect, and already affects, everybody. In the case of African Americans, the situation is worse. Poverty across black America is inextricably linked with, and is accentuated by, racism that is directly responsible for unemployment throughout black America. And it is worth examining the phenomenon of unemployment in a macroeconomic context to understand why blacks are not responsible for their condition.

To put it simply, unemployment is a situation where people who are normally part of the labor force, and are willing and able to work, cannot find employment. Large-scale unemployment, like racism, can and does cause serious social problems - including riots, "the power to disrupt," as Eldridge Cleaver put it - as the plight of black Americans clearly shows. Numerous factors are behind it, often beyond the control of the individual who is often blamed for his predicament. For example, there are layoffs. That is not an employee's fault.

There are different kinds of layoffs. For example, due to low demand or restructuring of businesses to streamline operations, layoffs occur in different parts of the United States and in other countries around the world. There are also layoffs in seasonal occupations. For example: in a northern state like Michigan or Pennsylvania that has prolonged periods of cold weather including freezing temperatures, construction work stops during winter months.

In Florida and California, migrant workers are laid off after the harvest; only the planters and the tillers remain at work as crops are introduced, and the land is cultivated to grow the crops - there may also be crop rotation.

Then, there is cyclical unemployment. It occurs during an economic depression or recession when production declines with reduced demand. Increased mechanization and automation in industries also causes unemployment. In the long run, technological innovations and advances create jobs for a small number of skilled workers, but during the short term they create unemployment by displacing large numbers of manual and semiskilled workers.

African Americans have always been hardest hit in that area because of their relatively low skills for a number of reasons. The primary reason is racism, and not low intelligence among blacks as Herrnstein and Murray claim, as did a Japanese prime minister who said the United States is less competitive and its economy is declining because of the despicably low and limited intellectual capacity of black Americans.

Another form of unemployment is structural unemployment. It is caused by shifts in a nation's demand for goods and services. Some declining industries, such as coal mining in West Virginia and Kentucky and Pennsylvania, may lay off workers or close down completely as alternative fuel - energy - sources become popular, or legislation limits how it is mined, used, or disposed of.

Without proper retraining, it is difficult for laid-off workers to find other jobs. Some are forced to relocate to another city or state. Others have to take pay cuts, change hours, or downgrade their standard of living. This has been the fate of manual and semiskilled workers for many years.

All these problems affect the individual and the nation's economic, social, and personal success and failure. They are not caused by genes or by race. Black Americans, more than members of any other race, have historically been singled out as the scapegoat for the nation's problems because they have never been fully accepted by other Americans as equals and probably never will be; other people think they are better, and blacks no more than a sub-species of mankind.

Even foreigners have joined the chorus to blame and condemn blacks as inferior, attributing America's problems to black people's "low" intelligence, as Japanese Prime Minister Nakasone did in 1986. A diplomat with little polish or understanding, he made his crude remarks publicly, claiming the United States was not only descending economically but had her standards of education falling precipitously   because of the low intelligence of black Americans.[73]

The implication of Nakason'e highly offensive remark was that the United States would be better off without blacks, a sentiment that has now and then through the years been articulated by many white racists telling black Americans: "Go back to Africa!" The logic of this other remark is, "After using you all these years, we don't need you now. Get the hell out and go back where you came from." They would love *The Bell Curve*, those who can read and understand it. Many of these racists are very ignorant and can hardly read and write. Plain stupid, with their "superior" genes and intelligence *The Bell Curve* claims they have simply because they are white yet, as the saying goes, can't tell A from B.

Undaunted, Herrnstein and Murray continue to argue in their book: "The average white person tests higher than about 84 percent of the population of blacks and the average black person tests higher than about 16 percent of the population of whites. The average black and white differ in IQ at every level of socioeconomic status. Attempts to explain the difference in terms of test bias have failed."[74]

Nothing is going to change. Blacks are stuck at the bottom, they can't help it, it's not their fault but their nature, and leave them where they are, at the bottom, because that's where they belong since they are inferior to whites and members of other races in terms of intelligence and socioeconomic status in general. It's all in the genes, a genetic thesis *The Bell Curve* articulates in the following terms:

> The universality of the contrast in nonverbal and verbal skills between East Asians and European whites suggests genetic roots. Another line of evidence pointing toward a genetic factor in cognitive ethnic differences is that blacks and whites differ most on the tests that are best measures of g, or general intelligence....
>
> Given a mean black IQ of about 85 and the link between socioeconomic status and IQ within ethnic populations, the implication is that the black inner city has a population with a mean IQ somewhere in the low 80s at best.[75]

An IQ of 85, which is said to be the IQ of an average black American, is bad enough. That is borderline intelligence, slightly above the retarded level of their people in Africa, at 70. Therefore an IQ in the low 80s is even worse. That is the IQ of most blacks, at best, since most of them live in the inner cities. And Herrnstein and Murray emphasize that, to make sure that the readers, white readers, understand its critical nature and their emphatic determination to define blacks as intellectually inferior beings. Simply, and succinctly put, Herrnstein and Murray are saying most blacks are retarded.

Since there is a distinct relationship between intelligence and socioeconomic status, as Herrnstein and Murray maintain, nothing short of divine intervention can be done to improve the condition of black Americans. Any attempt to help them, including providing them with equal opportunity under the law, is a waste of time and money.

It is irrational and downright wrong to give a black person the same employment or educational opportunities given to non-blacks who are people of normal intelligence unlike blacks whose intelligence is at the retarded level even if they don't act retarded. It is unfair to both; unfair to the mentally deficient, who is naturally black, because he is forced to compete against someone with superior intelligence, who is white or Asian or a member of another race except black.

And it is unfair to the intelligent individual because he is forced to go at a snail's pace to enable the retarded to keep up. It is equally unfair to the intellectually superior person because he is sometimes denied employment or educational opportunity that, instead of being given to him, is given to the mentally deficient for the sake of equality.

If nothing else, *The Bell Curve* has poisoned race relations and exacerbated racial tensions, twisting people's minds to justify racial inequality and discrimination against blacks. And the logic is simple, however irrational or immoral: Whites are on top, and deserve to be on top, because they are more intelligent. Blacks are at the bottom, and deserve to be at the bottom of the heap, because they are genetically, and intellectually, meant to be down there. They have weak genes, they are dumb.

That is the logic of Nazi Germany, and of the radical right in the United States which includes white supremacists and fundamentalist ministers who invoke scriptures using coded language when they preach before white congregations to justify racial separation and discrimination against blacks. And that is the logic of *The Bell Curve*. As the Reverend Jesse Jackson said about the book: "The last time such racist tripe received celebrity was in Nazi Germany."[75]

The Bell Curve is the *Mein Kampf* for this millennium. Just as Adolf Hitler declared in his magnum opus, "it is a sin against the will of the Creator to let hundreds and hundreds of thousands of His most talented beings degenerate in the proletarian swamp of today, while Hottentots and Zulu Kafirs are trained for intellectual vocations,"[77] Herrnstein and Murray contend in *The Bell Curve* that American blacks, like their African cousins, are unfit for higher training and vocations that demand rigorous intellectual discipline because they have weak mental faculties. As they emphatically state in their book, whites surpass blacks at every level in every mental test. The implication is obvious. Blacks are genetically inferior to whites. So why give them equal opportunity?

The fact that *The Bell Curve* was an instant best seller speaks volumes about the unspoken belief among most whites about blacks. The majority of whites are careful not to express their racial hatred and superiority publicly, although they have done so, covertly, according to polls and national surveys we cited earlier. Even the most timid have now come out of their racist closet, while the bold ones have become even more emboldened. As Jacob Weisberg put it: "You can hear a thousand David Dukes in the background saying: 'I told you so.'"[78]

An endorsement of *The Bell Curve* by black conservatives or by anybody else is equivalent to endorsing Hitler's *Mein Kampf* - and his dream of a "1,000-year Reich" but which barely lasted 12 years - and South Africa's diabolical institution of apartheid. And this is not a far-fetched analogy; in fact, that's why Hitler had a lot of support in apartheid South Africa, especially among Afrikaners. The message is the same.

The parallels are almost exact. As Hitler put it: "Everything that today we admire on this earth - science and art, technique and inventions - is only the creative product of a few peoples and...one race. On them now depends, also, the existence of this entire culture. If they perish, then the beauty of this earth sinks into the grave with them."[79]

Herrnstein and Murray have this to say along the same lines: "Whites are characteristically stronger than blacks on the subtests involving spatial-perceptual ability, and blacks are characteristically stronger than whites in subtests such as arithmetic and *immediate* [the emphasis is mine] memory, both of which involve retention and retrieval of information."[80]

That is a critical observation. It has to do exactly with the same thing that Hitler preached about: abstract comprehension and the inventive genius of the white race. Spatial-perceptual ability, which Herrnstein and Murray write about, entails abstract comprehension that is critical to the development and understanding of science. They say blacks are deficient in this area. They argue that this is the reason that there are few black inventors and scientists, compared with whites and Asians, in the United States (and hardly any, of course, in Africa).

The area in which blacks are particularly strong, the two conservative scholars claim, has to do with recalling information, like a parrot. In other words, whites generate, analyze and synthesize ideas. Blacks only memorize and parrot information; that's why they know songs so well, for example, as many white

233

racists would have us believe, which is a typical stereotype about blacks. Blacks, according to Herrnstein and Murray, are incapable of generating and coming to grips with ideas at a high level of abstraction.

Yet, what is so interesting is that for centuries, whites hardly made any advances in science in spite of their high intelligence, innate ability across the spectrum, inventive genius and superior spatial-perceptual ability which would have made them produce a disproportionately large number of scientists long before anybody else did. So what happened?

To understand civilization, one must first understand that history is cyclical. For example, while a number of Arab countries today have a high rate of illiteracy and are technologically backward, it is the same people from these countries who centuries ago were pioneers in science, medicine and other fields long before Europeans knew anything about all this.

Now, they are going through another cycle and re-emerging and may one day reach the pinnacle of success they once enjoyed hundreds of years ago, even if they may not be the only ones at the top this time.

All societies have socio-economic ups and downs. Skeptics, of course, scoff at this idea with regard to Africa. They say Africa has never enjoyed a reversal of fortunes - what did they ever have besides misery? Africa has always been static, never dynamic; a blank slate from the beginning. As Dr. Henry E. Garrett, who, for 16 years, was head of the psychology department at Columbia University stated: "Over the past 5,000 years, the history of Black Africa is blank....The Black African had no written language; no numerals; no calendar or system of measurement. He did not devise a plough or wheel."[81]

Did Europe have all that? Garrett says nothing about Europe. It did not have the inventions, innovations, and advances that he condemns Africa for not having over the same past 5,000 years. Europeans had no calendar, no numerals, and no written language until they got all that at a later date from the Middle East, China, India, and North Africa. Nor did Europeans invent the wheel; the Middle Eastern Sumerians did. Europeans also did not invent the plough; it came from the Middle East like many other inventions for which Europeans claim credit.

And some came from Africa, black Africa. Professor Garrett is more interested in glorifying his ancenstral homeland, Europe, for things it never had, than he is in pursuing scholarship which he has twisted in his warped racist mind to belittle and insult Africans. And his position is no different from Hitler's, or that of apartheid South Africa where whites tried to justify apartheid on the grounds that black people were inferior to them and were meant to be hewers of wood and drawers of water for members of the master race.

That also is exactly what *The Bell Curve* is talking about. Since blacks are inferior to whites, or are not as intelligent as whites, they have to be relegated to a permanent inferior status. They cannot have the same jobs as whites, or the same authority at work, in the government, or anywhere else, as whites. And why admit blacks to the same schools, colleges and universities as whites, where, according to Herrnstein and Murray, they cannot compete with white students because of their inferior genes?

They will only lower academic standards and slow down the other students from learning faster because professors will have to accommodate black students who can only learn at a slow pace; that's if they can learn at all.

And you can't have "separate but equal" schools or any other institutions and facilities because the doctrine of "separate but equal" is formulated and implemented on terms stipulated by the dominant race, that is, the white race, in the American context. And as the U.S. Supreme Court ruled in 1954 in *Brown vs. Board of Education*, "separate but equal" is "inherently unequal." Yet conservatives and millions other whites refuse to obey the ruling.

That's why schools are still segregated, mainly because of white flight, while at the same time a significant number of whites continue to espouse the doctrine of white supremacy or subscribe to the notion that races are inherently unequal, with the white race being the master race, and has the right to rule others, whether or not it is benevolent in its treatment of blacks and other members of the lesser breed: other nonwhites besides blacks, with blacks being on the lowest rung of the evolutionary ladder.

The Bell Curve has provided "scientific" justification for this kind of twisted thinking.

Also, besides schools and the work place, why allow blacks to

235

live in the same neighborhoods with whites? Blacks will only turn those areas into slums, destroying property, piling up garbage all over the place and committing "all that crime," because of their low intelligence. They cannot maintain property, or keep up property value; they cannot live as decent human beings - it's not in their nature to do so. And they are not supposed to integrate with whites who are superior to them.

Entire neighborhoods will be turned into a jungle if you allow blacks to move in. It makes no difference, none whatsoever, that they are middle- or upper-class. They are all the same, with the same low intelligence which determines everything in life as Herrnstein and Murray contend.

That is why blacks are in the ghetto, and that is why the ghetto is a ghetto: low-class, crime-ridden, with dilapidated buildings, no good role models except thieves and pimps, and much more. It is filled with retarded people, since all blacks have IQs at or near the retarded level, the two authors contend in *The Bell Curve*. Blacks in the inner cities have "a mean IQ somewhere in the low 80s at best," they say in their book.

There is no stronger indictment against an entire race of people. In one sweeping statement, they have condemned the whole race. The central message of *The Bell Curve* is no different from Hitler's *Mein Kampf* that black conservatives cannot help but endorse when they sanction its complement, *The Bell Curve*, as a work of genuine scholarship and not as a call for racial genocide in covert form. The parallels between the two works are, to say the least, frightening.

Articulating his position no different from that of *The Bell Curve*, Hitler in his magnum opus *Mein Kampf* goes on to talk about "preservation of the right of the victory of the best and the strongest in this world....The man who misjudges and disdains the laws of race...prevents the victorious march of the best race and with it also the presumption of all human progress."[82]

There is no better definition of social Darwinism. All talk of human equality is nonsense. And Hitler is brutally frank about it. So is *The Bell Curve*. It is an argument the authors of *The Bell Curve* have pursued with fanatical religious zeal throughout their book, contending: "People differ in intelligence for reasons that are not their fault, and intelligence has a powerful bearing on how well people do in life....The egalitarian ideal...underestimates the importance of the differences that separate human beings....[And] as soon as the differences are associated with membership in a group, censorship arises....The ideology of equality has done some good. But most of its effects are bad."[83]

Cumulatively, most of its effects have involved extending opportunity to blacks. If "most of its effects are bad," as Herrnstein and Murray argue in their book, then extending equal opportunity to blacks is wrong - according to the same rationale. One couldn't find a more racist argument, and a blatantly racist one at that, disguised as scholarship.

Hitler would be in good company, although he wound definitely wonder where black conservatives fit in. As he explicitly stated in his book *Mein Kampf* black conservatives have inadvertently endorsed by concurring with the thesis of *The Bell Curve* which is also Hitler's in support of white supremacy: "The Aryan alone was the founder of higher humanity as a whole....He is the Prometheus of mankind."[84]

The Aryan is definitely not a "Negro," the Fuhrer would have been quick to point out to the dark members of his new "family": black conservatives. Black conservatives would be no more welcome by Hitler than they are by David Duke or by any other white supremacists; nor would they be more welcome than other blacks.

When the Klan strikes a blow, that blow is intended for *any* black within reach, period, regardless of what label you wear, and however conspicuously. And that includes the label, "black conservatives." The Klan is impressed by none of that; nor are the neo-Nazis and other hate groups across the United States. You'll go just as fast. It is a question of race. As Cornel West says, "Race matters." And so do the authors of *The Bell Curve*: "It seems highly likely to us that both genes and the environment have something to do with racial differences."[85]

If external factors such as the environment also have to do with racial differences, let alone genes that are internal factors, then there is no hope for blacks. None. They cannot even manipulate the environment to improve their performance even if they were in full control of that environment. That is because they have weak genes, and therefore not intelligent enough to do anything positive that will have profound impact on their environment.

That is the same argument white racists used in South Africa during the era of apartheid when they said black people were incapable of managing their own affairs - let alone ruling the country. They probably make the same argument today, but mainly in private. If *The Bell Curve* became a best seller in the Union of South Africa as it did in the United States, racists among whites in that country, like their counterparts in America, would dig up gems like this one contained in *The Bell Curve*: "If it were known that the black/white difference [in IQ] is genetic, probably, human nature being what it is, some people would interpret the news as a license for treating all whites as intellectually superior to all blacks."[86]

Of course by putting it that way, Herrnstein and Murray imply that they mean the opposite; that it is wrong to think that way. But that is exactly their argument throughout the book: that the black/white difference in IQ is genetic, since they resolutely state that the environment does *not* account for the difference and has in fact failed to narrow the gap, let alone close it. That is also Hitler's argument. As he states in *Mein Kampf*: "The 'folkish' view recognizes the importance of mankind in its racially innate elements."[87]

Since those elements are innate, external forces such as environmental factors cannot manipulate them. That is why the environment has failed to close the gap between blacks and whites. The parallels between *Mein Kampf* and *The Bell Curve* are striking, and frightening even to some of the most hardened souls. Both are manifestos for racial genocide, a call to arms, and with blacks, in the American context, being the primary target.

And as someone who would never fail to talk about blacks, Hitler spewed his hatred in the most revolting manner, especially in his attacks on racial equality and integration. He described the twin ideals as suicidal for the members of the master race: "The 'folkish' view by no means believes in an equality of the races, but with their differences it also recognizes their superior and inferior values, and by this recognition it feels the obligation in accordance with the Eternal Will that dominates this universe to promote the victory of the better and stronger, and to demand the submission of

238

the worse and the weaker....In a hybridized and negrified world all conceptions of the humanly beautiful and sublime, as well as all conceptions of an idealized future for our mankind, would be lost forever."[88]

Herrnstein and Murray's *Bell Curve*, like Hitler's *Mein Kampf*, has delivered an equally devastating blow to the ideal of equality by invoking a genetic argument to justify the dominant position of whites over blacks. It is an argument that millions of whites find so appealing, especially when it is given academic respectability by the two conservative scholars who wrote the book. Its elitist message, also like Hitler's, is stark and clear: "People in different jobs have different average IQs. Lawyers, for example, have higher IQs on average than bus drivers....To be able to dig a ditch, you need a strong back but not necessarily a high IQ score."[89]

On top of the racism directed against them, blacks face a compound problem because of elitism that is so biased against them and is an integral part of the American way of life. For example, it is true that the majority of ditch-diggers, who are menial workers, are white in a nation that is predominantly white, but proportionally, more blacks are ditch-diggers and menial workers.

Blacks are expected by society, a white-dominated society, to do menial work that requires more brawn than "brains." Therefore the lawyer-versus-ditch-digger analogy applies more to blacks than it does to whites and is racist in all its implications because of its disproportionate impact on blacks. It is blacks who have "low" intelligence. Therefore, they are good only for manual labor.

The Bell Curve takes the genetic argument even further. Critics of IQ tests have argued that black people in the United States score lower than whites because of their disadvantaged status as a powerless minority who have endured racial oppression in the citadel of democracy for almost 400 years since August 1619 when the first African slaves arrived in Virginia, one year before the Mayflower.

They have therefore turned to Africa for vindication, hoping that since blacks on the African continent suffered less direct oppression under whites - except in South Africa - they will be able to find higher IQ scores to refute the racist argument about the genetic inferiority of blacks in the United States. The results have been disappointing, to say the least, as Herrnstein, Murray and others have testified.

Blacks in Africa score even lower, much lower, on IQ tests than blacks in the United States; in fact, lower than anybody else in the world. Instead, it seems that it is Herrnstein, Murray, Rushton and others like them who have been vindicated. But those findings are nothing new. Black people in Africa have always been considered to have meager intellect, at best, even before intelligence tests started to be used. Their low IQ scores, which are despicably low, only confirm that. Nobody likes to discuss the subject, as Herrnstein and Murray and even Philippe Rushton point out, because it is humiliating to blacks. As Herrnstein and Murray state in *The Bell Curve*:

> One reason for this reluctance to discuss [IQ] averages is that blacks in Africa, including urbanized blacks with secondary educations, have obtained extremely low scores....
> The median black African IQ [is] 75, about ten points lower than the current figure for American blacks. Where other data are available, the estimates of the black African IQ fall even lower.
> The IQ of 'coloured' students in South Africa - of mixed racial background - has been found to be similar to that of American blacks.[90]

Herrnstein and Murray have inadvertently admitted that IQ scores are *not* permanent when they talk about "the current figure" of IQ scores "for American blacks." By saying so, they imply that American black IQ scores could go higher or lower, thus casting doubts on their own genetic theory of intelligence and on the validity of IQ tests as genetic tools for measuring mental capacity. If it is genetically fixed, locked in place, it can't go higher or lower.

And as much as Herrnstein and Murray contend that intelligence has genetic roots, hence the gap in IQ scores between blacks and whites, they concede this much: "The most impressive of the findings is the the comparatively small black/white differences of only seven IQ points on the Ravens SPM (Standard Progressive Matrices) administered to 12-year-olds."[91]

That is a reduction by more than half of the 15-point gap in IQ scores between blacks and whites that existed since World war I. An 8-point gap has been erased, or closed, with only seven to go.

How has that been possible?

According to the genetic theory of intelligence propounded by the Herrnsteins, the Murrays, the Rushtons and others, it should be impossible to achieve that if IQ is indeed wholly genetic, hence permanent.

So what happened? Did those 12-year-old black children who narrowed the IQ gap, substantially, miraculously undergo genetic mutation and become smarter?

Even before the black children narrowed the IQ gap between themselves and their white counterparts, the question that has never been answered remains: If race is a factor inhibiting black performance, how is it that there are blacks who have higher IQs than whites? Millions do, even according to Herrnstein and Murray's own assessment, since, they concede,"the average black person tests higher than about 16 percent of the population of whites."[92]

Nature would make it impossible for them to do that because they are locked in a position of genetic inferiority by their inferior genes that account for their poor performance in general on IQ tests. Yet, Herrnstein and Murray make another significant concession, stating: "The American black population numbers more than 30 million people. If the results from the NLSY (National Longitudinal Survey of Youth) apply to the total black population as of the 1990s, around 100,000 blacks fall into Class I of our five cognitive classes, with IQs of 125 or higher. One hundred thousand is a lot of people. It should be no surprise to see - as one does everyday - blacks at high levels in every intellectually challenging field."[93]

How did that many blacks break through the genetic barrier if they are naturally and intellectually inferior to whites? What kind of genes do they have and which differ from those of other blacks who are "locked" at the bottom because of their weak genes as black people? It would be impossible even for one black person, just one, to do that, based on the genetic theory which explains intelligence exclusively as a product of genes, nothing else.

In fact, it is more than 100,000 blacks who have IQs of 125 or higher since there are about 35 million blacks in the United States today in a total population of more 280 million according to census figures.[94]

241

According to experts in the field, an IQ of 100 is a sign of average intelligence. An IQ of 115 signifies high intelligence; for example, of a sampling of university professors, doctors, and lawyers, on average. An IQ of 125 is considered to be very high intelligence; 130 and above, extremely high intelligence. Blacks are found across the entire range of IQ scores. According to Herrnstein and Murray's own charts, there are even blacks with IQs of 140 and above.[95]

They do, of course, admit that there are individual differences in IQ, just as there are group differences in IQ between blacks and whites; therefore, you are going to find blacks who are more intelligent than whites and some even at the highest levels of IQ. Since that is the case, and it is true, the genetic argument is invalid.

A duck is not going to soar as high as an eagle, no matter how hard it tries, for obvious genetic reasons. A cow is not going to outrun an antelope, or a donkey outrun a zebra. In the case of the duck and the eagle, it is true that they are different birds, just as in the case of the cow and donkey, the two are different from the other animals they are being compared to; while human beings are of the same species.

Even a racist like Arthur Jensen has conceded that much, saying there is no such thing as white genes or black genes determined by race. It is the frequency of genes in terms of combination that does the trick to determine racial features and identity.

Still, the genetic argument as it is used to explain differences in natural ability, for example between the duck and the eagle, is no less different from the one used by Herrnstein and Murray to explain natural differences between blacks and whites as a product of genes since the races are genetically different.

One can say that is an extreme case of contrast because there are birds that fly higher than the duck and as high as - and probably even higher than - the eagle. But this argument also applies to people of different races who are said to be on different levels of IQ on average for genetic reasons.

It is Hispanics and Native Americans who should soar as high as whites and Asians on IQ charts and even higher, as they do indeed sometimes, but not blacks blacks who, on average and according to genetic logic, have the lowest IQ. It is the Hispanics and Native Americans who are analogous to these other birds that fly as high and even higher than the eagle, with whites and Asians being analogous to the eagle.

Now, if some members of of a race that is lowest on the IQ scale, that is blacks, can score as high as and even higher than some of those belonging to races with the highest IQs, whites and Asians, it logically follows that some ducks, not just some other kind of birds besides ducks, should also be able to soar as high as the eagle, and even higher. But probably no duck has been able to do that, at least not to my knowledge. And the reason is simple: genes.

So why don't genes play the same role with regard to blacks, if they are genetically inferior, and make it impossible for *any of them* to score as high as and even higher than genetically superior beings, whites and Asians? There shouldn't be a single black person scoring as high as - let alone higher than - whites and Asians. That would be consistent with Herrnstein and Murray's genetic logic.

But since proponents of the genetic argument, such as Arthur Jensen, Richard Herrnstein, Charles Murray, and Philippe Rushton contend that race is the only reason why blacks score lower than whites on IQ tests, it should be just as much a factor in the case of millions of whites who score lower than blacks; they score lower *because* they are white.

Why should race apply only to blacks when they score lower than whites but not now when whites score lower than blacks if it is, indeed, the reason for IQ differences between races? If being black is a genetic defect, hence the low IQ of blacks, so is being white just as much a genetic deficiency in the case of millions of whites who score lower than millions of blacks on IQ tests.

The argument about group differences, besides not being fully explained, is also used to obscure reality. It is used to prove that whites - *including* the retarded - are more intelligent than blacks simply because, in terms of percentages, they belong to a group whose members collectively score higher on IQ examinations than blacks. That is very egalitarian for Herrnstein and Murray to do that, lifting every white up from the bottom and awarding all whites a high IQ score as members of a group whose average IQ is higher than that of blacks.

But does group membership make dumb whites smarter, and intelligent blacks less intelligent simply because they belong to a group? What makes white individuals in the white group more intelligent besides the fact that they share similar IQ scores? Today, America's per capita income is around $38,000. Does that mean every American earns that much? The United States is, of course, the richest country in the world with about 50 percent of the entire world's wealth; hence the high per capita income.

But while wealth is evenly "distributed" to every American in statistical computation in terms of per capita income, IQ cannot be shared the way a country's total wealth is. Intelligence is an individual attribute locked in one's head, while gross national product is computed collectively for very practical purposes, and it works. Collectivizing IQ on racial basis does not.

The justification for group intelligence as a meaningful criterion for measuring intellectual capacity of the races is that whites are more intelligent than blacks because, on average, they score higher than blacks. But that is running in circles because this question then arises:

How is it that there are blacks who score higher than whites who are more intelligent than blacks, if race is indeed a factor in the determination or distribution of intelligence? Are those blacks, who as individuals score higher than whites, any less black simply because they are counted as individuals and not as members of a group?

It is assumed by many people, because the genetic argument has so much appeal to millions of whites, that the logic of *The Bell Curve* is unassailable. But that is not the case. It is the same logic on which the edifice of apartheid was built. Yet, this abominable institution crumbled.

It was also the foundation of Jim Crow legislation in the United States, a contrived means to control, dominate, and humiliate blacks more than anybody else. Yet Jim Crow also, under sustained assault, was abandoned, at least in the legal sense. Also the logic of *The Bell Curve* is not impeccable.

In trying to prove that blacks are genetically inferior to whites, Herrnstein and Murray emphasize that the low intelligence of a particular group of people - blacks - is behind all the major problems that the United States, as a nation, faces. The problems range from high unemployment to drug use and trafficking, high school dropout rates escalating to skyrocketing illegitimacy in the black ghettoes across the nation, crime, and welfare dependency. These are major challenges, and it is the black community that is blamed for *all* these problems more than anybody else because they are all a result of inner-city chaos and maladies and the people who live there: blacks.

Nothing is put in its proper context by conservatives, with regard to the ghetto, in pursuit of their conservative agenda that ignores black America. For example, the high unemployment rate among blacks is a result of their low IQs. Even poor housing is blamed, not on white landlords who own most of the property in the inner cities, but on blacks because of their low IQs.

Racism is totally ignored in all these cases. Not only is racism is ignored by conservatives; it is given academic respectability, obviously itself being a product of low intelligence among blacks since they asked for it: people of higher intelligence, whites and others, have no business being on the same level with blacks, enjoying the same rights. Therefore they have the right to practice racism against backs. Keep blacks at the bottom, what black legal scholar Derrick Bell calls "faces at the bottom of the well." That is also the title of his book, *Faces at the Bottom of the Well: The Permanence of Racism.*[96]

It defies reason that Herrnstein and Murray go to great lengths to attribute the high unemployment rate among blacks - consistently twice the national average through the years - to their low intelligence. They even expound the theory that low intelligence is fixed among unskilled workers of every race. No mention is made of economic status. Nothing is mentioned about their inability to get quality education, equal opportunities in the job market, and the option to upgrade one's position above the line created by the individual's heritage.

And, in the case of blacks of course, racism is irrelevant in this context; only their low IQ is, as the cause of *all* their problems including unemployment and, by logical extension, racism itself, instead of the reverse being the case in a white-dominated society which continues to deliberately discriminate against blacks more than anybody else.

It is true that unskilled workers are found in every race. But a highly disproportionate number of them are black because of racism. Racism has nothing to do with low IQs except for those who practice it, arguing that they don't hire blacks because black people don't have the necessary skills needed at work; and because of their low IQs, of course, as Herrnstein and Murrary contend in *The Bell Curve*.

What about whites? If lack of skills, and not racism, is the main reason why blacks don't get jobs, why is it that the unemployment rate among unskilled whites is not as high as the unemployment rate among unskilled blacks? In fact, not all whites hired are smart, or have higher IQs and skills than all blacks who are not hired. A lot of skilled and educated blacks, some with college degrees, accept semi-skilled and unskilled jobs because they can't get better jobs. Their skin color or race is a barrier. And it is a permanent obstacle because they can't change it even if they wanted to. They will always be black in a predominantly white society.

The Bell Curve ignores all that. It could become the standard text for formulating conservative social policy that accentuates the inequalities Herrnstein and Murray attribute to genetic differences among the races, and which they try to justify by invoking the genetic theory of intelligence distributed along racial lines. They blame blacks for their socioeconomic status which, collectively, is lower than that of other groups. Yet, it is an empirical fact that many highly intelligent and motivated blacks have *not* been able to climb up the socioeconomic ladder simply because they are black.

Disputing this means racial discrimination does not exist and, if it does, it has no negative impact on the life chances of black people. That is an ingenious way of using Nazi logic without sounding like one. It is a racist argument. And the authors of *The Bell Curve* have gone through a lot of contortions to try and give it intellectual justification. In fact, they explicitly state that it is their intention to undo what has been achieved in terms of racial equality: "It is time for America once again to try living with inequality."[97]

They could not have been more explicit; blunt, to the point. If such a policy is to be supported by whites who would be inclined otherwise, the IQ-argument must be fortified with other statistics - beyond IQ scores - to "prove" that blacks are not entitled to the same equality as whites; not only because they are less intelligent, although that is good enough reason not to treat them as equals, but also because they are tearing the country apart. How? By milking the economy while sucking tightly on the welfare tit.

What else? By committing all that crime plaguing the nation, pushing dope, crack, cocaine, and much more. Anything else? By dropping out of school, thereby lowering standards and productivity at work, making the United States less competitive on the world market. Is that all? No. Blacks are also known to be very fertile. They are busy having all those babies all over the place, knowing full well that they are not going to be able to take care of them. Instead, they dump them on society, white society, on the laps of hardworking white men and women to take care of all those black babies.

The Bell Curve skillfully links all those charges to marginal IQs among blacks. As Herrnstein and Murray say about illegitimacy, pursuing their line of reasoning that black communities are plagued with high rates of illegitimate births: "Illegitimacy...is strongly related to intelligence....A woman's intelligence best predicts whether she will bear an illegitimate child....Fertility patterns among the smart and the dumb [are determined by IQ]....IQ is a factor in illegitimacy....There is a direct and strong relationship between low intelligence and the likelihood that a child will be born out of wedlock....Low intelligence is an important independent cause of illegitimacy."[98]

It is not, of course, an intelligent decision to have children one cannot support. But what is important to remember is the direct link the authors of *The Bell Curve* make between low intelligence and illegitimacy - and blacks. They do not say whites don't have babies out of wedlock - they concede that much. They emphasize that the highest rate of illegitimate births is among blacks because black people have the lowest IQs among all racial groups.

Regarding welfare, it is common knowledge that a disproportionately large number of blacks depend on the system, or what used to be welfare, now that the federal assistance programs have been repealed. But why such a high rate of welfare dependency among blacks? Herrnstein and Murray claim to have the answer: "Smarter women can more easily find jobs and resist the temptations of welfare dependency than duller ones....Welfare mothers have lower than average intelligence....The mean IQ of women who ever received welfare was 89. About 85 percent of them were below average in IQ. For chronic welfare recipients, defined as women who had received welfare for at least five years by 1990, the cognitive distribution was even lower....Just as low IQ was increasingly prevalent as the level of male unemployment increased, so is also low IQ more prevalent among mothers as their dependency on welfare rises."[99]

Welfare dependency and abuse of the system is not just a black problem. But because blacks are on welfare in disproportionately large numbers, Herrnstein and Murray contend that many blacks are on welfare because they have the lowest IQs among members of all races; therefore they abuse the system more than anybody else.

Yet, in terms of raw numbers, whites, especially white women, are the biggest recipients of welfare. And they also, not just blacks, abuse the system. In fact, Charles Murray has through the years advocated abolishing welfare, having launched his crusade with his highly influential book, *Losing Ground*,[100] first published in 1984 when Reagan was president. In *The Bell Curve*, he tries to justify his campaign on genetic grounds, together with Herrnstein who articulates the same position as the co-author of this work.

Reforming the system is noble, as long as people aren't left to starve especially in the richest country on earth. What is despicable is when such reform is conducted on genetic grounds, nefariously linking one race, the black race, to all the "evils" of the welfare system - laziness, illegitimacy, family disintegration, fraud - and to everything else that goes wrong in society.

The main culprit, we are told, is low IQ, and by implication, blacks, since they have the lowest. No wonder they commit "all that crime," wreaking havoc across the nation. As Herrnstein and Murray state in *The Bell Curve*: "Criminal offenders have average IQs of 92, eight points below the mean. More serious or chronc offenders generally have lower scores than more casual offenders....As a group, criminal offenders are below average in intelligence."[101]

Since they have already argued that blacks have "below average intelligence," there is little left than to read their thesis that blacks are responsible for the majority of the crimes in the United

States. To these conservative scholars, crime, of course, is aggravated by the prevalence of illegal drugs in the country. Drugs are directly linked to criminal activity, and blacks are considered to be the main culprits in the distribution, sale, and use of dope, especially in the inner cities.

Little is said about white people who distribute, sell and use drugs. In fact, statistically, more whites distribute, sell and use marijuana and more expensive "recreational" drugs including cocaine than do blacks or members of other races. It is also worth remembering that it is white people, not black people, who own most of the boats and planes which bring drugs into the United States. It is whites who run the Mafia. It is whites who are involved in laundering drug money, buying judges, the police and other law enforcement officers more than blacks do. It is also whites who cater to corrupt politicians by filling their campaign chests with soft money, including drug revenues.

But none of that concerns the authors of *The Bell Curve*. Their focus is on race and intelligence. As they state in their book:

> Let us conclude....inequality of endowments, including intelligence, is a reality....When the nation seeks to lower unemployment or lower the crime rate or induce welfare mothers to get jobs, the solutions must be judged by their effectiveness with the people most likely to exhibit the problem: the least intelligent people....
>
> Large portions of the people who exhibit the behaviors and problems that dominate the nation's social policy agenda have limited cognitive ability. Often they are near the definition for mental retardation.[102]

And they are black.

It is a book, a thesis, and a conclusion endorsed by Sowell[103] and other black conservatives who claim to express views and support policies which best serve the interests of fellow blacks across the nation. But most blacks disagree with that, as clearly demonstrated by their strong opposition to the conservative agenda and policies of the Republican party which has not even fully embraced black conservatives.

Chapter Six:

Black Conservatives and Race Relations

IT IS a common belief among black conservatives, unlike their liberal counterparts, that race relations in the United States are very good and even excellent. Not only is the sentiment widely shared among them; it is forcefully articulated by some black conservatives even if not fully supported by all their ideological compatriots.

In an interview with *Reason*, a libertarian magazine, controversial Los Angeles radio talk show host, Larry Elder, was asked:

Reason: "What's the state of race relations in the United States?"

Larry Elder: "Essentially, they are excellent. In our quotidian, day-to-day lives, people get along just fine. You walk up to the store and you see an integrated line. There's a black checkout clerk there and you get your stuff processed. We're getting along just fine. Most middle-class blacks live in integrated neighborhoods."

Reason: "But if you go to Chicago, or Detroit, or Los Angeles, segregation is still everywhere."

Larry Elder: "So what? Frankly, people choose to live where they're comfortable. I mean, if the housing patterns were a result of discrimination on the part of real estate agents, then that's one thing. But I see no evidence of that. Most of my friends who live in the Baldwin Hills and View Park areas of Los Angeles - which are predominantly black bourgeoisie [sic] areas - chose to live there because they want to live with other black people."

Reason: "So you don't think there is redlining in real estate and bank loans?"

Larry Elder: "It's crap; nonsense."[1]

Those are incendiary remarks in black America where passions are already high, as they always have been, flaring now and then over what many blacks consider to be unmitigated evils of racism being perpetrated, and perpetuated, against them by an unrepentant white America.

But Elder, like the rest of the black conservatives who delude themselves into believing that they are accepted by whites, remains undaunted: "Black paranoia, which is rampant in this country,...it's just absurd....The constant search for the great white oppressor has got to stop. A lot of this anger coming from inner-city blacks stems from a prevailing theory that the greater society not only doesn't even care about blacks, but actively seeks to hurt them....Nothing's going to change much until black leaders stop such reckless, careless, conspiratorial nonsense."[2]

Yet, more than a year later, contrary to what Larry Elder and other black conservatives say, *The Wall Street Journal*, itself a conservative paper, reported what the majority of Americans - according to polls we cited earlier and others - to be the nation's most intractable problem: "Americans share a pervasive sense that relations among the races are at best stagnant and at worst declining precipitously."[3]

Even members of the Religious Right, known for their conservatism, continuing message of hate and exclusivity, and opposition to racial equality throughout American history and during contemporary times, have, reluctantly and only to a limited degree considering the magnitude of the problem, belatedly joined the crusade to undo the damage they - and political conservatives - have done to racial justice:

[There has been a] manifestation of a profound and startling shift among [some of] the most conservative of religious believers [in] the all-white Southern Baptist congregations whose churches had been firmly separated since the day First Baptist's slave members departed to form their own congregation - in 1862....

The most energetic element of society may also seem the most unlikely: the religious right. Across the country, conservative congregations and denominations...are embracing a concept called 'biblical racial reconciliation' - a belief that as part of their efforts to please God, they are required by Scripture to work for racial harmony....

In 1995, the traditionally white National Association of Evangelicals - comprising 35,000 congregations - formally asked the National Black Association of Evangelicals to forgive its past racism....Skeptics abound both on the left and the right, warning that the new interest in race may be even less firmly rooted among conservatives than among liberals. Thus far, the movement has indeed been much wider than it is deep...and the conservative congregations - like those of liberal denominations - remain for the most part starkly segregated.[4]

The white congregations - both conservative and liberal - wouldn't be segregated if racism wasn't still a serious problem, and the Religious Right would not be trying to achieve racial reconciliation if race relations were as good as Larry Elder and other black conservatives claim they are. In fact, the Religious Right has, until recently, been very open about its racist beliefs: "The Religious Right fiercely resisted the civil rights movement and in the recent past showed a profound lack of interest in issues of race. As recently as the 1960s, church historians say, leaders in the Southern Baptist Convention, the nation's largest Protestant denomination, openly argued that the Bible ordained separation of the races and the Jim Crow laws that enforced it in the South."[5]

Little has changed since then. The hate-mongering message of the Southern Baptists still persists, keeping conservative congregations still segregated today. The congregations are only a microcosm of the larger society that maintains *de facto* segregation to perpetuate racial inequalities.

Collectively, the condition of African Americans is not very much different from what it was in the sixties because of racism, although a significant number of them have moved up into the middle class. But they are still behind whites in general in terms of income and home ownership; the gap being perpetuated by faster upward mobility among tens of millions of whites. As Adonis Hoffman, a lawyer and political commentator, stated in *The Washington Post*:

An epidemic of hate crimes and black church burnings, along with growing racial polarization, evidence a sharpening enmity between African Americans and whites on basic issues. As the last decade of the 20th century closes, the collective condition of African Americans may not be substantially better than it was before the enlargement of black political power in the 1960s, and many argue it is worse....

Race discrimination remains a daily fact of life for virtually every African American regardless of his or her economic station.[6]

Black conservatives sharply disagree with that assessment. To Larry Elder, that is just paranoia typical of the black community, exemplified by black people's reactions to a number of incidents including the burning of black churches during the 1990s. But is concern about black church burnings by racists, paranoia, when the racists themselves admit they did it, as they have in several cases in which they confessed? For example, according to the *International Herald Tribune*: "Two former Ku Klux Klan members face up to 55 years in prison for burning two black churches in South Carolina last year. Gary C. Cox, 22, and Timothy A. Welch, 24, both pleaded guilty to counts of conspiracy to violate civil rights and use of fire to commit a felony."[7]

Racism was definitely a factor in the burning of several black and interracial churches, contrary to what some people claim. As Dr. Joan Brown Campbell, general-secretary of the National Council of Churches of Christ in the USA, stated long after several of those burnings had taken place, more arson was still going on and the report on the burnings did not even cover all cases of racial arson. In response to one of the skeptics of the racial fires, Dr. Campbell stated in her letter to the editor of *The Wall Street Journal*, appropriately titled "Racism and the Burning of Churches":

Michael Fumento, in writing 'Who's Fanning the Flames of Racism?' pretends that the rash of arsons and fire-bombings of black churches has nothing to do with racism and everything to do with an elaborate 'hoax' foisted on the public....He abuses and misinterprets the first-year report of the National Church Arson Task Force to support his contention.

The report states clearly that its numbers are restricted by the ability to convict in a court of law, that its conclusions are preliminary, and that its investigations continue into questions of motivation and conspiracy. The task force further acknowledges that its numbers do not reflect all of the racism that is involved....

Attacks on houses of worship, particularly those against black churches, were receiving little national attention. Many investigations either were perfunctory or scapegoated the congregations....If Mr. Fumento were to listen,...he would know that racism is a powerful factor in the burnings. He would know about the racism, the repeated vandalisms, the hate mail and phone calls, and, yes, the white supremacist activity directed against many of these churches....Black and multiracial houses of worship still are being burned on a regular basis - six just last month.[9]

Racism is endemic to American society. That is why it is reflected even in the judicial system - that dispenses justice - as demonstrated by the disparity in sentences for blacks and whites; for example, in drug and murder cases. It is also reflected in institutionalized patterns of prejudice that perpetuate racial inequalities in the distribution of wealth, and access to opportunities in different areas of life even today - almost 40 years after the civil rights movement. As stated by *The Economist*:

> *The Washington Post* editorialized against the McVeigh sentence - the state 'should not have the authority to act as a killer has acted and to take a life for a life taken.' But a stance of that sort is rare.
> For many, a more convincing reason to oppose the death penalty is its seeming racial bias: blacks make some 13 percent of America's population, but account both for half of its prisoners and half of those who are executed. The Reverend Jesse Jackson calls this 'legal lynching'....[Blacks are not treated fairly in other areas, yet] the underclass [in the ghetto] riots only rarely, despite the country's glaring inequalities of wealth and opportunity.[10]

By downplaying and even denying the existence of racism, as Larry Elder does, black conservatives have incurred the wrath of many other blacks both in and out of the inner cities. Name-calling may be inappropriate and is not going to solve the problem. But it is an expression of anger, and of revulsion, the majority of blacks have toward black conservatives.

Black conservatives do have the right to believe what they want to believe. The majority of their brethren, in the inner cities and elsewhere, also have the right to reject them, as they consistently have, clearly demonstrated by their refusal to vote for black Republican candidates running for Congress, or for any other office in most cases.

As black conservatives continue to propagate their message, which has already been rejected by the majority of blacks, many blacks respond to this black conservative onslaught in more than one way including name-calling. For example, Larry Elder has been called an Uncle Tom - and other names - by people who listen to his radio talk show, honoring him as "without doubt, the most racist, anti-Black talk show host in southern California."11

Even some sponsors of the controversial talk show have withdrawn their ads in response to mounting criticism from members of the black community who called for an advertising boycott of the sponsors' products.12 But Larry Elder remains unperturbed. And he has his share of admirers, called Elderados. But they are far outnumbered by his opponents in the black community.

Even many of his admirers probably don't agree with him on the state of race relations in the United States today. Take, for example, his emphatic denial of racial discrimination in bank loans. The conservative *Wall Street Journal*, a highly influential newspaper which consistently publishes conservative editorials and endorses Republican candidates and policies without exception, is in total accord with Elder's draconian political philosophy.

Yet, not long after Larry Elder was interviewed by *Reason* magazine when he denied racial discrimination by banks, *The Wall Street Journal* reported that banks do indeed discriminate against blacks when they apply for loans. According to its report:

> The fears and accusations of black entrepreneurs just got some important confirmation: A new study shows that black business owners in one major banking market were more than three times as likely as their white peers to be rejected for a loan.
>
> Banks in Denver denied 51 percent of black business-loan applicants, while rejecting only 15 percent of white business owners, the study found. When researchers examined larger businesses, presumably the financially strongest and most established enterprises, banks still rejected more than half of black applicants, but rebuffed only 4 percent of the whites, the study found.13

But to Larry Elder, all that "is crap, nonsense" - and probably to many black conservatives as well, in spite of the evidence. Had the story appeared in a black newspaper, or in *The New York Times* or *The Washington Post*, black conservatives would have had a field day ridiculing it as nothing but but paranoia and liberal sensationalism spiced with conspiracy theories. But *The Wall Street Journal* that reported the story is one of *their* papers, conservative, and Republican. It went on to say:

Community advocates agree that the survey results reflect the national experience. As Denver's minority home-mortgage rejection rate tracks the national average, the city's minority-business loan activity probably does the same, they say. Many respondents to the survey, such as Harold Massop, think discrimination abounds.

Mr. Massop says that his eight-person architectural firm has been trying since late last year to get a loan. So far...three large Denver area banks have rejected his application. All claimed his company was financially unfit to borrow. One banker rejecting Mr. Massop's application asked, 'How do we know you are going to be around next month?' The firm is eight years old and has been profitable during most of its history....

Last year, the firm also won an $8.5 million contract to design a new main office for the owners of the National Basketball Association's Denver Nuggets. 'Harold has a very strong business and track record,' says Kent Morgan, a Denver procurement manager for the U.S. Small Business Administration who has consulted Mr. Massop's company. Mr. Massop, who has been practicing architecture for 26 years, reports, 'My white colleagues say their banks would find a way to work with them if they had a track record like mine.'[14]

The Denver study is just one among several that have found the same evidence. *The American Economic Review* reported findings by the Federal Reserve Bank of Boston that confirmed that race is a prime factor in determining eligibility for a loan even when legitimate criteria such as credit history were taken into account. *The Wilson Quarterly* reported the same study:

Blacks seeking to buy a home generally have a harder time getting a mortgage than whites do. Minority applicants are almost three times as likely to be rejected, according to data collected under the federal Home Mortgage Disclosure Act (HMDA)....

Analyzing additional data for 1990 gathered by the Federal Research Bank of Boston, [Alicia H.] Munnell, a member of the U.S. Council of Economic Advisers, and three colleagues from the Boston Fed [Geoffrey M.B. Tootell, Lynn E. Browne, and James McEneaney] contend that legitimate selectivity explains part of the gap - but not all of it. On average, the authors say, minority applicants have less wealth and weaker credit histories than white applicants do.

When these disadvantages are taken into account, minority applicants are still more likely to be rejected than comparable white applicants.[15]

Black conservatives like Larry Elder dismiss such reports of documented cases of racism as "crap, reckless, conspiratorial nonsense in search of the great white oppressor. That rhetoric has got to stop, the constant search for the great white oppressor has got to stop....When Jesse Jackson suggests that the difference between crack and powder [cocaine sentencing] is evidence of a racist criminal justice system, nothing's going to change much unless black leaders stop such reckless, careless, conspiratorial nonsense."[16]

Thomas Sowell also dismisses charges of racism against banks and other lending institutions, simply because blacks are rejected for loans, as "absurd." As he states in his book, *The Vision of the Anointed: Self-Congratulation as a Basis for Social Policy*:

> The fact that black applicants for mortgage loans are turned down at a higher rate than white applicants has been widely cited as proof of racism among lending institutions....
>
> This absurd conclusion is being taken in deadly seriousness when the conclusion fits the vision of the anointed....
>
> Implicit in the equating of statistical disparity with discrimination is the assumption that gross disparities would not exist in the absence of unequal treatment.[17]

Equally implicit in that kind of reasoning is the false assumption by Sowell and others of his ilk that gross disparities between blacks and whites in getting loans have nothing to do with racism at all.

It is this kind of twisted logic that leads Elder, Sowell and other black conservatives to make sweeping statements that there is no such thing as "the great white oppressor," as Elder puts it, and that racism is no longer a serious problem for blacks in the United States.

Yet Elder concedes: "I was in the headhunting business for 15 years. I have a friend who is in a similar business. She has clients that have told her not to send over black people: 'Don't send somebody black no matter how qualified. I don't want them in my house.' She told me this. I know it goes on. *60 Minutes* did a piece on a headhunting firm in New York. Black applicants were asked to fill out their application in black ink and white applicants were asked to fill out the application in blue ink so that counselors could identify the race of the applicant."[18]

Even Elder's interviewers of *Reason* magazine saw the contradictions in what he said.[19]

So where is the "crap [and] nonsense" when most blacks and their leaders complain about the racism that Elder himself admitted exists when he was caught off-guard contradicting himself in the interview with *Reason* magazine?

Thomas Sowell also knows racism exists, and that it is not a minor problem. He has experienced it himself as a black person; why other blacks except black conservatives?

Racists wouldn't care even if they saw black conservatives wearing labels proclaiming, "I am a black conservative"; "I am a Republican"; "I am a right-wing ideologue and fanatic"; "Racism no longer exists"; "We know you white folks love us as much as we love you"; "Liberals are lying about you, you are not racist"; "We adore you," and so on.

That is the collective sentiment of black conservatives, prompting other blacks to call them Uncle Toms. As Spike Lee described Supreme Court Justice Clarence Thomas, he is a "handkerchief-head, chicken-and-biscuit eating Uncle Tom."[20]

Julian Bond, chairman of the NAACP, has described them as mascots and ventriloquist dummies speaking in their master's voice - white racists whom they try to please by pretending that they are accepted by them, thus enabling white racists to deflect charges of racism directed against them. As he stated at the NAACP's national convention, in Houston, Texas, in July 2002:

> There is a right-wing conspiracy,...an interlocking network of funders, groups, and activists, who coordinate their methods and their message....They are...the movement behind vouchers, the legal assault on affirmative action and other remedies for discrimination, attempts to reapportion us [blacks] out of office, and attacks on equity everywhere.
> They've had a collection of black hustlers and hucksters on their payrolls for more than twenty years, promoting them as the new generation of black leaders. They can't deal with the leaders we choose for ourselves, so they manufacture, promote, and hire new ones. Like ventriloquist's dummies, [these blacks] speak in their puppet-master's voice.[21]

The renowned black psychiatrist Alvin Poussaint at Harvard University has diagnosed black conservatives as suffering from a mental disorder he calls "token black syndrome." He says it is a condition in which patients desperately try to impress whites by denying their blackness in order to become "white."[22]

And they cannot deny their blackness without denying racism exists even when confronted with solid evidence of racial discrimination, a nationwide phenomenon. For example, *The Wall*

Street Journal also had this to say about the Denver study cited earlier: "'[The] findings prove people of color are still being treated differently when trying to acquire a small-business loan,' says John Taylor, president and chief executive of the National Community Reinvestment Coalition in Washington, which represents community development advocates across the country....The University of Colorado study suggests that lending to minority owners has remained weak."[23]

Exactly three months later, the same paper carried another story that continued from where its previous report on the Denver study ended:

> A new study says discrimination may be widening the gap between the average wages of black and white males.
>
> In results published this month in the *American Sociological Review*, University of Cincinnati sociologist David Maume Jr. found the gap in hourly wages widened from $2.48 in 1976 to $2.66 in 1985, in constant dollars.
>
> Of these figures, Dr. Maume's model estimated that discrimination was responsible for 19 percent of the 1976 gap and 26 percent of the 1985 gap, after factoring out such variables as education, training and experience.[24]

In other words, discrimination got worse as years went by, contrary to what black conservatives say. In fact the 1980s, Reagan's era of alleged prosperity and trickle-down economic theory, was one of the worst decades in terms of overt racism and resurgence of hate groups such as the Ku Klux Klan, the American Nazis and skinheads; encouraged by Reagan's victory in the presidential election, the backlash of white voters voting for conservative candidates angry at blacks for the gains garnered since the civil rights movement including affirmative action, and by the rise of conservatism that gained momentum sweeping across the nation.

The Reagan administration itself was intimately involved in the resurgence of hate groups and other forms of overt and covert racism among many whites in general, countenancing racism in its most blatant form as shown by its hostility toward blacks clearly demonstrated by, among other things, the Equal Employment Opportunity Commission (EEOC) headed by Clarence Thomas.[25] During Reagan's tenure, the EEOC did nothing to combat racism and dragged its feet on the cases it already had on file, hiding behind the black face of Clarence Thomas as head of the comission to show that there was no racism going on within the EEOC or in the Reagan administration, or in the country itself.

Ironically, this rosy picture was disputed even by the conservative *Wall Street Journal* which showed that racism was a major problem across the nation before and during Reagan's presidency:

Dr. Maume analyzed the difference in earnings of 1,563 black and white men in the first study and 2,249 men in the second to see whether the gap narrowed, as predicted by [black] sociologist William Julius Wilson, who created a stir with his 1970s theory that race becomes less of a barrier to success as African-Americans gain more educational and professional opportunities....

Dr. Maume says Dr. Wilson's theory was correct until 1980, when the Reagan administration gutted the Equal Employment Opportunity Commission. 'White institutions no longer felt a penalty in discriminating,' Dr. Maume says.[26]

The existence of racism as a serious problem assumes greater significance when we look at national surveys that have been conducted through the years to determine the magnitude of the problem. The studies have gone beyond addressing specific cases such as employment and wage discrimination and discrimination against minorities by banks and other lending institutions in specific markets.

The national surveys came up with some disturbing findings about the state of race relations in the United States more than 30 years after the civil rights movement. As Katherine Johnson, an office worker in Mobile, Alabama, told *The Washington Post*: "Some ways things have gotten better, some ways they've gotten worse."[27] How worse? According to the survey:

The scar remains clearly and painfully visible in the South, and elsewhere in the country....

Following a rash of suspicious fires at predominantly black churches throughout the South and elsewhere, it is instructive to realize that polls show that millions of Americans support blatantly discriminatory laws as well as freely assert that blacks are inferior to whites....

According to a new *Washington Post* survey..., [the majority of] Americans view racism as a serious problem. Overall, 53 percent of those interviewed nationally and 54 percent of all Southerners said racism was 'a big problem,' while 35 percent in both cases identified it as somewhat of a problem.[28]

The study also found that the majority of Americans said

racism was greater in the South than elsewhere in the country. Southerners conceded that much, although by a lower percent.[29] Racism is just as devastating in many areas in the northern and western parts of the country as numerous racial incidents and other studies show.[30]

There has been no fundamental change in the beliefs millions of whites have about blacks, clearly demonstrated in national surveys through the years. *The Washington Post* asked one pertinent question in its analysis of various national surveys that focused on racism and got blunt answers:

> How many bigots are there in America?
>
> Results of public opinion polls offer one estimate, which is almost certainly an understatement because of people's reluctance to offer potentially inflammatory views to poll takers.
>
> Still, it's surprising how many Americans do openly claim in public opinion polls that blacks are inferior to whites, favor discriminatory laws or support a legal ban on marriages between the races.[31]

It is attitudes like that which lead even some whites to conclude that deep in their hearts, practically all people of Caucasian origin sincerely believe that they are genetically and intellectually superior to blacks; they just don't say it publicly or even to their fellow white friends afraid that word might get out about their true feelings.

And they believe they have proof: "How come black Africa is so backward if blacks are on the same level with us in terms of intellectual endowment?" "Why do we score higher than blacks on IQ tests if they're as smart as we are?" "White students do better in school than black students, don't they?" "Give an honest answer that excludes genetic differences as the only explanation." They say all that; at least feel that way. As Professor Andrew Hacker bluntly states: "Everybody of Caucasian descent believes that we belong to a superior strain. Most white people believe that persons with African ancestries are more likely to carry primitve traits in their genes."[32]

There are others, of course, besides whites, who feel the same way. Many Asians, if not the majority, do. For example, Japanese Prime Minister Yasuhiro Nakasone expressed a sentiment shared by more than just a few Japanese and other Asians.[33]

But even if there are whites who don't believe that blacks are inferior to them, those who openly espouse racist beliefs constitute a large segment of the American population:

> The General Social Surveys conducted by the National Opinion Research Center at the University of Chicago find that about one out of six Americans nationally say social differences between blacks and whites are due to 'less in-born ability to learn' [among blacks]....
>
> A slightly larger proportion of Southerners surveyed [19 versus 15 percent] say blacks are less intelligent than whites. This percentage of people expressing such views are [sic] relatively small. But when translated into people, these findings suggest that about 12 million Southern adults - and 28 million adult Americans nationally - hold at least some views that would be generally regarded as overtly racist.[34]

Those figures come from the 1996 national surveys and were therefore based on the 1990 census. There are more Americans today, about 300 million of whom 83 percent are white. Therefore the number of whites who are overtly racist is much higher than it was in 1996.

Now, add to this those who are reluctant to express their racist views to poll takers, including those who profess they like blacks knowing full well that they don't. You have a much higher number of racists, although no one is exactly sure how many. But one thing is clear:

> National surveys suggest that little consensus exists over integration as a goal, nationally or in the South.
>
> While Martin Luther King, Jr., a Southerner and a black, had a dream of an integrated society where African Americans and whites lived together in harmony, that dream is rejected by about half of all Americans in the South as well as in the country as a whole, according to surveys conducted by the Center for the Study of the American South at the University of North Carolina and co-sponsored by the *Atlanta Constitution*.
>
> Southerners were somewhat less likely than the rest of the country to support integration of the races.[35]

The study by the University of North Carolina also found that at least 4 percent of all Americans are in favor of legal segregation reminiscent of Jim Crow. Almost 11 million whites openly say so.[36] That was in 1996. You have more today who feel that way. Add those who are not so outspoken but still hostile toward blacks. The figure is not only much higher than 11 million; they are found in all parts of the country according to surveys.[37] And these are the results of different surveys.38 They all reach the same conclusion: Racism remains a big problem in America, contrary to what most black conservatives say.

Even Koreans and members of other racial groups whom Thomas Sowell claims don't start trouble with blacks in the inner cities where Orientals and other racial minorities own businesses,39 have been known to do that, contrary to what he says in his writings.40

That is one of the reasons, probably the main reason, blacks want them out of their communities in the inner cities, although their expulsion, if it ever happened, would probably never be as brutal as what Idi Amin did to Asians in Uganda. Sowell uses Amin as an analogy as much as he does Hitler. Amin, a black, ruled Uganda under black majority rule, while blacks in the United States remain powerless under white majority rule.

First of all, the vast majority of blacks in the United States don't even think in those terms or contemplate such a move, expelling Asian businessmen from their communities. I am black myself and lived in the inner cities for many years. So I know how fellow blacks feel.

But even if they did think in those terms and tried to force non-blacks out of the ghetto or any other parts of the inner city, whites are not going to allow that: do to Koreans what Idi Amin did to East Indians and Pakistanis in Uganda. As Sowell states in his book *Migrations and Cultures*:

> In August 1972, he [Amin] ordered 50,000 Asians expelled, citizens and non-citizens alike and severely limited how much money - 55 (British) pounds - they could take with them.
> The Asian population of Uganda, which had been 96,000 in 1968 [six years after Uganda won independence from Britain in October 1962], was estimated at only 1,000 at the end of 1972. Many landed destitute, in England or in whatever other countries would take them.41

Louis Farrakhan and others may be aspiring to do the same thing across black America, kick out "foreigners" - such as Koreans - whom he calls "bloodsuckers" of the black community. His motivation may be as racist as Idi Amin's, and just as wrong. But it is also wrong for Sowell and other black conservatives to argue that Koreans, Arabs, Vietnamese, and others don't initiate racial hostilities in the black communities without provocation from blacks; they have been known to, and many have publicly insulted blacks through the years. That is racism. Even if one chooses to call it verbal violence, which it is, as much as it is racism, it still leads to physical confrontation and violence in some situations.

And it has happened in a number of cases because of the insults hurled at blacks by Koreans, Arabs, Jews and other non-black business owners in black communities across the United States. For example, in Detroit, Arabs and other people from the Middle East have been known to insult blacks, taunting and treating them discourteously, and making disparaging remarks. It happened to me more than once when I lived in Detroit in the seventies. And it happened to others whom I know, and in my presence. Some blacks have even been shot dead, at gas stations, for example.42

Contrary to what Sowell says, these people have used physical violence against blacks in more than just a few cases. One of the best examples and most publicized cases is the Los Angeles incident when a Korean store owner shot and killed a black girl, inflaming passions in the black community. The result was a riot by blacks, leading to the destruction of Korean businesses and others.43 As this provocation continues, the obvious response from many blacks is: "See you in the next riot."

The contempt for blacks many of these people have is a matter of public record. As Dinesh D'Souza points out, although he hardly has anything good to say about black people in his book *The End of Racism*:

One Korean businessman in Los Angeles offered his blunt assessment of the reason for the black antagonism. 'Black people are jealous of the Koreans. They're lazy. We are working hard. They're not making money. We are making money'....

Certainly black and Korean ethnic styles differ. Blacks, as a group, are expressive and engaging [obviously, D'Souza's and other people's euphemism for - blacks talk too much and enjoy physical contact with all that hand-slapping and boisterous laughter]; Koreans as a group are reserved and taciturn: female merchants, for example, sometimes drop change on the counter to avoid physical contact with [black] customers....

Moreover, many Koreans...view with barely concealed distate, weird fascination,and fear an African American inner-city culture seemingly dominated by illegitimacy, profligacy, and violence. African American activists seize on these social characteristics to argue that Koreans refuse to offer them respect.[44]

The contempt for blacks is obvious, as D'Souza has shown, although he blames blacks for their hostility toward Koreans without pointing out that some of this hostility, perhaps most of it, has to do with the racist attitude of the Koreans.[45] Black conservatives - Sowell, Joseph Brown whom we cited earlier, and others - have taken the same stand, defending Korean and Asian racism toward blacks.[46]

If Asians don't have racist feelings toward blacks, there must be an explanation for that. Is it because they feel they are in the same boat with blacks as an oppressed people? Hardly the case. Some people claim this kind of solidarity exists among non-whites loosely identified as Third World Worlders. This is not very convincing either.

There just doesn't seem to be much solidarity among them beyond rhetoric especially by the leaders. Although Sowell blames blacks for their hostility toward Asians, and not vice versa, he concedes:

Asians have not been admirers of African culture, African habits, or African appearance. This was not peculiar to Kenya or even to East Africa. Despite the pious public 'unity' of Third World politics, a delegate from India at the famous Bandung conference of Third World nations summed up the relations between Asians and Africans to an Indian writer by confiding: 'We and the Africans couldn't care less for each other.'[47]

So what makes Sowell think the attitude of Asians toward blacks in the United States is any different? Black Americans are still African. That is why they call themselves African Americans: Africans born in America or Americans who are also Africans. And Asians are still Asian. That is why they call themselves, are also called and even Sowell himself calls them, Asian.

Ignoring racism by Asians, as black conservatives do, is not going to improve race relations by pretending that the problem does not exist, anymore than abolishing affirmative action will. In both cases, of affirmative action and Asian contempt for blacks, black conservatives gloat that that race does not matter, an observation that cannot be reconciled with what many perceive to

265

be the racist nature of the American society.

It is in this context that the attitude of many blacks toward black conservatives must be viewed. Vitriolic condemnation of black conservatives in their midst springs from real causes. And it should not be misconstrued as personal attacks.

The campaign to abolish affirmative action set the context for another clash between black conservatives and their brethren across black America most of whom support the program. Nowhere was the campaign more sustained than in the state of California.

It is precisely for this reason that Ward Connerly came under blistering attack from a number of blacks in California and other parts of the country, although their recriminations did not stop him from taking his crusade nationwide after he won in California in 1996.

In 2006, he led another campaign to abolish affirmative action, this time in the state of Michigan, and succeeded. The majority of the voters, that is white voters, supported Proposition 2 to abolish affirmative action. As California State Senator Diane Watson, a black, said about Connerly and his anti-affirmative action campaign in California: "He probably feels this makes him more white than black, and that's what he really wants to be."[48]

Michigan became the third state in the nation to abolish affirmative action. The other one was Washington which was the second to do so after California. And Ward Connerly played a major role in all those states campaigning to abolish affirmative action.

And he vowed to go on a nationwide crusade to abolish the program. None of this endeared him to the majority of blacks many of whom did not have very nice things to say about him.

Fred Jordan, a black San Francisco contractor, put it bluntly when he said about Connerly: "He's a hypocrite of the worst kind. He doesn't particularly want to be called African American or black, but he's using it very astutely to advance his own personal gains. For someone to stand within the ranks and say, 'I'm black,' but use it to destroy his own people - that's the kind we brand as a traitor."[49]

The Oakland Tribune published an editorial cartoon of a dry-cleaning shop, called "Connerly & Co - Ethnic Cleansers," complete with Ku Klux Klan outfits - hooded robes and all - hanging on the racks. One NAACP official told *The Los Angeles Times* that Connerly and Clarence Thomas are nothing but hypocrites: [They] thump their chest about merit, when neither of them operates in a realm where merit matters. It's political connections."[50]

And in a bitter op-ed in *The Los Angeles Times*, Richard Russell, a black and president of the California Alumni Association, said Connerly made it in business and enjoyed a high profile because of his connections to California's conservative Republican Governor Pete Wilson: "If I were in Connerly's position, I too might believe that the race card is largely irrelevant and had nothing to do with my successful position."[51]

A white supporter of the California Civil Rights Initiative (CCRI), which was the campaign launched to abolish affirmative action and succeeded in doing so, complimented Connerly in a way that may have made even hardcore white conservatives jealous: "He has an innate pro-Americanism that in a way makes him more in league with right-wing conservatives."[52]

Those are the kind of credentials that earn enemies in the black community because of the hostility and track record of right-wingers opposed to racial equality for blacks. And they are the very people Connerly identifies himself with as a *bona fide* right-winger himself. Another white conservative, Tom Wood who was one of the two academics who launched the abolish-affirmative-action campaign also praised Ward Connerly effusively, saying: "Without Ward and Pete Wilson, CCRI wouldn't have made it on the ballot."[53]

The battle between black conservatives and the rest of black America will never end. Not only are the two sides ideologically polarized, but they also disagree on fundamental realities of American life. Although black conservatives are outnumbered in the black community, they make their presence known on the national political scene using different forums including the media which they routinely denounce as "liberal," an epithet in the lexicon of right-wing ideologues.

One of the high-profile black conservatives who was also Pat Buchanan's running mate on the Reform Party ticket during the 2000 presidential campaign is Ezola Foster, a guest on two television talk shows, *CNN & Company*, and *Larry King Live*.

She has inflamed passions from coast to coast, especially among blacks, about whom she seems to know very little in terms of their daily lives in a white-dominated society, although she is black herself and should know about Jim Crow more than many other blacks since she came from Louisiana, a southern state notorious for racism and segregation, and moved to Los Angeles in 1960.

A former school teacher and administrator with the Los Angeles public schools for 33 years, mostly as a teacher, she is one of the leading women in the black conservative "movement" - a misnomer for such a small group - and remains unperturbed in the face of what she and her ideological compatriots consider to be vicious assaults on their black rightwing group. In relating her experiences with other blacks, she had the following to say in one of her articles in *Headway*:

> Responding to a December ad in *Radio-TV Interview Report*, radio talk shows from across the country booked me for a schedule that averaged two hours daily of talk show appearances.
> On one particular day, I found myself talking to radio listeners in North Carolina and Vermont in the morning and Detroit and Mississippi in the afternoon....
> Callers labeled me 'a liar' who was 'working with whites' to keep black leaders, like Farrakhan down,...A young black man began the onslaught by saying, 'It's blacks like you who hurt our cause, you are a traitor to the black race....You should be assassinated'....The caller became enraged and, more than once, shouted that I 'should be killed.'[54]

Of course to Foster and other black conservatives, such critics are playing a skin game, taking cover under their natural dress while dodging responsibility for their condition, a point underscored by Shelby Steele, who contends that many blacks are handicapped by the psychology of self-victimization.[55]

Foster argues that blacks who disagree with her believe more in the color of their skin than they do in God, their country, and their family. Such comments have further alienated her from the black community, causing her to lament:

> Just mention of our U.S. Constitution set ff one caller: 'How dare you, Mrs. Foster, supposedly a black woman, talk like the Constitution applies to us. You don't know your black history; black people aren't even mentioned in the U.S.

Constitution. We aren't even a part of the Constitution'....

Then there was the 31-year-old caller who first told how schools and community leaders in the South Central Los Angeles neighborhood where he grew up taught him to hate the white man. He went on to say how he had been a gang member and blamed the white man for everything. But then he found Jesus and realized he was taught wrong....Now he believes in God and family....

After congratulating him on his impending fatherhood, I added, 'I am curious, you said you now believe in God and family. What about your country?'...He snarled, 'How can I believe in this country, this white racist America, that enslaved and lynched my people?'[56]

Most blacks, and many whites, say America still is a racist society, despite the strides - and they are impressive in many areas - it has made toward racial equality. Black conservatives and their white counterparts say it is not. It used to be, but not anymore. Yet it can't be both. America is either racist or it is not. If it is not, it is color-blind and offers equal opportunity to all. But is this true?

Who is to blame for the confusion? Black conservatives contend civil rights leaders have warped the minds of their black followers into believing that racism is still a serious problem - if it is one at all - and that they don't have as much opportunity as whites and others do to succeed in life. Equal opportunity exists for everybody, black conservatives claim. A warped mind sees exactly the opposite. And that is the tragedy across America, they contend, prompting Ezola Foster to say: "Yes, a mind is a terrible thing to waste. And the political leadership of the 60's continues to take its toll on the minds and hearts of our young."[57]

Others have questioned her sanity, of course. For example, for a black person like her - or for any decent human being - to say God brought slaves to America so that their descendants could enjoy freedom, is unconscionable. And she has said more than that. According to *The Washington Post*:

If Ezola Foster is elected vice president of these United States, ladies and gentlemen, there won't be anymore free lunch in America! At least not in the public schools. The government won't be wasting money feeding poor kids. They're not hungry, anyway. 'This idea that you come to school hungry - *come on*! It's crazy!' Foster says. 'It's just so they can bring in all these lunch programs, breakfast programs - next, it's going to be dinner!...That's not the job of the schools - to feed the children. Let them pay for it or let them bring their own.'

Ezola is the black female John Birch Society member - [John Birch Society is a white racist organization] - who won the vice presidential nomination of the Reform Party, or at least the faction of the party that nominated [racist] Pat Buchanan for president....

In 1995, she organized a testimonial dinner for Laurence Powell, one of the [white] cops convicted of beating [black motorist] Rodney King....The city cancelled the dinner....She filed a lawsuit....She didn't get the money, but she did get lots of publicity.

She enjoys publicity, and she loves tweaking the black establishment. She says the civil rights movement has become 'a revenge-and-reparations movement.' She calls Jesse Jackson and other black leaders 'Leninist race-baiters.' Last January, she spoke at a 'Repudiate Jesse Jackson' rally, where she defended the Confederate flag and announced that God brought African slaves to America 'so that their descendants would know freedom'....

The 'government schools' have become 'socialist training camps,' she says. And a free lunch is just part of the problem. 'Now they have gone from feeding them to medicating them....These mental health programs are another thing that needs to be booted out of our schools! Every time there's a tragedy, they have to send for grief counselors. How totally ridiculous!'

Funny she should mention mental health. Her own mental health - or possible lack thereof - recently made news across the country. On August 24, *The Los Angeles Times* reported that Foster received workers' compensation payments for an unspecified 'mental disorder' after leaving her job as a typing teacher in 1996. It was the perfect gotcha story: Either Foster had a mental disorder or she was ripping off the workers' comp program. In other words, she's crazy or she's crooked.

'I'm perfectly sane,' she told *Times* reporter Doug Smith. But a few minutes later, she got mad and hung up on him.

The story went out on the news wires. It was printed all over the country. It made her look...well, nutty....

The exact nature of her 'mental disorder' is blacked out in the public records of the case, and Foster's attorney is fighting to keep those records secret. But Foster says her mental problem was simple - 'stress'....

Foster grew up poor in a little Louisiana town during the 1940s and '50s, but she says segregation wasn't really so bad. Sure, the law said black people had to sit at the back of the bus, but sometimes, she says, the less racist white drivers would let her sit wherever she wanted. And blacks could attend the local movie theater only one day a month, but that wasn't so bad either, she explains, because 'it was so exciting to have the theater all to ourselves.' And black folks were forced to sit in the back of her Catholic church and couldn't receive Communion until the whites were finished, but she didn't mind because, she says, 'after the Mass we saw the whites and blacks hugging and talking.'

'It's a gross distortion to say we were all ill-treated,' she wrote in her 1995 book, *What's Right for All Americans*. 'We were not sacrificial lambs.'[58]

If she did not see racism as bad back then, when the southern states including Louisiana where she grew up were as bad as apartheid South Africa in many fundamental respects, it's no

270

wonder she doesn't see racism as bad at all nowadays; that's if it exists at all according to her.

But to attribute her black conservative views like these to her "unstable" state of mind is to provide black rightwing ideologues like her with an excuse. They know what they are saying. And she may be "perfectly sane," as she said, despite her warped mind in the ideological sense according to the majority of blacks who don't subscribe to her views and those of other black conservatives.

By remarkable contrast, another black conservative, Shelby Steele, admits racism was bad when he was growing up in Chicago. They were segregated, they had to use second-hand books handed down to them from white schools, and the white teachers they had were the ones who had been rejected by white schools.

But, as a typical black conservative, he contends that there are virtually unlimited opportunities for blacks nowadays; which seems to be a contradiction in a country where even he himself admits racism still exists. As he states: "This is not to say there isn't racism. I still meet it everyday. It is simultaneously true that I have an enormous amount of freedom that I can pretty much take my life in whatever direction I want to take it."[59]

Can you live anywhere you want, or get any job job you want and for which you are qualified, as a black person? If you can do all that, and much more just like whites do, get loans and whatever else, why complain about racism then? Racism is no longer a problem. Black conservatives might respond by saying racism does not affect the lives of black people to the extent that it interferes with whatever they do or want to do. If racism does not have a significant negative impact on the lives of black people, that's if does at all according to black conservatives, then the United States does not have a race problem. It has been solved because whites now fully accept blacks as equals in all areas of life.

But that's not what even white people themselves say, as poll after poll through the years, and as everyday life in their encounter with blacks, clearly shows. And are all blacks lying when they say they suffer racial discrimination? Why just them and not black conservatives?

Black conservatives, of course, say black leaders and their

supporters and their white liberal counterparts still live in the sixties, with their minds trapped; hence their persistent claim that racism *still* is a serious problem that impedes black progress and denies black people full racial equality even today almost 40 years after the civil rights movement; when, in fact, it is a minor nuisance at worst in many, if not in most, cases.

And how do black civil rights leaders and other blacks respond to all that? They say it is the black conservatives, not they and their white liberal counterparts, who have warped minds. Racism *still* is a serious problem, they maintain. And every black person with even just a little common sense knows that because - "we *all* catch it. So let's stick together. We can't tolerate traitors."

At the NAACP annual convention in Minneapolis in 1995, U.S. Supreme Court Justice Clarence Thomas was branded a "traitor" to his race, "a pimp," and called other names by convention delegates because of his hostile conservative views toward blacks.[60] Myrlie Evers-Williams, widow of the slain civil rights leader Medgar Evers, who chaired the convention, put it poetically:

> How did his mind get so twisted
> And who does he think he is...
> And how can he imagine he is able
> To be anything but black?[61]

Jack White, a black columnist for *Time*, described Thomas as the "scariest of all the hobgoblins [in Washington]....The most disturbing thing about Thomas is not his conclusions, but his twisted reasoning and bilious rage."[62]

The question is why Thomas would do that in the name of justice. Black law professor Charles Lawrence, who testified against Thomas' confirmation for a seat on the U.S. Supreme Court, has tried to explain why. In his testimony, Lawrence praised Justice Thurgood Marshall, whom Thomas would replace, as an advocate of the least powerful members of society, while Thomas had chosen to serve "those who are the most powerful in this society, and has served them well."[63]

Dr. Joseph Lowry, who was then president of the Southern Christian Leadership Conference (SCLC), ridiculed Thomas during the 1995 SCLC annual convention when he described the

Supreme Court as having "three white males, one white female, and a whatchamacallit."[64]

Joseph H. Brown, a black editorial writer with the *Tampa Tribune* and columnist for the black conservative journal *National Minority Politics*, renamed *Headway*, has also come under blistering attack for his anti-black, specious views. As he stated: "The letters editor of my newspaper, a young white woman, came into my office recently with a stunned look on her face. She had received nasty letters before from black readers who disliked my columns, but this particular letter was beyond mean. The writer called me an 'Uncle Tom,' 'a house nigger,' the 'head nigger in charge,' and other things that I can't print here....At the beginning of 1995, *U.S. News & World Report* predicted that black conservatives would finally be heard by mainstream news media. Although it is far short of what I would like to see, there has been an increase. In reaction to this, the Soul Patrol - the Negro Thought Police, the Black Gestapo - has come out in force....Only the Marines can deploy its troops faster."[65]

As *U.S. News & World Report* pointed out at the beginning of 1995, black conservatives came to be heard more and more in the media and other forums. The reaction was swift when they got in the spotlight, but, to their dismay, there was not any large increase in the number of blacks who became conservatives. By the late 1990s, black conservative publications such as the Texas, Houston-based *Headway* and the Michigan, Lansing-based *Destiny* were being published. *Headway* ceased publication in the late 1990s for lack of readership. Financial backing from white conservative groups was not enough to save it; only large circulation in the black community more than anywhere else could have.

But the majority of blacks were not interested in what black conservatives had to say in this journal and other publications. They are a carbon copy of their white ideological fathers who not only don't care about blacks but don't mind starving people to death in the richest country on earth.

Much as black conservatives are beholden to white conservatives, they lack the courage to articulate new ideas which could provide a new perspective on what their white mentors say and try to convince fellow blacks why these new ideas provide a better alternative to the liberal ideas they have always taken for granted as the final truth. Instead, they only parrot what their godfathers say. As Timothy Lester, a white, said about black conservatives:

> I am a white man who lives in an overwhelmingly white state....I do concur with [the] assessment that black conservatives have a seriously deficient image....They echo the same old 'carbon copy, hard-line' rhetoric of the conservative right.
>
> This message is seen by many people even here in relatively conservative New Hmapshire as harsh, insensitive and unreasonable. An example of this mind set is conservative talk show host Armstrong Williams. Whenever I have seen Mr. Williams on television, he acts as if he is scared to death to say anything that may offend his right-winged friends. He dances and floats around issues instead of calling them what they are. On one program he was so bad that even the host had to tell him in so many words, 'don't be so damn bloodless.' He is not alone.
>
> Many black conservatives - I do not mean to be rude, but I have to be blunt - they come across as spineless, colorless individuals....Black conservatives must develop ideas that are going to convince Americans - particularly their own people - that they are a group that is worth to follow. Otherwise they will be seen merely as a group of naive, out-of-touch individuals with a useless message.[66]

Probably the most useful message black conservatives have delivered and continue to deliver as faithful messengers of white conservatives is: Ignore blacks, totally. They don't speak out even against what some whites in the Republican party, which is also the party of black conservatives, know are racist views of some of their most prominent leaders and lack of compassion by a party that claims to have a "Contract With America." The case of Republican House Speaker Newt Gingrich best illustrates this point. That was before this former history professor, later congressman, fell from grace and lost his job as speaker of the House. As Sandy Tadlock, a white Republican, said about Gingrich: "I don't think the man has any compassion."[67]

One would think that is a Democrat talking, saying all that about the House speaker who, in the eyes of many, symbolized what the Republican party stands for. But Tadlock was not only a Republican; she was only one of many Republicans who felt that way. As Richard Morin, a reporter, stated in *The Washington Post*: "Millions other Americans...don't like House Speaker Newt

Gingrich, according to a new *Washington Post* national survey. Only one in four survey respondents say they have a favorable impression of Gingrich. Nearly half hold an unfavorable opinion of the speaker, with the majority of those saying they have a 'very unfavorable' view. Even worse for the speaker, barely half of all Republicans and one out of four political independents say they view him positively."[68]

Michelle Ann Feavel put it more sharply: "I believe he is very hard on minorities. I don't like people being given the impression that Republicans are insensitive to people's needs. I feel that some people may feel that Newt Gingrich is insensitive to people's needs. I would tell him to become a little bit more compassionate and sensitive toward the needs of others."[69] Feavel's analysis speaks volumes about a leader and the policies of a party that has shown litle to no compassion for blacks since the end of Reconstruction - more than 100 years ago.

That is something black conservatives ignore when they oppose programs intended to fight racial injustice and include blacks in the mainstream of the American society from which they have been excluded for so long, restricted to playing a peripheral role as if they were not full citizens. Their hostility is directed against fellow blacks as if they are determined to prove to whites that it is only *they*, black conservatives among *all* blacks, who know what racism is, and what it means to be black. Their opposition to affirmative action is a typical example of this, calling it "racism in reverse."

But what they call racism is *not* racism. Affirmative action was instituted to fight racism, and was even implemented - although not formally launched - in 1970 by the Republican administration of Richard Nixon; its seeds had been planted earlier in the sixties by the Kennedy and Johnson administrations.

In March 1961, President John F. Kennedy issued an executive order which created the Committee on Equal Employment Opportunity and mandated that projects financed with federal funds "take affirmative action" to ensure that hiring and employment practices are free of racial bias. That is because of rampant discrimination against blacks.

Therefore the program initiated by Kennedy was intended to open up opportunities for blacks and others who had been left out.

275

But it was not until 1965 that President Lyndon B. Johnson defined the concept of affirmative action in his speech at Howard University in June that year. He made it clear that civil rights laws alone are not enough to remedy discrimination. As he stated in his speech:

> You do not wipe away the scars of centuries by saying: 'now, you are free to go where you want, do as you desire, and choose the leaders you please.' You do not take a man who for years has been hobbled by chains, liberate him, bring him to the starting line of a race, saying, 'you are free to compete with all the others,' and still justly believe you have been completely fair....
>
> This is the next and more profound stage of the battle for civil rights. We seek not just freedom but opportunity - not just legal equity but human ability - not just equality as a right and a theory, but equality as a fact and as a result.[70]

In September 1965, President Johnson issued an executive order to enforce affirmative action for the first time. The executive order required government contractors to "take affirmative action" toward prospective minority employees in all aspects of hiring and employment. Contractors must take specific measures to ensure equality in hiring and must document these efforts. The order was amended in October 1967 to cover discrimination on the basis of gender.

But it was the Philadelphia Order issued by Republican President Richard Nixon in 1969 that became the most forceful, up to that time, in implementing affirmative action, to guarantee fair hiring practices in construction jobs. Philadelphia was selected as a test case because, as U.S. Assistant Secretary of Labor Arthur Fletcher explained: "The craft unions and the construction industry are among the most egregious offenders against equal opportunity laws...openly hostile toward letting blacks into their closed circle." The executive order included definite "goals and timetables." As President Nixon asserted: "We would not impose quotas, but would require federal contractors to show 'affirmative action' to meet the goals of increasing minority employment."[71]

There would have been no need for affirmative action had there been no racism against blacks. But the people black conservatives single out as the greatest beneficiaries of "reverse discrimination," that is fellow blacks, are not even the ones who have benefited the most from these programs.

276

It is true that affirmative action has benefited many blacks and continues to do so. Still, the greatest beneficiaries, especially in the area of employment, have been white women, not black men or black women; something that is deliberately overlooked by black conservatives and others whose criticism is directed against blacks.

In the area of higher education, facts are twisted just as much to blame blacks. Again, black conservatives are more concerned about pointing out what is wrong with the blacks who are being admitted into colleges and universities under affirmative action than they are in presenting a balanced picture of what is really going on. As Professor Todd Gitlin states in his book, *The Twilight of Common Dreams: Why America is Wrakced by Culture Wars*:

> Consider the controversy over race-based admissions at Berkeley, one of Dinesh D'Souza's horror stories [in his best-selling book *Illiberal Education*]. The charge was that affirmative action was excluding thousands of worthy white and Asian candidates...that many blacks and Latinos were admitted to Berkeley with grade-point averages lower than those of whites and Asians - many of whom were being turned away with 4.0 averages.
>
> But hardly any protestors [including black conservatives] understood [or were willing to admit] that there were so many California high school graduates with 4.0 grade-point averages - more than 5,800 out of 21,300 who applied to Berkeley - that in 1989, even were there no affirmative action at all, 2,300 4.0s would have had to be turned away. With affirmative action, the number actually turned away was about 2,800.[72]

Statisticians, like economics professors Thomas Sowell and Walter Williams, using simple ciphers and numbers have no difficulty comprehending this reality but act as if these figures are buried in an ancient history archive that is inaccessible to them. The question is why black conservatives ignore this simple reality - and the benefits of affirmative action to minorities and to society as a whole that has seldom been fair to all its members.

This is not to say the numbers of those turned away as a result of affirmative action don't count or are a negligible factor - be it 50 or 500 white and Asian students denied admission - as was the case at Berkeley where 500 were. But all this must be weighed against the overall benefits to groups that historically and even in contemporary times have been denied - and continue to be denied - equality in a democratic society.

Black conservatives don't look at affirmative action in such a comprehensive way but, instead, focus on "injustices" perpetrated against white and Asian students, although those students still succeed in going to other schools that are just as capable of helping them harness their full potential. Even conservative economists such as Sowell and Williams will find that to be true when employing cost-benefit analysis techniques in an unbiased way. Nor are Sowell, Williams, Shelby Steele and other vehement critics of affirmative action, unfamiliar with inflated grades, being distinguished professors themselves who know what goes on in schools across the country. As Professor Gitlin states:

> Hardly any understood that in a most California euphemism, high school students got bonus grade-point credit for doing well in college preparatory courses, so that a 4.0 average did not mean that a student had gotten straight As. Hardly any students or faculty, let alone journalists, knew that alumni 'legacies' and athletic and special-skill admissions accounted for exceptions to the 'objective standards only' norm than affirmative action, so that in 1989, 24 percent of white students were admitted to Berkeley on criteria other than academic scores - a percentage not negligible....
>
> At Harvard, as late as 1988, preferences for children of alumni accounted for more admissions than all the African American, Mexican American, Native American, and Puerto Rican registrants combined.[73]

In spite of these facts, black students are still blamed for taking "all" the positions, in "all" the best schools that "should have" gone to "qualified" white and Asian students. In other words, so the argument goes, had it not been for "under-qualified" blacks being admitted into schools, "all" white students, and "all" Asian students, with 4.0 averages, would have been admitted - totally ignoring the fact that even if *no* blacks were admitted into colleges and universities, thousands and thousands of white and Asian students with 4.0 averages across the nation would *still* not have been admitted.

Critics of affirmative action also ignore the fact that thousands of white students are admitted into elite schools not only on criteria that have nothing to do with how well they did in high school and on the Scholastic Aptitude Test (SAT), or because they are sons and daughters or relatives of alumni; many of them are admitted because they have connections, other than ties of consanguinity with alumni and school officials, black students and their parents and relatives don't have in a society dominated by whites and which still practices racism.[74]

D'Souza ignores all this in his book *Illiberal Education* which Gitlin has dismissed as a product of "sloppy research." And black conservatives and others ignore these facts in their writings that could hardly be said to have been researched better, especially in the face of such incontrovertible evidence. This makes it extremely difficult for black conservatives to refute the charge that they downplay racism in a society where millions of whites openly espouse racist views.[75]

Others who don't openly do so are just as racist.[76] Even polls, with all the anonymity they guarantee, do not adequately gauge the sentiments of the people being interviewed, unless prodded further. As Bob Zelnick, although an opponent of affirmative action and probably a conservative himself, states in his book, *Backfire: A Reporter's Look at Affirmative Action*:

> The group's studies (done by Professor James H. Kuhlinski and others of the University of Illinois at Urbana-Champaign) had found evidence of rather acute anti-black attitudes in 42 percent of white Southerners and 12 percent of white non-Southerners, with milder prejudicial attitudes in perhaps an additional 10 percent of each population.
> The force of Kuhlinski's study was that its methodology was designed to avoid the 'social desirability' problem of poll taking, which is a phenomenon where people change their answers to match what they think is the 'right' or 'moral' answer.[77]

But even with all this, the unwillingness of even some of the most rabid racists to reveal their true feelings about blacks in polls, the level and intensity of bigotry is unmistakable, as shows by other surveys. As Gitlin states in *The Twilight of Common Dreams*:

> There remains plenty of bigotry, more than enough to indicate how far whites are from the color blindness commended as a value - even presumed as a fact - by those who think that the nation has done enough, or more than enough, to remedy the situation of blacks.
> In a 1990 survey, 29 percent of a national sampling of whites grouped blacks as unintelligent - four years before a best-selling book [*The Bell Curve*] lent this notion a certain degree of respectability with full pseudoscientific trappings. Whites who said they supported antidiscrimination laws in home sales increased from 34 percent in 1973 to 51 percent in 1990, an improvement of 50 percent; but this means that almost half were still not willing to support

279

open housing.[78]

The book Gitlin is talking about, *The Bell Curve* (now out of print obviously because of its pseudoscientific underpinnings that have been demolished by a number of scholars and others), generated no sympathy for blacks among the majority of its readers who felt vindicated in their belief of intellectual superiority over black people.[79] And it is understandable given the psychology of America.

What national surveys show about racism is bad enough. But even more disturbing is the fact that the people interviewed in the polls do not always reveal their true feelings about blacks.[80] All it takes to trigger racists of any color is to discuss welfare or affirmative action programs which benefit blacks "more than anybody else," according to conventional wisdom; or parley that "all that crime" is committed by "you know who." Affirmative action by itself is a hot rod that has sent sparks flying for quite some time since the seventies when the program went into full swing:

In 1989 Paul M. Sniderman of Stanford University and Thomas Piazza of the University of California, Berkeley, asked a random sample of whites their opinions of blacks. Twenty-six percent said blacks were 'irresponsible'; 20 percent, that they were 'lazy.'

An equal number of randomly sampled whites were asked their opinions of blacks only after they had been asked a question about affirmative action: 'In a nearby state, an effort is being made to increase dramatically the number of blacks working in state government. This means that a large number of jobs will be reserved for blacks. Do you favor or oppose this policy?'

In this population, the number who said blacks were 'irresponsible' rose to 43 percent; those who said blacks were 'lazy' rose to 31 percent. In other words, the mere mention of affirmative action, albeit attributed to 'a nearby state,' triggered an increase of more than 50 percent in the number of whites willing to express outright denigration.[81]

Almost ten years later, more than half of all Americans said they opposed racial integration.[82] Any talk of racial equality triggers an outflow of emotions even from some of the most timid whites but who are no less bigoted than their outspoken neighbors.[83]

Hostility toward blacks runs deep. And it is deeply rooted in

American history because of the perceived inferiority of black people more than anything else. And no legislation can end it. Affirmative action only fuels such hostility - which would exist, anyway, even without affirmative action. Affirmative action didn't start it. And that is the fundamental problem.

The problem already exists, with racists using affirmative action only as an excuse to justify their hatred of blacks, saying black people are unjustly taking this and that from them as a result of affirmative action favoring them. What about white women? Why don't they talk about them just as much if all they are against is affirmative action and nothing else? Yet they are the biggest beneficiaries of affirmative action. Blacks and other minorities, but especially blacks, are the only ones targeted:

> One may suspect that the 'mere mention' of affirmative action signaled to veiled bigots that the researchers might be receptive to otherwise taboo expressions of racial hostility. It is well known that survey interviewees are reluctant to own up to bigotry....
>
> In political campaigns, Republicans need 'merely mention' jobs, taxes, and welfare to get the attention of white males - the block accountable for their sweep in the midterm elections of 1994....
>
> The brutal fact is that the descendants of Africans seized and shipped to America where their ancestors were chained, sold, and lynched, they too, regardless of achievement, are often despised, belittled, or feared.[84]

Yet black conservatives either deny all that, or admit very little of it. Instead, they blame other blacks for stirring up trouble - complaining "for nothin'," about racism, even though millions of whites themselves admit they are racist. That is why they are opposed to racial integration, period, not just integrated housing or integrated schools. Survey after survey has shown that.

It is, of course, unfair, to say all whites are racist. Nobody knows what every white person thinks about black people to make such a bold assertion and sweeping indictment. Some whites have even died for blacks for reasons other than martyrdom. John Brown and his sons were not the only ones. Others died together with blacks during the civil rights movement in the sixties.

Even Malcolm X, who to many whites was the embodiment of black rage, did not condemn all whites as racist, as many of his critics, black and white but especially white, claimed. As he stated in his autobiography:

I don't speak against the sincere, well-meaning good white people. I have learned that there are some. I have learned that not all white people are racists. I am speaking against and my fight is against white racists. I firmly believe that Negroes have the right to fight all these racists.[85]

The majority of whites have negative feelings about blacks purely on the basis of race. And that makes them racist. Without affirmative action, many of them are not going to hire blacks out of their own goodwill. They don't have that toward blacks. They just *don't like* them. According to national surveys, "most whites retain negative beliefs about minorities..., they believe blacks prefer welfare to hard work and tend to be lazier than whites, are more prone to violence, less intelligent and less patriotic."[86]

Who would want to hire people like that, or have them as neighbors or rent to them? And they "all" steal, as the stereotype goes. They have nothing good to say about blacks. Yet some people, including black conservatives, say there is no need for affirmative action to open up opportunities for blacks and other minorities who have been locked out by these racists. Can you guarantee they are going to be fair without affirmative action? Civil rights laws are not enough. Experience has shown they are *not* enough.

And the tragic irony is that racism benefits *all* whites including those who are not racist and who fight racism. Many, probably most of them, are not going to give up or refuse to accept benefits in order to help a black person even if they know they are getting these benefits simply because they are white: employment, housing, services, what not. That is a function of racism, however inadvertent. But that is how it works. It is does not discriminate against any members of a privileged race. Therefore it is very democratic in that sense, to all of them.

But it can be hell for members of oppressed racial groups, especially blacks in the American context. And that is what many blacks see, which black conservatives don't. Yet when other blacks criticize them for ignoring racism, they accuse their critics of trying to control their minds and speech. As Joseph Brown, a black conservative journalist and editorial writer at the *Tampa Tribune*, states:

There is a price to pay when you deviate from the liberal Democratic path. You can be isolated and ostracized because you aren't 'black enough' to suit their taste....

A good example is the show 'Lead Story' on Black Entertainment Television. The regular panelists take turns with their name calling of black Americans who don't walk the Party line. They are called 'quislings,' 'sellouts,' 'buffoons' and 'traitors' for simply having ideological differences with the civil rights establishment, Democratic Party, or for having the nerve to be Republicans.

The show is so blatantly biased that the 'lead' in 'Lead Story' must be an acronym for Liberal Enforcement of Attitudes Department.'[87]

But it is more than just a question of ideological differences, as black conservatives claim, that has many blacks up in arms against blacks who are conservative. If the United States were an all-black nation, the terms of debate between black liberals and black conservatives would be profoundly different. The term Uncle Tom wouldn't even be in the vocabulary of political discourse, although the phenomenon so designated would undoubtedly exist since Uncle Tom is synonymous with traitor. Traitors are found in all societies and they don't always work for outsiders or for members of another race or ethnic group. All you have to do is betray the cause, from within or without.

Black conservatives have a tendency not only to downplay racism but also virtually deny its existence in spite of its malignancy across the spectrum. That is tantamount to endorsing, if not glorifying, white supremacy. Even some people who agree with them on a number of issues say black conservatives ignore racism and are no more than parrots on the shoulders of white conservatives echoing their views. As Ellen Rayner, who describes herself as "a political pragmatist [and] registered independent," states:

The image of black conservatives in the public eye is far from positive. Many of them are primarily seen as 'yes men and women' - I am being polite - who 'just happen to be black' as well as seem to bend over backwards in an effort to please their white conservative cohorts.

They are seen by many of their fellow blacks, as well as more than a few whites, as 'ideological puppets' who are being orchestrated by their right wing overseers. They seem to dismiss issues such as racism, sexism, poverty, discrimination, etc., as issues that are primarily nonexistent or, if they do exist, they are usually the victim's fault. Dr. Walter Williams and Armstrong Williams come to mind....

283

This is not going to garner black conservatives the admiration or respect that they will need from their own people in an effort to effectively promote their agenda that some claim they so desire to do. If they continue to travel down the perceived road of naivete, brashness, regressive conformity and lack of originality, they will eventually erode, become insignificant and evaporate into the cosmic, political dustbin.[88]

Black conservatives, of course, accuse other blacks and their liberal white supporters of "just blowing things out of proportion." Well, Rayner is not a liberal and in fact agrees with some of the things black conservatives say, although she is quick to emphasize that "as a matter of fact, I disagree strongly with some of them." And she is not alone in being highly critical of them. Many other non-liberals criticize black conservatives just as much.

But even if liberals do indeed "blow things out of proportion," which they don't concerning the pervasiveness and intensity of racism, does that mean conservatives should do the same thing?

One glaring example of such distortion by black conservatives and their white ideological compatriots has to do with the underclass phenomenon in the inner cities, a painful reality even blacks living in and outside the ghetto admit exists.   When black conservatives discuss it, they talk as if *all* of black America is saturated with the filfth many members - not all - of the underclass, black and white as well as others across the nation, are immersed in. For example, it is true that gang members roam the inner cities wreaking havoc. But where are the law-abiding citizens to balance the sheet of the virtues and vices of the inner cities in the record books of conservatives? Law-abiding citizens in the ghetto far outnumber gang members. But that is not the picture conservatives project. Why not?

Even most of the people who belong to the underclass in the ghetto are not criminals. As Charles Ogletree, a black law professor at Harvard, emphatically states: "Nine-nine percent of black people don't commit crimes."[89] There are at least 3 million blacks in the underclass, trapped in poverty.[90] Are all those people criminals, gang members, dope pushers, thieves, rapists, robbers and murderers?

It is also true that the number of high school dropouts across black America is alarming, as it is everywhere else across the nation. But what about the untold numbers of those who stay in school? They outnumber dropouts - otherwise classrooms in the inner-city schools would be almost empty. Yet you hardly hear about them, these ambitious black boys and black girls, except dropouts and troublemakers in class. What about the thousands and thousands of black students who graduate from college every year? Why don't conservatives talk about them just as much to give a balanced picture of black America?

It is also true that many blacks - but even more whites, of course - don't work, among whom are those who don't even look for jobs; some have simply given up for a number of reasons, including racism and lack of motivation and marketable skills. But what about the millions of blacks who work?

In fact, many blacks take jobs whites won't touch. As a superintendent of a Kentucky plough factory put it: "Negroes do work white men won't do, such as common labor; heavy, hot, and dirty work; pouring crucibles; working in the grinding room; and so on. Negroes are employed because they are cheaper....The Negro does a different grade of work and makes about 10 cents an hour less."[91] And that is not just in the south, or upper south as Kentucky and the other parts of that mid-region are called. A foreman at a steel mill in a northern city expressed similar views: "Blacks are well fitted for hot work, and we keep them because we appreciate this ability in them."[92]

But that is not the image we get, of the hardworking, overworked black man from the ghetto or the rural south. We hear more about lazy blacks, pimps, dope pushers, prostitutes and welfare queens in the ghetto. How many times do you hear conservatives, black and white, talk about lazy whites even in coded language? It is *always* blacks, with conservatives using code words and phrases - pimps, thieves, muggers, and dope pushers - to identify them, which automatically translate into "black" in the minds of most whites and others.

It is true that there are lazy blacks - you find lazy people in all races and ethnic groups. But there are even more lazy whites, in terms of raw numbers and probably even in percentage, in a predominantly white nation.

And are all those blacks who don't work, unemployed - *because* they are lazy? What about racism? Is it not a factor in many, if not in most, cases? Yet black conservatives and their white cohorts blame the victims.

Providing a balanced picture of the virtues and vices of black America, and of racism, is not a cover-up of black America's vices and failures; refusing to do so is a cover-up of lies about black America that are so common across the nation and accepted by most whites as gospel truth.

There is no question that black America is plagued with a multitude of problems all of which cannot be attributed to a single cause. But racism is definitely one of them, and a prime factor in many cases, and makes things worse, much worse for blacks than any other group of non-whites. Thomas Sowell, probably the most well-known black conservative and the patriarch of the black conservative "movement," contends otherwise. As he states in his book *Migrations and Cultures*:

> The political temptation is to overlook the differences in cultural capital which often go far back into history and, instead, attribute these disparities to current failures of society. For example, the head of the leading black civil rights organization in the United States declared in 1994: 'Almost half of all African-American children live in poverty. Black unemployment is twice that of whites. The infant mortality rate in many black communities is equal to that of many Third World nations. The statistics for housing, crime and education deliver a tragic statement of despair and inequality. Yet, in polls, more than 60 percent of whites say blacks now have equal opportunity.'
>
> The very possibility that these disparities might be due to cultural differences affecting behavior and attitudes, or to differences in the human capital brought into the workplace, rather than to the behavior of the larger society, received no attention whatsoever, either in this statement or in much of the media or the academic world.[93]

The black leader whom Sowell is talking about is Benjamin Chavis when he led the NAACP. The factors cited by Sowell do affect one's life chances, although in varying degrees. Yet he and other black conservatives cannot explain in a totally non-racial context why the unemployment rate among blacks is twice the national average consistently through the years, even when blacks have the same skills as whites; and why the rate of poverty for blacks is three times that of whites - the same it was in1959. Why all this, if it has nothing to do with racism?

That is also why a very large number of blacks, including many middle-class blacks who can afford to move out of the ghetto and are trying to, are concentrated in the inner cities. Whites won't allow them to move into their neighborhoods, predominantly white areas, because of racism. That is also why many blacks with education equal to whites - and with degrees from the same schools - earn less than their white counterparts doing the same job under the same employer.[94]

It is also because of racism that black businessmen with good credit histories and economically sound track records are denied loans while their white counterparts with the same - or weaker credit histories and business records - are awarded loans in substantial amounts from the same banks and lending institutions that turned down black applicants; as the studies in Denver and Boston cited earlier clearly showed.

The Denver and Boston incidents were not the only sordid cases. The same findings have turned up in New York, Chicago, Los Angeles, Detroit and other cities through the years.[95] But when blacks cite those cases, black conservatives dismiss their complaints as "just whining", saying, they are nothing but shallow excuses for black failure or even extortion attempts to get something for nothing from whites by making them feel guilty for "runnin' over" blacks.

The debate between black conservatives and many other blacks is also - besides the debate over racism - fundamentally a conflict of analysis of the black predicament.

Black conservatives, including the few who don't ignore racism, don't see race as a paramount factor; class is, in their analytic paradigm. For example, Shelby Steele in his book *The Content of Our Character* says "racism is in decline,"[96] although segregation is everywhere, employment discrimination remains a fact of life, hate crimes are just as real, and blacks - including the most successful ones like Steele himself[97] - are still treated with disrespect or contempt for no reason other than that they are black; all this almost 40 years after the civil rights movement.

Even liberal Professor William Julius Wilson stated in his book *The Declining Significance of Race* published in 1978, a few years after the turbulent sixties, that race didn't really matter that much anymore,[98] as blacks acquired more education and skills and moved up the economic ladder into the professions as part of the mainstream in upward social mobility (a class-versus-race

287

argument advanced by conservatives and Marxists); although the seventies proved racism was a significant factor as the outburst of emotions and violence over school busing in Boston clearly showed. And this was only one example.

I was in Boston in June 1975 at a mass rally addressed by Roy Wilkins, head of the NAACP, when the conflict over busing was going on in that city and elsewhere. Not only was racism a serious problem back then, when Professor Wilson said it had become increasingly insignificant among blacks moving up the ladder, triggering a heated debate over what he said; there were other serious racial incidents in different parts of the country just as there are today thirty years later.

Sowell also, in his books *Race and Culture*, and *Migrations and Cultures*, as well as in his other writings,[99] contends that a person's values, skills and behavior - work habits, savings pattern, culture - are more important than race in order to succeed in life; although untold numbers of blacks with strong values and needed skills have failed to make it in life simply because they are black. Otherwise racism is not a potent force, and blacks who don't succeed in life are just lazy, a favorite argument for conservatives.

It is true that values - what Sowell calls cultural or human capital - are critical. But so is racism. Sowell and other black conservatives know that not all blacks who fail in life, or who don't succeed, are lazy, or lack values conducive to achievement or are without skills. Even some whites with skills don't find jobs all the time. What about blacks then, in a society where racism still is a serious problem?

But that is something black conservatives and their white counterparts such Edward Banfield, a highly influential conservative scholar among conservative policy makers and academics, don't readily acknowledge; since they look at society - including black America - almost exclusively in terms of class analysis. As (the late) Banfield states in his book, *The Unheavenly City: The Nature and Future of Our Urban Crisis*:

Almost everything said about the problems of the Negro tends to exaggerate the purely racial aspects of the situation....

The importance of racial factors is exaggerated implicitly by any statement that fails - as almost all do - to take account of the many nonracial factors such as income, class, education, and place of origin....the continuing causes of the

Negro's problems...very often have little or nothing to do with race....

So long as the city contains a sizeable lower-class, nothing basic can be done about its most serious problems. Good jobs may be offered to all, but some will remain chronically unemployed. Slums may be demolished, but if the housing that replaces them is occupied by the lower-class it will shortly be turned into new slums. Welfare payments may be doubled or tripled and a negative income tax instituted, but some persons will continue to live in squalor and misery. New schools may be built, new curricula devised, and the teacher-pupil ratio cut in half, but if the children who attend these schools come from lower-class homes, they will be turned into blackboard jungles....

Our devotion to the doctrine that all men are created equal discourages any explicit recognition of class-cultural differences....Sympathy for the oppressed, indignation at the oppressor, and a wish to make amends for wrongs done by one's ancestors lead to a misrepresentation of the Negro as the near-helpless victim of 'white racism.'[100]

What Banfield does not explain is why race is not a prime determinant in the well-being of black people when all the factors he mentions - income, class, education, and place of origin - are determined by racism in a society where racial discrimination is a fact of a life. Blacks earn less, because of racism. They are stuck in the ghetto, because of racism.

Each point he makes can be answered as a result of racism. What he is really saying, by implication, is that there is something innately wrong with blacks: they are born that way. That is why they are in the condition they are in. They have only themselves, and their nature, to blame.

This is typical of conservatives, using coded language to describe and ignore blacks because "nothing can be done" to help them alleviate their plight or improve their condition. And it resonates well among millions of whites across the country, who are tired of seeing their tax money being wasted to take care of "you know who."

What Banfield has done, just like his ideological compatriots have and continue to do, with his class analysis, is take an approach that led Marxists to ignore the significance of race in the American context.

Like Marxists, black conservatives and their cohorts contend that class transcends race and ethnicity. They are talking as if they are promoting solidarity of the working class cutting across racial lines reminiscent of their nemesis: communists and socialists.

Strange bedfellows indeed.

Yet, history shows that white blue-collar workers have been, and still are, some of the most racist people around.[101] That was also the case in apartheid South Africa where white blue-collar workers and black blue-collar workers never worked together for their common interests as workers because white workers were treated better, and they thought they were better, than *all* blacks including black professionals.

That also has been the case in the United States where labor unions refused to admit blacks as members or treated them as outcasts. In fact, for years, white blue-collar workers refused to have anything to do with blacks, in labor unions or anywhere else. They didn't want them around and avoided them like the plague. They did not even want to sit with them at the same table. And they still complain about blacks taking "their" jobs, invading "their" neighborhoods and schools, and so forth; thus exploding the myth of workers' solidarity and of the working class as a monolithic whole submerging racial differences.

Class analysis ignores the realities of the American society where black people have been and continue to be discriminated against as a racial group, a reality ignored by conservatives who, together with their ideological foes of the Marxist persuasion, have become strange bedfellows and an explosive mixture employing the same analytical tool, *class*, in a futile attempt to comprehend the black predicament.

Class is important - but not paramount - in the black American context. It *must* incorporate race to form a comprehensive conceptual framework for analysis of the black dilemma, although a synthesis of the two dialectic paradigms - race and class - is a theoretical nightmare. They are inseparable. Dismiss one, you lose perspective.

The Black Panther Party was one of the black nationalist organizations that was aware of the importance of both race and class in the struggle for black liberation, but failed to achieve a synthesis of the two. Eldridge Cleaver, when he was the Black Panthers' minister of information, acknowledged the relevance of both race and class in the black American context and tried to put them in proper perspective in the following terms:

We recognize the problem presented to black people by the economic

290

system - the capitalist economic system. We repudiate the capitalist economic system. We recognize the class nature of the capitalist economic system and we recognize the dynamics involved in the capitalist system. At the same time we recognize the national character of our struggle. We recognize the fact that we have been oppressed because we are black people even though we know this oppression was for the purpose of exploitation. We have to deal with both exploitation and racial oppression, and we don't think you can achieve a proper balance by neglecting one or the other.[102]

By ignoring racism, black conservatives are neglecting black America. And by doing so, they justify oppression and exploitation of their own people - in the name of color-blindness which does not even exist in the United States. It may not be a conspiracy on the part of whites to keep blacks down, and there is none, as a conscious effort because there is no need for one. As Derrick bell, a nationally renowned black writer and law professor, states in his book *Faces at the Bottom of the Well: The Permanence of Racism*: "Americans achieve a measure of social stability through their unspoken pact to keep blacks on the bottom."[103] Conservatives dispute that, of course, although Professor Bell's cogent analysis is validated by experience, past and present.

If that's not true, why are millions of blacks below whites in terms of socioeconomic status in spite of the fact that blacks work as hard as whites, and even harder in many cases to make sure they keep their jobs? Why the pattern of inequalities, duplicated in every city and every state, if racism is not a factor and a major problem in the lives of black people as black conservatives insist? As Stokely Carmichael stated in his essay, "Toward Black Liberation," in the *Massachusetts Review*:

The ghetto is a product of a combination of forces and special interests in the white community....If one goes into any Negro community, whether it is Jackson, Mississippi; or Cambridge, Maryland; or Harlem, New York; one will find the same combination of political, economic, and social forces at work....

I do not suppose that at any point the men who control the power and resources of this country ever sat down and designed these black enclaves, and formally articulated the terms of their colonial and dependent status, as was done, for example, by the apartheid government of South Africa. Yet, one can not distinguish between one ghetto and another. As one moves from city to city it is as though some malignant racist planning-unit had done precisely this - designed each one from the same master blueprint.

And if the ghetto had been formally and deliberately planned, instead of growing spontaneously and inevitably from the racist functioning of various institutions that combine to make the society, it would be somehow less frightening. The situation would be less frightening because, if these ghettos were the result of design and conspiracy, one could understand their similarity as being artificial and consciously imposed, rather than the result of identical patterns of white racism which repeat themselves in cities as distant as Boston and Birmingham.[104]

Almost 40 years later, the ghetto remains an enduring reality of American life, a virtual concentration camp according to some people, where blacks are trapped by racism and can't get out even if they can afford to. It may not be a concentration camp, but it is definitely the black homeland, with its own liveliness, and not just misery. Still, it should not exist in a society that espouses racial integration. But there are no signs it is going to disappear. In fact, exactly the opposite is taking place: further deterioration of the inner cities, Detroit for example which is 83 percent black, and balkanization of the American society along ethnic lines.

Much of the dilapidated housing in the inner cities would not exist had the tenants been white, since most of the property owners in ghettoes across the nation are white who also favor white tenants providing them with better housing and facilities including nice carpet. The other houses they own and rent to whites in predominantly white neighborhoods are better kept than the ones they rent to blacks in the ghetto or anywhere else. Not only don't they care about poor housing for blacks; some don't even consider blacks to be full human beings. As one white slum landlord, accused of exploiting blacks, bluntly stated: "Who else but me would take care of the whores, pimps, winos, addicts, hoodlums, queers - the dregs of humanity that nobody wants? It's a lousy zoo and I take care of some of the animals - but that's more than the federal government [does]."[105]

All whites landlords, probably most, don't talk that way. But a very large number of them feel exactly the same about blacks. And that translates into action, ignoring blacks. But to most black conservatives, all this evidence of racism and the plight of the inner cities is not enough to convince them that racism still is a major problem across the country. Instead, they say all that kind of talk is nothing but an excuse blacks use to justify their own failures in life, obviously including the failure to build or buy their own homes so that they don't have to deal with racist landlords anymore.

A few conservatives in the mainstream - black conservatives are on the periphery although they delude themselves into believing they are not - disagree with that assessment, that racism is not a major problem the way black ideologues on the right contend. As Robert L. Maginnis, a white conservative and senior policy analyst with the Family Research Council in Washington, states:

Although there has been some progress in racial reconciliation since the 1960s, there are still serious, lingering examples of racial division. In the last 14 months, 19 black churches in the South have been torched, and federal authorities have ample evidence that racism is the motivation....

Two months ago, arson destroyed a black church in Knoxville, Tennessee. This was the fifth black church in Tennessee to be burned down in 13 months. The church's charred remains revealed spray-painted, racist graffiti. After the church burning, a racist letter was circulated promising that if interracial relationships continued, white supremacists would embark on a reign of terror....

That church burning wasn't Knoxville's only racially motivated incident. There was an unsolved cross-burning last year. Additionally, in another part of Tennessee in March, three white supremacists were sentenced under federal civil rights law for burning two black churches a year ago....Of the 19 church burning incidents since January 1995, seven occurred in the last two months in seven different states: North and South Carolina, Georgia, Alabama, Tennessee, Louisiana, and Mississippi. These church burnings have drawn national [and world] attention.[106]

According to *U.S. News & World Report*, Timothy Welch and Gary Cox, charged with burning two black churches - one in Greeleyville and the other in nearby Bloomville, South Carolina, in June 1995 - were also charged with beating and stabbing a retarded black man in the same month. The report goes on to say: "The existence of groups like the Lord of Chaos and the epidemic of church fires across the South are peeling the lid off an alarming phenomenon: Despite the gains of the civil rights struggle, in-your-face racism is bubbling to the surface again. 'There is in our society today, more so than 20 or 30 years ago, a greater tolerance for intolerance,' says Abraham Foreman, national director of the Anti-Defamation League of B'nai B'rith."[107]

Cox and Welch had been attending local Ku Klux Klan recruiting rallies. Welch was carrying a KKK membership card when he was arrested, part of an orchestrated campaign by racist groups to intimidate blacks into submission. In fact, whites commit most of the hate crimes, as reported by *U.S. News & World Report*: "Between 10,000 and 40,000 hate crimes are committed annually in America...about 60 percent by whites."[108] And as Professor Jack Levin of Northeastern University put it: "The bad news is that this is coming from the center where most of us live. We aren't talking about racism under a rock but in the mainstream of our culture."[109]

What is so terrifying is that racism is so widespread, and so subtle in many cases yet just as destructive if not more so, and not confined to one area or group as would be in the case of a conspiracy. In the words of Assistant U.S. Attorney-General Deval Patrick when talking about the church burnings: "It's plain that racial hostility is behind many. The prospect of a conspiracy is a chilling thing. But the prospect that these are separate acts of racism is even worse."[110]

It is worse since the pervasiveness of the phenomenon is everywhere. Each perpetrator acts out his hostility and hatred without the slightest concern for the lives and well-being of black people including babies. They are all fair game. The mentality is the same among racists across the nation who consider themselves to be the guardians of their race. And the existence and virulence of racism is taken for granted by the perpetrator and victim alike.

It is true that racial injustice is no longer sanctioned by law as a legal institution as it was in the past. Because of that, black conservatives delude themselves into believing that black people are guaranteed equality before the law simply because the law says so. They are therefore protected from the violence and virulence of racism. It is a very optimistic way of looking at things. But the world doesn't work that way. There is a big difference between theory and practice, fantasy and reality, something black conservatives fail to grasp, for whatever reason.

Black people don't have the power to make whites enforce those laws if whites don't want to. This is not South Africa. Today, blacks in that country have the political muscle to force their multi-racial government to go a little faster to achieve equality with whites especially in the economic arena where whites remain firmly in control.

The situation is exactly the opposite in the United States. Black people are at the mercy of the white majority who remain racist in spite of passage of civil rights laws. Racism is real. It is virulent and, in many cases, blatant. As Danielle Allen stated in one of those rare confessions by blacks on the ideological right in the *National Review*:

Passing a dormitory near mine [at Princetion University], I heard a shout from one of the upper floors: 'F...ing nigger!' The shout was directed at me.

About racism, at Princeton and elsewhere, I was already no innocent. Speakers standing directly in front of me, in small rooms, had managed to deliver entire presentations without once looking at my face. I had often encountered the word 'black' in a list of derogatory adjectives....

I do not fear racism. I know it exists. But I am not afraid that it will keep me from going anywhere I want to go. In this way I am not, it turns out, a typical black American.[111]

At least she admits racism exists and implies it is a serious problem. But she also believes that it can't stop her from doing anything she wants to do in life; which is being overly optimistic or not being realistic. If black people can do that, then they shouldn't worry about racism, and they should stop complaining about it since it's just one of those problems in life which can be overcome. That is the black conservative position.

Danielle Allen does not explicitly state that she's a black conservative but implies she is one; and not just because she wrote in the conservative weekly journal, *National Review*, the flagship of the conservative movement, but mainly because of her perspective on racism and her assessment that, because of the way she sees racism, she's not "a typical black American."

She expressed those views in her review of a book, *The Rage of A Privileged Class: Why Middle-Class Blacks Are Angry; Why America Should Care*, by Ellis Cose,[112] and made it very clear that she does not see racism as an insurmountable obstacle "like some blacks do," as she put it, obviously because she believes black people, and not just a few of them, have the opportunity to excel in life and do whatever they want to just like whites do, in spite of racism.

That is not a liberal perspective or the way the majority of blacks feel. And that puts her at the other end of the ideological spectrum where you don't find many blacks.

In her review, she noted that the author of the book wrote about middle-class blacks who "despite their success in the white world, do not trust the communities they live in. [Cose's] witnesses testify to the lingering anger and discomfort of black folks who have 'made it,' financially and professionally - academics, lawyers, and business executives who tell stories of snubs and insults experienced in the lobbies of expensive hotels, while driving in their own neighborhoods, and in other apparently safe settings...[for example] a house-hunting attorney who asked over the telephone whether an apartment was 'in a good neighborhood,' and heard: 'Yes, it's in a very good neighborhood. There are no black people here."[113]

What should be emphasized here is that all the middle-class blacks who complain about racism, as Cose has documented in his book, are not liberals paranoid about something that does not exist. Some of them are conservatives - although probably not like Thomas Sowell, Clarence Thomas, Larry Elder and others like that - and would find it difficult to believe that they are just busy looking for a white oppressor who does not exist; nor are their complaints about racism, "nonsense," and nothing but a product of a fertile imagination spawning conspiracy theories of black oppression as Larry Elder claims.

Other black conservatives do, of course, share his glossy assessment even if it does not correspond to reality. As he bluntly states: "[Blacks feel] the system is rigged against them....That's the way a lot of blacks feel and it cuts across economic lines. Blacks for the most part believe that racism remains a huge problem in America, that America remains corrupt, and the criminal justice system remains corrupt."[114]

Contrary to what Elder and other black conservatives say, Cose states in his book that race relations are not as good as some claim, although it will probably take more than empirical evidence to convince black conservatives, and many whites, of that. As he explains in his work: "Certain widespread and amiable assumptions held by whites - especially about the black-middle class but also about race relations in general - are utterly at odds with the reality many Americans confront daily."[115]

Cose contends that there is a "glass ceiling" deliberately installed to block many black professionals from advancing in their careers, although some have shattered it. Black conservatives vehemently disagree with that. If there is no such barrier as they claim, then, not only is racism no longer a serious problem but black people just want to make America look bad, a country that has been so good to them. As some black conservatives have asked, "Would you be better off in Africa?" "The white man has been good to you," is the obvious conclusion from this line of reasoning by black conservatives. They might as well add, "Also, the white man pays good, real good. Do you?"

And they challenge their brethren to disprove that. For example, if blacks can't move into white neighborhoods, don't blame whites - blame black people themselves for that. They are not trying hard enough or they simply don't deserve to be there for whatever reason. And whites have the right to fear them because of "all that crime" they commit, or because of their "unacceptable" life style, whatever that means. There *must* be other reasons, besides race, why whites don't want them in their neighborhoods, including lowering property value. That is the logic of black conservatives.

Cose talks about the hostility one black lawyer faced when he was looking for an apartment in a good neighborhood, only to be told - by implication - that he wasn't welcome once they found out he was black. Yes, the apartment was in a very good neighborhood, he was told, because no blacks lived there.

Was that an isolated incident? No. Housing discrimination is a nationwide phenomenon. It's everywhere, in every city, from New York to California, Michigan to Texas, Maryland to Oregon, Vermont to Florida; Grand Rapids, Minnesota, to Grand Rapids, Michigan. The list goes on and on.

The implication of the statement that the neighborhood was very good because it had no black people is obvious: "All" blacks are criminals, and everything else bad. And it is given credibility by black conservatives in a statistical context, of which this is typical as formulated by Larry Elder: "Whites have to tell blacks frankly and candidly why they are scared: 'We're scared because 45 percent of those arrested for violent crime in this country are black. I'm scared because I've been mugged by a black person. I'm scared because my purse has been taken by a black person. I'm sorry, but when I go into the inner city and interact and go to the [Los Angeles] Raiders' game, I've had some negative experiences. That is why I am afraid."[116]

But on the whole? "Race relations are excellent. We're all getting along just fine," Larry Elder says.[117] So do other black conservatives. In the words of former NAACP head, Benjamin Hooks, black conservatives are "some of the biggest liars the world ever saw."[118]

Legally, America is no longer a racist society. But racism still is a major problem across the nation. Black people don't have equal opportunity for one simple reason. They can't have equal opportunity in a country where racism still exists as a major problem.

The majority of whites don't like blacks. That is why they don't want racial integration, as the studies we cited earlier clearly show. Therefore they don't want racial equality.

You can't have racial equality without integration. As Nathan Glazer states in his book, *We Are All Multiculturalists Now*, the main problem is "the fundamental refusal of other Americans to accept blacks."[119]

Black conservatives deny that. They are dead wrong.

Chapter Notes:

Introduction

1. Roger Wilkins, quoted by Dinesh D'Souza, *The End of Racism: Principles for A Multiracial Society* (New York: Free Press, 1995), p. 246; cp., Lena Williams, "Growing Black Debate: Racism or an Excuse?" in *The New York Times*, April 5, 1992, Sec. A, p. 1.

2. Richard Morin, "What Americans Think: Southern Discomfort: Racially Bigoted Attitudes Linger in Many Parts of Dixie," in *The Washington Post*, National Weekly Edition, July 15 - 21, 1996, p. 35.

3. United Church of Christ, quoted by Dinesh D'Souza, *The End of Racism*, op. cit., p. 116; and "United Church of Christ Urges Fight Against Rising Racism," in *The New York Times*, January 15, 1991.

4. Kenneth B. Clark, quoted by Dinesh D'Souza, *The End of Racism*, op. cit., p. 17. See also Kenneth B. Clark, "Racial Progress and Retreat: A Personal Memoir," in Herbert Hill and James L. Jones, Jr., *Race in America: The Struggle for Equality* (Madison: University of Wisconsin Press, 1993), p. 18.

5. Harold Cruse, *Rebellion or Revolution?* (New York: William Morrow, 1968), pp. 100, and 95. See also, *The Crisis of the Negro Intellectual* (New York: William Morrow, 1967).

6. "College Freshman Attitudes," in *1992 World Almanac and Book of Facts* (New York: Pharos Books, 1991), p. 245.

7. Richard Morin, ibid; Todd Gitlin, *The Twilight of Common Dreams: Why America is Wracked By Culture Wars* (New York: Metropolitan books, 1995), p. 123.

8. *Report of the National Advisory Commission on Civil Disorders*, also known as the *U.S. Riot Commission Report*, and the *Kerner Report* (New York: Bantam Books, 1968), pp. 1, and 10.

9. Langston Hughes, "A Dream Deferred," quoted by H. Rap Brown, *Die Nigger Die* (New York: Dial Press, 1969); and Arthur L. Smith and Stephen Robb, editors, *The Voice of Black Rhetoric* (Boston: Allyn and Bacon, 1971), p. 304.

10. Malcolm X, "The Ballot or the Bullet," speech delivered on April 3, 1964, Cleveland, Ohio; and in Arthur L. Smith and Stephen Robb, *The Voice of Black Rhetoric*, op. cit., pp. 216, and 217; cp., George Breitman, editor, *Malcolm X Speaks* (New York: Pathfinder Press, 1965).

11. "Our Political Philosophy," in *Headway*, formerly *National Minority Politics*, Houston, Texas, April 1997, p. 2.

See also "Many Accept Racial Separation," in the *International Herald Tribune*, August 18, 1999, p. 3:

"About half of (American) young adults believe that separation of the races is acceptable as long as there are equal opportunities for everyone, according to a survey of attitudes about race relations.

The study, sponsored by the National Association for the Advancement of Colored People (NAACP) and conducted by Hamilton College in New York City and the polling frim Zogby International, asked adults 18 to 29 whether 'it's OK if races are basically separate' from one another. The survey did not specify what 'basically separate' meant.

About 50 percent of whites surveyed responded that general separation by race was acceptable, compared with about 40 percent of blacks. Analysts who worked on the study said the findings signaled that race relations could worsen unless social and political institutions continued to push for integration and equal opportunity among all ethnic groups."

See also "Youths' Shifting Attitudes on Race," in *The Christian Science Monitor*, August 18, 1999, pp. 1 and 10:

"They're the most multicultural generation ever, but most are also at ease with the old idea of 'separate but equal'....

The class of 2000 is full of young people who think that separation of the races - at school, in neighborhoods, on dates - is

OK. As long as there's equal opportunity, they feel, who cares about such social segregation? 'It's not necessarily a bad thing,' says Nicholas Flores, a Mexican-American. 'It's important to be with people who understand each other's experience.'

Today's young Americans are the first to grow up in a nation without formal barriers to racial equality....But some evidence suggests that they are also surprisingly comfortable with the idea of racial separation....A just-released Zogby International poll found that 50.3 percent of 18- to 29-year-olds agreed with the idea that it is all right for the races to be separate as long as everyone has the same opportunities....

'It may be that, especially among whites, a perception has developed that whites and blacks aren't meant to be together,' says Philip Klinkner, associate professor of government at Hamilton College and director of the Arthur Levitt Public Affairs Center, whose students helped draw up the questions used in the Zogby survey....

Almost three-quarters of the respondents at least somewhat agreed with the statement that blacks should work their way up without special treatment, as Irish, Italians, and other minorities have in the past....And fully 90 percent of the young people said they heard racist jokes at least occasionally. Jannett Matthews, a 1999 Hamilton graduate, who is black, says, 'People say we have come so far from the past, but we have so much farther to go'....

Nicholas Levine, a senior at Regis Jesuit High in Denver, says he would prefer to attend an integrated school. But others of his generation do not always feel that way, he agrees. 'Separate but equal might end up making things worse. But if that's how people are going to feel more comfortable, it might be a way to go,' he says.

The Zogby findings come at a time when there is rising support in the nation for the dismantling of government-led school integration efforts. A recent CNN/Gallup/USA Today survey found that...60 percent of the respondents felt that increasing funds for minority schools is a better way to help minority students than is integration."

12. Nathan Glazer, *We Are All Multicuralists Now* (Cambridge, Massachusetts: Harvard University Press, 1997).

Chapter One:

1. Kwame Nkrumah, quoted by Ali A. Mazrui, *Towards A Pax Africana* (London: Weidenfeld & Nicolson, 1967), p. 38.

2. Cornel West, *Race Matters* (Boston: Beacon Press, 1993).

3. Thomas Sowell, quoted by Neomi Rao, "One Writer's Battles," in *The Weekly Standard*, November 11, 1996.

4. Carl Rowan, loc.cit.

5. Thomas Atkins, loc.cit.

6. Thomas Sowell, *Race and Culture: A World View* (New York: Basic Books, 1994), pp. 94 - 95. Thomas Sowell, *Minimum Wage Escalation* (Stanford, CA: Hoover Institution Press, 1977), p. 4; this is a reprint of his testimony before the Subcommittee on Human Resources, U.S. Senate Committee on Labor and Public Welfare, August 3, 1977.

7. Thomas Sowell, *Race and Culture*, op. cit.; and T. Sowell, "The Twilight of Affirmative Action?," in *Headway*, May 1996, p. 20.

8. Walter E.Williams, *The State Against Blacks* (New York: McGraw Hill, 1982), pp. 32, 34; see also, W. E.Williams, *Youth and Minority Unemployment* (Stanford: Hoover Institution Press, 1977), p. 14. See also Williams' comments cited by Steve Yates, in *Civil Wrongs: What Went Wrong with Affirmative Action* (San Francisco: ICS Press, 1994), pp. 176 - 179; and Walter E. Williams, *All It Takes Is Guts: A Minority View* (Washington, D.C.: Regnery Publishing, 1988), a collection of his newspaper columns which have infuriated many blacks because of their insensitivity to racism. As one reviewer said about the book on Amazon.com: "All It Takes Is Politics. Written in a middlebrow style. Williams, a black, anti-black conservative, tends to the reactionary end of the political spectrum. As most things of his nature, you'll love it if you share his opinions, loath it if you don't."

The same can be said about other black conservatives, most of whose views don't reflect what the majority of blacks believe.

9. Walter E. Williams, "Politics' False Promises," in *Headway* (November 1966), p. 18.

10. Tom Wicker, *Tragic Failure: Racial Integration in America* (New York: William Morrow, 1996), p. 46.

11. "Curreent Population Reports," "Consumer Income," May 1996, cited in *1997 Almanac* (New York: Houghton Mifflin, 1996), p. 51.

12. Colin Powell, in *The Washington Times*, National Weekly Edition, June 9, 1996.

13. Jesse Jackson, quoted by Dinesh D'Souza, *The End of Racism: Principles for a Multiracial Society* (New York: Free Press, 1995), p.9. See also, John Harris and Dan Halz, "Affirmative Action Divides Democrats," in *The Washington Post*, March 10, 1995.

14. Ward Connerly, "You, Me, and CCRI: A Letter to Colin Powell," in *The Washington Weekly Standard*, August 19, 1996.

15. Errol Smith, "Time to Repackage Black Conservastism," in *Headway*, October 1996, p. 17.

16. Gary Franks, quoted by Sharon Brooks Hodge, "Peer Pressure at the Polls," in *Headway*, November 1996, pp. 22 - 25. See also, Gary Franks, *Searching for the Promised Land: An African American's Optimistic Odyssey* (New York: Harper-Collins, 1996).

17. Ibid.

18. Roger Wilkins, quoted by Dinesh D'Souza, *The End of Racism*, op. cit., p. 480. Cf., Lena Williams, "In a '90s Quest for Black Identity, Intense Doubts and Disagreement, in *The New York Times*, November 30, 1991, Sec. A, pp. 1, and 26.

19. Richard Morin, "What Americans Think: Southern Discomfort: Racially Bigoted Attitudes Linger in Many Parts of Dixie," in *The Washington Post*, National Weekly Edition, July 15 - 21, 1996; Lynne Duke, "Whites' Racial Stereotypes Persist: Most Retain Negative Beliefs About Minorities," in *The Washington Post*, January 9, 1991, Sec. A, p. 1.

20. Walter Williams, "A New NAACP - Maybe," in *Headway*, February 1996, p. 18.

21. Ibid.

22. Alphonso Pinkney, *The Myth of Black Progress* (New York: Cambridge University Press, 1984), p. 17. Cp. Alphonso Pinkney, quoted by Dinesh D'Souza, op. cit., p. 480.

23. Ralph Ellison, *Invisible Man* (New York: 1952).

24. James Baldwin, *Nobody Knows My Name* (New York: 1961).

25. William Clay, quoted in "Accusing a Black Republican of Murder," in *The Weekly Standard*, December 2, 1996; "Racist Insults of Blacks Are Ignored," in *Insight*, December 23, 1996; and "Washington Report," in *Headway*, December 1996. Cp. "Conservative and Black: Political Correctness Attacks Black Right Wing," in *Insight*, January 20, 1997.

26. William Clay, cited in "Washington Report," in *Headway*, December 1996, p. 29. Clay also had the following to say about black Republican congressman Gary Franks: "His six years in Congress were highlighted by support of legislation inimical to the permanent interest of black folk." He listed ten actions by Franks that hurt African Americans, including Franks' damaging testimony in a federal court against a newly created black-majority congressional district in Georgia that elected Representative Cynthia McKinney, and his votes for such Republican and conservative measures as abolishing welfare, drastic cuts in inner-city housing for poor blacks, and the extensive reduction of summer job programs that benefit young blacks in the ghetto and other disadvantaged youths.

27. Henry Louis Gates, quoted by Tom Wicker, *Tragic Failure*, op. cit., p. 155.

28. Tom Wicker, ibid., p. 131.

29. *1997 Almanac*, op. cit., p. 51.

30. Michael Selz, "Race-Linked Gap Is Wide in Business-Loan Rejections: Denver Study Shows Disparate rates Persist Despite U.S. Pressure on Banks," in *The Wall Street Journal*, May 6, 1996, Sec.B, p. 2. Cf., "Race and Real Estate," in *The Wilson Quarterly*, Summer 1996, p. 120; Alicia H. Hunnell, Geoffrey M.B. Tootell, Lynn E. Browne, and James McEneaney, "Mortgage Lending in Boston: Interpreting HMDA Data," in *The American Economic Review*, March 1996.

31. Jason Epstein, "White Mischief," in *The |New York Review of Books*, October 17, 1996, p. 31.

32. Martin Kilson, quoted by Dinesh D'Souza, *The End of Racism*, op.cit., p. 479; and, Martin Kilson, "The Anatomy of Black Conservatism," in *Transition*, Issue 59, 1993, pp. 14 - 16.

33. Malcolm X, "Message to the Grassroots," speech delivered

in New York, 1963; cf.,George Breitman, editor, *Malcolm X Speaks* (New York: Pathfinder Press, 1965).

34. Clarence Thomas, quoted in *1992 World Almanac and Book of Facts* (New York Pharos Books, 1991, p. 63. See also, "The Clarence Thomas Confirmation Hearings," Hearings Before the Committee on the Judiciary, United States Senate, One Hundred Second Congress, October 11, 1991; and Andrew Peyton Thomas, *Clarence Thomas: A Biography* (San Francisco: Encounter Books, 2002).

35. Jeffrey Toobin, "The Burden of Clarence Thomas, " in *The New Yorker*, September 27, 1993, pp. 38 - 51.

36. Clarence Thomas, cited by Jeffrey Toobin, ibid.

37. Manning Marable, quoted by Dinesh D'Souza, *The End of Racism*, op. cit., p. 479; Manning Marable, "Clarence Thomas and the Crisis of Black Political Culture," in Toni Morrison, editor, *Race-ing Justice En-gendering Power* (New York: Pantheon Books, 1992, p. 82.

38. Jeffrey Toobin, op. cit.

39. Ibid.

40. Ibid.

41. Ibid., pp. 41 - 42.

42. Carl Rowan, quoted by Dinesh D'Souza, *The End of Racism*, op. cit., p. 479.

43. Clarence Thomas, in a speech at Walter F. George School of Law, Macon, Georgia, May 1, 1993; quoted by Jeffrey Toobin, "The Burden of Clarence Thomas," in *The New Yorker*, September 27, 1993, p. 40.

44. John Henrik Clarke, quoted by Dinesh D'Souza, *The End of Racism*, op. cit., p. 480; John Henrik Clarke, "Black Pseudo-Scholars Are in with White America, but They Deserve to be Outed," in *City Sun*, New York, August 26 - September 1, 1992.

45. Larry Elder, in Nick Gillespie and Steve Kurts, "Elder Statesman: An Interview with Larry Elder," in *Reason*, Los Angeles, April 1996, p. 48.

46. Shelby Steele, quoted in Stephen Goode, "Political Correctness Attacks Black Right Wing," in *Insight*, January 20, 1997; and, Shelby Steele, *The Content of Our Character: A New Vision of Race in America* (New York: St. Martin's Press, 1990).

47. Jason Epstein, "White Mischief," in *The New York Review*

of Books, October 17, 1996, p. 31. See also, Tom Wicker, *Tragic Failure*, op. cit., pp. 9 - 10, 32, 87, 94 - 96; James T. Patterson, *Great Expectations: The United States, 1945 - 1974* (New York: Oxford University Press, 1996), pp. 375 - 406, 430 - 433, 732 - 735, 787.

48. Michael Lind, *Up from Capitalism: Why the Right is Wrong for America* (New York: Free Press, 1996); Jason Epstein, "White Mischief," loc.cit.

49. Jason Epstein, loc.cit.

50. Michael Lind, loc.cit.

51. Tom Wicker, *Tagic Failure,* op. cit., pp. 17 - 18, and 19.

52. Ibid.

53. Ronald Reagan, quoted by Tom Wicker, *Tragic Failure*, op. cit., p. 15; Randall Kennedy, "Persuasion and Distrust: A Commentary on the Affirmative Action Debate," in *Harvard Law Review*, April 1986, p. 1342, cited by Tom Wicker, ibid., p. 196.

54. T. Wicker, ibid., p. 15.

55. Ibid. See also, *The New York Times*, and *The Washington Post*, on the Dr. Martin Luther King national holiday.

56. T. Wicker, *Tragic Failure,* p. cit., pp. 3 - 4, 6 - 11, 12 - 13, 16, 17, 32, 38, and 193; Richard Morin, "What Americans Think: Southern Discomfort: Racially Bigoted Attitudes Linger in Many Parts of Dixie," in *The Washington Post*, National Weekly Edition, July 15 - 21, 1996, p. 35.

57. Tom Wicker, *Tragic Failure*, op. cit., p. 16.

58. Ibid.

59. Jesse Jackson, quoted by Tom Wicker, ibid., p. 13.

60. Tom Wicker, ibid., pp. 13, 16; cf., p. 12.

61. Shelby Steele, *The Content of Our Character*, loc.cit.; Stephen Goode, ibid.

62. Nikki Giovanni, quoted by Dinesh D'Souza, *The End of Racism*, op. cit., p. 479; and, Nikki Giovanni, *Racism 101* (New York: William Morrow, 1994), p. 52.

63. Willie A. Richardson, "From the Publisher," in *National Minority Politics*, October 1995, p. 4.

64. Colin Powell, quoted by Tom Wicker, *Tragic Failure*, op. cit., p. 89.

65. Thomas Sowell, "The Twilight of Affirmative Action?," in *Headway*, May 1996, p. 20.

66. John N. Doggett, "I Still Believe in Clarence Thomas," in *National Minority Politics*, October 1995, p. 8.

67. Paul Craig Roberts and Lawrence M. Stratton, *The New Color Line: How Quotas and Privilege Destroy Democracy* (Washington, D.C.: Regnery, 1995).

68. John N. Doggett, "The Issue is Equal Opportunity, Not Race," in *Headway*, June 1996, p. 24.

69. Thomas Sowell, *The Vision of the Anointed: Self-Congratulations as a Basis for Social Policy* (New York: Basic Books, 1995), p. 209.

70. J.N. Doggett, "I Still Believe in Clarence Thomas," loc.cit.

71. J.N. Doggett, "The Issue is Equal Opportunity, Not Race," loc.cit.

72. Ibid.

73. Robert Dole, in an interview with CNN, June 10, 1996, quoted by John Harwood, "Dole Campaign Tries to Regain the High Ground on Affirmative Action and Other Thorny Issues," in *The Wall Street Journal*, June 28, 1996, Sec. A, p. 24.

74. Thomas Sowell, "The Twilight of Affirmative Action?," loc.cit.

75. Charles Murray, *Losing Ground: American Social Policy, 1950 - 1980* (New York: Free Press, 1984).

76. Deroy Murdock, "Media Machinations," in *Headway*, January 1996, p. 16.

77. "Our Philosophy," in *Headway*, 1996 - 1997, p. 2.

78. Joseph H. Brown, "Children Held Hostage in Welfare Reform," in *Headway*, August 1996, p. 24. Brown also contends: "Black politicians and self-appointed leaders...will go to great lengths to undo the stereotype of the unmarried black woman on the dole...[and then] turn around and reinforce these stereotypes when it is politically expedient....'The majority of the AFDC population is white, not African American,' Representative Maxine Waters (Democrat-California) told 'USA Today' late last year in attacking Republican proposals to change the welfare system. So why then do Waters and other black elected officials fight welfare reform tooth and nail? To protect the white majority?" Cf., *The Wall Street Journal*, September 1994.

79. Shelby Steele, *The Content of Our Character*, op. cit., p. 27.

80. Armstrong Williams, "Race and History," in *Headway*, July 1996, p. 17.

81. Shelby Steele, *The Content of Our Character*, op. cit., pp. 26, and 31.

82. Ibid., p. 118; cf., Steven Yates, "Civil Wrongs," op. cit., pp. 126 - 127.

83. Joseph H. Brown, "Bloodsuckers Come in Many Colors," in *Headway*, January 1996, p. 28.

84. Michael Selz, "Race-Linked Gap Is Wide in Business-Loan Rejections: Denver Study Shows Disparate Rates Persist Despite U.S. Pressure on Banks," in *The Wall Street Journal*, May 6, 1996; "Race and Real Estate," in *The Wilson Quarterly*, Summer 1996; Alicia H. Munnell, Geoffrey M.B. Tootell, Lynn E. Browne, and James McEneaney, "Mortgage Lending in Boston: Interpreting HMDA Data," in *The American Economic Review*, March 1996; Joel Glenn Benner, "A Pattern of Bias in Mortgage Loans," in *The Washington Post*, June 6, 1993; Paulette Thomas, "Blacks Can Face A Host of Trying Conditions in Getting Mortgages," in *The Wall Street Journal*, November 30, 1992; Jesse Jackson, "Racism is the Bottom Line in Home Loans," in *The Los Angeles Times*, October 28, 1991.

85. Charles B. Rangel, "Crack Law Is Biased and Flawed," in *The Wall Street Journal*, May 13, 1997, Sec. A, p. 23; cf., "Mandatory minimum jail sentence, in years, for possession of five grams of crack: 5. Chances that an American sentenced for crack-related offenses is white: 1 in 25. Mandatory minimum sentence for possession of five grams of cocaine: 0. Chances that an American sentenced for cocaine possession is white: 1 in 3," in *Harper's*, 1997.

86. Shelby Steele, quoted from his essay in *The New York Times* by *National Review*, April 4, 1994. See also, Shelby Steele, *The Content of Our Character*, loc.cit.; and Shelby Steele, *A Dream Deferred: The Second Betrayal of Black Freedom in America* (New York: Perennial, 1999).

In his first book, *The Content of Our Character*, Shelby Steele, a black professor of English and self-described black conservative, launched a blistering attack - even if sometimes in disguised form - on liberal policies which helped alleviate the plight of blacks and other minorities and what he considers to be unjusfitied complaints of racism by African Americans and their supporters, white liberals.In *A Dream Deferred*, his unrelenting attack on the liberal establishment has reached a new level, contending that government programs to help blacks and other disadvantaged groups amount to a form of slavery and segregation against the very people for whom they are intended to help.They have compromised standards of excellence and robbed blacks of the incentive to work and to be self-reliant and be the best they can be like the rest of the members of the American society; a compelling thesis in theory, and in the ivory towers of academia, but one that does not stand up to scrutiny or correspond to reality on the ground.

87. Martin Luther King, Jr., "I Have A Dream," a speech he delivered on August 28, 1963, in Washington, D.C.; coincidentally, the day before, Dr. W.E. B. DuBois died in Accra, Ghana, where he had become a citizen after renouncing his American citizenship. He was 93. The news of his death was passed on Dr. King and his colleagues just before he delivered his speech, itself a landmark in American history on the long journey towards racial equality which still remains a dream today.

Chapter Two:

1. *Harper's*, May 1995.

2. Ronald W. Walters, *White Nationalism, Black Interests: Conservative Public Policy and the Black Community* (Detroit, Michigan: Wayne State University Press, 2003).

3. Joe Davidson, "Reagan: A Contrary View," on American television web page MSNBC, June 7, 2004.

4. Dinesh D'Souza, *The End of Racism: Principles for a Multiracial Society* (New York: Free Press, 1995), pp. 10, 11, and 12.

5. Ibid., p. 13.

6. J. C. Watts, quoted by Nancy E. Roman, "GOP Blacks Emphasize Economy in House Bids," in *The Washington Times*, National Weekly Edition, August 4, 1996.

7. Malcolm X, "Message to the Grassroots," speech delivered

in New York, 1963.

8. Milton Bins and Faye M. Anderson, "Grand Old Party: Free At Last?," in *Headway*, Houston, Texas, October 1996, p. 15.

9. Faye M. Anderson, quoted in "Washington Report," in *Headway*, August 1996, p. 29. Cf., Faye M. Anderson, op-ed, in *The New York Times*, July 16, 1996.

10. Faye M. Anderson, in her article, op-ed, in *The New York Times*, July 16, 1996. For a contrasting view, see Ann Coulter, "Another Damascus Road to Conversion," TownHall.com: Conservatives Columnists, August 18, 2000: "The substantive points on which Ms. Anderson ('former' Republican) accused the republican party of racism were - funnily enough - many of the same things Democrats are constantly harping on, such as Bob Jones University and the Confederate flag....All these Damascus Road conversions are nothing but liberal street theater....There will probably be another ersatz 'former' Republican on the op-ed page next week - some phony who once registered as a Republican and intends to use that curiosity combined with a later sorrowful resignation to create the illusion that we are witnessing a vast migration from the Republican party over this or that issue....Larry Rockefeller, Lawrence Walsh, Arianna Huffington, the list of Damascus Road conversions goes on - this is the hoax the media can't help falling for because if anyone in the media were a Republican he'd be resigning from the Republican party for the exact same reason."

Ann Coulter does not believe or simply refuses to admit that the Republican party is insensitive to minorities, to put it mildly, and is sometimes openly hostile toward them, as its track record clearly shows. Republicans use coded language when playing the race card to mobilize whites against blacks and other minorities, besides formulating and implementing policies which hurt African Americans and other groups and don't take their interests and well-being into account.

11. Terry Neal, "Talking Points Live," on washingtonpost.com, *The Washington Post*, May 20, 2004.

12. Vincent Watkins, "A Defining Moment for Black Conservatives," in *Headway*, March 1997, p. 37.

13. Clarence Thomas, quoted in Ramesh Ponnuru, "Republicans Like Me: Invisible Men: The GOP's Black Voters,"

in *National Review*, April 22, 1996, p. 21.

14. George McGovern, cited by Jonathan Aitken, *Nixon: A Life* (Washington, D.C.: Regnery, 1993) , pp. 447 - 448.

15. Robert Franklin, "Civil Rights," in *Headway*, January 1996, p. 5.

16. Richard Lugar, in "Men Who Would Be President," in *National Minority Politics*, Houston, Texas, November 1995, p. 13.

17. Jerry T. Burley, "GOP Displays Uncompromising Harshness Toward Poor," in *Headway*, February 1996, p. 10.

18. J.C. Watts, quoted in "Washington report," in *Headway*, June 1996, p. 30. Watts, who had one of the most conservative voting records in Congress, also claims that the Republican party reaches out to [white] small business people even though some differ with the party, but ignore blacks: 'Should we not do the same with the black community?,' he questions. Watts estimated that only 8 to 12 percent of blacks voted Republican in the 1992 elections at the local, state, and national levels. See also, Nancy E. Roman, "GOP Blacks Emphasize Economy in House Bids," in *The Washington Times*, National Weekly Edition, August 4, 1996.

19. Quoted by Walley Naylor, "GOP Must Again Become A Beacon of Hope," in *Headway*, February 1996, p. 8.

20. Quoted by Vincent B. Watkins, "A Defining Moment for Black Conservatives," in *Headway*, March 1997, p. 37.

21. Nancy Reagan, during the 1980 presidential campaign in Hampshire, quoted by the media, print and electronic.

22. Harold Cruse, *The Crisis of the Negro Intellectual: A Historical Analysis of the Failure of Black Leadership* (New York: William Morrow, 1968).

23. *National Minority Politics*, December 1995; *Headway*, January 1996; Jerry T. Burley, "GOP Displays Uncompromising Harshness Toward Poor," in *Headway*, February 1996; *Headway*, December 1996 - January 1997.

24. Robert L. Woodson, "Misconceptions About Race and Poverty," in *Headway*, April 1997, p. 25.

25. Stephen A. Holmes, "New Survey Shows Americans Pessimistic on Race Relations," in *The New York Times*, June 11, 1997, Sec. A, p. 12.

26. Fredrick D. Robinson, in his review of Star Parker, *Pimps,*

Whores, and Welfare Brats (New York: Simon & Schuster, 1996), in *Headway*, April 1997, p. 34.

27. Fredrick Robinson, in his review of Dinesh D'Souza, *The End of Racism*,op. cit., in *National Minority Politics*, October 1995, p. 36.

28. Richard Morin, "What Americans Think: Southern Discomfort: Racially Bigoted Attitudes Linger in Many Parts of Dixie," in *The Washington Post*, National Weekly Edition, July 15 - 21, 1996, p. 35. Cf., Todd Gitlin, *The Twilight of Common Dreams: Why America Is Wracked by Culture Wars* (New York: Metropolitan Books, 1995), p. 123.

29. Tom Wicker, *Tragic Failure: Racial Integration in America* (New York: William Morrow, 1996), p. 46.

30. Cornel West, *Keeping Faith: Philosophy and Race in America* (New York: Routledge, 1993), p. 236.

31. Harold E. Ford, quoted by Michael Myers, "Franks Tries to Overcome Cold Shoulder Treatment," in *The Washington Times*, National Weekly Edition, June 30, 1996, p. 11. Gary A. Franks, who had the dubious distinction of having the most conservative voting record of the entire Connecticut's congressional delegation and who was one of the most conservative members of Congress, also commented, "[Michigan black Democratic Congressman] John Conyers called me imbecile. Jesse Jackson had a sit-in in my office, singing 'We Shall Overcome'." See also, Gary A. Franks, *Searching for the Promised Land: An African American's Optimistic Odyssey: The First Black Conservative Member of Congress* (New York: HarperCollins, 1996).

32. Paul Craig Roberts and Lawrence M. Stratton, *The New Color Line: How Quotas and Privilege Destroy Democracy* (Washington, D.C.: Regnery, 1995), pp. 145 - 146.

33. Jerry T. Burley, "GOP Displays Uncompromising Harshness Toward Poor," in *Headway*, February 1996, p. 10.

34. Ibid.

35. Haley Barbour, *Agenda for America: A Republican Direction for the Future* (Washington, D.C.: Regnery, 1996).

36. Arthur Fletcher, Jr., quoted by Hazel Trice Edney, NNPA Washington correspondent, "Black Republicans Question Party's Commitment," in *The Grand Rapids Times*, Grand Rapids, Michigan, June 11 - June 17, 2004, p. 1.

37. Edward W. Brooke, quoted, ibid., p. 15.

38. Terry McAuliffe, quoted, ibid.

39. Hazel Trice Edney, ibid.

40. Edward Brooke, ibid.

41. Hazel T. Edney, ibid.

42. Manning Marable, "How Children Learn Racism: Along The Color Line," in *The Grand Rapids Times*, Grand rapids, Michigan, June 11 - June 17, 2004, pp. 3, and 14. See also, L. Hirschfeld, "The Conceptual Politics of Race: Lessons from Our Children, in *Ethos*, 1997, cited by M. Marable; Kenneth Clark, *Dark Ghetto* (New York: HarperCollins Publishers, 1967).

43. Lynn Martin, "The Next Step in the Republican Revolution," in *Headway*, February 1996, p. 7.

44. Leon Panetta, cited by John F. Harris, "The Man Who Squared the Oval Office," in *The Washington Post*, National Weekly Edition, January 13, 1997; and David S. Broder, "Farewell, Leon Panetta," in *The Washington Post*, National Weekly Edition, January 27, 1997, p. 4.

45. Leon Panetta, quoted, ibid.

46. Robert L. Woodson, "Conservatives Have Lost Battle of Public Perception," in *Headway: Defining Conservatism*, May 1996, pp. 7 - 8.

47. Sandra Day O'Connor, quoted by Pennsylvania Republican U.S. Senator Arlen Specter, in *National Minority Politics*, November 1995, p. 14.

48. Willie A. Richardson, "From the Publisher," in *Headway: The Republican Gender and Race Gaps*, January 1997, p. 4.

49. Gwen Daye Richardson, "The Men Who Would Be President," in *National Minority Politics*, November 1995, p. 6.

50. Ibid.

51. Malcolm X, in a speech in New York, 1963.

52. Malcolm X, in a speech in New York, 1963.

53. Nathan Glazer, *We Are All Multiculturalists Now* (Cambridge, Massachusetts: Harvard University Press, 1997).

54. Janice Rhodes, quoted by Stephen Harmon, "Conservative West Michigan Is Gaining Blacks," in *The Grand Rapids Press*, Grand Rapids, Michigan, June 20, 2004, Sec. D, p. 1.

55. Ibid., pp. D1, and D5.

56. Gwen Daye Richardson, "GOP: A Party Out of Balance,"

in *Headway*, February 1996, p. 6.

57. Walley Naylor, "GOP Must Again Become Beacon of Hope," in *Headway*, February 1996, p. 8.

58. James T. Patterson, *Grand Expectations: The United States, 1945 - 1974* (New York: Oxford University Press, 1966), p. 759.

59. Derrick Bell, *Faces at the Bottom of the Well: The Permanence of Racism* (New York: Basic Books, 1992).

60. Robert Woodson, "Conservatives Have Lost Battle of Public Perception," in *Headway: Defining Conservatism*, May 1996, p. 7.

61. Clarence H. Carter, "Need to Diversify the Face of Conservatism," in *Headway*, May 1996, pp. 10 - 11.

62. Joint Center for Political and Economic Studies poll, Washington, D.C., cited by *The Washington Post* and *The New York Times*, January 1996. Cf., "Political Attitudes of Black Americans," in *Headway*, April 1996, p. 34.

63. John H. McWhorter, *Losing the Race: Self-Sabotage in America* (New York: Perennial, 2001).

64. John H. McWhorter, *Authentically Black: Essays for the Black Silent Majority* (New York: Gotham Books, 2003).

65. Joint Center for Political and Economic Studies poll, op. cit.

66. Adam Meyerson, "The Growing Conservatism of Black America," in *Policy Review*, Spring 1994, p. 4.; cf., ibid, pp. 4 - 6.

67. Gwen Daye Richardson, "Defining Conservatism," in *Headway*, May 1996, p. 6.

68. Jimmy Carter, quoted on television during the 1980 presidential campaign.

69. Barry Goldwater, at the Republican National Convention, San Francisco, July 16, 1964, during which Ronald Reagan delivered the keynote address; quoted by David C. Whitney and Robin Vaughn Whitney, *The American Presidents* (Garden City, New York: Guild America Books, Doubleday, 1993), p. 322: "In July 1964, the Republican National Convention named Senator Barry Goldwater of Arizona as its candidate for president. He was the leader of the conservative wing of the party....Goldwater had voted against the Civil Rights Act of 1964, and in his acceptance speech he appealed to ultra-rightist organizations with the phrases

'extremism in the defense of liberty is no vice' and 'moderation in the pursuit of justice is no virtue'....The Democratic National Convention that met in Atlantic City, New Jersey, in August adopted a platform plank that denounced 'extremism' and named such organizations as the Ku Klux Klan and the John Birch Society as examples of extremist groups."

The White Citizens' Council, founded in Mississippi, was another extremist group notorious for its opposition to civil rights for blacks through intimidation, economic reprisals, and murder. It played a critical role in helping Goldwater win Mississippi, where he captured an astounding 87 percent of the vote against President Lyndon B. Johnson in the 1964 presidential election. See also, Barry Goldwater, in James T. Patterson, *Grand Expectations*, op. cit., pp. 548 - 550, 561, and 564.

70. David Bositis, "African Americans and the Republican Party," Joint Center for Political and Economic Studies, Washington, D.C., 1996.

71. Edward W. Brooke, "Crisis in the Two-Party System," in Arthur L. Smith and Stephen Robb, editors, *The Voice of Black Rhetoric* (Boston: Allyn and Bacon, 1971), pp. 156 - 157.

72. Ed Vaughn, in *Proceedings of the Ad Hoc Democratic Party Platform Hearings: La Rouche's Committee for A New Bretton Woods*, Washington, D.C., June 2000, pp. 52, and 53.

Chapter Three:

1. Faye Anderson, quoted by Michael Tomasky, "Not a Lott-a Shakin,'" in *New York Magazine*, March 22, 1999; and in *National Interest*, 1999.

2. Michael Tomasky, ibid.

3. Trent Lott, quoted, ibid.; "Council of Conservative Citizens: Extremism in America," Anti-Defamation League, 2004.

4. "Council of Conservative Citizens: Promoting A Racist Agenda," Anti-Defamation League, February 1999; "Council of Conservative Citizens: Extremism in America," Anti-Defamation League, 2004.

5. Faye Anderson, quoted by Ann Gerhart, "Armed with Razor

Wit, the GOP Chairman Is Out to Draw Votes and Blood, in Ed the Quipper, Washingtonpost.com, April 5, 2004.

6. Richard Dixon, in *Black Oklahoma Today*, quoted by Jon Dougherty, in "NAACP: Racist to blacks," in *WorldNet Daily*, July 19, 2000.

7. John L. Wilks, quoted by *The New York Times*, December 22, 1991.

8. Sherri Smith, quoted in "Blacks Wary of New Black 'Conservatives,'" the University of Alabama, Huntsville: www.uah.edu/research/resrev96/Liberal/blacks.html

9. Glenn Loury, *The Anatomy of Racial Equality* (Cambridge, Massachusetts: Harvard University Press, 2001).

10. Michael Harrington, *The Other America* (New York: Scribner, 1997).

11. Richard J. Herrnstein and Charles Murray, *The Bell Curve: Intelligence and Class Structure in American Life* (New York: Free Press, 1994).

12. Dinesh D'Souza, *The End of Racism: Principals for A Multiracial Society* (New York: Free Press, 1996).

13. Stephan Thernstrom and Abigail Thernstrom, *America in Black and White: One Nation, Indivisible* (New York: Simon & Schuster, 1999).

14. Glenn Loury, quoting his uncle Fred, in Richard Higgins, "Breaking Ranks: Glenn Loury's Change of Heart - and Mind: *The Anatomy of Racial Inequality*: Book Review," in *Christian Century*, December 18, 2002.

15. G. Loury, ibid.

16. Richard Higgins, "Breaking Ranks: Glenn Loury's Change of Heart - and Mind," ibid.

17. Paul Krugman, "Glenn Loury's Round Trip: The Travails and Temptations of A Black Intellectual," The Unofficial Paul Krugman Web Page:
www.pkarchive.org/economy/loury.html.

18. Glenn C. Loury, *One by One from the Inside Out* (New York: The Free Press, 1995), p. 16.

19. William Julius Wilson, *The Declining Significance of Race: Blacks and Changing American Institutions* (Chicago: University of Chicago Press, 1978).

20. Thomas Sowell, *Race and Economics* (New York: Davic

316

McKay Co., 1975).

21. Paul Krugman, "Glen Loury, Round Trip: The Travails and Temptations of A Black Intellectual," Ibid.

22. Glenn C. Loury, "Leadership Failure and the Loyalty Trap," in *One by One from the Inside Out*, op.cit., p. 190. See also Stephen Steinberg, "Two Cheers for Glenn Loury - Or Maybe Just One," in the *New Republic*, vol. 9, no, 1 (new series), whole no. 33, Summer 2002.

23. Loury, *The Anatomy of Racial Inequality*, op. cit., p. 106.

24. Loury, *One by One from the Inside Out*, op. cit., p. 134.

25. Loury, *The Anatomy of Racial Inequality*, op. cit., pp. 105, and 104; Stephen Steinberg, "Two Cheers for Glenn Loury - Or Maybe Just One, in the *New Republic*, op. cit.

26. Cornel West, "Unmasking Black Conservatives," in *Christian Century*, July 16 - 23, 1986, p. 644.

Chapter Four:

1. Walter Williams, "A New NAACP - Maybe," in *Headway*, February 1996, p. 18. See also Dinesh D'Souza, *The End of Racism: Principles for a Multiracial Society* (New York: Free Press, 1995).

2. Walter Williams, "Souring Racial Relationships," in *Headway*, August 1996, p. 18.

3. Ibid.

4. Steven A. Holmes, "New Survey Shows Americans Pessimistic on Race Relations," in *The New York Times*, June 11, 1997; Richard Moring, "What Americans Think: Southern Discomfort: Racially Bigoted Attitudes Linger in Many Parts of Dixie," in *The Washington Post*, National Weekly Edition, July 15 - 21, 1996, p. 35.

5. Bruce White, *Black Robes, White Justice: Why Our Legal System Doesn't Work for Blacks* (New York: Carol Publishing, 1987).

6. Ibid. See also, Randall Kennedy, *Race, Crime and Law* (New York: Pantheon, 1997); Raymond S. Franklin and Solomon Resnik, *The Political Economy of Racism* (New York: Holt,

Rinehart and Winston, 1973), p. 18 - 19; and *Southern Patriot,* February 1971, p. 7:

"Statistics show that the death penalty is almost exclusively reserved for black men - and then, usually only if the victim is white....A study by the NAACP Legal Defense and Educational Fund a few years ago showed that the 20 death penalty cases in Alabama involved 19 black defendants. All of the victims were white. No sentence of death was imposed in Louisiana during 20 years except upon a Negro convicted of raping a white victim. No available factor other than race satisfactorily accounts for this disproportion."

Commenting on this, the authors, Franklin and Resnik, make a significant observation: "It should be pointed out that the NAACP study was only concerned with actual sentencing; it was not concerned with the possibilities of frame-ups or with the extent to which 'rape' was properly defined in the convictions of blacks."

See also, Sam Howe Verhovek, "As Texas Executions Mount, taking Life Becomes Routine," in *The New York Times,* May 25, 1997. It should be noted that the Texas executions escalated draconially during the governorship of George W. Bush, a man who claimed to believe in "compassionate conservatism," and who later became president of the United States after winning a deeply flawed election following the invalidation of thousands of black votes in the state of Florida that was under the governorship of his brother Jeb Bush.

7. Tom Wicker, *Tragic Failure: Racial Integration in America* (New York: William Morrow, 1996), pp. 144 - 145.

8. Charles S. Rangel, "Crack Law is Biased and Flawed," in *The Wall Street Journal,* May 13, 1997, Sec.A, p. 23.

9. Tom Wicker, loc.cit.

10. Larry Elder, in Nick Gillespie and Steve Kurtz, "Elder Statesman: An Interview with Larry Elder," in *Reason,* April 1996, p. 46.

11. Tom Wicker, *Tragic Failure,* op. cit., p. 145.

12. Ibid., pp. 145 - 146.

13. *Harper's,* 1997.

14. Joseph Brown, "Bloodsuckers Come in Many Colors," in *Headway,* January 1996: "Why, Reverend Jackson should care about the sentencing disparities that these scoundrels

receive?....Let them rot in jail." See also Larry Elder, in Nick Gillespie and Steve Kurtz, "Elder Statesman: An Interview with Larry Elder," in *Reason*, April 1996: "When Jesse Jackson suggests that the difference between crack and [powdered] cocaine [sentences] is evidence of a racist criminal justice system...nothing's going to change much until black leaders stop such reckless, careless, and conspiratorial nonsense." See also Ezola Foster, "Is There A 'Cultural War' in America?" in *Headway*, April 1996, and E. Foster, "Can America Survive Another Civil War?" in *Headway*, March 1997, pp. 14 - 15.

15. Foster keeps strange, white company, as seen in her affiliation and endorsement by the radical right racist oganization, The John Birch Society. See http://www.jbs.org/speakers%201999/foster-sp99-materials.htm. She was also the running mate of Pat Buchanan, a known racist, in the 2000 presidential campaign on the Reform Party ticket. Buchanan was the party's presidential candidate, and Foster ran for vice president of the United States. Neither was taken seriously by the voters, as shown by their poor showing in the polls.

16. Ezola Foster, in *National Minority Politics*, and her comments on CNN & Company and the Larry King Live Show in 1992.

17. Ibid. See also related articles in *National Minority Politics* and *Headway*, 1996 - 1997.

18. American Scene: www.wsws.org/public-html/prioriss/iwb12-4/amscen.htm. See also *Pittsburgh Post-Gazette*, October 13, 1995; *Pittsburgh Tribune-Review*, October 13, 1995; *Philadelphia Inquirer*, October 13, 1995; *The New York Times*, October 15, 1995; *The Washington Post*, October 16, 1995.

19. "4000 Protest Police Acquittal in Pittsburgh": www.wsws.org/public-html/prioriss/iwb 12-2/prote.htm. See also CNN: "White Officer Acquitted in Death of Black Motorist," November 13, 1996.

20. Malice Green killed by the police on November 5, 1992, in *Detroit Free Press*, November 6, 1995; Betsy Miner, "'Racism' Killed Detroit Man, Mourners Told at Funeral," *USA Today*, 13 - 15 November, 1992. As Reverend Charles G. Adams said, "Racism killed Malice Green. And if it is not destroyed, nobody in

the U.S. can be   safe."

21. Lee F. Berry, Jr., killed by Detroit police, in *Detroit Free Press*, June 25, 1987; Joe Davidson, "Have Police Declared War on Blacks?," in *Emerge*, Issues 27 - 30, Washington, D.C., May 1993.

22.. Jerry White, "Detroit Police Kill Deaf-Mute Man", August 31,   2000,   World   Socialist   Web   Site: www.wsws.org/articles/2000/aug2000/det-a31.htm.   See   also *Detroit Free Press*, September 1, 2000. See also, Larry Roberts, "Detroit Police Kill Again," September 15, 2000, World Socialist Web Site; *Detroit Free Press*, September 9,   2000.

23. Joe Davidson, "Have Police Declared War on Blacks?," ibid.

24. Tom Wicker, *Tragic Failure*, op. cit., p. 146.

25. Tom Wicker, ibid., pp. 146 - 147.

26. Andrew Hacker, *Two Nations: Black and White, Separate, Hostile, Unequal* (New York: Ballantine Books, 1992).

27. E. Franklin Frazier, *Black Bourgeoisie* (New York: Collier, 1957).

28. George M. Fredrickson, *Black Liberation: A Comparative History of Black Ideologies in the United States and South Africa* (New York: Oxford University Press, 1995), p. 320.

29. Andrew Hacker, *Two Nations*, op.cit., pp. 218 - 219.

30. Bill Hardman, "Diversity Has Much to Offer," in *The Grand Rapids Press*, Grand Rapids, Michigan, February 15, 2004, Sec. F, pp. 1, and 5.

31. Walter Williams, "Souring Racial Relationships," in *Headway*, August 1996, p. 18.

32. Gordon Parks, *Born Black* (New York: J.B. Lippincott, 1971), p. 137.

33. U.S. Department of Justice, "Uniform Crime Reports, 1994," cited in *1997 Almanac* (New York: Houghton Mifflin, 1997), p. 851.

34. "Youths Thought Targets Were Racists," in *The Nashville Banner*, January 20, 1995.

35. Dinesh D'Souza, *The End of Racism*, op. cit., p. 8. See also, Southern Poverty Law Center, "Klanwatch Intelligence Report," February 1994; James Martinez, "Two Whites Convicted in Burning of Black Churches," in *The Washington Times*,

september 8, 1993.

36. Dinesh D'Souza, *The End of Racism*, op. cit., pp. 8, 394; Southern Poverty Law Center, loc. cit.

37. *The Wall Street Journal*, August 15, 1996; "Pride and Prejudice," in *U.S. News & World Report*, July 15 - 22, 1996.

38. Dinesh D'Souza, *The End of Racism*, op. cit., p. 393; Morris Dees, *A Season for Justice* (New York: Simon & Schuster, 1991), p. 337.

39. Jon Dougherty, "Blacks Arrested More for 'Hate Crimes': FBI Report Confirms Higher Rate Than Whites for Racial Attacks," in *WorldNetDaily*, March 6, 2001.

40. Dinesh D'Souza, *The End of Racism,* op. cit.; Southern Poverty Law Center, loc.cit.

41. Richard Morin, "What Americans Think: Southern Discomfort: Racially Bigoted Attitudes Linger in Many Parts of Dixie," in *The Washington Post*, National Weekly Edition, July 15 - 21, 1996. See also Todd Gitlin, *The Twilight of Common Dreams: Why America is Wracked by Culture Wars* (New York: Metropolitan Books, 1995), p. 123.

42. Dinesh D'Souza, *The End of Racism*, op. cit., p. 395.

43. Walter Williams, "Souring Racial Relationships," in *Headway*, August 1996, p. 18.

44. Gwen Daye Richardson, "Media Machinations," in *Headway*, February 1996, p. 12.

45. Ishmale Reed, "Stats, Lies and Videotape," in *Emerge*, April 1994.

46. Martin Luther King, Jr., *Where Do We Go From Here: Chaos or Community?* (New York: Harper and Row, 1967), chap. 2 for full text; for excerpt, see Robert L. Scott and Wayne Brockriede, editors, *The Rhetoric of Black Power* (New York: Harper and Row, 1968), pp. 35 - 36. To compare what happened in apartheid South Africa with the lives of black people in the United States, see, "Will the Truth Set Them Free? Confronting Their Terrible Past, South Africans Seek Reconciliation," in *U.S. News & World Report*, April 28, 1997, pp. 42 - 44.

47. Whitney Young, *Beyond Racism* (New York: McGraw-Hill, 1969), p. 85; Diniesh D'Souza, *The End of Racism*, op. cit.

48. Malcolm X, ibid.

49. Walter Williams, "A New NAACP - Maybe," in *Headway*,

February 1996, p. 18.

Probably the most volatile issue in race relations today is the conduct of the police toward blacks of all classes, especially those living in the inner cities. It was this conduct that triggered and will continue to trigger riots, sparking the riots in the 1960s, and the Los Angeles uprising in 1992, considered to be the worst in the nation's history.

While black conservatives contend that blacks, and not racism, caused the Los Angeles riot and other forms of civil unrest, other observers blame racism and police brutality for the strife and bad race relations between blacks and whites. And there is ample to demonstrate that. A few cases illustrate that, as we have shown in this study. And as Bruce Shapiro stated in "When Justice Kills: Police Brutality is on the Rise, Sparking a Reform Movement," in *The Nation*, June 9, 1997:

"Two young men not long out of high school are chased in their car by police, who completely surround them. They have no weapons, no drugs. Their offense is an ill-considered run after being pulled over for speeding. In a panic, the driver shifts into reverse. Suddenly two police officers shatter the car's window with their revolver butts. Then the officer on the driver's side shifts the gun in his hand, sticks it inside the window and fires - one, two, three, four times - at the upper body of the young man at the wheel, who throws himself over his friend in a gesture of protection and whispers, with bewildered, dying breath, 'Sam, they're shooting at us.'

Most of the facts are straightforward. At dusk on April 14, 21-year-old Malik Jones and his friend Samuel Cruz were driving along a man drag in East Haven, Connecticut, a quiet suburban town. East Haven is famously hostile to people with dark skin: Though adjacent to 40-percent minority New Haven, the town deos not have a single black police officer or firefighter, which has provoked a suit by the NAACP....

At 6:15 p.m., an East Haven police van driven by Officer Robert Flodquist tried to pull Jones and Cruz over. The East Haven police claim a motorist had complained that Jone's car was speeding, though it may also have beena case of 'D.W.B.' - Driving While Black. Malik made a U-turn and raced onto Interstate 95 back over the city line, followed within moments by a high-speed convoy of East Haven and state police. The frightened young man was apparently trying to get home; After ten minutes the chase ended with Jones and Cruz cornered just a few blocks from Jone's mother's house. Officer Flodquist leaped from his van. Later he claimed Jones tried to back into him; Cruz says Jones was trying to avoid colliding with a cruiser ahead.

Whatever reason, it was Flodquist who broke Jone's window and shot him. Cruz, drenched in blood, was first dragged handcuffed back and forth between squad car and ambulance as police officers and E.M.T.s argued over who should have custody; then he spent the night in the lockup, still in his bloody clothing, because of a motor-vehicle warrant.

Even taking the suburban police account at face value, the shooting of young Malik Jones has all the incendiary elements of the odney King case: a black driver pulled over by a white officer, adrenaline-powered cops, an unarmed and outnumbered victim. But in its particulars it also opens a window into political and legal nuances of police brutality, which is on the rise again around the country.

It's not just famously thuggish police departments like L.A.'s. In Prince George County, Maryland, outside Washington, 24-year-old Archie Elliot was shot fourteen times while handcuffed in police custody, after being pulled over for drunk driving. In a Pittsburgh suburb, 31-year-old Johnny Gammage, cousin of a Steeler's defensive lineman, was pulled over for repeatedly touching his brakes and somehow edned up strangled. And in New York City, civilian complaints of excessive force have risen 41 percent since Mayor Giuliani intoruced his 'zero tolerance' policies - widespread arrests for minor violations. Three-quarters of those complaints are filed by black and Latino citizens, against a police department that remains 75 percent white....Amnesty International charges that many cases of police violence in New York violate basic international human rights standards....

In the days after Malik Jone's killing, the *New Haven Register* ran dozens of comments from readers to its call-in-line; the remarks from suburban readers [nearly all of whom are white] were vicious and hostile: 'The officer was completely justified in what he did. He was dealing with criminals.' 'The police cannot properly do their job because they always have to worry about racism and brutality.' 'As soon as someone gets shot they say it's racism.'

Officer Flodquist himself had to beg East Haveners not to stage a support rally sure to raise tensions....Malik Jones's killing and the growing epidemic of police violence of which it is a part, reveals a deep racial chasm....'All the family wants is justice,' Jone's survivors said. Yet how to trust in justice when justice itself does the killing?"

Such butal conduct by the authorities, as catalogued here by Bruce Shapiro as much as others have done the same investigations, has striking and frightening parallels to the diabolical iniquities perpetrated by the apartheid regime of South Africa against its own black citizens; which is what prompted us to draw an analogy between the two in this chapter. For comparison, see: "Will the Truth Set Them Free? Confronting Their Terrible Past, South Africans Seek Reconciliation, " in *U.S. News & World Report*, April 28, 1997. On police brutality in the United States, see William F. Schultz, "Cruel and Unusual Punishment," in *The New York Review of Books*, April 24, 1997. As he states:

"Brutality is not difficult to document when it comes to police officers' behavior towards suspects, particularly racial minorities. Within the past ten months human rights groups have reported on apparent increases in the number of police shootings and the number of people who have died in custody in New York City."

See also "America's Constant Curse: Race rears Its Head Again," in *The Economist*, June 14th - 27th, 1997: "On June 10th a judge released Elmer 'Geronimo' Pratt, a former Black Panther who was imprisoned more than 25 years ago for allegedly murdering a Santa Monica [white] school teacher, on $25,000 bail. Two weeks earlier the judge, Everett Dickey, had overturned Mr. Pratt's conviction in the light of new evidence that the chief witness against him was a police and FBI informant who lied about his connections with the authorities to the jury.

The Pratt case will no doubt confirm ordinary blacks in their skepticism of America's commitment to fairness. A Gallup poll published on June 6th found that 70 percent of black males aged 18 - 34 felt that they had been discriminated against the previous month. The case will also fan the theory, raging through

America's law school departments, that racial prejudice is so pervasive in America's legal system that it is almost impossible to produce objective judgement about guilt or innocence....As David Troutt, a law professor at Rutgers University, points out, the Pratt case does much to support the theory's main contention: that it is not unreasonable to take race into account when testing the soundness of a legal ruling....

Nathan Glazer, a former professor at Harvard and one of the earliest critics of affirmative action [says], America's failure to integrate blacks into the mainstream society has been so dramatic that multiculturalism may be the only alternative to social breakdown....To read some stories in the press in the past few days was to discover that race pollutes every institution, even the law courts."

For more information on the Pratt case, see B. Drummond Ayres, "An Ex-Leader of Black Panthers is Freed on Bail," in *The New York Times*, June 11, 1997, Sec. A, p. 12. See also Greg Goldin, "Pratt's Fall, and Rise," in *The Nation*, June 30, 1997. For more information on racism and the burning of black churches, and analysis of the issue, see Joan Brown Campbell, "Racism and the Burning of Churches," in *The Wall Street Journal*, June 25, 1997, Sec. A, p. 23; cf, Tom Wicker, *Tragic Failure: Racial Integration in America*, loc. cit.

50. Larry Elder, *The Ten Things You Can't Say in America* (New York: St. Martin Press, 2001). See also, Larry Elder, *Showdown: Confronting Bias, Lies, and the Special Interests that Divide America* (St. Martin's Press, 2002).

51. Nathan Thill, quoted by James Brooke, "Killing Wasn't Much, Skinhead Says: Slaying of West African Leaves Denver Stunned, and Frightened," in *The New York Times*, November 22, 1997, Sec. A, p. 7.

52. On March 17, 1990, Jeremiah Barnum, 25, was found guilty of murder and sentenced to life in prison without a chance of parole. The jury also found Barnum guilty of ethnic intimidation. He was one of two white men accused in a shooting at a Denver bus stop that killed Oumar Dia, an immigrant from Mauritania, West Africa, and left Jeannie Van Velkinburgh paralyzed. More details are on the Internet at http://blackvoices.com/news/99/03/17/nat03.html.

53. Nathan Hill, ibid.

54. Ibid.; see also Lynda Gorov, "In Denver, the Hate Has Surfaced Oce Again: Hate Crimes Make Denver Look Within," in *The Boston Globe*, November 24, 1997, Sec. A, p. 10.

55. Robert Shelton, quoted by the Ati-Defamation League of B'nai B'rith, *Hate Groups in America* (New York: B'nai B'rith Press, 1998), p. 18; Dinesh D'Souza, *The End of Racism*, op. cit., p. 12.

56. Jeannie Van Velkinburgh, quoted in *The Boston Globe*, and *The New York Times*, op. cit. See also, *Denver Post*, November 24, 1997.

57. Mary Boyle, "Teenager Offers TV Confession in Racist Slaying, " in *The Boston Globe*, November 22, 1997, Sec. A, p. 5.

58. Wellington Webb, quoted ibid.

59. Lynda Gorov, "In Denver, the Hate Has Surfaced Again," loc. cit.

60. Gail Gains, quoted ibid.

61. Carl Raschke, ibid.

62. "Skinheads Accused in Denver Beating," in *The Boston Globe*, November 29, 1997, Sec. A, p. 7.

63. Ibid.

64. Ann Scott Tyson, "It's A Date: Young Love Bridges Race Divide," in *The Christian Science Monitor*, December 3, 1997, p. 18.

Chapter Five:

1. Richard J. Herrnstein and Charles Murray, *The Bell Curve: Intelligence and Class Structure in American Life* (New York: Free Press, 1994).

2. Carl Rowan, *The Coming Race War in America: A Wake-Up Call* (New York: Little, Brown & Co., 1996). Rowan discusses, among other things, black conservatives who endorsed *The Bell Curve*, giving special attention to the specious remarks of Glenn Loury, Professor of economics at Boston University and formerly at Harvard, although Loury is reported to have been critical of *The Bell Curve* and the American Enterprise Institute for sponsoring Dinesh D'Souza's *End of Racism*. He found D'Souza's book to be

intellectually flawed and full of "sneering, cartoonlike provocations" about race. Concerning *The Bell Curve*, Loury said the book was rife with errors and contained "sweeping conclusions based on por science." He was also critical or another highly influential conservative book, *America in Black and White*, by Stephan Thernstrom and Abigail Thernstrom, saying he was disturbed by its intellectual lapses and racist assumptions.

See also Paul Krugerman, "The Unofficial Page of Paul Krugerman": www.pkarchive.org/economy/loury.html, on what he he has to say about Glenn Loury and *The Bell Curve* among other things:

"The final straw (for Loury with the conservative establishment) was surely the grotesque affair of Richard Herrnstein and Charles Murray's *The Bell Curve: Intelligence and Class Structure in American Life*. This book came close to claiming that, given your genes, it makes no difference to your economic success whether you grew up in Scardale or the South Bronx. The implied subtext was that this absolves society from any responsibility to do something for children growing up in the South Bronx. Since *The Bell Curve* was published, it has become clear that almost everything about it was inexcusably wrong: suspect data, mistakes in statistical procedures that would have flunked a sophomore - Murray (Herrnstein is dead) clearly does not understand what a correlation coefficient means; deliberate suppression of contrary evidence, you name it. Yet conservative publications such as *Commentary*, which was always happy to publish Loury when he criticized liberal evasions, would not grant him space to critique *The Bell Curve*."

3. Thomas Sowell, *Race and Culture: A World View* (New York: Basic Books, 1994).

4. Sowell, ibid.

5. Walter Rodney, *How Europe Underdeveloped Africa* (Dar es Salaam, Tanzania: Tanzania Publishing House, 1974).

6. Conservative Book Club, Selection 195 (Harrison, New York, 1994).

7. Barbara R. Bergmann, "Affirmative Action: Still the Best Way," in *The Wall Street Journal*, May 15, 1996, Sec. A, p. 15. See also, Barbara R. Bergmann, *In Defense of Affirmative Action* (New York: Basic Books, 1996). For a contrasting view, see Terry

Eastland, *Ending Affirmative Action: The Case for Colorblind Justice* (New York: Basic Books, 1996); Richard D. Kahlenberg, *The Remedy: Class, Race and Affirmative Action* (New York: Basic Books, 1996); and, David Greenberg, "Affirmative Action in the Positive and Negative," in *The Washington Post*, National Weekly Edition, July 8 - 14, 1996.

8. Thomas Sowell, *The Conservative Book Club Bulletin* (Harrison, New York: Conservative Book Club Press, 1994).

9. W. Fitzhugh Brundage. From 1997, Brundage was affiliated with the University of Florida at Gainsville, where he was associate professor of history (1997 - 1999); and since 1999, chair and professor of history. The article cited here is not chronicled in his curriculum vita; it is on his home page on the internet: http://www.clas.ufl.edu/users/brundage/1998cv.htm.

10. W. Fitzhugh Brundage, "The Return of Respectable Racism," in *The Queen's Quarterly Journal*, Toronto, Ontario, Canada, 1996; cf., *National Review*, May 6, 1996.

11. *National Review*, May 6, 1996.

12. J. Philippe Rushton, "IQ: Why Africa is Africa - Haiti Haiti," SouthAfrica.com Discussion Forum: South African Politics, March 10, 2004. See also,Richard Lynn and Tatu Vanhanen, *IQ and The Wealth of Nations* (Westport, Connecticut: Praeger Publishers, 2002); and J. Philippe Rushton, *Race, Evolution, and Behavior: A Life History Perspective* (Port Huron, Michigan: Charles Darwin Research Institute Press, 2000).

13. Herrnstein and Murray, *The Bell Curve*, op. cit., pp. 51, 64, 91, 127, 167, 191, 235, 269 - 270, 297, 317, 341, 369, 447 - 448, 590 ff.

14. Jared Taylor, in Dinesh D'Souza, *The End of Racism*: *Principles for a Multiracial Society* (New York: Free Press, 1996), pp. 387 - 389. Jared Taylor expressed his racist views in the *American Renaissance*, January, May, August, September-October, November, December 1993; June and September 1994. See also Carl Rowan, *The Coming Race War* loc.cit.

15. Jared Taylor, *Paved with Good Intentions: The Failure of Race Relations in Contemporary America* (New York: Free Press, 1994).

16. Walter Williams, in *Conservative Book Club Bulletin* (Harrison, NY: Conservative Book Club, 1995).

17. *The New York Times Magazine*, October 9, 1995.

18. J. Philippe Rushton, *Race, Evolution, and Behavior*, op. cit.

19. Transaction Publishers, Rutgers University, quoted in *National Review*, February 26, 1995.

20. *Columbia Encyclopedia* (New York: Columbia University Press, 1993), pp. 1343 - 1344, 1748.

21. Jared Taylor, loc.cit.

22. Jared Taylor, in anexchange with Phil Donahue, MSNBC, 2003. See also Jared Taylor in Dinesh D'Souza, *The End of Racism*, op. cit.; and *American Renaissance*, ibid.

23. Thomas Sowell, *Race and Culture,* op. cit., pp. 176 - 177.

24. Ibid.

25. Ibid., pp. 16, 159, 172. See also, "Race, Class, and Scores," in *The New York Times*, October 24, 1982; College Entrance Examination Board, *Profiles, College-Bound Seniors, 1981*(New York: College Entrance Examination Board, 1982), pp. 27, 32, 36, 41, 45, 51, 55, 60, 70.

26. Myron Weiner, "Nations Without Borders: The Gifts of Folk Gone Abroad," in *Foreign Affairs*, March/April 1996, p. 131.

27. Ibid., pp. 131 - 132; cf., pp. 128 - 134.

28. "Are Immigrants A Drag?: The Golden Door - Foreign Born Median Household Income, 1998," a chart, in *The Economist*, March 16 - 22, 1996, p. 33.

29. Ibid.

30. Thomas Sowell, *Race and Culture*, op. cit., pp. 167 - 169.

31. Ibid., pp. 173 - 174.

32. Ibid., p. 169.

33. Ibid., p. 167.

34. Ibid., p. 162.

35. Ibid., p. 163.

36. Ibid., pp. 164 - 165.

37. *The Bell Curve*, op.cit.

38. http://www.marvacollins.com/mar-info.html.

39.Lynne Duke, "Whites' Racial Streotypes Persist: Most Retain Negative Beliefs About Minorities," in *The Washington Post*, January 9, 1991, Sec. A, p. 1.

40. Professor Glenn Loury earned his Ph.D. at the Massachusetts Institute of Technology, Cambridge, Massachusettts

in 1976. He got a bachelor's degree in mathematics from Northwestern University, Evanston, Illinois. His field of expertise is Applied Microeconomic Theory, Political Economy of Race. A short list of his publications includes: *One By One, From the Inside Out: Essays and Reviews on Race and Responsibility in America* (New York: The Free Press, 1995); "Self-Censorship in Public Discourse: A Theory of 'Political Correctness' and Related Phenomena," in *Rationality and Society*, October 1994; "Rotating Savings and Credit Associations, Credit Markets and Economic Efficiency," in *The Review of economic Studies*, October 1994; "The Economics of Rotating Savings and Credit Associations," in *American Economic Review*, September 1993; "Will Affirmative Action Eliminate Negative Stereotypes," in *American Economic Review*, December 1993.

41. Tom Wicker, *Tragic Failure: Racial Integration in America* (New York: William Morrow, 1996), pp. 189 - 190.

42. Ibid., p. 190. See also, Wallace Kaufman, "Racism and the BBC Controversy," in the *Carolina Alumni Review*, p. 21.

43. *The Bell Curve*, p. cit., p. 399.

44. Ibid., p. 130.

45. Ibid., p. 308.

46. Ibid.

47. Jay Ambrose, "The Flynn Effect," in *The Washington Times*, 1996.

48. *The Bell Curve*, op. cit.

49. Jay Ambrose, op. cit.

50. *The Bell Curve*, op. cit. Cf., chart in *The Bell Curve*, "The Black and White IQ Distributions in NLSY, Version I," on frequency distributions of equal size, showing IQs of some blacks going past 140 and approaching 150, if blacks do indeed have weak genes and are therefore genetically inferior to and less intelligent than whites, Asians and mebers of other races as Richard Herrnstein and Charles Murray contend in their highly inflammatory book. What kind of genes do these blacks with such high IQs have? Are they no longer black simply because they score so high on IQ tests?

51. *The Bell Curve*, ibid., pp. 642 - 643, and 772.

52. *The Economist*, July 13 - 19, 1996.

53. Donald Hebb, in Jack Fincher, editor, *The Brain: Mystery*

of Matter and Mind (New York: Torstar Books, 1984), p. 72.

54. Nelson Mandela, *Long Walk to Freedom: The Autobiography of Nelson Mandela* (New York: Little, Brown and Company, 1994), p. 204.

55. Thomas Sowell, *Race and Culture*, ibid.; and Dinesh D'Souza, *The End of Racism*, ibid.

56. *The Bell Curve*, ibid.

57. ibid., pp. 23, 105, 106, 110, 217.

58. J. Philippe Rushton, "IQ: Why Africa is Africa - and Haiti Haiti," op. cit.

59. Albert Schweitzer, *The Primeval Forest* (New York: Pyramid Books, 1974), p. 99.

60. John L. Wilks, in *The New York Times*, December 22, 1991.

61. *The Bell Curve*, op. cit., p. 527.

62. "The Farrakhan Sideshow," in *The New York Times*, July 12, 1994, Sec. A, p. 13.

63. Sowell, *race and Culture*, op. cit., pp. 169 - 170.

64. Arthur Jensen, "How Much Can We Bost IQ and Scholastic Achievement?," in *Harvard Educational Review*, Winter 1969, pp. 1 - 123.

65. Jack Fincher, *The Brain: Mystery of and Matter and Mind*, op. cit., p. 72.

66. *Conservative Book Club Bulletin* (Harrison, New York: Conservative Book Club, 1995).

67. Peter Brimelow, in *National Review*, op.cit.

68. Peter Brimelow, in *Conservative Book Club*, and *National Review*, ibid.

69. Jared Taylor, *American Renaissance*, loc.cit.

70. Jared Taylor, *Paved with Good Intentions*, loc.cit.

71. Louis Uchitelle, "Black Americans Hit Hard by Loses in Manufacturing: The Booming 1990s Gave Many Blacks Jobs in Factories and Plants. Now They Are Being Let Go," in *The New York Times*, July 12, 2003, and in *The Grand Rapids Press*, Grand Rapids, Michigan, July 12, 2003, Sec. A., p. 13.

72. *The Bell Curve*, op. cit., pp. 91, 105, 127, 370, 371, and 375.

73. "Nakasone's Ugly Remark Says A Lot About Today's Japan," in *Business Week*, October 13, 1986, p. 66.

74. *The Bell Curve*, op. cit., p. 269.

75. Ibid., pp. 270, 522.

76. Jesse Jackson, "'Bell Curve' Exemplifies the Retreat on Race," in *The Los Angeles Times*, October 23, 1994, quoted by Dinesh D'Souza, *The End of Racism*, op. cit., p. 432.

77. Adolf Hitler, *Mein Kampf* (Boston: Houghton Mifflin, 1939), p. 640.

78. Jacob Weisberg, "Who? Me? Prejudiced?," in *New York*, October 17, 1994, quoted by Dinesh D'Souza, *The End of Racism*, op. cit., p. 432.

79. Hitler, *Mein Kampf*, op. cit., p. 396.

80. *The Bell Curve*, op. cit., p. 302.

81. Henry E. Garrett, quoted in Felix N. Okoye, *The American Image of Africa: Myth and Reality* (Buffalo, New York: Black Academy Press, 1971), p. 3.

82. Hitler, *Mein Kampf*, op. cit., pp. 396 - 397.

83. *The Bell Curve*, op. cit., pp. 527, 532 - 533.

84. Hitler, *Mein Kampf*, op. cit., pp. 397, 398.

85. *The Bell Curve*, op. cit., p. 331.

86. Ibid.

87. Hitler, *Mein Kampf*, op. cit., p. 579.

88. Ibid., pp. 579 - 580, and 581.

89. *The Bell Curve*, op. cit., p. 51.

90. Ibid., p. 289.

91. Ibid., p. 290.

92. Ibid., p. 269.

93. Ibid., p. 278.

94. *2004 Almanac* (New York: Houghton Mifflin, 2003).

95. *The Bell Curve*, op. cit., p. 279.

96. Derrick Bell, *Faces at the Bottom of the Well: Persistence of Racism* (New York: Basic Books, 1992).

97. *The Bell Curve*, ibid., p. 551.

98. Ibid., pp. 177, 179, and 189.

99. Ibid., pp. 191, 193, and 379.

100. Charles Murray, *Losing Ground* (New York: The Free Press, 1984).

101. *The Bell Curve*, ibid., pp. 235 - 236.

102. Ibid., pp. 385, 386, and 551.

103. Thomas Sowell, *Conservatives Book Club Bulletin*, ibid.

Chapter Six:

1. Nick Gillespie and Steve Kurtz, "Elder Statesman: An Interview with Larry Elder," in *Reason*, April 1996, p. 46. See also, "This Elder Gets Respect," in *U.S. News & World Report,* October 16, 2000, p. 16: "Some critics say Elder benefited from the affirmative action he condemns. Others say his incendiary stance is merely glib posturing."

2. Ibid.

3. Douglas A. Blackmon, "For Heaven's Sake: Racial Reconciliation Becomes A Priority For the Religious Right: Reasons Are Strictly Biblical, Not the Social Ideals of Liberal Congregations," in *The Wall Street Journal*, June 23, 1997, Sec. A., p. 1.

4. Ibid.

5. Ibid. The Southern Baptist Convention's premier pastor of hate was Dallas, Texas, First Baptist Church leader Wallace A. Criswell. For decades, Criswell preached from his pulpit that God not only demanded racial segregation, but religious segregation. He urged people of different congregations and persuasions to "stick to their own kind." This bible-thumping racist preacher "suggested strongly that black people did not possess the same kind of soul before God that white people owned, attacking the 'spurious doctrine' of national church groups preaching the 'universal Fatherhood of God and brotherhood of man.'" See Jim Schutze, *The Accommodation: The Politics of Race in an American City* (Secausus, New Jersey: Citadel Press, 1986), pp. 91 - 92.

6. Adonis Hoffman, "Clinton's Black Problem: Image vs. Reality," in *The Washington Post*, National Weekly Edition, August 19 - 25, 1996.

7. *International Herald Tribune*, August 16, 1996, p. 3.

8. Reverend Dr. Joan Brown Campbell is the General

Secretary of the National Council of Churches (NCC), the first woman to serve in that post. She is also a minister in both the Christian Church (Disciples of Christ) and American Baptist Churches; and responsible for refocusing the NCC's attention in broad national issues such as violence, health care, welfare reform, the urban crisis and the proper role of religion in public life.

9. Joan Brown Campbell, "Racism and the Burning of Churches," in *The wall Street Journal*, June 25, 1997, Sec., A, p. 23.

10. "The Death Penalty: Death and the American," in *The Economist*, June 21 - 27, 1997.

11. Gillespie and Kurtz, *Reason*, loc.cit.

12. Ibid.

13. Michael Selz, "Race-Linked Gap is Wide in Business-Loan Rejections: Denver Study Shows Disparate Rates Persist Despite U.S. Pressure on Banks," in *The wall Street Journal*, May 6, 1996, Sec. B, p. 2.

14. Ibid.

15. "Race and Real Estate," in *The Wilson Quarterly*, Summer 1996; Alicia H. Munnell, Geoffrey M.B. Tootell, Lynn E. Browne, and James McEneaney, "Mortgage Lending in Boston: Interpreting HMDA Data," in *The American Economic Review*, March 1996.

16. Gillespie and Kurtz, *Reason*, loc.cit.

17. Thomas Sowell, *The Vision of the Anointed: Self-Congratulation as a Basis for Social Policy* (New York: Basic Books, 1995), pp. 33, and 35.

18. Gillespie and Kurtz, *Reason*, loc.cit.

19. Ibid.

20. Quote attributed to Spike Lee, in Dinesh D'Souza, *The End of Racism*, op. cit., p. 479.

21. Julian Bond, in his speech at the NAACP national convention, Houston, Texas, July 8, 2002; quoted by John Perazzo, "How the Left Trashes Black Conservatives," FrontPageMagazine.com, July 10, 2002.

22. Alvin Poussaint, quoted in Dinesh D'Souza, ibid., p. 480. See also Arch Puddington, "Clarence Thomas and the Blacks," in *Commentary*, February 1992, p. 150.

23. Michael Selz, *The Wall Street Journal*, loc.cit.

24. Leon E. Wynter, "Business and Race," in *The Wall Street*

Journal, August 7, 1996. see also the study on wage discrimination by Professor David Maume, Jr., in the *American Sociological Review*, August 1996.

25. Tom Wicker, *Tragic Failure: Racial Integration in America* (New York: William Morrow, 1996), p. 14.

26. Leon E. Wynter, "Race Still Plays Role in Wages, Study Shows," in "Business and Race" section in *The Wall Street Journal*, August 7, 1996. See also David Maume, Jr., *American Sociological Review*, August 1996.

27. Katherine Johnson, quoted by Richard Morin, "What Americans Think: Southern Discomfort: Racially Bigoted Attitudes Linger in Many Parts of Dixie," in *The Washington Post*, National Weekly Edition, July 15 - 21, 1996, p. 35.

28. Ibid.

29. Ibid.

30. Southern Poverty Law Center, *Klan Intelligence Report, 1994 - 1997* (Montgomery, Alabama: Southern Poverty Law Center, 1998); Dinesh D'Souza, *The End of Racism*, op. cit., pp. 393 - 395; Tom Wicker, *Tragic Failure: Racial Integration in America*, loc. cit.

31. Richard Morin, "What Americans Think: Southern Discomfort: Racially Bigoted Attitudes Linger in Many Parts of Dixie," loc. cit.

32. Andrew Hacker, *Two Nations: Black and White, Separate, Hostile, Unequal* (New York: Ballantine Books, 1992), p. 24; Dinesh D'Souza, *The End of Racism*, op. cit., pp. 17 - 18.

33. "Nakasone's Ugly Remark Says A Lot About Today's Japan," in *Business Week*, October 13, p. 66.

34. Richard Morin, "What Americans Think...," loc.cit.

35. Ibid.

36. Todd Gitlin, *The Twilight of Common Dreams: Why America is Wracked by Culture Wars* (New York: Metropolitan Books, 1995), p. 123. See also Bob Zelnick, *Backfire: A Reporter's Look at Affirmative Action* (Washington, D.C.: Regnery, 1996), p. 239.

37. Richard Morin, "What Americans Think...," loc. cit.; Tom Wicker, *Tragic Failure: Racial Integration in America*, loc. cit.

38. Ibid.

39. Haki Madhubuti, editor, *Why L.A. Happened: Implications*

of the '92 Los Angeles Rebellion (Chicago: Third World Press, 1993); Cornel West, *Race Matters* (Boston: Beacon Press, 1993).

40. Thomas Sowell, *Migrations and Cultures: A World View* (New York: Basic Books, 1996); Sowell, *Race and Culture: A World View* (New York: Basic Books, 1994).

41. Sowell, *Migrations and Cultures*, ibid., pp. 321 - 322. See also Yashpal Tandon, *Problems of A Displaced Minority* (London: Minority Rights group, 1973), pp. 5, 7, 29; Allison Butler Herrick, et al., *Area Handbook for Uganda* (Washington, D.C.: Government Printing Office, 1969), p. 67.

42. See *The Detroit Free Press* from the seventies to the nineties, for some of the cases.

43. *The Los Angeles Times*, April 1992.

44. Dinesh D'Souza, *The End of Racism*, op. cit., pp. 416 - 417.

45. Ibid.

46. Thomas Sowell, *Migrations and Cultures*, loc.cit.

47. Sowell, ibid., p. 327. See also Agehananda Bharati, *The Asians in East Africa: Jayhind and Uhuru* (Chicago: Nelson-Hall Co., 1972), pp. 150 - 151, 154, 157, 160, 164, and 178.

48. Diane Watson, quoted in Rich Lowry, "Rolling Back Quotas," in *National Review*, September 2, 1996. Senator Diane Watson represented Los Angeles in the California state legislature from 1978 to 1998. She was ineligible to run for an additional term in 1998.

49. *National Review*, ibid.

50. Ibid.

51. Ibid.

52. Ibid.

53. Ibid.

54. Ezola Foster, "Surviving Media Assaults," in *Headway*, February 1996, p. 28.

55. Shelby Steele, *The Content of Our Character: A New Vision of Race in America* (New York: St. Martin's Press, 1990), p. 27.

56. Foster, "Surviving Media Assaults," ibid.

57. Ibid.

58. Ezola Foster, quoted by Peter Carlson, "Ezola Foster: Pat Buchanan's Far Right Hand," in *The Washington Post*, September

13, 2000, p. C01. See also, Ezola Foster: Pat Buchanan's Far Right Hand: washingtonpost.com.

59. Shelby Steele, in an interview by Peter Robinson, "Shelby Steele: The Content of Our Character," in *Hoover Digest Selections*, No. 2, 1996.

60. "Clarence Thomas," in *National Minority Politics*, loc.cit.

61. Ibid.

62. Jack White, in *Time*, June 26, 1995.

63. Charles Lawrence, quoted in *The World Almanac and Book of Facts 1992* (New York: Pharos Books, 1991), p. 59.

64. Joseph Lowry, quoted by Gwen Daye Richardson, "The Attack on Clarence Thomas," in *National Minority Politics*, October 1995, p. 6.

65. Joseph H. Brown, "Running Afoul of the Soul Patrol," in *National Minority Politics*, October 1995, p. 24.

66. Timothy Lester, "Black Conservatives," in *Headway*, september 1996, p. 5.

67. Sandy Tadlock, quoted in Richard Morin, "They Just Don't Like Newt: A National Survey Finds Many Americans Have Harsh Words for the House Speaker," in *The Washington Post*, National Weekly Edition, August 19 - 25, 1996, p. 33.

68. Richard Morin, "They Just Don't Like Newt...", Ibid.

69. Michelle Ann Feavel, quoted, ibid.

70. President Lyndon B. Johnson, in a speech at Howard University, Washington, D.C., June 4, 1965, defining the concept of affirmative action.

71. The Philadelphia Order by President Richard Nixon enforcing affirmative action, issued in 1969. It was the most forceful affirmative action plan up to that time and set in motion what became a sustained effort to use racial and gender preferences to correct injustice across the spectrum, triggering a white backlash that led to the election of Ronald Reagan and the resurgence of the conservative movement that gained momentum and swept across the country, putting liberals on the defensive for years. The word "liberal" became an epithet in the lexicon of conservatives, and they used it effectively to smear their political opponents - mostly Democrats - and mobilize white voters to support a conservative Republican agenda hostile toward blacks and other minorities.

72. Todd Gitlin, *The Twilight of Common Dreams: Why America Is Wracked By Culture Wars* (New York: Metropolitan Books, 1995), p. 179. See also, Jerome Karabel and David Karen, "Go to Harvard, Give Your Kid a Break," in *The New York Times*, December 8, 1990.

73. Todd Gitlin, ibid.

74. Karabel and Karen, ibid.

75. Morin, op. cit. See also Lynne Duke, "Whites' Racial Stereotypes Persist: Most Retain Negative Beliefs About Minorities," in *The Washington Post*, January 9, 1991, Sec. A, p. 1.

76. Ibid. See also Bob Zelnick, *Backfire: A Reporter's Look at Affirmative Action*, op. cit.

77. Morin, "What Americans Think...," ibid.; Todd Gitlin, *The Twilight of Common Dreams*, op. cit.; Bob Zelnick, *Backfire*, loc. cit. As Zelnick states: "The group's studies (done by Professor James H. Kuhlinski and others of the University of Illinois at Urbana-Champaign) had found evidence of rather acute anti-black attitudes in 42 percent of white Southerners and 12 percent of white non-Southerners, with milder prejudicial attitudes in perhaps an additional 10 percent of each population. The force of Kuhlinski's study was that its methodology was designed to avoid the 'social desirability' problem of poll taking, which is a phenomenon where people change their answers to match what they think is the 'right' or 'moral' answer."

78. Gitlin, *The Twilight of Common Dreams*, op. cit.

79. Herrnstein and Murray, *The Bell Curve*, op. cit.

80. Morin, "What Americans Think...", loc. cit.; Gitlin, *The Twilight of Common Dreams* loc.cit. ; Zelnick, *Backfire: A Reporter's Look at Affirmative Action*, loc. cit.

81. Gitlin, ibid.

82. Morin, ibid.

83. Gitlin, ibid.; Nathan Glazer, *We Are All Multiculturalists Now* (Cambridge, Massachusetts: Harvard University Press, 1997). See also, *The Nation*, May 12, 1997, pp. 38 - 42.

84. Paul M. Sniderman and Thomas Piazza, *The Scar of Race* (Cambridge, Massachusetts: Harvard University Press, 1993), p. 102 - 104. Gitlin, op. cit., pp. 123 - 124, 229, notes that in a personal communication with Piazza, Piazza told him on

December 23, 1994, that there was no significant difference between white men and white women in their racial attitudes toward blacks.

85. Malcolm X, with Alex Hailey, *The Autobiography of Malcolm X* (New York: Grove Press, 1966), pp. 366 - 367.

86. Lynne Duke, "Whites' Racial Stereotypes Persist: Most Retain Negative Beliefs About Minorities," in *The Washington Post*, January 9, 1991, Sec. A, p. 1.

87. Joseph H. Brown, "Running Afoul of the Soul Patrol," in *Headway*, loc. cit.

88. Ellen Rayner, "Defining Conservatism," in *Headway*, July 1996, p. 5.

89. Charles Ogletree, a black law professor at Harvard, emphatically states: "Ninety-nine percent of black people don't commit crimes." See Dinesh D'Souza, *The End of Racism*, op. cit., p. 260; and, Howard Kurtz, "Some Journalists Link Crime Coverage, Racism," in *The Washington Post*, July 29, 1994.

90. Jim Powell, "A Stirring Battle cry for Equal Rights," in *Laissez Faire Books*, San Francisco, June 1996. He states: "[There are at least] 3 million blacks in the underclass. Total black population in the U.S. is around 31 million."

91. S.D. Spero and A.L. Harris, *The Black Worker* (New York: Athenaeum, 1968), p. 169; see also, Raymond S. Franklin and Solomon Resnik, *The Political Economy of Racism* (New York: Holt, Rinehart and Winston, 1973), pp. 23 - 24.

92. H.M. Baron, "The Demand for Black Labor: Historical Notes on the Political Economy of Racism," in *Radical America*, Vol. 5, No 2, 1971, p. 23.

93. Thomas Sowell, *Migrations and Cultures*, op. cit., p. 382; cf., Chavis, loc. cit.

94. Keith Gilyard, "Would Ebonics Programs in Public Schools Be a Good Idea?" in *Insight*, March 31, 1997. Gilyard, a professor at Syracuse University, states: "African-American college graduates...earn a fraction of what white college graduates earn."

95. Michael Selz, "Race-Linked Gap is Wide in Bunsiness-Loan Rejections: Denver Study Shows Disparate rates Persist Despite U.S. Pressure on Banks,' in *The Wall Street Journal*, May 6, 1996; "Race and real Estate," in *The Wilson Quarterly*, Summer

1996; Alicia H. Munnell, Geoffrey M.B. Tootell, Lynn E. Brown, and James McEneaney, "Mortgage Lending in Boston: Interpreting HMDA Data," in *The American Economic Review*, March 1996; Nick Gillespie and Steve Kurtz, *Reason*, April 1996; Joel Glenn Brenner, "A Pattern of Bias in Mortgage Loans," in *The Wasington Post*, June 6, 1993; Paulette Thomas, "Blacks Can Face a Host of Trying Conditions in Getting Mortgages," in *The wall Street Journal*, November 30, 1992; and, Jesse Jackson, "Racism is the Bottom Line in Home Loans," in *The Los Angeles Times*, October 28, 1991.

96. Shelby Steele, *The Content of Our Character*, op. cit.

97. Ibid., p. 169.

98. William Julius Wilson, *The Declining Significance of Race* (Chicago: University of Chicago Press, 1978).

99. Thomas Sowell, *Migrations and Cultures*, and *Race and Culture*, as cited.

100. Edward C. Banfield, *The Unheavenly City: The Nature and Future of Our Urban Crisis* (Boston: Little, Brown & Co., 1970), pp. 68 - 70, 73, 210 - 211, nd 256.

101. Raymond S. Franklin and Solomon Resnik, *The Political Economy of Racism* (New York: Holt, Rinehart and Winston, 1973), op. cit.; James C. Wilson, "The Negro in Politics," in Talcott Parsons and Kenneth B. Clark, editors, *The Negro American* (Boston: beacon Press, 1970), pp. 435, and 443.

102. Eldridge Cleaver, in *The Guardian*, April 13, 1968. see also Robert L Allen, *Black Awakening in Capitalist America: An Analytic History* (Garden City, New York: Anchor Books, Doubleday & Co., 1970), p. 265.

103. Derrick Bell, *Faces at the Bottom of the Well: The Permanence of Racism* (New York: Basic Books, 1992), p. 152.

104. Stokely Carmichael, "Toward Black Liberation," in the *Massachusetts Review*, Autumn 1966, pp. 639 - 651; and, "Stokely Carmichael Explains Black Power," in Robert L. Scott and Wayne Brockriede, editors, *The Rhetoric of Black Power* (New York: Harper & Row, 1969), pp. 103 - 104.

105. Quoted by Arnold Schuchter, *White Power/Black Freedom: Planning the Future of Urban America* (Boston: Beacon Press, 1968), p. 100; Raymond S. Franklin and Solomon Resnik, *The Political Economy of Racism*, op. cit., p. 32.

106. Robert L. Maginnis, "Burning of Black Churches is National Disgrace," in *Headway*, May 1996, p. 24.

107. "Pride and Prejudice," in *U.S. News & World Report*, July 15 - 22, 1996.

108. Ibid.

109. Jack Levin, quoted in "Pride and Prejudice," in *U.S. News & World Report*, ibid.

110. Deval Patrick, quoted, ibid.

111. Danielle Allen, "Class Conflict," in *National Review*, April 4, 1994.

112. Ellis Cose, *The Rage of A Privileged Class: Why Middle-Class Blacks Are Angry; Why America Should Care* (New York: HarperCollins, 1993).

113. Ibid., quoted by Danielle Allen, "Class Conflict," in *National Review*, April 4, 1994.

114. Larry Elder, in *Reason*, op. cit.

115. Ellis Cose, *The Rage of A Privileged Class...*, quoted by Daniell Allen, in *National Review*, loc. cit.

116. Larry Elder, loc cit.

117. Ibid. See also, Larry Elder interview, "'Correctness' Not A Concern for Black Conservative Talk-Show Host," in *The Washington Times*, October 2 - 8, 2000, pp. 26 and 28.

118. Benjamin Hooks, "Civil Rights and Wrongs," in *The Wall Street Journal*, July 19, 1990, Sec. A, p. 10, quoted by Dinesh D'Souza, *The End of Racism*, op. cit., p. 479; cf., "Conservatives on Race," in *National Minority Politics*, July 1994.

119. Nathan Glazer, *We Are All Multiculturalists Now* (Cambridge, Massachusetts: Harvard University Press, 1997). See also, Richard Delgado, *The Coming Race War?: And Other Apocalyptic Tales of America After Affirmative Action and Welfare* (New York: New York University Press, 1996); Carl Rowan, *The Coming Race War in America: A Wake-Up Call* (New York: Little, Brown & Co., 1996).

See also, Jonathan Yardley, "Lament for A Common Culture," a review of Nathan Glazer's *We Are All Multiculturalists Now*, in *The Washington Post*, National Weekly Edition, March 31, 1997, p. 34:

"*We Are All Multiculturalists Now* is a sad book, and it is difficult to imagine how it could have been otherwise....Glazer's faith in the capacity of government to protect...equality and liberty [for all] in effective ways has diminished; his faith in the good intentions of the American people themselves where race is concerned has, if anything, diminished even further.

That at least is the conclusion to be drawn from this brief but densely packed book, the essential argument of which is that multiculturalism 'is the price America is paying for its inability or unwillingness to incorporate into its society African Americans, in the same way and to the same degree it has incorporated so many groups....The [multicultural] movement is given its force and vigor by our greatest domestic problem, the situation of African Americans.' As Glazer puts it elsewhere:

'Blacks...feel the issues most urgently, their problems are the most severe....Why have so many blacks moved against assimilation as an ideal...? The answer, I am convinced, is to be found in black experience in America, and in the fundamental refusal of other Americans to accept blacks...'

All the evidence indicates that this choice 'not to assimilate' has been made less as a positive assertion of black pride than in reaction to white America's refusal to honor, in full, the legal and moral pledges it made in the 1950s and 1960s....As Glazer points out...'the apartness of blacks is real; for this one group, assimilation, by some measures, has certainly failed.'"

See also, Michael A. Fletcher, "The Kerner Report at 30: The 'Separate and Unequal' Warning Has Come True Despite Black Gains, An Updated Study Asserts," in *The Washington Post*, National Weekly Edition, March 9, 1998, p. 35:

"Thirty years after a presidential commission declared 'our nation is moving toward two societies, one black, one white - separate and unequal,' that dire warning has become a reality, according to a report released last week.

'The Kerner Commission's prophecy has come to pass,' states the report from the Milton S. Eisenhower Foundation, a group founded to continue the work of the commission, which was appointed by President Lyndon B. Johnson to probe the causes of rioting in urban America in the 1960s....Inequalities with troubling racial dimensions are becoming more deeply rooted in American society, the report concludes.

'The richer are getting richer, the poor are getting poorer and minorities are suffering disproportionately,' said the report....The report lists racial and economic statistics to back its bleak conclusions. While the American economy booms, most adults in inner cities do not work in a typical week. The top 1 percent of Americans have more wealth than the bottom 90 percent, the report says, placing the United States first among industrialized nations when it comes to wealth inequality.

In addition, 40 percent of minority children attend urban schools, where more than half of the students are poor and fail to reach even 'basic' achievement levels. With 1.5 million prisoners, the United States incarcerates people than any nation in the world, and one in three young African American men are in prison, on parole or probation. 'The private market has failed the inner city. The prison system is a symbol of discrimination. A class and racial breach is widening again as we begin the new millennium,' the report said....

Former Democratic senator Fred R. Harris of Oklahoma, who served on the original Kerner panel, says the report merely reflects some sad realities of American society. He credits affirmative action, civil rights laws and anti-poverty programs with fueling the expansion of the black middle class in the three decades since the original Kerner report was written. 'But the progress we've made on race and poverty really stopped toward the end of the 1970s,' he says. 'Then, we began in many ways to go backward.'"

This grim assessment of America's racial dilemma is also shared by many other analysts, including Mark Nathan Cole, professor of anthropology at the State University of New York and author of *Culture of Intolerance*. As he stated in his article, "Racism: An Undeniable Fact," in the *International Herald Tribune*, May 15, 1998, p. 11:

"It is certainly true that one physical encounter between police and a person of color does not make racism. But what is undoubtedly racism is the fact that such instances involve black individuals far more often than their numbers or behavior would warrant.

It is also true that urban flight need not be racist and that people of all colors are attempting it. What is undeniably racist is that the suburbs to which people flee are still segregated. A black cannot live or buy a house in a white community even if he or she is a successful middle-class professional.

It is true that nobody [including blacks] much likes quotas for college admissions or hiring. But they are needed because even qualified black individuals too often cannot be hired or admitted. Sometimes this represents sheer racism; other times, even well-meaning white employers are unable to separate differences in style from differences in ability and are unable to see quality or potential when it comes in minority - or female - form.

In colleges there have long been 'set asides' or quotas for athletes, legacies (children of alumni), and the wealthy. Even people from different areas of the country are routinely granted preferential admission because they add richness and variety to a campus. No one challenged such preferential admissions until they were applied to minorities. That is   racism.

At a much subtler level, the failure of white society to see the arbitrary nature of its admissions tests and the fact that tests themselves discriminate against minorities, or to recognize the impact of poor schooling on performance, is also a form of racism that needs to be addressed.

It is racism, too, if once established at a corporation minority group members are still denied advancement, as has been amply documented at Texaco."

See also, "Black Lawyers Not Likely to Warm to [Clarence] Thomas: Speech Today is Expected to Renew Civil Rights Debate," in *The Boston Globe*, July 29, 1998, Sec. A, p. 3; Jewelle Taylor Gibbs, *Race and Justice: Rodney King and O.J. Simpson in A House Divided* (San Francisco: Jossey-Bass, 1998); Jonathan Coleman, *Long Way to Go: Black and White in America* (New York: Atlantic Monthly Press, 1997); David K. Shipler, *A Country of Strangers: Blacks and Whites in America* (New York: Alfred A. Knopf, 1997).

Appendix:

Reparations for African Americans

Ten Reasons: A Response to David Horowitz
by Robert Chrisman and Ernest Allen, Jr.

David Horowitz's article, "Ten Reasons Why Reparations for Slavery is a Bad Idea and Racist Too," recently achieved circulation in a handful of college newspapers throughout the United States as a paid advertisement sponsored by the Center for the Study of Popular Culture. While Horowitz's article pretends to address the issues of reparations, it is not about reparations at all. It is, rather, a well-heeled, coordinated attack on Black Americans which is calculated to elicit division and strife.

Horowitz reportedly attempted to place his article in some 50 student newspapers at universities and colleges across the country, and was successful in purchasing space in such newspapers at Brown, Duke, Arizona, UC Berkeley, UC Davis, University of Chicago, and University of Wisconsin, paying an average of $700 per paper. His campaign has succeeded in fomenting outrage, dissension, and grief wherever it has appeared.

Unfortunately, both its supporters and its foes too often have categorized the issue as one centering on "free speech." The sale and purchase of advertising space is not a matter of free speech, however, but involves an exchange of commodities. Professor Lewis Gordon of Brown University put it very well, saying that "what concerned me was that the ad was both hate speech and a solicitation for financial support to develop antiblack ad space. I was concerned that it would embolden white supremacists and antiblack racists." At a March 15 panel held at UC Berkeley, Horowitz also conceded that his paid advertisement did not constitute a free speech issue.

As one examines the text of Horowitz's article, it becomes apparent that it is not a reasoned essay addressed to the topic of reparations: it is, rather, a racist polemic against African Americans and Africans that is neither responsible nor informed, relying heavily upon sophistry and a Hitlerian "Big Lie" technique. To our knowledge, only one of Horowitz's ten "reasons" has been challenged by a black scholar as to source, accuracy, and validity. It is our intention here to briefly rebut his slanders in order to pave the way for an honest and forthright debate on reparations.

In these efforts we focus not just on slavery, but also the legacy of slavery which continues to inform institutional as well as individual behavior in the U.S. to this day. Although we recognize that white America still owes a debt to the descendants of slaves, in addressing Horowitz's distortions of history we do not act as advocates for a specific form of reparations.

1. There Is No Single Group Clearly Responsible For The Crime Of Slavery

Horowitz's first argument, relativist in structure, can only lead to two conclusions: 1) societies are not responsible for their actions and 2) since "everyone" was responsible for slavery, no one was responsible. While diverse groups on different continents certainly participated in the trade, the principal responsibility for internationalization of that trade and the institutionalization of slavery in the so-called New World rests with European and American individuals and institutions.

The transatlantic slave trade began with the importation of

African slaves into Hispaniola by Spain in the early 1500s. Nationals of France, England, Portugal, and the Netherlands, supported by their respective governments and powerful religious institutions, quickly entered the trade and extracted their pieces of silver as well. By conservative estimates, 14 million enslaved Africans survived the horror of the Middle Passage for the purpose of producing wealth for Europeans and Euro-Americans in the New World.

While there is some evidence of blacks owning slaves for profit purposes--most notably the creole caste in Louisiana--the numbers were small. As historian James Oakes noted, "By 1830 there were some 3,775 free black slaveholders across the South. . . . The evidence is overwhelming that the vast majority of black slaveholders were free men who purchased members of their families or who acted out of benevolence." (Oakes, 47-48).

2. There Is No Single Group That Benefited Exclusively From Slavery

Horowitz's second point, which is also a relativist one, seeks to dismiss the argument that white Americans benefited as a group from slavery, contending that the material benefits of slavery could not accrue in an exclusive way to a single group. But such sophistry evades the basic issue: who benefited primarily from slavery?

Those who were responsible for the institutionalized enslavement of people of African descent also received the primary benefits from such actions. New England slave traders, merchants, bankers, and insurance companies all profited from the slave trade, which required a wide variety of commodities ranging from sails, chandlery, foodstuffs, and guns, to cloth goods and other items for trading purposes.

Both prior to and after the American Revolution, slaveholding was a principal path for white upward mobility in the South. The white native-born as well as immigrant groups such as Germans, Scots-Irish, and the like participated. In 1860, cotton was the country's largest single export. As Eric Williams and C.L.R. James have demonstrated, the free labor provided by slavery was central to the growth of industry in western Europe and the United States;

347

simultaneously, as Walter Rodney has argued, slavery depressed and destabilized the economies of African states.

Slaveholders benefited primarily from the institution, of course, and generally in proportion to the number of slaves which they held. But the sharing of the proceeds of slave exploitation spilled across class lines within white communities as well. As historian John Hope Franklin recently affirmed in a rebuttal to Horowitz's claims:

"All whites and no slaves benefited from American slavery. All blacks had no rights that they could claim as their own. All whites, including the vast majority who had no slaves, were not only encouraged but authorized to exercise dominion over all slaves, thereby adding strength to the system of control.

If David Horowitz had read James D. DeBow's "The Interest in Slavery of the Southern Non-slaveholder," he would not have blundered into the fantasy of claiming that no single group benefited from slavery. Planters did, of course. New York merchants did, of course. Even poor whites benefited from the legal advantage they enjoyed over all blacks as well as from the psychological advantage of having a group beneath them."

The context of the African-American argument for reparations is confined to the practice and consequences of slavery within the United States, from the colonial period on through final abolition and the aftermath, circa 1619-1865. Contrary to Horowitz's assertion, there is no record of institutionalized white enslavement in colonial America. Horowitz is confusing the indenture of white labor, which usually lasted seven years or so during the early colonial period, with enslavement. African slavery was expanded, in fact, to replace the inefficient and unenforceable white indenture system. (Smith).

Seeking to claim that African Americans, too, have benefited from slavery, Horowitz points to the relative prosperity of African Americans in comparison to their counterparts on the African continent. However, his argument that, "the GNP of black America makes the African-American community the 10th most prosperous "nation" in the world is based upon a false analogy. GNP is defined as "the total market value of all the goods and services

348

produced by a nation during a specified period." Black Americans are not a nation and have no GNP. Horowitz confuses disposable income and "consumer power" with the generation of wealth.

3. Only A Tiny Minority Of White Americans Ever Owned Slaves, And Others Gave Their Lives To Free Them

Most white union troops were drafted into the union army in a war which the federal government initially defined as a "war to preserve the union." In large part because they feared that freed slaves would flee the South and "take their jobs" while they themselves were engaged in warfare with Confederate troops, recently drafted white conscripts in New York City and elsewhere rioted during the summer of 1863, taking a heavy toll on black civilian life and property.

Too many instances can be cited where white northern troops plundered the personal property of slaves, appropriating their bedding, chickens, pigs, and foodstuffs as they swept through the South. On the other hand, it is certainly true that there also existed principled white commanders and troops who were committed abolitionists.

However, Horowitz's focus on what he mistakenly considers to be the overriding, benevolent aim of white union troops in the Civil War obscures the role that blacks themselves played in their own liberation. African Americans were initially forbidden by the Union to fight in the Civil War, and black leaders such as Frederick Douglass and Martin Delany demanded the right to fight for their freedom. When racist doctrine finally conceded to military necessity, blacks were recruited into the Union Army in 1862 at approximately half the pay of white soldiers--a situation which was partially rectified by an act of Congress in mid-1864. Some 170,000 blacks served in the Civil War, representing nearly one third of the free black population.

By 1860, four million blacks in the U.S. were enslaved; some 500,000 were nominally free. Because of slavery, racist laws, and racist policies, blacks were denied the chance to compete for the opportunities and resources of America that were available to native whites and immigrants: labor opportunities, free enterprise, and land. The promise of "forty acres and a mule" to former slaves was effectively nullified by the actions of President Andrew Johnson. And because the best land offered by the Homestead Act of 1862 and its subsequent revisions quickly fell under the sway of white homesteaders and speculators, most former slaves were unable to take advantage of its provisions.

4. Most Living Americans Have No Connection (Direct Or Indirect) To Slavery

As Joseph Anderson, member of the National Council of African American Men, observed, "the arguments for reparations aren't made on the basis of whether every white person directly gained from slavery. The arguments are made on the basis that slavery was institutionalized and protected by law in the United States. As the government is an entity that survives generations, its debts and obligations survive the lifespan of any particular individuals. . . . Governments make restitution to victims as a group or class." (San Francisco Chronicle, March 26, 2001, p. A21).

Most Americans today were not alive during World War II. Yet reparations to Japanese Americans for their internment in concentration camps during the war was paid out of current government sources contributed to by contemporary Americans. Passage of time does not negate the responsibility of government in crimes against humanity. Similarly, German corporations are not the "same" corporations that supported the Holocaust; their personnel and policies today belong to generations removed from their earlier criminal behavior. Yet, these corporations are being successfully sued by Jews for their past actions. In the same vein, the U.S. government is not the same government as it was in the pre-civil war era, yet its debts and obligations from the past are no less relevant today.

5. The Historical Precedents Used To Justify The Reparations Clain Do Not Apply, And The Claim Itself Is Based On Race Not Injury

As noted in our response to "Reason 4," the historical precedents for the reparations claims of African Americans are fully consistent with restitution accorded other historical groups for atrocities committed against them. Second, the injury in question--that of slavery--was inflicted upon a people designated as a race. The descendants of that people--still socially constructed as a race today--continue to suffer the institutional legacies of slavery some one hundred thirty-five years after its demise. To attempt to separate the issue of so-called race from that of injury in this instance is pure sophistry. For example, the criminal (in)justice system today largely continues to operate as it did under slavery--for the protection of white citizens against black "outsiders."

Although no longer inscribed in law, this very attitude is implicit to processes of law enforcement, prosecution, and incarceration, guiding the behavior of police, prosecutors, judges, juries, wardens, and parole boards. Hence, African Americans continue to experience higher rates of incarceration than do whites charged with similar crimes, endure longer sentences for the same classes of crimes perpetrated by whites, and, compared to white inmates, receive far less consideration by parole boards when being considered for release.

Slavery was an institution sanctioned by the highest laws of the land with a degree of support from the Constitution itself. The institution of slavery established the idea and the practice that American democracy was "for whites only." There are many white Americans whose actions (or lack thereof) reveal such sentiments today--witness the response of the media and the general populace to the blatant disfranchisement of African Americans in Florida during the last presidential election. Would such complacency exist if African Americans were considered "real citizens"? And despite the dramatic successes of the Civil Rights movement of the 1950s and 60s, the majority of black Americans do not enjoy the same rights as white Americans in the economic sphere. (We continue this argument in the following section).

6. The Reparations Argument Is Based On The Unfounded Claim That All African-American Descendants of Slaves Suffer From The Economic Consequences Of Slavery And Discrimination

Most blacks suffered and continue to suffer the economic consequences of slavery and its aftermath. As of 1998, median white family income in the U.S. was $49,023; median black family income was $29,404, just 60% of white income. (2001 New York Times Almanac, p. 319) Further, the costs of living within the United States far exceed those of African nations. The present poverty level for an American family of four is $17,029. Twenty-three and three-fifths percent (23.6%) of all black families live below the poverty level.

When one examines net financial worth, which reflects, in part, the wealth handed down within families from generation to generation, the figures appear much starker. Recently, sociologists Melvin L. Oliver and Thomas M. Shapiro found that just a little over a decade ago, the net financial worth of white American families with zero or negative net financial worth stood at around 25%; that of Hispanic households at 54%; and that of black American households at almost 61%. (Oliver & Shapiro, p. 87) The inability to accrue net financial worth is also directly related to hiring practices in which black Americans are "last hired" when the economy experiences an upturn, and "first fired" when it falls on hard   times.

And as historian John Hope Franklin remarked on the legacy of slavery for black education: "laws enacted by states forbade the teaching of blacks any means of acquiring knowledge-including the alphabet-which is the legacy of disadvantage of educational privatization and discrimination experienced by African Americans in 2001."

Horowitz's comparison of African Americans with Jamaicans is a false analogy, ignoring the different historical contexts of the two populations. The British government ended slavery in Jamaica and its other West Indian territories in 1836, paying West Indian slaveholders $20,000,000 pounds ($100,000,000 U.S. dollars) to free the slaves, and leaving the black Jamaicans, who comprised 90% of that island's population, relatively free. Though still facing racist obstacles, Jamaicans come to the U.S. as voluntary immigrants, with greater opportunity to weigh, choose, and develop their options.

7. The Reparation Claim Is One More Attempt To Turn

African Americans Into Victims. It Sends A Damaging Message To The African-American Community

What is a victim? Black people have certainly been victimized, but acknowledgment of that fact is not a case of "playing the victim" but of seeking justice. There is no validity to Horowitz's comparison between black Americans and victims of oppressive regimes who have voluntary immigrated to these shores. Further, many members of those populations, such as Chileans and Salvadorans, direct their energies for redress toward the governments of their own oppressive nations--which is precisely what black Americans are doing.

Horowitz's racism is expressed in his contemptuous characterization of reparations as "an extravagant new handout that is only necessary because some blacks can't seem to locate the ladder of opportunity within reach of others, many of whom are less privileged than themselves." What Horowitz fails to acknowledge is that racism continues as an ideology and a material force within the U.S., providing blacks with no ladder that reaches the top. The damage lies in the systematic treatment of black people in the U.S., not their claims against those who initiated this damage and their spiritual descendants who continue its perpetuation.

8. Reparations To African Americans Have Already Been Paid

The nearest the U.S. government came to full and permanent restitution of African Americans was the spontaneous redistribution of land brought about by General William Sherman's Field Order 15 in January, 1865, which empowered Union commanders to make land grants and give other material assistance to newly liberated blacks. But that order was rescinded by President Andrew Johnson later in the year. Efforts by Representative Thaddeus Stevens and other radical Republicans to provide the proverbial "40 acres and a mule" which would have carved up huge plantations of the defeated Confederacy into modest land grants for blacks and poor whites never got out of the House of Representatives. The debt has not been paid.

"Welfare benefits and racial preferences" are not reparations. The welfare system was set in place in the 1930s to alleviate the poverty of the Great Depression, and more whites than blacks received welfare. So-called "racial preferences" come not from benevolence but from lawsuits by blacks against white businesses, government agencies, and municipalities which practice racial discrimination.

9. What About The Debt Blacks Owe to America?

Horowitz's assertion that "in the thousand years of slavery's existence, there never was an anti-slavery movement until white Anglo-Saxon Christians created one," only demonstrates his ignorance concerning the formidable efforts of blacks to free themselves. Led by black Toussaint L'Ouverture, the Haitian revolution of 1793 overthrew the French slave system, created the first black republic in the world, and intensified the activities of black and white anti-slavery movements in the U.S.

Slave insurrections and conspiracies such as those of Gabriel (1800), Denmark Vesey (1822), and Nat Turner (1831) were potent sources of black resistance; black abolitionists such as Harriet Tubman, Frederick Douglass, Richard Allen, Sojourner Truth, Martin Delany, David Walker, and Henry Highland Garnet waged an incessant struggle against slavery through agencies such as the press, notably Douglass's North Star and its variants, which ran from 1847 to 1863 (blacks, moreover, constituted some 75 % of the subscribers to William Lloyd Garrison's Liberator newspaper in its first four years); the Underground Railroad, the Negro Convention Movement, local, state, and national anti-slavery societies, and the slave narrative. Black Americans were in no ways the passive recipients of freedom from anyone, whether viewed from the perspective of black participation in the abolitionist movement, the flight of slaves from plantations and farms during the Civil War, or the enlistment of black troops in the Union army.

The idea of black debt to U.S. society is a rehash of the Christian missionary argument of the 17th and 18th centuries: because Africans were considered heathens, it was therefore legitimate to enslave them and drag them in chains to a Christian nation. Following their partial conversion, their moral and material lot were improved, for which black folk should be eternally grateful. Slave ideologues John Calhoun and George Fitzhugh updated this idea in the 19th century, arguing that blacks were better off under slavery than whites in the North who received wages, due to the paternalism and benevolence of the plantation system which assured perpetual employment, shelter, and board. Please excuse the analogy, but if someone chops off your fingers and then hands them back to you, should you be "grateful" for having received your mangled fingers, or enraged that they were chopped off in the first place?

10. The Reparations Claim Is A Separatist Idea That Sets African Americans Against The Nation That Gave Them Freedom

Again, Horowitz reverses matters. Blacks are already separated from white America in fundamental matters such as income, family wealth, housing, legal treatment, education, and political representation. Andrew Hacker, for example, has argued the case persuasively in his book Two Nations. To ignore such divisions, and then charge those who raise valid claims against society with promoting divisiveness, offers a classic example of "blaming the victim." And we have already refuted the spurious point that African Americans were the passive recipients of benevolent white individuals or institutions which "gave" them freedom.

Too many Americans tend to view history as "something that happened in the past," something that is "over and done," and thus has no bearing upon the present. Especially in the case of slavery, nothing could be further from the truth. As historian John Hope Franklin noted in his response to Horowitz:

"Most living Americans do have a connection with slavery. They have inherited the preferential advantage, if they are white, or the loathsome disadvantage, if they are black; and those positions are virtually as alive today as they were in the 19th century. The pattern of housing, the discrimination in employment, the resistance to equal opportunity in education, the racial

355

profiling, the inequities in the administration of justice, the low expectation of blacks in the discharge of duties assigned to them, the widespread belief that blacks have physical prowess but little intellectual capacities and the widespread opposition to affirmative action, as if that had not been enjoyed by whites for three centuries, all indicate that the vestiges of slavery are still with us.

And as long as there are pro-slavery protagonists among us, hiding behind such absurdities as "we are all in this together" or "it hurts me as much as it hurts you" or "slavery benefited you as much as it benefited me," we will suffer from the inability to confront the tragic legacies of slavery and deal with them in a forthright and constructive manner.

Most important, we must never fall victim to some scheme designed to create a controversy among potential allies in order to divide them and, at the same time, exploit them for its own special purpose."

Ernest Allen, Jr. is Professor of Afro-American Studies at the University of Massachusetts, Amherst; Robert Chrisman is Editor-in-Chief and Publisher, *The Black Scholar* (April 2, 2001).

Bibliography

1. *2001 New York Times Almanac* (New York: Penguin Books, 2000).

2. Richard F. America, *Paying the Social Debt: What White America Owes Black America* (Westport, CT: Praeger, 1993).

3. J. D. B. DeBow, "The Interest in Slavery of the Southern Non-Slaveholder," in *Slavery Defended: The Views of the Old South*, ed. Eric L. McKitrick (Englewood Cliffs, NJ: Prentice-Hall, 1963), 169-77.

4. Ira Berlin and others, *Slaves No More: Three Essays on Emancipation and the Civil War* (Cambridge [England]; New York: Cambridge University Press, 1992).

5. Dalton Conley, Being Black, *Living in the Red: Race, Wealth, and Social Policy in America* (Berkeley: University of California Press, 1999).

6. LaWanda Cox, "The Promise of Land for the Freedmen," *Mississippi Valley Historical Review 45* (December 1958): 413-40.

7. Dudley Taylor Cornish, *The Sable Arm: Black Troops in the Union Army, 1861 - 1865* (1956; reprinted, Lawrence, Kansas: University Press of Kansas, 1987).

8. Eric Foner, *Free Soil, Free Labor, Free Men: The Ideology of the Republican Party Before the Civil War* (New York: Oxford University Press, 1970).

9 John Hope Franklin and Alfred A. Moss, Jr., *From Slavery to Freedom: A History of African Americans*, 7th ed. (New York: McGraw-Hill, 1994).

10. Andrew Hacker, *Two Nations: Black and White, Separate, Hostile, Unequal*, revised edition (New York: Ballantine Books, 1995).

11. James Oliver Horton and Lois E. Horton, *In Hope of Liberty: Culture, Community, and Protest Among Northern Free Blacks, 1700 - 1860* (New York: Oxford University Press, 1997).

12. James L. Huston, "Property Rights in Slavery and the Coming of the Civil War," in the *Journal of Southern History 65* (1999): pp. 249-86.

13. James Oakes, *The Ruling Race: A History of American Slaveholders* (New York: Vintage Books, 1983).

14. Melvin L. Oliver and Thomas M. Shapiro, *Black Wealth/White Wealth: A New Perspective on Racial Inequality* (New York: Routledge, 1995).

15. Benjamin Quarles, *Black Abolitionists* (New York: Oxford University Press, 1969).

16. Benjamin Quarles, *The Negro in the Civil War* (Boston: Little, Brown, 1953).

17. Walter Rodney, *How Europe Underdeveloped Africa*, revised edition (Washington, DC: Howard University Press, 1981).

18. Jack Salzman, David Lionel Smith, and Cornel West, eds., *Encyclopedia of African-American Culture and History, 5 vols.* (New York: Macmillan Library Reference USA: Simon & Schuster Macmillan; London: Simon & Schuster and Prentice Hall International, 1996).

19. Diana Jean Schemo, "An Ad Provokes Campus Protests and Pushes Limits of Expression," in *The New York Times*, 21 March 2001, pp. A1, A17.

20. Abbot Emerson Smith, *Colonists in Bondage: White Servitude and Convict Labor in America, 1607 - 1776* (Chapel

Hill: Pub. for the Institute of Early American History and Culture at Williamsburg, Va., by the University of North Carolina Press, 1947).

21. Barbara L. Solow and Stanley L. Engerman, eds., *British Capitalism and Caribbean Slavery: The Legacy of Eric Williams* (Cambridge [Cambridgeshire]; New York: Cambridge University Press, 1987).

22. Eric Williams, *Capitalism & Slavery* (1944; reprinted, New York: Russell & Russell, 1961).

About the Author

GODFREY MWAKIKAGILE has written several books on politics, economics and social issues including race relations. They are found in public and university libraries around the world. His forthcoming books on race relations include *Resistance to Racial Equality*, and *Conservatives and Black America.*

He has always been interested in race relations and was affiliated with a civil rights organization when he was a student in college.